This book is a masterpiece; a compelling read full of timeless wisdom and practical truths. Russ Moore is a wordsmith and a poet but don't let that deceive you. Just because this book is a delight to read, it is also hilarious, and his transparency will make you both blush and cringe. He knows insecurity from the inside and is willing to let God use his own "tortured stuff" to lighten your journey. In my opinion, CONFIDENCE is destined to become a Christian classic.

—Kay Kasburg, LPCC–S Professional Clinical Counselor, Supervisor, Director

In his familiar and brilliant style, Russ tackles one of the more elusive concepts to master. This book contains spiritual and practical insights on growing your confidence without falling into the ditches of false humility or arrogance. Once again, Russ uses his wit, charm, and self–deprecating humor to create the ultimate how–to guide for developing God–honoring confidence. This is the book we never knew we needed.

—Tim Moore, Lead Pastor of
Scary Faith

CONFIDENCE by Russ Moore is a must read for every believer and a must have resource for every Christian counselor and pastor. Russ Moore brilliantly lays out, in his witty and relatable style, what confidence in Christ is, and what it is not. He invites readers to go on a journey where grief, guilt, shame, fear, and the effects of past trauma are confronted, and replaced by confidence found only in Christ. Through his funny and relatable personal stories, readers can feel less alone, and find hope in spite of the past and in the midst of today's struggles. Relax, prayerfully break open the pages, and begin a journey where you will laugh, cry, pause, and find Jesus waiting to love you back to the confident person He created you to be. This is one of those books you will want to keep close and read over and over.

—Kim M. McMillan, LPC / Damascus Road Counseling, LLC

I've seen Russ's words work miracles in my own heart and mind—they're timely, powerful, and transformative. Selfishly, I claim him as my personal hype man! Every conversation makes me want to run through a brick wall — this book is no different. These words are crucial for anyone who feels their biggest roadblock is their own sometimes debilitating view of self. Russ powerfully connects scriptural narratives along with his personal journey to help readers dismantle insecurities and discover true freedom. Highly recommended for those who are hungry for personal breakthrough.

—Kevin Ilich, Real Estate Influencer / Owner of Indigo

My dear friend, Pastor Russ pushes you to trust Jesus in every situation, whether it's a joyful season or a dark one. His writing is convicting but warm, honest, transparent, filled with hope and wrapped in truth.

—Joel Leggett, Lead Pastor, Cor Church

Russ has yet again tackled a topic that can either hold us in complacency or unlock the greatness latent in us all. Finding hope when we can't seem to; now, finding the confidence to take the next step. Through his transparency, Russ puts himself out there to show firsthand what it looks like when we have confidence and what it looks like when we don't. Russ has such a way with words . . . you feel all the emotions he is describing. I am proud to call him a friend and mentor in my own journey.

—Brock Everhart, Ultramarathon runner

Humans are complex. There are endless variations of personality type. But there is one variable that is consistent throughout all personality types . . . and that is confidence. With very few exceptions, the commonality among all people is a lack of confidence. In CONFIDENCE, Russ lays out a clear Bible–based rationale for why confidence is valuable for one's quality of life. But there is more than just a rationale for confidence; there is a clear "How to" component. You will be divinely encouraged and elevated in your confidence by following the teaching in this book.

—Dr. Wes Beavis, Psy. D, Clinical Psychologist, Pastor, Author

This book came at a much needed time in my personal faith journey. Confidence has always been one of those topics of tension: "Am I being humble enough?" "Is this divinely gifted confidence or walking in my own self esteem?" This book helped me tackle those questions, discover inner peace, but most importantly, find the courage to embrace confidence.

—Addie Overla, Podcast Host of Christ in Me with Addie, Discipleship Director

CONFIDENCE

Destroy *Insecurity*.
Discover *Freedom*.

RUSS MOORE

Contents

PROLOGUE: Give It Away

Foreword

Confidence.

Something everyone wants but not everyone has. It's one thing to recognize it; another to obtain it.

What comes to mind when you even hear the word? Some mistake it for loud or cocky or even as a personality. I would argue it's none of that. The confident people I follow embody a quiet strength. A sense of confidence not from the projection of a false self, but from the authenticity of knowing one's true self.

Imagine for a moment a life where this type of confidence is available to you—not just in theory or concept but integrated into your very being. As you will discover in the pages ahead, it is. There is a confidence that awaits you. A strong confidence. One not based not on the circumstances around you but on something greater within you.

It's one thing to read an author's work; it's another to know them personally. I've had the privilege of calling Russ a close friend for a long time. I've never met a more winsome person.

I am honored to personally know Russ and have watched him wrestle with and learn to live out the truths he shares in this book over the years. He is a man of integrity and character, with a heart to help people reach their full potential. Few people I know possess the ability to be authentically themselves and embrace their calling the way Russ does. He is a rare breed—both an extremely gifted communicator on stage

and a deeply engaging author on page. That's exactly what
you'll find in this book.

After obtaining my review copy, I began reading and found it
to be captivating. From the insightful truths he pulls from
Scripture to the hilarious stories you'll relate to in his
humanity, you'll be both inspired and motivated to apply these
principles to your everyday life. You'll overcome lies that often
hold us back from becoming who we were created to be.

When it comes to this subject, I've had individuals tell me
they've lost their confidence. The truth is, we can't lose our
confidence; we just choose to give it away. The good news is
we can always choose to take it back. Russ will guide you step
by step to do just that in what I consider his best work yet.

A more confident you is closer than you think. Let today
begin that new journey. A journey toward discovering the you
God had in mind since before the foundations of the earth.

—Logan Claypoole
Pastor of Culture & Direction, Oaks Church
Raleigh, NC

Preface

WHEN WAS THE LAST TIME YOU EXPERIENCED TRUE confidence? You know. That sweet, sure-of-yourself kind.

Seriously, find the moment. Zero in. *Feel* it.

Maybe it was at work, in a meeting, or giving a presentation. Perhaps on a date or with friends. Or even alone, doing your thing, content in your own skin.

Relive it in slow motion. Take in how you felt, how you walked, how you interacted with others and yourself.

Smiling yet?

I don't know about you, but I can *tell* when I'm confident.

It feels amazing.

I have a pep in my step and a shine in my eyes. I feel joy. I walk taller. My instincts soar, and I trust them. I look people in the eye and engage, fully present, like I have something to offer.

I walk into rooms secure in soul, with a humble, bold assurance that my voice matters and people like me. I move with purpose and peace. I operate from a sense of expectancy instead of dread. I dream big about my tomorrows. I'm assertive and innovative and bring my best to the table.

I even feel a mature, optimistic perspective when I look at problems or survey past failures.

Not to sound like a modern poet, but when I'm feeling confident, food tastes better and colors shine brighter.

Oh, and also . . . when I'm confident, I tend to *like myself*.

However.

I'm also just as aware when I'm insecure. It's miserable.

I walk with my head down and make less eye contact. I don't think people like me. *I* don't like me.

I'm hesitant, constantly second-guessing myself. I get needy to prove and itchy for acceptance. I don't speak up or bring my best. I hoard my time. I get lethargic. I connect less with others.

My happiness tanks. Faith becomes a job instead of a joy. I feel busy but not productive. I don't think as clearly. I get edgy and create narratives and interpret a microexpression as evidence someone wishes I had never been born.

I think you get the point.

Any of that sound familiar?

This much I know about you: You are at your best when you are full of confidence. And life is too short to not live full, free, and at your best.

. . . . .

CONFIDENCE MATTERS.

You know that, or you wouldn't have picked up the book.

It's a strange thing, too. You might feel like you have very little going for you, like Kevin from *The Office* thrust into a last-minute spelling bee. Or the whole universe tilted your way, like The Rock walking a Miami beach shirtless at sunset. The thing is, without confidence, it won't matter.

Because without confidence:

You can have the optimal advantage . . . but you won't tap into it.

You can have beautiful potential . . . but you won't step into it.

You can have incredible gifting . . . but you won't rise into it.

All because you lack confidence.

I'll never forget opening a *Men's Health* magazine at a BI-LO grocery store my freshman year of high school. I saw the headline about an article of how to attract amazing girls if you're an average guy.

That's me!

I looked both ways to make sure my mom hadn't already found the peanut butter or Amy from biology class wasn't looking. Then I opened the magazine like I was handling the Dead Sea Scrolls. I flipped to the article. I swear the page began to glow.

The writer claimed he had an average-looking friend that consistently dated the most beautiful, wonderful women. He repeatedly emphasized how underwhelming his friend was (I *really* wish I could have seen his friend's reaction).

"He's not attractive," the author repeated. "Or talented. Or smart." (*I get the point*, I hear his friend say.)

So how did he do it? One reason, the writer claimed. Only one reason.

His friend was completely unafraid of rejection. He was so secure and unfazed by the prospect of *no* that he asked girls out with abandon until he received the kind of *yes* that made everyone else delirious with envy.

In other words, he was *confident.*

He got more *yeses* than most of us because he had the nerve to withstand more *nos* than most of us.

I wonder what all *yeses* we might be missing out on in life. In our careers, marriages, and dreams.

If only we were secure and unafraid. If only we were confident.

See, confidence is how you get life to say *yes.*

The writer of Hebrews makes a forceful case about it, too. In Chapter 10, he contends for a confidence to *connect boldly with God,* a confidence to *endure hardship,* and a confidence to *move forward instead of shrinking back.*

In the middle of it all, he writes:

"So don't throw away your confidence, which has a great reward."[1]

The context is spiritual, but the concept's universal. In fact, if we step back and observe life from just a broad, human level, it becomes exceedingly clear that this principle—*confidence brings reward*—translates to *every arena of life.*

Deep down, we know it.

For starters, it translates to the arena of *you.* To live your optimal life, thrive at work, take on opportunities, experience the world, bloom in your gifts, ask out the cute coworker, even make more money.

It's essential in relationships, too. To flourish in marriage and love people well. Without confidence, you're too shrunken to serve. You're paralyzed with self-doubt, unable to fully expend yourself. After all, it's hard to give people all you've got when you're convinced you don't have a lot to give. In fact, without confidence, you'll even be unable to *receive* love properly from those who wish it to give it.

And yes, strangely enough, confidence matters when it comes to your spiritual health. I won't make assumptions about your faith journey and what you believe. But if you desire to enjoy a relationship with God and fulfill a divine mission on earth, you'll need the self-esteem and courage to do so.

"Don't throw away your confidence," the writer says.

Right now, some of us don't have a lot to throw away. That's what this book is for.

· · · · · ·

AS WE TRAVEL TOGETHER, I'LL

intertwine some of my own bumbling, lurching journey through confidence and insecurity with that of Saul and David from Scripture.

Saul. Not the one from the dark show about meth. And not the New Testament, assassin-turned-church-planter. No, the Old Testament Saul. King Saul. The complex, heroic, tragic Saul.

And David. The also complex, deeply flawed, warrior-king-poet described by God Himself as "a man after my own heart."[2]

From Saul's life, we'll keep a clipboard on just how serious insecurity can be in our lives, its fallout when unchecked and micro-radiating in our system. We'll see Saul's contrast in David and extract insight, letting golden help and wisdom spill from the hills.

The truth is, I don't know the state of your confidence in this particular moment. I don't know if you feel like Taylor Swift blazing through an Eras Tour or more like your neurotic aunt biting her nails at the post office. But I can tell you this, regardless where you find yourself: I've written the book I wish I'd had.

A gritty, holistic guide to develop well-rounded esteem, internal resilience, and psychological well-being. A deeply spiritual, deeply personal, deeply practical wisdom book on how to actually *dismantle insecurity* and *build and maintain confidence.*

The true kind, not the contrived or narcissistic. No trying to make you an extrovert if you're an introvert. And no faking. See, we tend to think confidence is one of those things you either have or you don't. And if you don't? Well, then, you better learn to put on the act. But true confidence is not an act; it's an essence. And it's possible to develop that essence in a way that's organic, healthy, and powerful.

So, these are the things I've learned—and am learning—along the way. These are the stories of my successes and my many, many defeats. This is where Ephesians, Mark Manson, modern psychology, and timeless wisdom collide into something that can actually help you.

A couple things as we get started.

The book is divided into three main sections. Themes will overlap, but in general the first section builds a framework designed to free us from the claws of *insecurity*. The second builds foundational health into our *identity*, the kind we can construct our lives from. The third gets uber practical with how to build and implement that *confidence* in our day to day.

On that note, I encourage you to go in order without skipping. The concepts stack on each other like stories in a home. And I want to tell you in advance I can almost guarantee, depending on how you're wired, you will find some parts too spiritual or too practical. We'll make it through.

This much I know: If you take time to absorb the principles in this book and integrate them into your life, insecurity will loosen its grip around your heart and you will step into a bolder, freer, and more purpose-filled life than you thought was possible.

Of that, I'm confident.

With you in the journey,
John Russell Moore

Part 1

THE TRAP OF
INSECURITY

G IBEAH.

1020 BC.

Modern-day Tall al-Ful, located just north of Jerusalem. Land home to the tribe of Benjamin.

It's late in the day, and a man walks up a hill. Gibeah, of course, is a hill. But there's a hill among the hills. This Benjamite's secret hill.[1]

As his foot hits the final elevating step, a familiar view rises to greet him. A small body of water shimmering back to him the dying hues of a red-orange sun. Calm permeates his body, and he breathes deep. This is his safe place.

He comes here to remember the past. To dream of the future. To reflect on his days.

He reminisces on the forbidden adventure a few months back when he snuck all the way to the Dead Sea thirty miles out. What was he thinking? His mind predictably slows at the woman he'd passed along the way, his thoughts lingering back over her high cheekbones and the smile she'd flashed as he walked by.

He looks down at the dirt and suppresses a Cheshire grin. He's attractive, and he knows it. The subtle whispers and grins are not so subtle. Nor is the fact he's a foot and a half taller than anyone he knows.

The grin fades, however, at the thought of his father.

Kish.

A great man. A well-to-do member of the tribe. Noble standing and reputation.

And a man of whom he would never be worthy.

Was it ever spoken out loud or just inside his own soul? Either way, he somehow knows no physical stature will ever grow him out of the shadow of the man he both respects and resents.

He looks out over the water and sighs, kicking a small rock over the precipice to break the liquid surface. The thoughts and questions slip out loud:

"Really?

Thirty years old and still can't get past my father's opinion.

Taller than anyone around and still feel like a little boy.

Who am I, anyway?

What will my future be?"

Little does he know tomorrow will begin to answer that question.

Tomorrow will change Saul's life.

Insecurity kills more dreams than failure ever will.[1]
—Rich Wilkerson Jr.

Be strong. Take courage. Don't be intimidated.[2]
—Moses to Israel

Sometimes, God opens doors. Other times, He waits for us to kick them down.[3]
—Bob Goff

1)

How I Got into College

I'd like to begin by telling you a secret.

When I say *secret*, I'm not being cute or hyperbolic. No, an actual secret. My parents and a couple friends know, and that's it. Until now.

It may not seem like a big deal to some, but for me, the secret's a bit embarrassing.

And it's this:

I never graduated high school.

Those who know me may have just tilted their head like a Labrador. They know my affinity for learning, how I value the life inside the mind, or the fact I began my master's degree a few years ago.

But it's true.

In high school, my study habits were piteous.

Read multiple books a week on my own regarding historical

theology or far-reaching astronomy? No problem. Finish mandatory reading on Steinbeck's most overrated work? Not a chance on Lennie's poor life.

Thus, I ended up in the *top* ten percent of my class for SATs and the *bottom* ten percent for my GPA.[4] That's called *lazy*. I kept telling myself I had plenty of time to turn it all around before the end of senior year, but I didn't.

That next year, I trudged through a depressing semester in a charter school, then decided I'd had enough. I wanted to go to North Greenville University. A beautiful college up in the mountains, twenty minutes from home. My best friend was there. Girls were there. The beginning of the rest of my life was there.

I made the drive one sunny fall morning to inform the dean I'd be attending his school.

"Hey, man," my buddy Colt started carefully on the drive. "You do realize there's a problem with your plan."

"Yeah? What's that?"

"You haven't graduated high school."

I smirked. A cocky, nineteen-year-old smirk.

"Not a problem."

"Not a *problem*?"

Colt stared at me like I'd just waved off the idea of gravity.

Sitting across from the dean, I heard Colt's same objections repeated back to me by the dean himself, albeit in much more eloquent, emphatic, and confused tones.

"Son, in the century of this school, we have *never* let a student in here without a high school diploma or GED. I'm sorry, it's just not possible."

I don't remember what all was said next. I just know twenty minutes later, I walked out enrolled at North Greenville University.[5]

A dumb, shocked grin covered Colt's face like saran wrap on the walk back to the dorm.

"Only you, man," he repeated, shaking his head. "Only you."

Now, look. I didn't hypnotize the dean. And yes, I've already broken a cardinal rule of communication: *Don't make yourself the hero of your own story.*

But the truth is, I'm still embarrassed. Twenty years removed, I look back on that season with regret over my immaturity and that I didn't honor God with my best. I also cringe at my presumption. And trust me, I've had entire *seasons* of insecurity alongside those moments of boldness.

All that to say, I'm so glad I chose to step into *that* moment with confidence.

See, that moment led to memories at NGU, to my year in Argentina, where I learned Spanish, worked on a ranch, met people I'll never forget, and had spiritual encounters that changed my future.

I can tell you I've watched insecurity close doors that could have been opened. And I've watched confidence open doors that would have *never* been opened.

Because that's what confidence does.

It opens doors that remain shut to everyone else.

It opens the door to the life you were meant to live.

. . . . .

IF *CONFIDENCE* IS NUCLEAR ENERGY, *insecurity* is kryptonite.

It comes through different doors and wears different clothes.

It can sneak through the backdoor of childhood rejection, adolescent abuse, or adult trauma.

Or just life, for that matter. Personality. Quirks. A certain amount of confidence or lack thereof already baked in the cake of your DNA.

Perhaps you're overly cerebral and find it easier to escape Alcatraz than your own head. There behind the iron bars of your thoughts, you pace, constantly second-guessing yourself, over-analyzing your every interaction.

Maybe your appearance causes you angst. When God worked with the playdough of your form, He stretched you too long or wide or scrunched you too short or narrow. Or He hooked the clay too sharply on your chin or sneezed, clumping your cheeks into mounds where dimples could have been. Or perhaps, tragically, He excessively packed in your core, forever protecting you from the possibility of visible abs.[6]

I'm sure there's a mother reading this who's ready to chuck the smartphone—along with her sanity—out the window. You've resigned yourself to the fact your family will never be as Facebook-perfect as all the legging-wearing, organic-cereal-eating families you secretly hope wake up tomorrow with horrible acne. Or it's deeper, a gnawing ache that there's more than the safe, suffocating routines slowly decaffeinating all your dreams.

You may feel understaffed in the talent department. Everyone else seems gifted by the stars. Or even by measure of intelligence. I know people who were told early in life they were dumb and have worn that label like a grade on their forehead ever since, forever hesitating to open their mouths in public settings for fear of saying the wrong thing.

Maybe you used to beam with esteem like the sun. Then, a spouse cheated on you or walked out. The psychological damage has left you wilted.

How about this? You're a man's man. I mean, a real Marlboro one, enamored by sport and gun, smelling of cedar and cigar, radiating testosterone like a teenager's cologne. And no one knows you're still an eight-year-old boy inside. That if it were late at night and you were feeling honest and maybe had a finger or two of whiskey in you, you'd admit you feel lost and scared. That your words and actions rise from the abyss of your father's absent affirmation.

It could be a nagging sense of *otherness* based on gender, race, age, personality, fill in the blank. Or you've always felt like you don't quite fit.

You don't make enough money. You're from the wrong side of the tracks. Or what others would label the "right side" of the tracks, all propped up by privilege and opportunity, and yet you feel you'll just never measure up.

Not trying to overwork the point here. I just want to gather us all around the table before we grab coffee and start talking. Maybe it's all the above, none of the above, or a mixture of the above. Honestly, I think being a human in and of itself gives you a hall pass to insecurity.

The truth is, *all of us*—to some degree or another—are insecure.

. . . . .

INSECURITY IS FUNNY.

I have a friend named Steve who's never met a stranger. He's run local radio stations, lunches with mayors and sports heroes, makes horrible O.J.-will-kill-you jokes with every server at breakfast, and oozes a loud, buoyant gravitas in every room he enters. He's also incredibly kind and generous. And a perfect example of *intrinsic confidence*. He loves to retell the story of the day he and his dad got home from yet another social setting Steve had loved and his dad had dreaded.

> Steve's father (exhausted): *Son, you know the only difference between you and me?*

> Steve (hesitating): *Yes, Dad, I think I do.*

> Steve's father: *I know you do. The only difference is you have confidence.*

It's striking.

And yet, if you get Steve alone in an honest moment, there's an other side to him. A side that still hears the echo of harsh voices in his youth constantly correcting him. To this day, he has to work hard to ensure he doesn't mix up current voices with those voices and begin to feel like he can't do anything right.

I guess you could say he's a mixed bag in the confidence/insecurity department.

Maybe like you. Definitely like me.

In some ways, it's hard even to assess this area of myself.

A few years back, I felt a bit melancholy as the weather grew cold and the Christmas green increased. If you want the real story, I was sad over a love that got away. My friend sent me an Avett Brothers song. He said it reminded him of me and the charisma and assuredness I'd always carried. He said he knew I'd be fine, highlighting the following lyrics:

> *I meant what I said when I said I would rearrange my plans and change for you. You know me; I've always been the kind with easy confidence. Confident enough to honestly believe that nothing out there's stopping me, especially not someone who's not loving me.*[7]

The kind with easy confidence.

In a way, I suppose he's right.

I have always possessed a decent measure of confidence. And

it's grown over the years as I've accrued experience and a few wins.

I'm confident in speaking, for example. Hand me a mic and I'm in my bag. Ask me to talk to a room or convince a polar bear to buy suntan oil, I'm golden. I'm not saying I'm great. I'm just saying it feels natural.

The speaking confidence dovetails into some leadership confidence. I've always been pulled into executive roles, be that school council, corporate management, or ministry leadership. Or even middle school days where I got so obsessed with martial arts and professional wrestling, I created my own choreographed fight scene organization and convinced fifty students to sign ironclad contracts to be a part of it. That last one sounds pretty strange now that I type it out.

For the most part I also embrace how I'm wired, with my own unique, out-of-the-box traits and quirks. And I confess I've experienced a wild optimism my entire life, a near-dangerous and perhaps delusional belief that I can do whatever I set my mind to, that no dream is too high, no fantasy too fantastical, no obstacle insurmountable.

But I've grappled with insecurity too. Like *bad*. From self-consciousness around my appearance, my personality quirks, bank account, or relational turmoil, all the way to ring-dinger mistakes that made me think my life was over.

On the low-grade level, I used to never feel handsome enough. In fact, quite embarrassing to admit now, I remember spending hours in my parents' basement my sophomore year mapping out plans to increase my attractiveness. No kidding. I laid out magazine cutouts on a chipped coffee table with articles on how to improve my skin, hair, muscles, you name it. Like a mad accountant, I created checklists. I'd watch the way Brad Pitt moved his jawline in *The Mexican*, so tough and nonchalant and appealing.

"One day," I'd promise myself, pen adding to checklist. "One day."

Medium-grade, I slip into funks. I can fall deep down a well of my own thinking, where I *feel* insecure based on my self-perceived performance, leadership failures, relational dynamics at work, or whatever. And then spend a week scraping my palms against the brick of the well to heave myself back out.

More often than not, though?

Shame.

I'm actually convinced it's the secret, rotten ingredient inside all our insecurities.

We had an incredible worship night at church a few months back. We'd been in a Sunday series on mental health, so in between songs, all the worship leaders grabbed stools and shared vulnerably about their own journeys with depression and anxiety. It was beautiful. One of my good friends, Kevin, an *extremely* confident person, hit home inside me with his words:

"If you're not careful, you can get really good at building a case against yourself. Really good at stacking up evidence about all the ways you suck, all the ways you're a horrible person."

This is true for me. I think I'm good at stacking evidence. I remember all the ways I should be better by now, the ways I don't measure up, the ways I keep letting myself down. I remember my worst moments, sins I regret, even times I've misspoken to my wonderful parents, and I conclude I'm irreversibly flawed. I begin to believe my church would be better off without my leadership, my relationships better off without my influence.

Then I'll have a life-giving morning in prayer, go on a long run, receive the most affirming text about who I am from a close friend, hear someone say my book or sermon changed their life, and feel grounded as the earth below.

Crazy, huh?

Maybe I can say it this way:

For me, confidence has been both a *lifelong strength* and a *lifelong struggle*.

The struggle's not always a bad thing, either. Sometimes it's a good thorn in the flesh to keep me humble.

More often than not, though, it's an unhealthy sabotaging of my energy, time, relationships, and overall happiness.

. . . . .

SAUL WAS A MIXED BAG TOO.

And mixed bag or not, he was about to be given the weight of a nation.

The runway had been long leading up to this moment: God delivering His people from Egypt, decades in a hot desert, one generation dying out, another finally stepping into the promised land, then a long stretch of wars and ups and downs, and a whole era of judges leading the country.

Eventually, "All the other nations have a king" became Israel's version of "All the other kids have a bike." God waved a warning finger but finally in essence said, "You want a king? Here you go."[8]

Enter Saul. One day his father, Kish, lost his car (donkeys). He sent Saul and a servant to fetch them. After a long, frustrating string of bad luck, the servant remembered a man nearby with near-magic insight and predictions. Maybe he could help.

Enter Samuel. The most famous prophet in Israel. As it turns out, he'd had a conversation with God just yesterday about the nation's future and their desire for a king. And God told him *today* he would bump into the man to anoint for the job.

Screen-cut, Saul and his servant go looking for the "seer." Sure enough, they find him. The first dramatic scene in this movie comes early:

> "When Samuel caught sight of Saul, the Lord said to him, 'This is the man I spoke to you about; he will govern my my people.' Saul approached Samuel . . . and asked, 'Would you please tell me where the seer's house is?' 'I am the seer," Samuel replied. '. . . you are to eat with me, and in the morning I will . . . tell you all that is in your heart. As for the donkeys . . . do not worry about them; they have been found. And to whom is all the desire of Israel turned, if not to you and your whole family line?'"[9]

What a moment. And what a *line*. "To whom is all the desire of Israel turned . . . "

A pinnacular, defining scene for Saul. The eyes of destiny turn his way. He will be Israel's first king. And Samuel told him where to find the car.

Can I be honest? I wish life always made announcement like this.

How much is at stake. The opportunity. The weight of our choices.

There are moments and seasons in our lives where so much rests in our hands. And just like Saul, what we choose to do with certain moments can shape not just *our* future but *the* future.

In fact, I want to remind you right up front that you have an insane, once-in-a-lifetime opportunity in front of you.

An opportunity more important than college or even a kingly role in Israel.

That opportunity?

Life. *Your* life.

Your one brief, mad, beautiful, fleeting-down-the-hourglass life.

The question is, what will you do with it?

Will you close your own doors out of fear and self-doubt?

Or will you open those doors and walk into the future God has waiting?

Note Saul's response to *his* opportunity:

> "Saul answered, 'But am I not a Benjamite, from the smallest tribe of Israel, and is not my clan the least of all the clans of the tribe of Benjamin? Why do you say such a thing to me?'"[10]

On the surface, this is moving. Saul's in awe. He responds the way you *hope* someone would respond in this situation. His response is even reminiscent of King David's years later:

> "Who am I, Sovereign Lord, and what is my family, that you have brought me this far?"[11]

Same with Saul.

I'm just a Benjamite . . .

Such humility.

Except not everything that looks like humility is humility.

Samuel invites Saul into a meeting hall for a big ribeye dinner, followed by a private rooftop chat full of instructions and prophetic heads-ups.

Then Samuel takes a flask of oil and pours it over Saul's head, anointing him king, and declares, "Has not the Lord anointed you ruler over his inheritance?"[12]

You can read the rest yourself. For now, just know that this handsome, tall, promising young man will be king. He has the prophet's approval and God's anointing. He's got it made in the shade.

What could go wrong?

The big day arrives. Inauguration Day, fat with pageantry and every reporter from Israeli Broadcasting. All the tribes are there. Saul's moment has come. Mom's crying, Dad's beaming.

Sure enough, Saul is announced.

Drumroll . . .

Nothing.

Saul's not there.

Long silence. Stiff smiles and nervous glances permeate the crowd. As the seconds collect, I imagine someone nodding furiously at one of the directors to stall with a few jokes. In all the confusion, they even began to pray, asking God if *He* knew where Saul was. And God responded:

". . . Yes, he has hidden himself among the supplies."[13]

Wow.

Saul was hiding.

Hiding instead of being highlighted.

At his unveiling as king, he was veiling *himself* behind airport luggage.

It doesn't take the imagination of James Cameron[1] to grasp the weight of this moment. It would be like the new pastor of your church, the new CEO of your company, or, yes, even the new President of the United States being announced and then they're just not . . . there. They never come out. Then the janitor finds them crouched behind a mop bucket in the storage closet.

And remember, Saul wasn't thirteen like many of Israel's kings to come. Saul was thirty. A grown man with his own car insurance.

They finally find him, and Samuel brags on him and everyone sees he's a foot taller than everyone, and people chant "long live the king" and on and on.

But we've just seen something: Saul is a man whose heart is *filled with insecurity*.

. . . . .

IN THE CHAPTERS TO FOLLOW, WE will have an uncomfortably close seat to observe just how insecure Saul is and just how much it will cost him.

Look. I don't know you, your past, your present, or your future.

I just believe when it comes to the life God has for you, there is more inside you and in front of you than you could dream.

And insecurity will steal and deplete that life more than you could imagine.

It's unlimited what God can do with your life. The future awaiting you isn't safe and pain-free but it *can* be filled with beauty and purpose and divine grace.

Without confidence, though, you will never fully step into what God has. You will never be fully postured to love those beside you, rise into the gifts inside you, and serve the world around you. You will never fully step into life itself. You will never be fully yourself. You will never be free.

Let's go.

It's time to get your confidence back.

Confidence isn't walking in a room and thinking you are
better than everyone; it's walking in and not having to
compare yourself to anyone at all.[1]
—Jay Shetty

. . . Let's just go ahead and be what we were made to be,
without enviously or pridefully trying to compare ourselves
with each other, or trying to be something we aren't.[2]
—Paul

I feel like . . . a shape that will never matter, a color that will
never flatter.[3]
—AVA ("Saturday Love")

2)

Zero Sum

I N A W A Y , I N S E C U R I T Y D O E S N ' T SEEM LIKE THAT BIG OF A DEAL.

I guess I shouldn't say that. I've written a whole book on it, and you're cutting into Netflix to read it. But insecurity sort of feels like a first-world problem, like trust-fund kids with too much money, or the way WiFi is criminally bad in airports, or how people no longer know how to whisper in movie theaters.

If anything, insecurity just seems an unfortunate weakness, like a darker, less honorable version of humility. Perhaps even endearing.

On the subject, what are *you* insecure about?

Looks? Growing older? Relational status?

We all have something. Even the ones you think wouldn't. Apparently, Kate Moss is self-conscious about her "bowed legs," Beyonce dislikes her feet and ears, and Post Malone got tattoos all over his face because he thinks it's ugly.

Me? I have a small charcuterie board of insecurities. Just depends which aged cheese you want to start with.

I remember the first time I felt it, too. Third grade, walking down the hall, thinking about Velociraptors from *Jurassic Park* when a group of girls walked toward me, grinning.

They must be thinking about Velociraptors, too.

But the "mean girls" leader spoke up:

"Russ, you're a witch!" Then she laughed like one.

Witch? I'd always been told I'm such a nice kid . . .

It wasn't my personality, she clarified. It was my pointy nose.

I don't think I'd ever been made aware of this particular feature of mine. Not to worry, she took painstaking pleasure in pointing out the distinct sharpness of my snout from its right silhouette.

My face went white. I stammered out something about me being rubber and her being glue and then hobbled off to a corner to process this new information.

Such a small thing. Yet the spears of that particular "truth" sunk succinctly into my psyche like fork into butter.

For years and years after—okay, still to this day—I make sure pictures are taken from my left profile and don't laugh, but on any date, particularly at movies, I make sure to sit on the right side so my date can view me from the best possible angle.

Confusing conversations have ensued. For example, if my date has sat down on the "wrong" side, or, to my horror, attempted to *switch* sides.

Through slick maneuvering or plain, adamant refusals, the obvious question's asked:

"Uh . . . why do you so badly want to sit on that side?"

"Protection," I reply simply. "I need to protect you from intruders."

Occasionally, tragically, the girl will point out the unfortunate fact the entrance is on the *other* side, in which case I smirk and simply shake my head like what she said didn't make sense.

Yes, I've been to therapy.

Crazy, though, isn't it, how one moment, one word from childhood can shape your self-view for years and decades to come?

But again, the question begs to be asked: Is insecurity *that* big of a deal?

We'll circle back to that in a few chapters, but first, a quick *Lost*-style flash forward in this movie on Saul. A couple of decades, actually.

By now, time has dramatically spotlighted both Saul's strengths and weaknesses. There have been some remarkable political achievements and some heart-wrenching personal failures.

Most amazingly, all those years of kingship haven't melted away an ounce of his insecurity. On the contrary, it's been growing into an avalanche. And a young man named David is unknowingly about to provide the final, snowy push.

Even if you didn't grow up religious, you've probably heard of

David. Lion and bear assassin, most famous king in Israel's history, did most of the heavy lifting for the book of Psalms, Jesus came from his bloodline, Da Vinci made a big, naked statue of him. That guy.

By Samuel 18, he's killed wild beasts, dropped Goliath, and become best friends with Saul's son Jonathan.

A bourgeoning reputation has grown around David. And not just for all the giant-killing. After Goliath's defeat, Saul recruited the young man into his administration and began to send him on military missions. He performed splendidly. Crushed every assignment. So much so, Saul eventually gave him a top-tier rank in the service, which made the troops and officers ecstatic.

David was on a *roll.*

Maybe too much so.

Ever met someone that seemed to have *too* much going for them? So annoying. And a little suspicious.

One day, David came home from battle with another blistering victory, and the reception went Times Square on New Year's Eve:

> "When the men were returning home after David had killed the Philistine, the women came out from all the towns of Israel to meet King Saul with singing and dancing, with joyful songs . . ."[4]

To bring this home, Saul's in his BMW, Instagram model beside him, smiling behind Prada shades. She presses the radio. A new hit plays on Jerusalem's 106.5 Top 30. The beat's good. Saul's head bobs.

The lyrics:[5]

> As they danced, they sang: "Saul has slain his thousands . . ."

Saul's eyes light up. He tries to play it cool, concealing a grin, turning the volume to the right. His wife unmoved, he gently taps her knee with a knuckle and gestures toward the speaker.

> "Not a big deal, honey, they're singing about me. It's whatever . . ."

But then the next line hits.

> ". . . and David his *tens of thousands*."

Uh oh.

Saul palm strikes the radio off, muttering that they don't make music like they used to. His hands tremble. A blaze of suffocating panic swarms down his brain and into his stomach.

The women of Jerusalem are making music videos about how Saul has killed thousands but David his tens of thousands.

He could feel the sea change beneath his feet.

Now. We'll ignore the different times and what passes for office-place bragging. What's not new is this thing we call comparison.

Thousands versus tens of thousands, huh?

Ever felt like Saul?

Talented until you got around someone more talented?

Attractive until someone came around more attractive?

Intelligent until someone walked in more intelligent?

Secure in your job until that new employee blazed in, hot off the press, taking everyone by storm? Ever tried not to notice the boss has given them *three* compliments already but hasn't thanked you for your work in *weeks*? You golf-clap through a closed smile but deep down would *not* be mad if they tripped on the way to high-five the boss, hot coffee in hand.

A leader I respect, Larry Brey, says, "Insecurity grows in the land of comparison."

So true. In the land of comparison, we get distracted and spend much of our time, well, comparing. We hold up areas of our life against that of others and become deflated when we come up short. Which leaves us feeling sad, anxious, and inadequate. Even threatened.

And let me tell you, this new song and reality made Saul feel so threatened it drove him mad. Literally.

We read:

> "Saul was very angry; this refrain displeased him greatly. 'They have credited David with tens of thousands,' he thought, 'but me with only thousands. What more can he get but the kingdom?' And from that time on Saul kept a close eye on David."

The following verses show a leader spiraling into a paranoid depression and torment that could only be relieved by music and eventual thoughts of harming David.

As that face-tatted prophet Post Malone once said, "A paranoid man makes paranoid plans."

Oh, what a daisy chain insecurity can be.

. . . . .

IT'S PROBABLY A CHICKEN–OR–THE– egg scenario as to whether insecurity causes comparison or comparison causes insecurity. I know this much: The two go hand in hand. And they're a miserable cycle to live in.

The Apostle Paul wrote to friends at one of his seaside churches and warned them plainly:

"They measure themselves by themselves . . . not wise."[6]

Comparing is expected, of course, on one hand. We all do it. Let's acknowledge that. There's even a healthy kind of comparison (topic for another book), one that Paul also talks about, that spurs us on in personal development, elevating our standards and progress, one where iron sharpens iron, and our values are deepened by people who inspire us.

Here, however, Paul is speaking to *insecurity-fueled comparison*. The kind where we envy someone's results instead of embodying their process. The kind where we feel angst over someone else's good fortune instead of gratitude over ours. The kind where we compare someone's different lane of work with our own unique contribution.

That kind of comparison is *always* unwise.

Why?

For starters, it's a lose-lose. When we compare, we tend to come up *less than*, feeling inadequate and discouraged, or *better than*, feeling haughty and arrogant. Superior or inferior. Pride or insecurity. Lose-lose. No bueno either way.

It's also the wrong scoreboard, not to mention a misleading one.

The truth is we're all wired, gifted, and purposed differently. What someone else does is a non factor in both my significance and ability to fulfill my own God-given purpose. When things are wonky and missing in our souls, though, to the comparison trap we run. There, we drink its salt, thinking it'll quench our thirst.

· · · · ·

I BELIEVE PART OF OUR ISSUE IS WE'VE unknowingly been formed by zero-sum philosophy. If you're unfamiliar with zero-sum, it's a concept popular in game theory. It's any situation in which one person's gain is equivalent to another's loss. In the end, the net change in wealth or benefit equals zero.[7]

Your gain is my loss, and my gain is your loss. For me to win, you must lose.

Examples include poker, chess, tennis, and so forth. All strictly zero-sum games with clear winners and losers. It makes the stakes high and puts the players on defense.

Theoretically, how would zero-sum play out in everyday affairs?

Like this:

> *Your attractiveness takes away from my attractiveness. Your popularity takes away from my popularity. Your talent takes away from my talent. Your recognition takes away from my recognition.*

Sound familiar? *Feel* familiar?

After all, there's only so much of all that to go around. Right?

It's said Alexander III wouldn't tolerate any praise given to his generals, convinced it distracted from his glory.

It's a scarcity mindset. A fear-based mindset. A zero-sum mindset.

I'm just shooting out a possibility: Could that describe us? The posture of our post-Eden, glory-missing souls? That in our vulnerable, dysfunctional state of disconnection from God, we've adopted zero-sum thinking in how we assess our value with each other and ourselves? Always clamoring for bigger fruit to show and bigger leaves to hide?

I think so. And it's a small way to live.

There's a different way.

Another game theory.

Positive-sum theory.

These are circumstances in which the total net gains and losses
are *more* than zero. It's when resources are so increased and an
approach so formulated that the needs and wants of all are
fulfilled.

It's an abundance mindset. A faith-based mindset. A positive-
sum mindset.

I'm convinced this simple truth would set us free if we
embraced it:

Human value is not a zero-sum game; it's a positive-sum game.

In other words, with God, there's always enough to go around.
There is enough abundance and diversity in God's ecosystem
and your eternal value that no one on this planet could ever be
fortunate enough, attractive enough, or rich enough to take a
single point from your worth.

This must sink in.

When you realize someone else's gift doesn't diminish your gift,
you become freed up to celebrate them instead of being
shrunken back with sadness, feeling threatened and insufficient.

In your friend group, your gifts don't detract from each other;
they enrich each other.

When individuals tap into this, they flourish.

When cultures tap into this, they soar.

I'll say it again: *No one can detract from your value.*

That's zero-sum thinking. No, there's enough room for all your awesomeness *and* theirs. The moment that truth slips into your soul, shackles loosen and life expands.

If someone around me does something better than me, that's great. No skin off my nose. No skin off my beautiful, pointy nose at all.

No, I can stand there with quiet confidence and clap, knowing God has made me unique in my own right, and continue to develop my own skills while baseball-whistling for theirs.

Everyone around us is going to have different areas of strength and struggle. We must release people to be imperfect in their own ways and impressive in their own ways without letting it frustrate our day or press into our self-worth. When we do that, we're headed toward freedom.

. . . . .

IF "INSECURITY GROWS IN THE LAND of comparison," then dang, what a swampland we currently live in. I trust I don't need to belabor the point on the effects digital media and current societal values have on us.

Books[8] and documentaries[9] abound. As do the stats.[10]

Just as a pinch of salt to taste:

Between 1997 and 2007, the suicide rate among ten to twenty-four-year-olds was stable. And then Facebook—founded in 2004—became available to the public in 2006, rising quickly and meteorically. From 2007–2017, the suicide rate in that same age range rose *fifty-seven percent.*

That's crazy talk.

Social media consumption has proven time and again to negatively impact mental health in virtually every arena.[3] And research points to one primary, shared cause:

Comparison.

Think about it. Social media is the largest "land of comparison" humanity has ever ventured into. Inside that land, many of us starve, die, or pick each other off.

You've probably heard it a thousand times: We tend to compare our *behind-the-scenes footage* with everyone else's *highlight reel.*

Nowhere is this truer than Instagram.

Few post their tedious, mind-numbing study hours; they post swinging tassels in front of Colgate® teeth. Few post the cuss-filled argument on the way to church; they post the adorable family posed in their Sunday best with an out-of-context verse. And few post the ugly picture; they post the attractive one (and if their friends look bad in it to help with contrast, even better).

More importantly, hardly anyone posts their weaknesses; no, they present their best angle and the areas where they're killing it.

Or, how about number of likes, views, and followers? None of us would ever be superficial enough to notice *that*. Right?

So, we see others' dream vacations and got-it-together lives and contrast it with a keen awareness of all our areas we wish were different.

Anyone?

Let's face it: The "grass is greener" effect is real. It just is. And here's the thing, I can promise you *right now* even as you read these words, there are people who want *your life*, or at least some part of it. You know that, right?

I have friends in another state who called a couple of summers back and said the concert of the century was about to take place.[11] All our favorite punk rock bands of the early 2000s were about to descend onto multiple stages from sunup to sundown in Las Vegas to shake the earth with their wonderful, melodic angst.

We *have* to go, they said. So we hopped on a group call as the ticket sale counted down and put our fingers to the submit button. Apparently, the whole world had the same idea. It sold out instantly.

All that to say, my purchase went through but my friends' didn't. I was stuck with a stupendously expensive, nonrefundable ticket to a music festival in Vegas. Could've sold it, I guess. But I hadn't been to Vegas since middle school with my parents, so I decided to make a trip out of it. I researched all the best shops and views and restaurants and even found deals on seeing my favorite magicians (no laughing).[12]

That first morning, I found a coffee spot with great vibes and bright aromatic roasts and felt my soul come alive as I walked in.

I was so excited.

But I also felt a little lonely, if I'm honest. Maybe even a teaspoon of self-pity. No friends there with me. And when will

I have a wife and kids to experience these things with?

That's when my friend Joel called. Joel's a church planter in Atlanta with a wife and kids and a great life. He asked what I was doing and I told him. Without pause he laughed,

"Man! You are going to the grave with no regrets, my friend. I'm serious. Do you know how often I want your life?"

Isn't that funny?

There's green grass everywhere. It's just hard to see ours.

. . . . .

ON OUR JOURNEY TO CHIP AWAY insecurity, let me ask: What would it look like to live in a world free of comparison?

One can only imagine it.

Some are trying to create it.

The well-known *Onsite* workshop in Tennessee has seen tremendous success, notably among many celebrities. One of the hallmarks is their strict rule that no one can tell anyone what they do for a living. Sounds simple. But I've read stories of people in the program who describe the surprising level of detox and struggle to not define your value with each other by what you produce. To be Adam and Eve without leaves.

Yesterday a friend sent me an article about a similar experiment. Strangers in test groups connecting with each other. In the first, they could reveal their occupation. In the second, they couldn't.

Guess what? The latter remained lifelong friends.[13]

You can't help but wonder . . . What kind of connection do we miss with other human beings when tricked into believing they're our competition instead of fellow sojourners to explore life with?

A friend and I even wondered aloud the other day about our context in the faith community. What would it be like to experiment with a small group where no one can say what they do for a living?

I don't know. Maybe one day we'll try.

What I do know is *today* we can all take steps to leave the dry, devious land of comparison and head toward the sweet perfume of open field.

A practical action step?

Detox from digital media.

Seriously. If you've been feeling that comparison pinch, take a break from it until you've finished the book. Or better yet, a month after. Give your soul some silence, rest, and reset. (Just do us all a favor and don't make a dramatic announcement about it.)

Then if you come back, have a plan first.

Maybe no screentime before Scripture (or meditation, journaling, whatever) in the morning. Or only fifteen minutes a day of social media and only *after* exercise, time with friends, and a focused day's work. That alone could spread Harry Potter magic all over your land.

Another thing. If your current community is a bit toxic and Tommy-topper about everything, I hate to say it, you might need a detox from that too. And to find some new circles if they refuse to shift.

I recognize some contexts are impossible to escape, your place of work being one. And this obviously isn't an excuse to ghost your friends or ditch a marriage.

But in the fight for a healthy, confident soul, we probably all need some sort of *intentional detox* followed by an *intentional direction.*

In the circumstances you can't avoid? For now, when you see that person get more attention and those familiar, unpleasant feelings begin to flutter, simply smile to yourself and whisper, "Oops, playing the wrong game again. This isn't zero-sum. It's positive sum. And life has enough room for us both."

The jealous are troublesome to others, but a torment to themselves.[1]
—William Penn

Nobody who knew who God meant them to be would ever want to be anybody else.[2]
—Bill John

You can be the moon and still be jealous of the stars.[3]
—Gary Allan

3)

Green-Eyed Monsters

A S WE SAW LAST CHAPTER, DAVID'S RISE INADVERTENTLY put the spotlight on Saul's heart and all the moss that'd been growing there.

One of the first dastardly creatures to scurry from the shadows was insecurity's bitter cousin:

Jealousy.

That slimy, green-eyed monster.

Even the word is icky, isn't it?

But we all know it.

We've all felt the familiar sludge fill our veins when our significant other laughs a little *too* hard with that attractive friend or when our coworker's praised a little *too* highly by the boss or when our friend continues to hit the jackpot a little *too* much in life.

But while jealousy might be natural to experience, it's something to keep binoculars on and shoo from the door.

When Proverbs says to guard our hearts, you can bet this is one of the intruders Solomon had in mind.

In fact, left unchecked, the story of jealousy terminates in devastation.

Take our protagonist, Saul. From the moment jealousy entered his heart toward David, the relationship was never the same. And neither was Saul.

In fact, Saul ended up trying to *kill* David.

You read that right. And not just once. Saul spent years on a single-mission manhunt, no matter how many times David proved his innocence and loyalty.

It's vital we see jealousy's corrosive, spiraling effect.

Saul, the God-ordained, God-anointed leader over God's people, shifted all his mental and emotional energy to undermine, resist, and even murder another person. And not just any person. God's next in line to be king. A humble, kind young man who had *benefited Saul.*

Madness.

But in the words of Lawrence Durrell, "It is not love that is blind, but jealousy."[4]

See, there's a verse I used to raise an eyebrow at. It just seemed a stretch:

> "Anger is cruel, and wrath is like a flood, but jealousy is even more dangerous."[5]

Another translations ends with, "Who can stand against jealousy?"[6]

Come on. I know jealousy is suboptimal, but more dangerous than *wrath*?

Then I received a call one night that rattled me to the marrow. A friend from church had driven over and murdered his brother at his own house. The police found him in the rain on the side of the road, yelling into the night. Jarring anecdote, I know. And look, other issues factored in, marital suspicions and dissatisfaction in life among them. But front and center? A lifelong jealousy and resentful inadequacy towards his brother.

If you want the real truth, the verse finally clicked when I saw *The Count of Monte Cristo*.

I watched the film in my *wanderjahr* by a South American lake, losing myself in the tale. And oh, what a tale. Feels like *Indiana Jones*, *Shawshank Redemption*, and *Taken* had a baby.[7] And the baby has it all: romance, adventure, mystery, and the complex friendship of Edmond Dantes and Fernand Mondego.

Though naïve and poor, Edmond has the affection of the girl of his (and Fernand's) dreams. The stars favor him. He keeps scoring lucky escapes and surprising promotions. And unlike rich, well-heeled Fernand, Edmond's simply and stupendously *happy*.

Evidence of Fernand's resentment creaks throughout the movie like trespass signs, obvious and disconcerting until, spoiler alert, Fernand betrays Edmond, scheming him into lifelong imprisonment on a remote island while running off with his former fiancé.

The movie fills out nicely from there with seaside castles, grandiose revenge plans, and *Princess-Bride*-level sword fights.

But to me, the personal tragedy eclipsed everything else: The light left Edmond's soul. The once-kind, joyful, wide-eyed man became cold, cynical, and shut off in heart to any mission besides vengeance.

In a scene that stays with me even now, Edmond, between flashes of steel, cries, *demands*, a reason for such betrayal:

"Why! In God's name, why!"

His former friend gathers himself and with resigned but emotional calmness, sighs,

"Because you're the son of a clerk. And I'm not supposed to want to be you."

Jealousy. Who can stand against it?

This is Cain and Abel stuff.

David and Saul.

Me and Colt.

Colt and I have been friends since middle school. We're like brothers. And honestly, we've enjoyed a pretty healthy relationship. And I've never tried to kill him with a Spanish sword.

But there were a couple of seasons, looking back, it's obvious insecurity got its teeth in me.

And can you blame me? Take my human journey and put me beside a tall and handsome Romeo with blue eyes and long blond hair, not to mention football player, homecoming king, guitarist, singer, oh, and anointed young man of God . . . and well, I'd be lying if I said there weren't moments I was Saul and he, David.

I'll never forget one parking lot night with friends and girls. It'd be hard to explain what happened or how I did it. It was so subtle. I just know I wielded my charm in a way that stole the attention from Colt, that oh-so-subtly excluded him, diverting interest away from his efforts. Then I garnered time with the girl we both liked, making her laugh, even stealing sarcastic glances his way.

May sound trivial. But it's the little paper cuts that sting.

Later that night as he began to drive away, I started feeling bad and ran to his driver's side window to say bye. When I did, I was gut punched. This carefree friend had tears shining off both cheeks.

I "won" that night. Good job, Russ.

Jealousy is *ugly*.

I also remember a better moment. A healing moment. Ninthgrade, bleachers, end of gym class. I don't even remember how I started the conversation. But it poured like lava.

"I've felt jealous of you," I confessed.

He was gracious. Thanked me for telling him and said it made us closer. He even lied and said he'd felt jealous too.

That was hard to imagine, of course. But assuming he wasn't just making me feel better, it highlights what we mentioned last chapter.

"Grass is greener" syndrome.

Rock stars want to be movie stars and movie stars want to be rock stars. Married people envy a single person's freedom, and a single person thinks marriage will complete them. The intelligent person envies good looks and the attractive person envies another's skill.

On and on the useless cycle goes.

Jealousy eats our lunch.

. . . . . .

THERE ARE SEVERAL SUBNARRATIVES inside of jealousy.

Romantically, it indicates greed, not love. A desire to possess, not serve.

Internally, it reveals a sad disbelief in ourselves. It's actually a lack of ownership we take in our own lives, a lack of confidence in our ability to build the future we want, that makes us resent the reality others experience.

And theologically, it is a strangely scandalous thing.

In his now classic book *Enemies of the Heart*, Pastor Andy Stanley outlines four great invaders of the human spirit. In trademark clarity, he reveals how they boil down to debt-and-debtor relationships. The four enemies, he contends, are guilt, shame, anger, and jealousy.[8]

The debt-doomed dynamics are thus:

Anger says, "You owe me."

Guilt says, "I owe you."

Greed says, "I owe me."

But jealousy—watch this—says, "*God* owes me."

That might need a minute to metabolize.

I watched Andy give a talk on this once. He brought up volunteers and, announcing he had gifts, handed them each a brown paper bag. One by one, they opened them. Inside the first, a pencil. Inside the second, an apple. Inside the third . . . a brand-new *Apple iPad* . . . Then, he told them to sit down and enjoy their gifts. Awkward laughter ensued.

Even watching it from a distance, the "That's not fair!" feelings rose in us all.

The point, of course, is those gifts were Andy's to give. He could give them however and to whomever he wanted. If anyone had a problem with "fairness," their real problem wasn't with each other; it was with Andy, the one who distributed the gifts.

In this framing, jealousy, in short, says, "God, I don't like what You've given me, and I wish I had what You've given *them*."

We don't think of it that way, of course. But if you're a
follower of Jesus who believes God is the One who made us
and gave us our lives, that *is* the unspoken meta-narrative of
jealousy.

And that might be a needed perspective shift. A heart check to
realize my real problem might be a dissatisfaction and distrust
in how God made *me*. A convicting insight, for sure. But one
that could open us up to a heart-to-heart with a gracious
Father, marked with honesty, confession and healing.

. . . . .

BACK TO ISRAEL'S NEW HIT SONG.

The story continues:

> "Saul was very angry; this refrain displeased him greatly.
> 'They have credited David with tens of thousands,' he
> thought, 'but me with only thousands. What more can he
> get but the kingdom?' And from that time on Saul kept a
> close eye on David."[9]

If you keep reading, you'll be shocked how quickly Saul's
mental health deteriorates. He becomes *tortured* by it all.

Ever felt *tortured* by insecurity? *Tormented* by jealousy?

It's not fun stuff.

Saul's so tortured, in fact, that he ironically beckons David—
the source of his paranoia—to serenade him with the harp for

some ancient, ASMR[10] soul relief. Even then, his mind goes sideways. Superficial relief only lasts so long. As the private concert closes, he grabs a spear and hurls it at David, barely missing.

But look back at that line:

". . . From that time on Saul kept a close eye on David."

Such fascinating insight into human psychology.

Think about it. Saul's now hell-bent on keeping tabs on David even though *David hasn't done anything.*

The only thing David's done is continue to honor Saul and prove himself trustworthy. Yet the moment Saul became unhealthy in soul, he viewed David through the lens of suspicion.

I don't think we're aware how often we do this.

How often our *projection of others* is actually a *reflection of ourselves.* A mirror to what's inside *us.*

When we are untrustworthy, we think others can't be trusted.[11] When we aren't generous, we suspect others are stingy or their motives dodgy. When we don't feel good about ourselves, we don't feel good about anyone.

As the German polymath Goethe said, "We see in the world what we carry in our hearts."[12]

Saul began to keep a close eye on David when he should've kept a closer eye on his own spirit.

He reached a disturbing place. Not only was he unable to celebrate David's success; he viewed it as a threat. That's how small and dark his interior world became.

Can we see it now? How devious jealousy truly is? How this trifecta of insecurity, comparison, and envy can ruin our lives?

. . . . .

IN ANDY'S BOOK I REFERENCED, HE gives a practical weapon to combat each heart invader.

The one for jealousy is timeless and powerful and has served me well.

I present to you this simple sword:

Celebration.

When you feel jealous of someone, celebrate them.

Oof. Tough, I know.

Look, we have a lot of inner work ahead. But practically, if you want to cut away the chains of jealousy wrapped around your soul, practice celebrating other people. *Especially* those you feel jealous of.

I probably don't have to tell you this takes intentionality. In the baser parts of our nature, our inclination is to do the opposite. When we feel less than others, we shut down and minimize a person's success. Or worse, we find excuses to criticize or even sabotage. We look for chinks in their armor to make sure everyone knows that, come on, they're not *that good* . . .

But if we want to be free? Then, just like any other area of life, we need to train ourselves to do the opposite of what we *feel* like doing.

So today, tomorrow, next week, when that person gets extra attention or scores big, and you feel that familiar torture-nerve-pinch on your heart, do your soul the favor and fight back: Celebrate the heck out of 'em.

Send them a gift. Look them in the eye and tell them how proud you are. Make a post on social media (here's your permission to get back on for two minutes). Send a text. Brag on them in front of their coworkers.

It doesn't have to be big or fake. Find the good. Find something specific. And recognize it.

It may be challenging at first. But if you do it, you'll notice something. It won't just make their day; it'll make yours. You'll find your soul becoming free and light. You'll find that the universe God made has enough room for them *and* you.

Shall we warm our muscles now? Quick challenge: Before the next paragraph, put the book down and send a text to someone hard for you to celebrate. Try it.

If you did, notice how you feel. Your pulse. Your shoulders. I'm telling you, it's better than a half-day at the Sky Lagoon Spa in Iceland. Almost.

By the way, more on this later, but I have to say it because I feel the tension as I type. It seems a lot of our current culture, due to an odd obsession/misunderstanding of "authenticity," is convinced they have to *feel* something in order to *do* something or it's "fake."

It's not.

It's called maturing into the optimal version of yourself regardless of your lesser impulses. It's called wisdom. It's called growth. And if you're stuck in the "have to feel it in order to do it" phase, I need to level with you: You will remain in emotional prisons the better part of your life waiting to *feel* like taking the right action before you do it. I say we bust out of prison now, regardless of goosebumps.

. . . . .

I TRULY BELIEVE A SPIRIT OF
celebration is one of the most powerful things you can cultivate as a person. For you, the people around you, and the culture of your life.

In fact, all over Scripture, God commands people to pile up stones to do just that. To remember. To celebrate.

I'm convinced our society would be infinitely healthier if we observed a fraction of the celebratory feasts God gave the children of Israel. Maybe some of us should start with actually taking our PTO. Or at least having fun.

We take this stuff seriously where I work. We have staff standards, one of which is literally, "Celebration: We celebrate a lot."

We kick off Mondays in a circle where we honor each other and fist-pump about what God is doing. This way, we *see* each other, accentuate the positive like Paul directed the Philippians,[13] practice gratitude toward God, and maintain unity. I can't even explain what it's done for our culture.

A couple of years ago, I took this further with the team I lead. I thought our culture was good but noticed most of us still tended to only show up to or post about "our thing." I told them I didn't just want us to have a *celebratory* spirit; I wanted us to have a *championing* spirit. I wanted us to root each other on like crazy, personally and professionally, just as much as if "their thing" was "my thing."

That year, a team member came out with a book.[14] It was a terrific but modest endeavor with no real plan to promote it. A personal accomplishment for friends and family and anyone out in the ether.

Still, I knew my first book was launching later that year. I asked myself what I'd want in his shoes. So, at our volunteer rally that next Sunday, I schemed a few surprises. I had this coworker step forward, and with his book in hand (which I read), I bragged on his accomplishment and encouraged everyone to buy it. We had a cake custom-made with the book's theme, which his wife brought out with candles like it was his birthday. Then his daughter stepped forward and read a note about how much her dad meant to her and how much the book reflected the enormity of his heart. She cried, he cried, others cried.

It was a good morning.

You may be wondering if I've popped a joint reaching to pat my own back. Look, I've failed in the jealousy category plenty. But I'm telling you: Choosing to be someone who celebrates others is one of the most fun, liberating, life-enlarging decisions you'll ever make. And that morning, it didn't just make my coworker's day; it made mine.

I know life's tough. With some people, it's tricky to find the good. Everything isn't roses. Another standard of ours is, "Evaluation: We evaluate everything." We're a high-feedback culture.

But, especially in church, can I be honest? As important as it is to hold to truth and keep each other accountable and all that jazz, I can't escape the feeling a lot of our critique is just ill-disguised jealousy.

In one of my favorite stories, a faith hero of mine found himself in a meeting with semi-famous pastors who all began criticizing even-more-famous pastors who weren't in the room and the megachurches they lead.[15] Finally, he spoke up:

"Hey, guys—why don't we just own up to the fact we're probably just jealous? That we hate the fact they're more talented and it might be why their churches are bigger?"

I imagine the delicious silence that followed.

But as H.G. Wells once said, "Moral indignation is jealousy with a halo."

I think it's true. I think in the same way we dress up gossip with "prayer request" and "concern," we often massage our ego by using religious language to tear down other churches, leaders, and each other.

Only you can decide what the spirit and conversation of your life will be. I'm just telling you, the secure people I respect are too busy working hard in their lane to do much else besides encourage their peers and celebrate others' unique expressions.

That's the kind of person I want to be, at least.

And I'm convinced it was the kind of person Jesus was.

Remember when His disciples got all flustered over another group that wasn't in their little tribe and was doing things differently? Remember what Jesus said? He told them to cut it out and not discourage them. Whoever wasn't against them was for them.[16]

Apparently, Jesus wasn't into the zero-sum game.

As for me? I've decided other people and organizations aren't my competition. I know hate sells and outrage builds followers. But celebration builds my heart. I'll take the latter.

What if you took this on as a new personal code, part of the ethos of your life? A championing spirit. The kind who champions people. A celebratory attitude, not a corrective kind. An encouraging spirit, not a jealous one.

There's other weaponry against jealousy, of course.

Gratitude. All day, every day. Jealousy and gratitude can't even coexist in the same space.

And pray for the people you're jealous of. Pray happiness and health over them every morning. Do it for a week, take your emotional vitals, and get back to me.

Also, if your people speak poorly of other people, you might need new people.

That's tough to hear. And tougher to do. But the health of your soul and future depends on it. Be kind. Don't cancel people; invite them into your new way of life. But you can't force them to go with you. Cultivate an inner circle that's healthy and self-aware and that spends their "improvement energy" on themselves.

Above all, if you want to enrich your life, add value to others. Prop up their efforts and toast their successes. And when you feel that old enemy of jealousy pick a fight, go to freaking war against it with the sword of celebration. It'll take you from the prison to the castle.

I sometimes think that shame, mere awkward, senseless shame, does as much towards preventing good acts and straightforward happiness as any of our vices can do.[1]
—C. S. Lewis

Let the ghosts get loud. Let the tears fall down.[2]
—Amy Stroup ("As Long as You're with Me")

A not-so-perfect past does not give you permission to indulge in a passive future.[3]
—Clint Claypoole

4)

Haunted & Hiding

YOU KNOW THE CRAZIEST THING ABOUT SAUL'S INSECURITY?

He had nothing to be insecure about.

Seriously. Quite the opposite.

Let's put the Legos in place: In 1 Samuel 9, we're told Saul's as *fine and handsome* a man as any other and a *foot taller* on top of it.

Then he's anointed with God's Spirit, crowned king, and given the nation.

So—Saul's the *hottest* guy around, the *tallest* guy around, the most *anointed* guy around, arguably the most *gifted* guy around, now the most *powerful* guy around, *and* the *wealthiest* guy around.

And yet he's the most *insecure* guy around.

Crazy, huh?

This is important.

See, if you're anything like me, you might be tempted to believe you'll feel confident *when* . . .

Ever felt that?

When I lose this amount of weight . . . *then* I'll feel comfortable.

When I get that job . . . *then* I'll feel like I made it.

When I can prove myself to my mom/dad/ex . . . *then* I'll feel like I'm enough.

Doesn't work, though, does it?

I mean, sometimes for a minute. There's a practical sense in which success breeds confidence in an already healthy soul. The trouble comes when we use it as a mask. Success is a great *ingredient* when we have meaning; a terrible fix-all without it.

We keep chasing the carrot anyway, don't we?

I once heard actor Matthew McConaughey call this the *ta-da* moment.[4] The imaginary moment people believe comes when they get rich enough or famous enough, and . . . ta-da! I feel good now!

Ta-da! I'm married and now I'll never be lonely or scared again.

Ta-da! I've achieved that income/promotion/award and now my self-belief is permanently settled.

Ta-da! I've reached a certain age/job and now I finally feel like an adult.

    CONFIDENCE

It's madness any of us continue to buy into this myth no matter how many immortals come back from the velvet curtain of success/fame/sex/talent to tell us, "Nope, doesn't work." Or when those who should be the most confident perpetually find themselves in rehab, multiple marriages, or worse.

And here we have Saul. The whole package on the outside. But he never became a whole person on the inside. And so not only does none of that stuff heal his soul; it only magnifies the dysfunction that's in it.

We should mark this down somewhere inside us:

> *There is no imaginary line I will ever cross through external accomplishment that will convert my insecurities into confidence.*

It didn't work with Saul. It doesn't work for anyone in Hollywood. And it won't work for you or me.

And that's because true confidence is not an *external circumstance*; it's an *internal condition*.

No amount of leaves a human being accumulates will ever be enough to cover the interior vacancy.

Confidence is an inside job.

On a superficial level, I've experienced this phenomenon when getting in shape for trips or checking social media after communicating. But chasing validation to feel value is chasing the wind.[5]

I think first-time writers experience this. A shiny fairy tale of what "being published" will do for their soul.

I wrote my first book because I genuinely sensed I should. The fire of its message burned inside me, the coals demanding to be unbagged and lit. And I wanted all those flames to honor God and help people.

I also really love to write. I can't not write. I'm outright obsessed with the art and beauty of words and love the process so much that even if no one read those words, I would still write them.

But also . . .

Somewhere inside me, I wanted the validation of being an author. I wanted the clapping that would come with making something beautiful, something important. I wanted to feel significant through the praise of what others would say about my work.

I imagined the texts that would come of, "Oh, Russ, that was so wonderful. Oh, Russ, that was brilliant! Oh, Russ, that changed my life! Oh, Russ, we've all been discussing the majesty of your prose, and it's clear you are the new Steinbeck!" I haven't heard that last one yet.

So, a big part of me did it for good. And a small part of me did it for clapping.

Yucky to admit. But God already knows. What's the point of acting pious? And here's what I've discovered: As long as I stay honest, especially about the ugly in my heart, asking Him to scrub and help, He can continue to work with even someone like me.

So, releasing a book is fantastic. It really is. There's a rich sense of accomplishment in it, not to mention deep meaning when your simple words can add to someone's life.

But most days are just days. Days I forget I have a book out there and I'm stuck with being me. All that thunderous clapping fades to silence and I have to get off the stage and live life.

So yeah, I don't have going for me what Saul did. Not by a thousand desert miles. But I do get it, these weird contradictions of life. And the next time you look at someone and assume they feel constantly amazing inside because of all that's happening outside, realize there are people who feel that way about *you*.

I *know* they felt that way about Saul.

. . . . .

SO THEN WHAT GIVES? WHY WAS SAUL so insecure?

That's up for grabs, of course. But I do think we have a powerful hint to work with. Something enclosed in a moment we've already discussed. Something that doesn't just explain Saul but explains us.

So, let's rewind. All the way back to his inaugural day, fetal position behind a few Samsonite suitcases. Recall the phrase God used when they couldn't find him. God said Saul had,

> ". . . hidden himself among the supplies."[6]

Another translation says it better:

"He is hiding among the *baggage*."[7]

Now we're down to brass tacks.

What a picture of Saul. What a picture of us.

Saul never broke out of his *insecurity* because he never broke out of his *issues*.

He had baggage.

Ever heard that?

> *He has baggage. They have baggage. Oh, be careful not to date her . . . she has baggage.*

The truth? We all have baggage. I know I do.

Some of our baggage is simply messier than others. And some of us choose to address our baggage, while others do not.

Saul did not.

To the point that as the imminent king of Israel, he was *hiding in his baggage* instead of *heading toward his future.*

That's what unaddressed trauma and chronic insecurity will do, by the way. It'll drive you into hiding. You'll stay stuck on the sidelines instead of moving forward in the game. You'll hide in emotional scars instead of opening up again. You'll sabotage the good thing God wants to do in your life because deep down you don't think you deserve it.

Unprocessed issues lead to unfulfilled potential. Yesterday's infections become tomorrow's insecurities.

See, insecurity is not an isolated reality. Insecurity is usually *connected to something.*

What baggage was Saul's insecurity connected to?

Again, who knows? Could've gone back to his dad. Kish was a man of noble standing.[8] Maybe Saul felt he could never measure up. It's conjecture, but interesting nonetheless that when Saul gets back from meeting Samuel, he tells his uncle about it,[9] but his dad is never really mentioned again. Either way, I can't count how many guys I talk to that feel like, at the end of the day, it doesn't matter what they do—it'll never be good enough for their old man.

Maybe there was something in Saul's past. Thirty years is *way* more than enough time to accumulate mistakes and scars. The kind that can warp how you see yourself and dampen your outlook with shame.

Shame, by the way, is the confidence *destroyer.*

Ever felt shame's poison weaken your emotional immune system whenever you think about putting yourself out there? Shame grabs you by the ankle and whispers, "Tsk-tsk, not so fast. Where do you think you're going?" and "Who do you think you are?" and, "Don't you remember what you did?"

It's incredibly difficult to step into a possibility in front of you when you can't drown out the soundtrack of your worst moments behind you.

On top of that, in today's world, shame can also whisper,

"What if you're found out?" If Saul's day was anything like our current cancel culture, then *yikes*.

Or maybe it wasn't something Saul did *to* someone but something someone did to *him*. Maybe when he was younger, a relative did something in the dark so atrocious, Saul wanted to forget it and muster through instead of bringing it into the light. Maybe a leader in the community physically abused him. Or a young Gibeonite gal shattered his poor heart into a thousand pieces.

Perhaps there was a tragedy. Life dealt him a sour hand in the passing of a loved one or the discovery of a life-altering disease.

A word spoken over him took root.

A stray thought molded his identity.

We have no idea what Saul's baggage was.

All we know is he never addressed it.

. . . . .

SOMETHING WEIRD ABOUT ME?

In moments I should feel fear, I experience anger or excitement instead. Even in early childhood, noises outside the house caused me to walk out into the dark and investigate, the thought of some intruder doing something to my parents infuriating me into action.

I'm pretty high on the fight part of fight-or-flight.

But my John Wayne fades to Gumby when it comes to scheduling a doctor's appointment. Or facing a relational loss. Or being *thoroughly* honest about just how deep a struggle has been.

I bring this up because as I've studied Saul's journey of insecurity, I've noticed an interesting nuance. Saul ran *away* from some things in life and ran *toward* others.

He was brave in battle, even heroic. In 1 Samuel 13, for example, when the entire Philistine army attacks the few conscripted battalions of Israel, most men "ran for cover, hiding in caves and pits, ravines and brambles and cisterns." They retreated in fear across the Jordan. But not Saul. Saul stood his ground.

Jealous, insecure Saul. Going all William Wallace *Braveheart* against the Philistines, despite how enormously outnumbered.

Strange, isn't it? Except . . . that's us.

More willing to fight a stranger who cuts us off in traffic than conquer our selfishness or lust at home.

More eager to confront the service worker who inconvenienced us than to address the person in our lives we keep putting off conversations with.

Happier to sweat in the gym or distract ourselves at work than engage with the fear, anger and unforgiveness rotting out our souls.

Anything but go to therapy, do the inner work, and deal with our demons.

We are an odd species.

We'll muster the strength to face monsters. And do anything but face the mirror.

I heard someone say the other day that when we talk about confronting our fears, what we're really talking about is confronting ourselves. The scariest haunted house of all.

The truth is, we tend to *hide* as long as we're *haunted*.

While ghosts and demons roam, we crouch behind couches instead of running through doors.

See, Saul felt comfortable in his physical dominance and combative skill. So he stayed there, far away from the discomfort of ever having to address the wounds inside. And just like it does with us, it eventually cost him.

I don't mean to pry, but what space in you do you keep avoiding? What excuse do you keep making not to address it?

What is your baggage?

Here's the harsh truth: *Our baggage is costing us our boldness.*

And blessing, too, while we're at it.

So, what do you do?

Well, like we learn as kids, the only way to get rid of ghosts is to *turn on the lights.*

Don't stay in the dark. Don't pretend the scaries aren't there. Flip on the overhead switch.

     CONFIDENCE

In Jeremiah 6.14, the prophet reminds us, "You can't heal a wound by saying it's not there."[10]

Healing can't reach the space of hiding. Healing can only reach the space of honesty.

. . . . .

TO STEP OUT FROM BEHIND THE airport carousel of all our baggage, we must step onto three carousels of honesty.

Honesty with God.

Honest with others.

Honesty with ourselves.

These only work in tandem, by the way. Our hearts tend to be used-car salesmen, laced with all kinds of subterfuge and deflection. We lie to ourselves, and we do it well. As we do, we lie to others. And as we do that, we hide from God in post-modern gardens, sewing on leaves and constructing papier-mâché castles to feel safe inside. All the while God calmly whispers, "Where are you?"

But since hiding ourselves is hurting ourselves, it's time to machete our way out of the jungles and into open field.

So, let's walk these three backward.

Get honest with yourself.

This is so hard. This usually only comes when we force

ourselves to slow down. To get quiet. To practice some silence and solitude. That's when the demons come out and we see their actual shape.

Fortunately, there are a multitude of helpful resources to lead you by the hand into your inner ocean.[11]

Then, get honest with people. Safe and trusted ones.

In fact, if you're serious about getting healthy inside, recruit a power team I call *The Three P's*: a peer, a professional, and a pastor. Assemble these "avengers" and watch your life elevate ten Manhattan stories in a matter of months.

A *peer*. A wise, faith-filled friend you can text before this chapter ends and say, "Hey, let's get coffee this week." Someone who believes in you and knows how to listen well but also how to speak truth into you.

Second, a *professional*. Yes, remove whatever taboo you have and find a clinical, faith-based counselor or psychologist and do the work of talking through your stuff. We tend to be foolish enough to think we don't need anyone. Ironically, the most inspirational leaders I know, the ones who should "have all the answers"—all see counselors. That's an example to follow. You can't pull yourself out of a pit and see your own blind spots. The sooner we quit pretending we have a third hand or third eye to do so, the better for everyone involved. As they say in the clinical world, "It's hard to see the label when you're stuck inside the bottle."[12]

Finally, a *pastor* or *pastor figure*. An older, godly mentor. It may be a mother or father figure or leader at your church. Someone with the benefit of age and experience who can point out the choppy air[13] ahead and give some air traffic suggestions.

Six months ago, I began to see the pale yellow of *check engine* light up across my soul. I called a former pastor-mentor in another state, one who knows me well, and asked if for a season we could schedule a standing phone call appointment every six weeks. I caught him up to speed on where I was, my highs and lows, some embarrassing recent failures, reminded him of my weaknesses and escapes, then gave him permission to ask hard questions and speak hard truth. As I write this, my next "soul check in" is scheduled for Tuesday. And I have work to do.

Listen, I'm busy. And I'd rather not. But the older I get and the more aware of my humanity I become and the more I see leaders fall apart, can I just tell you—I really, *really* want to finish well. The other day, I saw a simple verse that struck a resonating fork deep inside: "Live well before God."[14]

I so want to live well. Honest. Pure. Whole. Healthy.

So, get honest with people. That may be the most significant step you take this year.

And get honest with God.

There is nothing more powerful than pouring out your soul in the Presence of the One who knows you best and loves you most. He made you. He knows how to heal and change you. He knows how to speak to you. He knows how to help you.

If you don't know where to start, leave your phone in the car and take a walk. On the walk, imagine what you'd say to your best friend about everything you're feeling if there were no filters, then begin saying it *to God*. Out loud.

Ask Him to speak to you. Take time to listen.

Another power tool for processing with God is journaling. Try writing to God and *naming* what you feel. Be specific. Be transparent.

The Psalms are great too. The Psalms are King David's gut-level, lying-on-the-couch-with-a-psychologist, pounding-on-the-floor-in-frustration, screaming-into-the-sky vents and complaints to God about all the crap he's feeling. Join him. Read the Psalms and personalize them into gritty prayers, using them to get specific about your own issues, fears, anger, and shame.

Get in the habit of bringing your rawest issues and emotions into the presence of God and reflecting on them there. I've discovered in my own life that what I don't process in *God's Presence* will eventually turn to poison in *my perspective*.

And you know what's crazy about all this? It feels so weak to think about being vulnerable. But when you do it, strength follows. Strength really does come from vulnerability, and God's grace really does rest on our weakness.

And long term, we set ourselves up for a foundation of wholeness and a deep, mature confidence that's actually unshakeable.

I cannot emphasize this enough. The greatest gift you will ever give to yourself and those around you is to address your issues. To step out of your baggage and into your future. To step out of hiding and pursue health. To face your past so you can face your future.

Who knows? Samuel might be calling your name even now,

with a whole lot of people waiting for you to rise into the fullness of your purpose.

The number one addiction in the world right now is the addiction to other people's opinions of us.[1]
—Ed Mylette

You are masters at making yourself look good in front of others, but God knows what's behind the appearance.[2]
—Jesus

I've been trying to find a reason to get up . . . the baggage in my heart is still so dark.[3]
—Lauv ("Modern Loneliness")

5)

Better Call Saul

IN THE EARLY 1800S, A COMET BLAZED ACROSS THE MAP OF history, igniting the globe.

Napoleon Bonaparte.

Born in the French port city of Ajaccio, he was raised by a rather snobbish family, one who considered themselves among the elite class, though they drudged their days away frugally in a cramped, ramshackle home.

Perhaps because of that, Napoleon nursed a shameful resentment toward his father. He also distrusted women and had difficulty relating to others, especially when he left for northern France at an early age to enter the military. His French was repugnant and his personality quirks bristled against his new, more sophisticated companions.[4]

In a way, his distinct aloneness spurred him on to climb higher than others, outwitting them through his cleverness. He rose quickly. Shot through the ranks like a cannon by his military genius, falling in love with gold and money along the way.

Before long, he'd become a statesman and general who helped

revolutionize France, appointed himself Emperor, and took over most of Europe.

With the exception of Egypt, Greece, Russia, and a few other nations, a large swath of the known, civilized world lay like puzzle pieces at Napoleon's fingertips.

He became famous for his conquest.

And famous for his insecurity.

Complexes have even been named after him (though historians debate if he was short for his time). He reserved a crisp, arrogant distance from others, struggled socially, and was petrified of ever coming across as weak. He was also tortured by sexual insecurity, and the first woman he ever fell for, famous Miss Josephine, cheated on him egregiously.

You could say he had baggage.

It's interesting, by the way, when you observe the lives of high-charging leaders, performers, and CEOs. For many, if unaddressed, the same baggage that becomes jet fuel to early greatness causes them to combust in the sky by age thirty.

Also, one can't help but wonder if Napoleon *knew* his power came solely through fear instead of affection and secretly desired the intimacy that evaded him his whole life. This painful awareness even seemed to creep into his admiration for another leader:

> "I know men, and I tell you Jesus Christ was not a man. Superficial minds see a resemblance between Christ . . . and other religions. That resemblance does not exist. There is . . . the distance of infinity. Alexander, Cæsar,

Charlemagne, and myself founded empires. But on what did we rest the creations of our genius? Upon sheer force. Jesus Christ alone founded His empire upon love; and at this hour millions of men will die for Him."[5]

This kind of love is the one thing Napoleon never experienced.

So he settled for self-glory. And the most powerful man in the world got wrapped around the axle of his insecurity.

Several factors coalesced for the downfall, but on April 12, 1812, after Napoleon led his men, against warning, through a treacherous Russian winter, he found he'd bitten off more than he could chew. His insecurity-fueled quests for more had led him from hubris to debris.

The man had to surrender. France had to retreat. Napoleon had to be exiled.

What a swipe the claws of insecurity can make at us all.

Even at kings.

Wild, isn't it?

Napoleon had all of Europe before him.

Just like Saul had all the Middle East before him.

. . . . .

BY NOW, INSECURITY HAS THE POINT of its sword at Saul's back, leading him away from the life he could've had.

Before we step under the yellow tape, it's important to point something out. Contrary to how he's often painted, Saul wasn't *all* bad.

Undisciplined character and tragic ending? Yes.

Complete vilification? Not so fast.

More Han Solo than Thanos.

Saul did some good. He had significant military and political success, for starters. He bested the Philistines out of the central hills and campaigned successfully against the Amalekites in the south, ensuring a monopoly of the Arabian trade for Israel.

These feats gained him favor with the people,[6] and he became the first leader to reunite all the tribes under one rule.

And while his character may have been Swiss cheese, he was not generally self-promoting nor lascivious, nor did he commit a *fraction* of the evils of most of Israel's kings to come. No Baals, Asherah poles, or golden calves on his watch. In fact, there was no known idolatry in Israel at all during his lifetime. He even avoided the moral disaster of his successor, David, the one actually known as "a man after God's heart."

We also catch glimpses of spirituality, times of worship and sacrifice and even moments of prophecy, where God's Spirit came on him in power.

Tricky, huh?

In fact, the more you press into Saul, the more his relatability becomes unsettling.

He's *not* black-and-white. He's not 2D. He's not all good or all bad. He's complex. A bit like me. Probably a bit like you.

I'm glad Scripture doesn't bevel off the edges of its characters to make them clean, like the one-dimensional villains of Old Hollywood.

No, it records them as they are. To help us see ourselves as *we are*.

This is why for thousands of years now, with a hand ready to cover our eyes, we study hard the lives of Saul and David. They're almost *too* close to home. The more we sweep aside the contextual veneers of their time and keep walking into the inner core of their lives, we eventually smash into a mirror where we see our own hearts.

Eight years ago, I sat in the corner of a Starbucks in my hometown of Greenville, South Carolina and wept. I had read Chapter 1 of Gene Edwards's classic *A Tale of Three Kings*. A heart-rending expose on King Saul, King David, and King Absalom.

Exploring themes of ambition, humility, toxic leadership, and how to respond to authority, the book fillets open the heart like a fish. It aromatizes the spirit with sweetness for God while also destroying presumption about who you are in the story (one always imagines they are David), and even reveals how God often uses a Saul *over* you in leadership to kill the Saul *in* you. Can't recommend it enough.

All that to say, study of Saul is a good EKG for the heart.

Especially if we're anything *like* Saul, who had *just enough* good and *just enough* religion to act as a smokescreen for the hypocrisy, compromise, and insecurity eroding him away from the inside. The very anointing and blessing on his life *deceived* him into thinking he was okay and kept him from attending to things beneath the surface.

Samuel might have anointed Saul's skin. But the oil never absorbed into the spirit.

. . . . .

IN 1 SAMUEL 13, IT ALL GOES SOUTH.

The baggage becomes blatant.

Saul's son, Jonathan, who led one of Saul's military companies, attacked and killed the Philistine governor. Word got out and the Philistines went ballistic. They immediately set out for a rampage of revenge. In response, Israel's soldiers hightailed it for the hills.

To his credit, Saul stuck it out, along with some remaining men. There they waited on the prophet, holding down the fort in their own ancient Alamo. But there was a problem. The man of God—who had instructed Saul to wait—was late. The heat of it all got to Saul. He became squirmy, stress ball in hand, and hurried through a religious ritual strictly reserved for priests.

That's when Samuel arrived and let him have it.

On his heels, Saul justified,

> "I saw my men scattering . . . and you didn't arrive when
> you said you would, and the Philistines are . . . ready for

battle. So I said, 'The Philistines are ready to march against us . . . and I haven't even asked for the Lord's help!' So I felt compelled to offer the burnt offering myself before you came.'"[7]

Saul was commanded to wait, but the weight of it crushed him. Samuel put the proverbial sword to his throat, announcing God's judgment for his action, that his kingdom would come to an end.

Needless to say, it's incredibly sad it came to this.

And also ironic that Saul's impulsive actions expedited his worst fear: David becoming king.

Also, I know this isn't trending, but we shouldn't miss the importance of simple *obedience to God*. A Father who exudes love, but also a King who radiates holiness and is to be held in the kind of esteem that corresponds with follow-through.

But I want to land on Saul's *reaction*. His frantic reply for why he got so antsy.

Again:

> "When I saw that the men were scattering, and that you did not come . . . and that the Philistines were assembling . . . I thought . . ."

Can you feel the hot panic of these sentences?

"When I saw everyone wasn't with me . . ."

People-pleasing

"And they seemed to be leaving . . ."

Codependence/abandonment

"And to be honest, you weren't there like you said you'd be . . ."

Blame/victimhood

". . . And my enemies were getting in attack position . . ."

Fear/doubt

"And I realized it'd been a minute since I prayed, so I felt *compelled* to offer a sacrifice . . ."

Shaky conscience/spiritual instability

Are you catching this?

We are getting a crystal-clear picture of an insecure leader.

Saul's kingship is collapsing because *he* is collapsing under the weight of his insecurity.

Because *insecurity is a trap.*

A trap that sends us into foolishness instead of wisdom, defeat instead of victory, and haste instead of assurance.

Now. Let's board the train from 1 Samuel 13 down a couple of stops to 1 Samuel 15, from Saul's *rebuke* to Saul's *removal.*

The pin's been pulled from the grenade, and here it lands.

For context, God had commanded Saul to execute justice on the Amalekites, a wicked, Nazi-esque people who'd been terror-reigning for 500 years without remorse.

Moment of reckoning. And Saul obeyed. Kind of.

He wiped out *almost* everything. Everything except the king and a few choice cattle, for which he even leveraged a spiritual excuse. He was going to use it as fuel for worship, after all. How noble.

So, the prophet confronts him. Again. And Saul spins excuses. Again.

Finally, "Saul gave in and confessed, 'I've sinned . . . *I cared more about pleasing the people.*"[8]

In desperation he begs Samuel to absolve his sin, to make him feel better, to go back with him to church and act like it's all alright. Brokenhearted, Samuel has to refuse. Saul's panic worsens and his dignity leaves, and he shifts from verbal pleading to physical clutching, literally grasping at Samuel's clothing, holding on for dear life.

Another insight for us: When we don't stay *close to God*, we get *clingy with people.*

It's truly a sobering, terrifying moment. King Saul—handsome, powerful, anointed—now falling, pleading, clasping.

In chilling cinematography, the robe tears and Samuel turns and declares, "In the same way that this robe just tore, God is tearing the kingdom from you today and is going to replace it with somebody after his own heart."[9]

A.k.a. David.

See, it's one thing to have insecurities; it's another thing for insecurities to have you.

So, yes. To answer our question from a few chapters back . . .

Insecurity *is* a big deal.

The price tag is high.

. . . . .

FEEL UPLIFTED?

Look, we could make one messy, depressing list of side effects to wrap around insecurity's bottle—chokes you with fear, provides you a spirit rife with paranoia and skewed perspective, makes you a bad friend, stymies your progress, causes you to play the short game instead of the long game, distorts your personality, ruins your relationships. And those are just beginning symptoms after headache and nausea.

But can I tell you what I've *really* been feeling in my gut at night?

The speed of life.

The pace at which time is passing is *unnerving*.

The other evening after a long day, I meandered a stroll around Schiller Park in German Village, an idyllic neighborhood here in Columbus. I walked and walked. I walked by wych elm trees, running dogs, landscaped gardens, over short bridges and cobblestoned alleyways, around the enchanted brick homes that make one feel like a child, the stooped cottages, and finally the two-story Italianates and Queen Annes with their soft, garden lighting.

I'd left my phone behind so my soul could exhale. Eventually, my restless bones forced themselves onto an iron bench and I watched the late summer sun die slow around branches and water. Evening thickened to dusk. My childhood snuck out then in the form of fireflies. So many fireflies. I sat there for an hour or so, watching them, hundreds of them, flashing up like yellow suns out of the grass in twilight.

And felt how quickly life is passing.

I felt how long it had been since I felt the dewy glow of a firefly in my fingers, felt the decades it had been since I'd slowed down long enough, got off my phone long enough, stopped worrying about stupid crap long enough to *live*.

I want you to know insecurity plays this trick too. It may be the worst theft of all. It distracts us, diverting our hearts from the gold in us and in front of us. Insecurity distracts us from *life*.

I look back on seasons when I just wasted way too much time caring what people think. Too much time fretful, too much time in my head instead of engaging with loved ones, too much time missing the world in front of me. Way too much time small in my old prison of inferiority instead of climbing new hills in bold intensity.

Don't get me wrong. I've had a great life. I *have* a great life. And I don't live in regret. But that doesn't mean I don't *have* regret.

The older I get, the more acutely aware I am of just how short life is, how big God is, how precious people are, how much divine material God has deposited in me.

And it makes me want to fight with everything in me to stomp "Saul" out of my system.

To eradicate the petty, life-reducing, peace-robbing mental impasses so I can live in mind-melting joy and intention. I don't want to miss one more second of this fleeting life stuck in my head.

Not one. More. Second.

I am dying. And so are the people around me. And so are you.

I know I sound like a Christian movie trailer now, but let me say it again:

Life is short.

God is big.

People are precious.

And there is so much in you. More than any Disney Imagineer could ever dream up.

There's no telling what God might do in you. For you. Through you.

It's time for a shattering.

A shattering of everything keeping you small and held back. A shattering of internal limitations. A shattering of intimidation and inferiority.

Yes, for all that low glass ceiling over your life to be smashed to bits. And for you to rise like a phoenix, empty eyes filled with fire.

Next chapter, we'll see how.

I was invincible many years ago when I was so much stronger.[1]
—Gaslight Anthem

For they loved human praise more than praise from God.[2]
—Jesus

Go confidently in the direction of your dreams. Live the life you have imagined.[3]
—Henry David Thoreau

6)

The Coin

S AUL FUMBLED THE BAG. NO WAY
AROUND IT.

If I've got you self-medicating with a tub of peanut butter, I'm sorry. But there's gold in that fumbled bag.

We looked at Saul's rebuke and removal. Now let's double-click on a couple of images around the crash. In 1 Samuel 15.12 we read,

> "Early in the morning . . . Samuel went to meet Saul, but was told, 'Saul has gone to Carmel. There *he has set up a monument in his own honor . . .*'"

Two observations.

First, the level of deception that's entered Saul's heart.

It's striking how much this verse contrasts with the one above it. God just told Samuel He regrets having made Saul king and Saul spends the night weeping over his fate. Meanwhile, Saul climbs a hill like a whistling Michelangelo to construct his own statue of honor. Oh, man.

Second, the level of presumption to *construct your own statue of honor* . . . (I imagine how this would go over with my team in the office tomorrow . . .)

Okay. Sticky-tab that verse and run a quick finger to the bottom where Saul backpedals once confronted:

> ". . . *I was afraid of the men* and so I gave in to them. Now I beg you, forgive my sin and come back with me, so that I may worship the Lord." (1 Samuel 15.24–25)

Hmm.

Okay, the two statements together, this time with the invisible ink showing:

"Has set up a monument in his own honor . . ." *Pride*

"Was afraid of the men, so I gave into them . . ." *Insecurity*

We see here, in the exact same chapter, both the *heights of pride* and the *depths of insecurity*.

So, which was it? Pride or insecurity?

Here's the mind shift:

Insecurity is not, in fact, a harmless, benign kind of humility. And insecurity is not the opposite of pride.

Insecurity and pride are inextricably *linked.*

If you take the branches of pride and insecurity, palm your

way down the trunk, and dig beneath the surface, you'll find the roots eventually merge.

Where?

Self.

Preoccupation with self is both the problem and the source.

To quote well-known author C.S. Lewis, "Humility is not thinking less of yourself; it's simply thinking of yourself less."[4]

Yes, pride and insecurity are connected. They're two blades of the same scissors. Two wings of the same bird. They are, don't make me say it,

Two sides of the same coin.

If you have a coin nearby, grab it. Hold it between your fingers. Roll it around, even. Run the give of your thumb against its brassy edges and analyze both sides. Indulge me and keep it on you as a reminder until the book ends.

Observe this circuitous, domino effect in your life. Ego swells you, then failure deflates you. *Pride* props you up, then *insecurity* knocks you down. The two always travel together. I just know: When I'm mired in insecurity, pride is in the mix.

It's a big deal. We can't understand confidence without seeing this insidious, symbiotic relationship between pride and insecurity.

For that matter, we can't understand Saul himself without seeing the symbiotic *contrast* between him and David. In Saul, the clear expression of insecurity; in David, the vivid display of confidence.

The truth is, we could do a whole *Encyclopedia Britannica* series on these two, beginning with how they responded to failure.

It's interesting (and encouraging) when you peruse David's biography that God ever called him a man after His own heart. His rap sheet's a bit dark.[5] Yet, uncomfortable as David's blunders are, the arc of his story is that of a heroic narrative. One who finished well. One we (mostly) want to be like. One not defined by his worst moments. One whose proverbial headstone was carved with the greatest words ever to describe a human being: God Himself saying, "This guy has My heart."

That moves me even as I type it. One of my deepest longings is to know I have God's heart.

So how did these two respond to failure?

Saul said, "Yeah, you're right. I shouldn't have done that. But now, *please honor me in front of the people.*"[6]

David's response?

He wept. And said, "God, against You and You alone have I sinned and done what is wrong . . . I trust you to do what is right . . . but whatever you do, *please don't take your Presence from me.* Create in me a clean heart, oh God . . ."[7]

Saul wanted to make sure his image was still intact. David wanted to make sure his intimacy with God was still intact.

It's in the rubble of our failure that our hearts unfold like flowers.

And it couldn't be more obvious: These two men lived from different coins.

In David's darkest moment, his eyes were still on God. In Saul's darkest moment, his eyes were still on himself. David was miserable over God's broken heart. Saul was just consumed with his own broken ego.

Saul's attention never left self. It's the coin he lived from.

. . . . .

FOR A COUPLE DECADES NOW, I'VE studied, listened to, and even taught the contrasting biopics of these two legends. But a year ago, contemplating their lives, a paradigm opened like a mirror to Hogwarts. When I saw it, it caught my breath. And I pray it sweeps through vents in your soul.

Of all his faults, the most damning thing about Saul is *he never lived from a place of purpose.*

Think about it.

He was king. He had a divine assignment. But when you canvas the frames of his life, you never see him operate from any sense of destiny. Just driven moment to moment by a desperate sense of uncertainty—moment to moment, with some version of *Do I have what it takes?* and *Everyone is against me* and *Please clap for me* and *Please don't leave me* and *Samuel, please approve of me.*

But pulled by purpose? Not once.

Then you flip the page to David, a man who *lived from a different coin*. A coin formed not of *ego* and *self* but of *purpose* and *service*.

Audiences did not seduce David. He was not captivated by kingship. He was a man forged by solitude with God and then branded with a mission from God. A flawed but secure man with the attitude of, *You know what? As imperfect as I am, I know: God's called me. And if God's called me, it doesn't matter how big the giant or fierce the army.*

A man *seared with purpose*. A man faithful over every small thing given to him. A man who knew God from an early age, passionate about Him *before* he had a clue he'd be king.

Even in battle, we smell the smoke of his calling. "Who is this uncircumcised Philistine who would *dare* to defy God's armies . . . The Lord who gave me bear and lion will give you to me . . ."[8]

Even in line to be king, instead of avenging himself, he exercises self-restraint, trusting God.

Even when threatened, instead of "being fearful of the men," like Saul, he lives with bold assurance, penning words like,

> "The Lord is my light and my salvation—whom shall I fear? The Lord is the stronghold of my life—of whom shall I be afraid? When the wicked advance . . . it is my enemies . . . who will stumble . . . Though an army besiege me, my heart will not fear; though war break out against me, even then I will be confident." (Psalm 27.1–3)

Come *on*.

Even then, I will be confident.

What a declaration to hide away for a rainy day.

And if the greatest compliment given to David was that he possessed God's heart, the second greatest was given by the physician Luke thousands of years later:

> "Now when David had *served God's purpose* in his own generation . . . he was buried with his ancestors . . ."[9]

This is a statement I want etched over my epigraph: that I *served my generation*, fulfilling the call of God on my life.

Want to know where confidence comes from? I mean, true iron-in-your-blood confidence that can't be taken away by defeat-victory rollercoasters or the changing tide of others' opinions?

True confidence comes from calling.

This is the flag to rally your strength around.

This is the *coin* David lived from.

If you want to shatter insecurity and explode into an expectant life, *exchange the coin of self for the coin of calling.*

When you live from that place, you become unstoppable.

When you live from that place, courage follows.

Apart from the grace of God and a handful of core principles, I'm convinced it's the only reason I'm still standing.

For me, in long nights of the soul, opposed by people, tripped up by mistakes, cussed out behind that old church in Georgia, I go back to calling.

I go back to that D.A.R.E. officer who accidentally prophesied over me in elementary school that "You will find your path in 7th grade and never leave it." How could I have known in two years my trajectory would change? How could I have known my mom would secretly pray a new best friend into my life who burned for God? It may sound small to you, but when God began to whisper my name at Northwood Middle School, I bottled up that Voice and memory. They still echo.

When ministry feels discouraging or I feel inadequate, I go back to calling. Back to that peculiar night over Mexican food with Colt's dad who began praying strangely under his breath, sensing *God's about to speak.* We drove out to a distant church where the preacher interrupted my daydreams mid-sermon, invited me forward, and shared specifics he saw over my future, things God had already been percolating in my young soul like single-origin brew. And again, six months later, in the Dominican Republic, when a preacher spoke the same things to me verbatim through a translator.

When I've fallen shamefully and made painful confessions and had to claw my way back to health, I go back. I go back to every book-worthy miracle and nature-bending answer to prayer, every secret whisper by God, every changed nature inside my ever-inconsistent, creaky character. I'm telling you, I go back.

I go back to moments as an eighth-grade kid so passionate to reach my school for Jesus but so overwhelmed by how many there were, then did the stupid Bible-roulette thing you should not do, opening scripture and pointing randomly, begging God to speak, and bam:

> "Do not be afraid or discouraged because of this vast army. For the battle is not yours, but God's."[10]

"The king" might as well have been "Russ," and the words might as well have been audible.

When I'm feeling stuck, afraid, or wounded, I go back to these. I return to calling. To serving others. I tap back into purpose. It's the fuel that moves me forward on dull days and the light I hold close on moonless nights.

I believe it's God's desire that we *all* be pulled by this unstoppable power. This invincible sense of purpose.

In fact, the deepest calling I feel is this right here. To convince any human who'll listen, through lunch, coffee, message, or book, there's so much more. So much more to God. So much more to life. So much more to *you*. So much more *in* you.

I don't care how young or old you are or how broken or imperfect you feel; I want you to know God has a sacred beckoning over your life. Every next breath and step you take contains possibility and purpose.

And you've probably sensed it.

It doesn't matter if it's dramatic like some of the moments I noted. It doesn't need to be.

It's often an inner nudge or moment of clarity. Passions crystallizing as you search Scripture. Gifts affirmed as you operate in community. Things you're good at or interested in.

Steps becoming clear as you endeavor to do your best in every way *today*.

I'm just telling you, despite my many failures and inadequacies, I'm here because *God put me here*. God used people along the way to affirm, but as much as I'm sure this table underneath my computer is real, I know *God* called me to the mission I'm living.

In fact, I feel like *flipping* this table and yelling until we hear it: When the storm is severe and the road is lonely and the results seem far away, there is a deep-seated assurance that only comes from calling. The knowing, deep in your sinews that,

God is for me.

God is with me.

God has called me.

I feel its fire singeing my fingers as I type.

If God is for you, who in God's name can be against you?

If God has called you to this work, what demon in hell can stop you?

If God is inside you, what flesh-and-blood mortal can stand in your way as long as you engage God's work in God's way?

I think we give spiritual darkness too much credit, but I *do* believe there's an enemy in this dark world and I *do* believe he knows something:

He can't take your calling;[11] *so he tries to take your confidence.*

He knows without confidence you won't have the strength to walk in that calling.

"Do not throw away your confidence," Hebrews says.[12]

It's time to get it back.

It's high time to lift your head, feel God's wind at your back, fan His fire in your chest, and get a little holy attitude about why you were put on earth and Who put you here to do it.

If you don't know where to start, start where David did.

So often when we talk about purpose, we immediately skip to *career field*. The *field* of science, the *field* of education. But David received his calling in a different field. In a field with smelly sheep, connecting in a meaningful way to the God of the Universe. That's the field where we receive our divine compass.

Life is about connections and the deepest callings flow out of the most profound connections. Especially with God. Since He designed us, our purpose emanates most richly as we get to know Him most fully.

You could say it this way:

We find our future in the field.

The material for David's future was birthed out of his close-knit friendship with God. His greatest calling wasn't to kill Goliath or defeat a foreign army or sit on a throne any more than your greatest calling is to become a doctor or get on a podcast or make millions. His ultimate calling wasn't to be a king; his ultimate calling was to know God.

See, a page or so back we read Psalm 27.1–3 about David being confident no matter what, knowing God is on his side. But we see where that holy confidence oozed out of in the next few verses:

> "One thing I ask . . . this only do I seek: that I may dwell in the house of the Lord all the days of my life, to gaze on the beauty of the Lord and to seek him . . ."
> (Psalm 27.4–5)

David had one request—one burning, desirous ask of God. And it wasn't for riches or notoriety or to be on the speaking circuit.

He wanted to be in God's Presence. To look at God Himself. To seek His face.

Every secondary calling emanated from that first calling, "That my soul follows close behind You,"[13] and "As the deer pants for streams of water, so my soul pants for you . . ."[14]

Decades before David owned land, he was making melody to God from a harp in his father's field. God had stolen the young man's affections long before he knew of the "positions" lesser men lust after.

So don't let the word "calling" throw you. I've found people who don't believe in God still believe in calling. They just call it destiny, or the "universe," or worse yet, fate.

And if you're a church person, don't fall into the trap of thinking vocational ministry is the peak of purpose.

There is a first, primary calling for every human being: to know and love God. To give yourself fully to Him, a white-flag surrender of heart and life. Out of that, with communal wisdom and awareness of how you're wired, secondary callings flow.

For some, that will be spreading an irrepressible joy through acting or singing. For others, radiating the brilliance of God in a medical field. For others, creating a home where people find hospitality and kids are raised to be world-changers. Teacher, carpenter, entrepreneur, cook, pastor, accountant, doesn't matter.

If you follow Jesus closely, you'll find your what. But more important than *what* is *why*. More important than craft is the calling behind it.

I cannot encourage you enough: If this chapter stirs you, but you feel a bit lost in purpose, move that onto your radar. No need to get panicky. Just go on an adventure with God. Pray and fast. Listen and journal. Read and think. Serve where you are.

And pay attention to what's already in you . . .

What makes you mad? What gets you up in the morning? What gifts and talents and opportunities? What do the people in your life affirm in you? Ask a person of faith in your hemisphere what they see on your life.

And trust: As you *follow Jesus*, your purpose will *find you*.

Also, if you don't feel an intrinsic sense of purpose *in* your current job, for now, bring meaning *to* your job.

As I left retail to step into full-time ministry, my manager gave me one of the best and strangest compliments. She told me she'd loved working with me because I was the most passionate person she'd ever met. I *cherished* that compliment. I cherished that, imperfect as I was, though I hadn't yet stepped vocationally into my dream, she saw me bring joy, creativity, and enthusiasm into everything in my care.

The reciprocal, replenishing reward of doing that is beyond calculation.

So until [fill in the blank], make every task an opportunity to sharpen your excellence, every duty a moment to elevate your gifts, every interaction a chance to refine your people skills, every day a chance to serve others.

These are the bricks that pave the path for calling.

. . . . .

I SHOULD PROBABLY LET YOU IN ON something.

Calling can cure insecurity.

And it also can cause it.

It's like wading into choppy water in that way.

If you weren't insecure *before*, and then you hear the reality-defying future God calls you into, you *will* be. You'll become immediately aware you don't have what it takes, aren't big enough, talented enough, connected enough.

It's what happened all over Scripture. When presented with a big calling:

Jeremiah says he's only a youth.[15]

Moses says he can't speak well.[16]

Isaiah says he's too unholy.[17]

Abraham says he's too old.[18]

Calling drives you forward but also creates a gap between who you are and who you need to be. And that's a *good thing*. That gap creates our dependence on God. That gap is what God fills in with His grace. That gap is where God does the impossible to show He's the sun this story orbits around. That gap is what God uses to transform us.

And that gap is where we tap into a deeper confidence. A confidence that doesn't just rest in *me* but in the *God inside of me*.

This is where faith comes in.

I know we've been getting heavy on the spiritual (I warned you). But the etymology of the word "confidence" in Latin literally unwraps to "with faith."

Confidence is a faith issue.

It's just about where we place it.

When we place "faith" in a negative prognosis of the future, the result is *fear*.

When we place "faith" solely in ourselves, the result is
limitation, insecurity, or even *narcissism*.

When we place "faith" in the past, the result is *shame* or
regret.

But when we place "faith" in an all-powerful God who loves
us and has a wonderful future in store, the result is *joyful
confidence.*

So, I don't want to mislead you: The goal of this book isn't to
never feel insecure again. That's unrealistic and would be
concerning. If you never care what anyone thinks, you might
be a sociopath. And if you never feel insecure, your dreams are
too small.

Sometimes a little insecurity means you care.

The problem isn't when we *care* what someone thinks or how
good a job we do or how something turns out. The problem is
when we are *controlled* by those things.

We have to make sure we're only *controlled* by faith in a God
who beckons us into a future beyond our wildest imagination.

. . . . .

FOR SOME OF US, THIS WON'T BE
about discovering a calling but returning to the heart behind it.

Whether you're a dentist, cop, or engineer, it's so easy to start
with pure motives and then lose yourself along the way.

We must return to our *why.* Over and over. Our core motive, that sense of, *This is what I was made to do*. And operate from there.

We must remind ourselves, *I'm called to this*.

If you're alone, try it out loud:

I'm called to this.

This job I'm in, it may not seem significant, but until next becomes now, *I'm called to this*. Called to be salt and light in every sphere I walk into.

This current season of life, be it great, horrible, dull, or confusing—*I'm called to this*. And because I'm called, I have everything I need to flourish right in the middle of it.

Don't be cocky but get sassy. Let new fire rise from the furnace of calling. Cultivate a spirit that's too called to need compliments.[19] Thank God for encouragement. It's great seasoning. But it's not my meal. You have to get that in your spirit. After all, *If you live by praise, you'll die by criticism*.

There's a mom reading this who needs that grit in her gut that says, "I'm too called to let the 'do extra' mom in the neighborhood make me feel less than. God's given me this child and *I am called to this*. With God's help, I will bring my best and do what is right."

Your life can change right now if you decide to trade the coin of self (insecurity, ego) for the coin of calling confidence, purpose).

To say, *You know what, line in the sand. I refuse to take up mental real estate with, Did they look at me weird? What are they thinking? I saw them whispering . . .* No, I'm no longer *entering rooms itching for their approval; I'm walking into rooms already dripping with God's approval. Collected and secure. Enjoying people because I don't need anything from them.*

Confidence is not a fleshly pride we muster up. It's an internal assurance that swells with, *God has called me, and if God has called me, He's going to equip me and see me through.*

You might need to write over your life a brand-new mission statement, a brand-new articulation of your purpose.

And keep that coin in your pocket as a reminder.

A reminder you're destined. A reminder God's with you. A reminder to live off calling, not compliments. Off assignment, not affirmation.

The question's simple: What coin will you live from?

Self or calling?

The choice will determine your future, David.

Part 1 // Reflection

We've absorbed a lot. Change occurs when we move from absorption to application. Before we rush on, let's take space to reflect and apply.

ASSESSMENT

What stood out? Where has comparison and jealousy crept in? Where have you bought into Zero Sum? What baggage needs to be addressed? What has insecurity cost you? What calling can you begin to step into?

____

____

____

____

____

____

____

APPLICATION

What steps can you take this month, this week, and today?
Who can you call and what systems can you implement to keep
you accountable?

____

____

____

____

____

____

____

Part 2

FOUNDATION OF WORTH

EDEN.

Near Mesopotamia.

Once upon a time, a young couple lived in a garden untouched by age.[1]

They were naked and free. They wore glory instead of clothes, breathed God instead of oxygen, and dwelled in eternity instead of years. Concepts like worry and death were nonexistent, as foreign as calculus to an ant. Their cells never aged, their hair never fell, their hearts never sank. And they never fought—not with each other, not with nature, and not within their own souls. They talked with God, made love to each other, explored the world, and named the animals. They were happy.

A Creator, dripping in love and intention, had dreamed them up and breathed them out.

But a shadow slipped across the sunlight. An enemy, cloaked in scales, spoke words of venom, distorting the Maker's heart. He lied to them about God and they bit into it. Poison exploded from the fruit of their betrayal, pervading the universe.

They unplugged from the Source of life in that moment, plunging their bodies and hearts into ruin.

Before this, they had never wondered who they were, never questioned their value. But now glory was missing, their souls untethered from Meaning Himself.

The scramble began.

The quiet desperation of men and women searching the earth to feel okay inside.

We have a lot of people in this city who are in love with themselves. But very few people in this city who love themselves.[1]
—Erwin McManus

Earth is polluted by its very own people, who have broken its laws, disrupted its order, violated the sacred and eternal covenant. Therefore, a curse, like a cancer, ravages the earth.[2]
—Isaiah

Can the child within my heart rise above?[3]
—Fleetwood Mac ("Landslide")

7)

Don't Ask Eve

IN THE LAST SECTION, WE LOOKED AT HOW TO DISMANTLE insecurity. In the next, we'll talk functional confidence.

But first, it's vital we lay a foundation for our psychology. We must get some bearings—and health—to the world inside us.

We've seen how Saul's insecurity was connected to his baggage. And how *our* insecurity is connected to *our* baggage.

But our baggage goes past our childhood.

It reaches back to humanity's childhood.

I've thought about it for years, and I have to tell you: The longer I live, study, counsel, spend time with humans, and observe my own soul, the more I'm convinced our entire anthropology as a species can be explained by the first three chapters of Genesis. The ache inside us screams to that garden behind us.

I don't care how you interpret the prose or timeline. Our ailment, the ripped fabric of the universe, the tear in our psyches, the tension between sexes, the explanation for our striving, it's all there.

God blanketed our skin, our very *souls*, with His presence and love, and then we unhooked, opening a pandora's box of cancer that's been metastasizing ever since.

And the human spirit became naked.

In fact, Adam and Eve's first post-fumble reaction is fascinating. Not, "We've screwed up." Not, "We've dishonored our Maker." Not, "Will there be punishment?"

Their first thought was,

"We're naked."

They'd always been naked, of course. But now that their souls were naked, they burned with shame that their bodies were naked. Everything in them had gone wrong and felt exposed.

And everything they did next is everything we still do.

They scrambled to cover up, frantically looking around for anything nearby to conceal the most vulnerable parts of themselves. Then they found a place to hide. From each other. From God.

This is us.[4]

You don't have to scour a nude beach in France to observe it. Our behaviors give us away. Welcome to the naked club of humanity. Our leaves have just gotten fancier. Social media scorecards, cars to impress, names to drop, corporate ladders to climb.

Nicer leaves. But still, leaves.

Fifteen years ago in Colorado, I read Donald Miller's lesser-known book *Searching for God Knows What*. In it, he imagines aliens coming to Earth to observe the human race. The report he imagines back to the chief alien is striking:

> *Humans, as a species, are constantly, and in every way, comparing themselves to one another, which, given the brief nature of their existence, seems an oddity . . . a waste . . . It is as though something that helped them function . . . has gone missing, and they are pining for that missing thing in all sorts of odd methods, none of which are working . . . very few people understand they have the disease . . . seems strange . . . because it is obvious. To be sure, it is killing them, and yet sustaining their social and economic systems. They are an entirely beautiful people with a terrible problem.*[5]

Miller goes on to analyze the alien's report, connecting everything we do—from the condos we buy to the music we listen to—back to what happened at the fall.[6]

Our collective and individual pain emanates from that seminal moment. At the fall, we fell. And have been falling ever since.

. . . . .

THE DISEASE FROM THAT TREE DIDN'T just wrap its way into weather patterns and cell function. The poison flooded our souls, pumping strychnine into our relationships and identities.

A while back, I lived in Argentina.

I'd been clamoring for an adventure-escape. Loved ones had passed, God felt distant, sin crept in, and I was achy inside over a girl no longer there. The wounds had gotten down like plaque that wouldn't come off.

I was also getting to the age I needed to address some things. Everyone kept shoving a trending book in my hands.[7] A memoir-treatise about the deep, passionate longings of a man's soul. I read it and felt like a city-caged Huckleberry Finn.

I needed to get back out in the wild. You know, kill some things. Collect scars worth telling stories about at a bar. Maybe begin to spit again like I did when I played baseball.

I heard about a cattle ranch by this school in Argentina where you could work to pay tuition. I imagined finding my heart among rough-and-tough *gauchos* whispering the secrets of life by an open fire. Mark Twain once said, "The best thing for the inside of a man is the outside of a horse." I didn't know if it was true, but I had to try.

All that to say, that year by the little pier in San Miguel del Monte, I devoured book after book on fatherhood and the wounded heart.

I can't remember who, but at some point, one author spoke through the pages about what we need to receive from our fathers. That every young girl needs, somewhere inside them, to know they're treasured, wanted, beautiful even. That a father's words are supposed to pour into that space. In slight contrast, every man needs to be approved of, to know they have what it takes, that they're enough.

The role of a mother—biologically and fundamentally—remains without needed defense. This author-psychologist

　　　CONFIDENCE

proposed, however, that these two questions, *Am I enough?* and *Am I desired?*—are hardwired in us to be *answered by a father*.

I have caution tape in hand as I type this, trust me. I'm just one person, a male at that, and right now any conversation around gender seems fraught with radioactive danger.[8] And thank God we live in a time where unhealthy gender stereotypes are being challenged.[9] (You don't have to love horses and guns to be a man; you can love poetry and photography.)

But while I tread cautiously, it's important I tread. I'm convinced more than ever of the mysterious impact of father figures, their words and presence in our lives, especially in formative years. And honestly, the stats are in. Eighty-five percent of youths in prison, 71 percent of high school dropouts, and 90 percent of homeless and runaways all come from fatherless homes. Not to mention mounds of academic literature connecting the role of fatherhood with emotional well-being, bullying, and risky sexual behavior.[10]

Whether or not they were involved, absent, extraordinary, or horrible, our fathers have left their fingerprints all over the glass. It's so deep, it seems we *all* have father issues, even from the great ones.

And these preloaded questions of value are tantamount to our base of confidence. If we don't experience an answer, we'll take the question somewhere.

Usually the opposite sex.

Cue the common scenarios:

A young girl doesn't receive that crown of confidence from that first man, instilling in her the dignity, beauty, and value of who she is. So she takes it to an immature boy who uses her, making her feel worth even less.

Or, because of abuse, she runs in the opposite direction, shirking off any appreciation for what she perceives as femininity. She might even construct a reactionary theology that women are weak and/or men are bad.

It can be similar but different with males. A father doesn't impart his strength and approval. Ergo, the son spends his life in aggression or proving himself or goes through other human beings just to feel like a man.

Or he walks out a spirit of weakness resembling kindness because he desperately needs the affirmation of a woman to fill what's missing. Which can start relationships out lovely until, skip a few scenes, that thinly veiled insecurity gives way to neediness, the woman no longer respects him, and the young man is further wounded.

Any of these feel familiar?

Oh, Adam and Eve. We've been trying to get our clothes back from each other ever since.

. . . . . .

I'LL NEVER FORGET READING THE following phrase as a nineteen-year-old, hopeless romantic: "When young men don't receive deep down from their father the answer to the question, 'Do I have what it takes,' they will take that question to Eve."

Wow.

Let me tell you, that phrase, "Take the question to Eve" has haunted me ever since. How often I used to do this. Maybe still do. And I'm one of the fortunate ones with a terrific father.

I now remind young men, "Don't take your question to Eve.

She doesn't have the power to answer that. And the moment you put pressure on another human being to be Jesus, the relationship's doomed."

Ironically, when a man puts his worth in Eve's hand, he forfeits any inner brawn he had left.

In fact, King Lemuel's mother gives an odd admonition in Proverbs 31.3:

> "Do not give your strength to women."

If you're a woman, stick with me. This is for both of us.

There's a sexual layer to this verse. Sex is "more than skin-to-skin contact."[11] It's a mingling of souls, a divine, human-Velcro moment, and when we pull apart, parts of us do too.

But there's a deeper layer.

The writer's not telling men to close up their hearts toward their wives. Nor, as a woman, is she implying anything negative about women.

She's issuing a fundamental question to all of us:

What source do you go to and draw from?

Where do you go for your value, well-being, and identity?

Wherever you draw from is where you expend your strength.

And vice versa.

The implication is obvious. *If you're a man, don't try to get that from Eve.* And *If you're a woman, don't try to get that from Adam.*

When a man doesn't cultivate his own inner strength, he'll give it *away* to soothe the emptiness, *losing* that strength and hurting the other person.

Such a sad inversion of the original plan. God designed a man to *bring* strength to a relationship so he can *serve* that person, not come parasitically to a relationship and *deplete* that person.

The same is true for women. When a girl forfeits the force of nature she is because she doesn't know the fountain of value she has, creation weeps. I'm convinced of it. Women are designed to bring power and beauty to the world; not manipulate that power and beauty or be used for it.

It's sad, isn't it, when we use each other to get what only God can give? Only bad things happen.

This dynamic plays out in marriage, too. When two broken people tie the knot and fly off into the Jamaican sunset, thinking they'll complete each other, someone better hide the kids once the euphoric high dies. I once heard someone say the picture of most marriages today is two people fighting underwater over a single oxygen tank, clawing at masks and tubes.[12] All along, the invitation is for each to bring their own emotionally healthy tank and breathe easy together as they serve the world.

As the adage goes, the best relationship is where your *want* for each other exceeds your *need* for each other.

Humans were designed for connection. But to *complement* each other, not *complete* each other.

So, let these words tumble off the page and into your soul:

Eve doesn't have what you need.

Adam doesn't have what you need.

The reason relational fractures can feel like an existential crisis? If we put our soul's chief question into the fickle hands of another human and they decide *No, I don't want you* . . . then it *is* an existential crisis. Someone better call an ambulance.

All that codependency, trauma, neuroticism, and dysfunction. All tracing back to the Adam or Eve inside.

. . . . .

"EVE" ISN'T ALWAYS A PERSON.
Maybe your "Eve" is your bank account. Every day you go to that app to ask Eve your value. Or the like count on your last post. Or your career status and popularity among peers. Maybe your Eve is your Cain and Abel, living vicariously through your kids. Or whatever crumbs of affirmation fall from an authority figure's table.

When we do any of this, we become fragile, a cork in the storm of passing emotions, circumstances, and other people's actions and opinions.

I could hear this in my friend's voice the other day over the phone. I was at a cafe when she called and I could feel her anxiety, thick and tense, dripping through the line. Reading too much into her boss's every spoken or unspoken word. Over-analyzing people's seeming approval or disapproval. I've been there myself. In this state, we walk into rooms and situations aching to have value pressed into us from the outside in. The thing is, resilience and freedom only come when we decide to live from the *inside* out. And we can make that choice *today*.

We must take our questions back from the places that leave us empty. We must have our primordial questions answered.

And I can't answer them for you.

Well, I can, but I can't.

To every woman, I could write that you're the affection of God's eye. That I am so sorry for anyone, especially any man, that's ever made you feel less than. God Himself made you, wonderfully and intentionally, clothing you with dignity and strength. The poetry of Genesis creation crescendos with woman as the crown. You are that crown. You should wear it with lifted head, radiant smile, and confident heart. You are beautiful, powerful, and deserving. You were created with purpose, and—stamped with God's image—you have infinite worth.

And it would be true. Every last word.

And to every man, I could write that you have what it takes. Strength comes from God and you're His workmanship. He has enough in the tank as a Divine Father to impart His approval over your soul. He's not easily irritated by you, even if an earthly father was. He's not distant, but looks at you through a smile, glad to have you around. He'll walk you through all life's land mines, like a broad-shouldered dad with His son. In Him, you're competent and fierce. Through Him, you can do all things by the might of His power, including the ability to love well. If you don't know who you are yet, notice the resemblance you bear as you walk with God. You favor your Father. And you're going to be okay.

And that would be true too. Every last word.

And sometimes that's enough. I've known people vice-gripped by lust and bondage who heard one simple message about their identity, realized the root of dysfunction was insecurity, and were set free immediately.

Sometimes healing rushes in like a finger snap.

But only sometimes.

Often, the deepest answers don't come through answers. They come through relationship.

Certain revelations have shifted things in me instantly, it's true. But mainly I've been changed along the way. In the *journey* of walking with God as Father, wholeness has come gradually, lies dissolving, identity elucidating. In the *journey* of walking with community, through painful ups and downs, hurts and reconciliations, confession and forgiveness, challenge and encouragement, a healthy sense of self has developed, and I've discovered who I am.

God promised to love us, reveal Himself, and transform us. But some promises only actualize in process.

It's strange, really, how textured our relational dynamics become with time. The shapes they take. How you relate to a parent from two to twenty-two to forty-two is vastly different. Same with God.

As a seventh-grade kid, God exploded into my brain like a supernova. Sounds dramatic, perhaps. All I know is the universe inside me seemed to expand, and I walked around many days in what felt like a trance. I read passage after passage and book after book. One particular book—*A God to Call Father*[13]—settled over my new journey like a northern snowfall. A mountain allegory upward into the clouds, high, high into the rare air of the Father's heart. I fell into this tale, fell into this truth. I fell into this new Father's journey with God.

I've been stumbling along that mountain ever since. At times with bloodied knees or hypothermia. Sometimes a foolish prodigal returning to a waiting lantern in snow. Occasionally, in hilly fields of sun so full of glory, I think it can't be real. It's been a tale of returning to a Father over and over.

I can tell you this Father is patient and wonderful.

Sometimes He feels far. And sometimes as close as skin. And sometimes there are moments in His Presence, so near and so hard to put into language, I can feel the kid inside me being renewed as if my soul is growing new cells. As if I am finding my way back to Eden. As if I am becoming whole again.

I share this, personal and even sensational as it may sound, to press the point that God is a Father we can walk with in

   CONFIDENCE

actual, dynamic experience. Some moments may be extraordinary, some not so much. It doesn't matter.

What matters is that while we learn the Father's heart in *Scripture*, we are changed in Father-child identity in the *journey*. Our Edenic wounds begin to mend in the shade of intimacy. In both earthly and divine friendship, transformation happens in Someone's *Presence*, not just on *pages*. Even neurology shows we are *healed in loving relationship*.[14]

I don't know your view of faith, much less how any experience with an earthly father has filtered your view of a perfect Father who made you and loves you.

But if I could nudge you, feel my elbow to your heart: Why not walk up the mountain with God? I wish I could offer something more formulaic. The thing is, it might be accurate, but it wouldn't be true. Formulas don't form us. Only an actual faith journey does.

The following could be a prayer for this next season: "God, reveal Yourself to me as a Father. Show me your heart. Come really close. And show me who I am too."

I'm convinced you'll find Him. I'm convinced you'll find *you*. Along with the answers your soul craves.

. . . . .

BARCELONA, 1992.

Derek Redmund, twenty-six, bounds around Lane 5 of the Olympic track. His first of two four-meter semifinals as part of Britain's gold-medal relay team.

Tragedy strikes. Pain hits like lightning, and he pulls up, grabbing the back of his leg, writhing. Face wincing, tears streaming, he eventually gets up and tries to hobble down the track. Then, the moment that captured millions.

An older, burly man somehow evades the tight, controlled security and bursts onto the track in a white T-shirt, heading Derek's way. A man built like a truck. A machinery shop owner in London.

Derek's father.

Sprinting toward his son.

Shouting, "Derek, it's me."

Derek turns and buries his head in his father's shoulder, sobbing.

Together they finish, while agony paints the son's face and the father whispers, "You have nothing to prove. I'm here. You're already a champion."

The International Olympic Committee called it one of the most inspirational moments in Olympic history.

I just watched the whole thing on YouTube for the thousandth time and again batted away the tears.

Because that's me.

And that's God.

Leaping over the barricade of eternity, splitting through the crowd of time and space, entering our same track on earth.

Running to where we are. Even when we're grown and running, He sees where we're naked and limping. And He's ready to draw close if we'll only open our souls enough to draw close in turn.

Even now, He's ready to run to you. To father you. To place gentle hands on open wounds. To begin to heal you from what happened in Eden. And what's happened since.

You need it too much.[1]
—Matthew McConaughey

Is anyone thirsty? Come and drink.[2]
—God through Isaiah

I care too much about what other people think. And sometimes it makes me drink until I don't care at all.[3]
—Quinn Lewis ("Everyone But Me")

8)

Thirsty

T HE ALIENS WERE RIGHT.

Something is missing.

We were designed to live in God's presence like fish in water. Now we're all on land, gulping at rain, taking medicines to stave off thirst.

It's why connection to God is so vital.

He's our air, bread, and water.

When Jesus taught people about this on earth, He used agricultural terms to resonate. He said things like:

> "I am the vine; you are the branches. Those who remain . . ."[4]

Jesus invited them to envelop their lives in His, hang there, and find energy and nutrients through Him. Not only could they throw away those pesky leaves; they could even begin to *bear fruit*. They could produce wondrous things because of the divine link pulsating through them.

No doubt if Jesus were to connect over coffee or a TED Talk today, He'd skip the farming lingo altogether and pull out an iPhone. (God knows it wouldn't be Android.)

I think He'd remind us what we already know, the mind-boggling potential hidden inside all that aesthetic plastic. A GPS to anywhere in the world, connector to anyone on earth, global internet at our fingertips, not to mention music and movies and work and anything one could dream up.

Then I think He'd pull out that off-white cord and remind us none of it matters if disconnected. All that power irrelevant if unplugged.

We were unplugged from the Source in Eden. And we've been glitching ever since.

But Jesus has come. And His invitation isn't religion; it's reconnection. He invites us to step back into actual life through Him.

. . . . .

THE YEAR 2020 REVEALED ALOT.

How prone we are to echo chambers. How people raise tigers in their spare time. How little toilet paper we keep on hand. And for me, how dehydrated I've really been.

Seriously. On Carey Nieuwhof's leadership podcast, leader after leader called him for advice, struggling, burnt out, anxious.[5] He surprised them all by asking how much sleep they'd been getting and water they'd been drinking. He told them to take two weeks, fix that first, then call him back about the rest. Staggeringly, the majority said that did the trick. No kidding. Once rested and water-filled, their perspective calibrated, and they had strength of mind to face their problems.

We enormously underestimate the synchronistic nature of our mind, body, and soul. Sometimes when I think I'm *depressed*, I might just be *dehydrated*.

Apparently, seventy-five percent of Americans *are* chronically dehydrated.[6] Call me a gym rat if you'd like, but I've been carrying around a gallon jug of water almost every day for a couple of years now. The effects of under-hydration on health, mood, energy, and focus are just too visceral.

The effects of a dehydrated spirit are even worse.

Thousands of years ago, God told the prophet Jeremiah:

> "'My people have committed two sins: They have forsaken me, the spring of living water, and have dug their own cisterns, broken cisterns that cannot hold water.'"[7]

Humans walked away from Niagara Falls as the water source for their souls. Then stuck some hole-riddled Styrofoam™ cups into their own shallow mud puddles to satiate the remaining thirst.

It's madness.

But we do it, don't we?

And the result of leaving God-waters and bootlegging our own makeshift wells?

We walk around thirsty.

I'm sure you've heard the slang *"thirsty."*

"He's so *thirsty."*

It has sexual connotations, but it also describes someone someone needy, someone desperate for attention. Someone who brags or stretches for validation. Someone who namedrops or doesn't know how to be normal around a celebrity without getting a picture. Someone who constantly posts revealing or braggartly pictures—aptly called "thirst traps"—to get the liquid serotonin relief of likes and comments.

It's, *Hello… does anyone see me?*

Thirsty.

Honestly, it's solid theology. We're all thirsty. And the thing about thirst? If not quenched, we'll take it somewhere.

. . . . .

IN WAR, REFUGEES ARE OFTEN DRIVEN to drink unsanitary water. The same thing happens when there's a civil war in the human heart. We tend to visit poisoned wells in desperate attempts to slay our thirst. We may never post a thirst trap, but we probably all know what it's like to be trapped by our thirst.

We see an absolute Rembrandt of this in John 4.

Jesus journeys from one human thirst well to another. The

Pharisees had been keeping score of baptism numbers and started comparing notes. Like Religious Olympics, they were grieved to have a silver medal and were taking their thirst to a religious cup of self-importance.

So, Jesus left. He headed for Galilee, veering oddly out of his way into Samaria, resting His legs at a well. A woman approached and Jesus stunned her by asking for a sip of still water. The subtext of racism and sexism that pervaded that day would've elicited hand-over-mouth, me-oh-my kind of gasps. And He didn't care.

When she asked why He'd dare even speak to her, he went for it:

> "If you knew the generosity of God and who I am, you would be asking me for a drink, and I would give you fresh, living water."[8]

It's beautiful. She'd been thirsty all her life and then crashed into water.

Jesus supernaturally discerned the details of her life, that she'd had five ex-husbands and was living with someone even now.

There's so much to the context in this culture. The truth is, it's possible she was victimized by the system. It's also possible she'd taken her inner thirst to men, leaving behind a trail of immorality and pain. Either way, instead of beating her up for self-medication, Jesus offered a deeper solution:

> "Everyone who drinks this water will get thirsty again and again. Anyone who drinks the water I give will never thirst—not ever. The water I give will be an artesian spring within, gushing fountains of endless life."[9]

He offered her fresh water instead of the saltwater that kept her coming back.[10]

For her, it may have been the saltwater of dysfunctional love. For us, it may be an extra pain pill. Or job-hopping. Or digital comparison. Licking at the screen for every drop we can get, the dopamine addiction growing stronger and stronger. After all, we crave what we consume.

We're a thirsty species.

It's interesting. The woman seemed to trip over the water metaphor at first, doubting Jesus's optimistic claims, and, looking skeptically down the earthen well, accidentally made a very profound statement:

"This well is deep."[11]

The well *is* deep right now.

There's a collective canyon in the human soul.

In fact, not long ago, the US Surgeon General issued warnings of a new epidemic:

Loneliness.

We are an isolated and disconnected society. And doctors are telling us it's not good for us. That it's even more harmful than a pack of cigarettes a day.[12]

It's worth reflecting on: We've never had more places to take our thirst—apps for attention, sexual outlets for release, substances for relief, shopping highs on every device. And yet we've never been thirstier, have we? We've never been more depressed, medicated, and alone.

That's because only real wells work. Only living water quenches.

. . . . .

SPEAKING OF WATER, THERE IS A healing compound to be extracted from the river of Jesus' baptism. If it can swim through our veins, it can set us free.

See, to know where to drink, we should ask where Jesus drank.

There is, after all, a dazzling, mysterious dance between Jesus's humanity and divinity.

On earth, He was God but also Man. He was tempted but never sinned, felt emotion but wasn't controlled by it, had authority but was submitted to the Father. He performed miracles, but not as God; rather, as the Son of Man anointed by the Spirit of God.

Here's why I bring it up. Have you ever wondered, "How confident was Jesus?"

It's a bizarre question. And you might be tempted to answer, "Well, probably super confident. After all, He was *Jesus* . . ."

But I think we'd be missing something about that dazzling dance. The Scriptures go out of their way to tell us Jesus stripped Himself of all divine privileges and made Himself a servant.[13] Jesus didn't just show us what *God* looked like; He showed us what an optimally healthy and confident *human* looks like.

And as the Son of Man dressed in skin and bone, I'm convinced Jesus had to draw His strength and confidence from *somewhere*. Just like us.

Watch His rhythms. The more He pours *out* (teaching, healing) the quicker He ninjas back onto a mountain with His Father to fill back *up*. His very own Tesla charge station.

Recall the suffering woman who snuck up behind Him with life-altering faith and touched His clothes. Healing energy *left* Him. And He felt it. So much so, He turned around and asked, "Who touched Me?" The disciples, never the brightest crayons, helped clarify that there were, in fact, *a lot* of people currently touching Him.

"Thanks," I imagine Him muttering.

But Jesus knew what He meant. There'd just been an extraction of His soul's divine virtue.

When it came to Jesus's power, energy, even emotional wellspring, there seemed to be a drawing and withdrawal.

So . . . where *did* Jesus get His energy and confidence?

I believe we get a hint at His baptism.

Thirty years old, knowing He's about to begin His ministry, Jesus wades into the murky waters of the Jordan and,

> "As soon as Jesus was baptized, he went up out of the water. At that moment heaven was opened, and he saw the Spirit of God descending like a dove and alighting on him."[14]

The Spirit had been *with* Him. But now the Spirit is *on* Him, anointing Him with power for ministry.

But that's not all. And I don't think that was the key to His deepest, internal confidence of heart. With divine, voyeuristic pleasure, we read next,

And a voice from heaven said, "This is my Son, whom I love; with him I am well pleased."[15]

Let the timing slip in like medicine:

These words poured over Jesus *before* He'd done one miracle, cast out one demon, preached one rock-star sermon, proven one leadership instinct, organized one helpful activity.

The Father's pleasure was irrelevant to the Son's performance.

He didn't have to hit a home run to hear an attaboy. He didn't need a perfect scorecard to see an approving smile. No one had to look pretty enough or win homecoming queen or marry up to see the doting look of love.

No, before any of that, Jesus hears the affirmation of His Father ring out in His soul:

    I love you.

        I'm proud of you.

        I approve of you.

It's from this place Jesus moves, operates, and lives.

He doesn't grit His teeth and work tirelessly for the fuel of His father's approval, wondering day after day if He's done enough.

No, tank already filled up with the gasoline of God's pleasure, He catapults from *there* into every room, endeavor, and challenge.

And we—you and me—as sons and daughters of God are invited to do the same. This is how Jesus can say things like, "Come to me all who are weary and burdened, and I will give you . . . rest for your souls, for my yoke is easy and my burden is light."[16]

Surely, part of that easy burden is that the performance-covenant has been cancelled and the relationship-covenant is underway.

See, when you live *for* approval, it's exhausting; when you live *from* approval, it's energizing.

We've been "accepted in the Beloved," Paul reminds us.[17] Which means we don't need to keep trying to prove our worth; we just need to accept our worth.

In Christ, the audition's been called off.

I once met someone at a coffee shop that I ended up dating for a few months. A real rom-com scenario. There were a couple of times toward the beginning when I wanted an excuse to send her one of my preaching messages. Or podcasts or books. You know, find a way to impress her. Embarrassing to admit.

Even though we weren't right for each other, I did experience an interesting phenomenon along the way. I realized I *liked* that she didn't seem all that impressed by me (not that anyone should be).

I guess at the end of the day, and maybe it's taken me way too long to get here, I don't want someone to perform for. I want someone who, in the words of Donald Miller, will take me by the hand and pull me off the stage. Who will see me and choose me for me.

I long to vulnerably and authentically love someone and, God help me, if it's possible, in spite of all my demons and tragic imperfections, have them know me and somehow love me, too, anyways.

I think that's what we all want.

"Love says: 'I've seen the ugly parts of you, and I'm staying.'"[18]

And that's what Jesus does.

Only God knows why.

In Jesus, we don't perform for water. We get to drink it endlessly.

· · · · ·

THIS ALL REMINDS ME OF THE MOVIE Hitch.[19]

In college, I fell pretty hard for someone. She made my stomach warm and my words dyslexic.

As our dates approached, I'd get so nervous I could barely sleep. The good nervous. The kind that lets you know it matters. The "nervous like a knife fight" kind Tom Delongue sings about.[20]

To help those nerves, I watched *Hitch* at night.

It's an older rom-com. Alex (Will Smith) is the love doctor, helping poor saps like Albert (Kevin James) connect with women out of their league. Sure enough, he helps Albert score a date with Allegra Cole. But then Albert has a near-panic attack in the back of the cab.

Alex shakes him:

"Tonight, when you're wondering what to say or how you look or whether or not she likes you, remember: *She is already out with you.* That means she said yes when she could have said no. . . . It is no longer your job to make her like you."

I guess I'm giving away all my tricks, but this is one I've kept close to the chest. A phrase that's helped me a time or two when nervous:

She already said yes.

When you know someone's already said yes, you can relax. You can enjoy yourself. You can stop auditioning. You can even switch the focus to them.

And that's what I hope to do in this book if you'll let me: shake you a bit and remind you, *God has already said yes.*

The tryouts are called off. Performance cancelled. When Jesus said, *It is Finished* . . . that meant no more auditioning for acceptance.

There is a giant *yes* hanging over your head.

A *yes* that goes before you into every room and opportunity you walk into.

Run the rest of your life inside that *yes*.

When you do, you breathe easier in the proverbial cab on the way to your life.

Your shoulders relax. Your head lifts. Your lips smile.

In fact, while we're tossing out secrets like candy, here's another. A decade ago, a friend could tell I was anxious before preaching. He spoke to my value, then, a bit cliché, added: "Russ, you got *nothing to lose and nothing to prove*."

To this day, whenever I face something that could get me in my head, I take a deep breath, smile, and whisper to my already-accepted, already-secure soul: *nothing to lose, nothing to prove*. Then I step forward and give it my all, knowing God's yes was spoken over me before I took the platform, will be hanging over me while I'm there, and will be waiting for me when I get off, whether I bomb or do great.

Try it. Right where you are, out loud:

Nothing to lose, nothing to prove.

It's true. And liberating.

It's taken a while, but I've been slowly relearning the art of living as a *secure son* instead of a *stressed servant*.

So why was Jesus confident?

It had little to do with the baptism waters, as important as that moment was. I think it was because He knew He was loved. Loved for who He was, not what He did. It's because He knew how to draw from the well. Draw from the well of His Father's Presence, the well of His purpose, and mostly, the well of His pleasure. He'd learned to drink that affirmation and walk in that security.

Can I press a little?

Every time you feel the need to promote yourself, you might just be operating out of the fear no one sees you. That's called a father wound.

A few years back, I polished off my favorite grilled sandwich at an Atlanta bistro with a church planter friend when he wiped soup from his mouth and took the breath out of me with,

"Russ, always remember—self-promotion is usually the cry of an orphan spirit."

Cue knife in gut.

What if it's true?

What if like kids constantly in trouble because of lack of attention at home, we express more civilized, adult-flavored tantrums of our dysfunction?

What if we're plagued by a deep *unseenness*?

What if we're thirsty because we feel abandoned?

And what if that's why intimacy with God is essential, not supplemental?

Maybe, just maybe, we can draw strength from the words Jesus poured over His disciples before He left:

> "I will not leave you as orphans; I will come to you."[21]

Jesus, of course, was referring to putting His Spirit inside His friends. He'd now be close to us forever because He wouldn't just be walking *with* us, but by His Presence dwell *within* us.

It's why Paul told us later:

> "So you have not received a spirit that makes you fearful slaves. Instead, you received God's Spirit when he adopted you as his own children. Now we call him, Abba, Father. For his Spirit joins with our spirit to affirm that we are God's children. And since we are his children, we are his heirs."[22]

This latch must click in place. I must capture the image of God as Father cheering me on like an out-of-his-mind dad at a child's tee ball game or recital. I must hear the cries of heaven surrounding me, hands cupped around mouths, yelling for my success.[23]

Look, I won't pretend I don't appreciate affirmation. It's my love language.

In fact, another secret. I have a Notes *Affirmations* folder. The kindest, most life-giving things people have said to me—about my character, personality, gifts, future, what I mean to these people, how I make them feel.

Occasionally, if I'm down on myself, I'll fish them out like electrolyte packets for the spirit. I'll never minimize how God uses others to speak life into me.

But relying on affirmation is like quick-fading sunscreen. It's an outward-pressing-in approach. While it feels good to apply external compliments into the ego-skin, it washes away in the water of life by midafternoon.

The confidence God desires for us is inside *out*. Not something we get *from* a room but something we bring *to* a room. Something spoken over us that continues to echo inside of us.

. . . . .

MUCH OF OUR JOURNEY COMES DOWN to this: *the daily decision of what bucket we draw from.*

The bucket I draw from will determine the life I experience. How full I stay and for how long. Whether or not my peace goes up and down like the stock market.

So let's get into the nitty gritty. Today—not tomorrow—what bucket will you draw from for strength and peace of mind?

Your own fledgling sense of esteem? Your latest win? Will you let your mind splinter between different people's feelings toward you in this particular moment? Will you let your mood derive from how talented, popular, or successful you feel today?

Or will you draw from the bucket of God's ardent, unrelenting love for you?

What will it be?

I'm believing Paul's prayer over you:

> "I fall to my knees and pray . . . that you have the power to understand . . . how wide, how long, how high, and how deep his love is."[23]

Swim there. Drink there. Live from there.

. . . . .

BACK TO BEING NAKED IN THE garden.

As odd as Adam and Eve's first reaction was—"We're naked"—God's response seems even stranger.

Not, *How could you?* Or, *I'm so mad.*

No, right on the heels of, *Where are you?*, God asked:

> *Who told you that you were naked?*

In other words,

> *Who are you listening to now?*

> *When did you let another voice become your narrative instead of mine?*

> *When did you start hiding instead of living?*

Today, we hide in all kinds of gardens. Shame drives us to numb inside a Netflix series or medicate with a third glass or isolate behind screens.

In the garden of relationships, we run behind bushes of silent treatment, passive aggressiveness, and other dysfunctional mechanisms handed down by unhealed families. Or we turn the bushes into walls, never fully letting anyone in, retreating into our minds for escape.

All along, the loving voice of God whispers and whispers:

Where are you?

And, *Who told you?*

Who told you you were naked?

Who told you you weren't enough?

Who told you you can't rise above it all?

Who told you you should be more like somebody else?

Who told you you have to audition for love?

It's important to locate the origin of those serpentine voices. And dislodge them. And realize whose voice didn't say those things. The Lord never said them. We must go back to a garden and allow His voice to shape our souls. A voice that says:

You have unending value.

Your story isn't over.

You can be forgiven and changed.

You have ardent design and purpose painted over your coming days.

I can take every piece of your life and create beauty and meaning from it.

I know everything about you, and I still ruthlessly love you.

Regardless of who hasn't chosen you, I choose you.

Regardless of how thirsty you are, I stand calling:

"If anyone thirsts, let him come to me . . ."

It is not the question, what am I going to be when I grow up;
you should ask, who am I going to be when I grow up.[1]
—Goldie Hawn

Right out of the gate, I'm super confident. But I'm also an
idiot. It's a brutal combination.[2]
—Steve (Stranger Things)

Without a musket to raise, a barricade to storm, a flag to wave,
the question hit me in the face like the cold air: Who am I?[3]
—Gary Ackerman

9)

Mystery in the Mirror

IT CAUSES REAL PROBLEMS WHEN YOU DON'T KNOW WHO YOU ARE.

I walked a quaint downtown the other day, coffee in hand. Sunlight broke around an arched sign that caught my eye, the letters warm and ancient.

The Majestic.

It took me back to a movie with the same name.[4] One that haunted me long after the credits rolled.

Jim Carrey's character, Peter, an aspiring screenwriter, gets blacklisted during the Russian "Red Scare" era of the 50s. Career derailed and girlfriend gone, he drives off one night into liquor and rain. And crashes so hard his mind wipes clean.

A smiling old man finds him washed up on the beach and takes him into town for breakfast. "Lucy makes a mean egg," he winks.

Heads in Lawson turn. Person after person remarks that he looks "strangely familiar." In an eerie but enchanting serendipity, Peter—the done for screenwriter—is the absolute doppelganger of Luke, a local hero assumed to have died in war.

The grieving father, fiancé, and town grapple to come to grips with this young man suddenly back to life. And as for Peter—now Luke—who remembers nothing of his past life, he begins a new one.

I won't spoil the ending—or whether the two characters are the same—but in a strange way, I find this odd, beautiful, heartbreaking story to be our odd, beautiful, heartbreaking story.

Peter had a crash and spent the rest of his days trying to remember who he was. Scrambling to find his bearings. Resigned to act out any script handed to him by those nearby.

Same with us. Long ago we had a collective crash under the foliage of that ancient, exotic garden. And we've been spinning out ever since.

Trying to remember our names. Contact tracing all the ancient longings inside us. Discovering who we were meant to be. Meanwhile, living out the narratives passed out by parents, peers, and society.

To add confusion to the cosmic amnesia, we experience all the subsequent mini crashes that follow.

No wonder we grasp for scripts to make meaning. No wonder we devolve into political tribalism, make sports teams our burning association, and curate online images. No wonder we get addicted and scared.

We've all forgotten who we are.

. . . . .

HOW DO YOU DEFINE YOURSELF?

With cultural identity? Familial? Religious? Racial? Occupational?

Many own theirs proudly:

Third-generation farmer.

Progressive thinker.

Proud American vet.

TikTok influencer.

Single dad with the best tee-ball-playing kindergartner in town.

On one hand, it makes sense. We pull identity from association, community, and wherever we gain value.[5]

Look no further than the shirts people wear or the stickers they slap on computers or cars. Some people want you to know they believe in evolution or that people who love Jesus should honk or that their child is on honor roll or that they really love this political candidate or really, *really* hate that one.

And don't get me started on vehicular stick-figure art.

Point is, there are core aspects of identity we broadcast, while others remain tied up in deeper waters and never brought above surface, much less named.

I experienced a paradigm shift around this ten years ago when I heard a psychologist nuance "belief" as not just the *faith* inside our heart, but the *film* around it.[6] A film by which we receive and perceive life. A film often formed in childhood. A film we usually don't realize we have.

For example, someone may experience neglect from a mother and form the unspoken *belief* that "women are cruel" and/or "only the strong survive." They'll never recite the belief like the Nicene Creed in a Presbyterian church, but make no mistake—unless addressed, that *belief* will be the filter and fulfillment of the rest of their days.

I bring it up because belief and identity are connected. And identity works the same way.

Whatever you believe deepest about who you are will determine how you receive and perceive everything around you.

It was Solomon, not Eckhart Tolle, who said, "As a man thinks, so is he."[7]

In this sense, your self-view sets the limits for your story.

Whatever you believe about *who you are* will determine *how you live.*

Even more poignant: Whatever you believe about *who you are* will determine *who you become.*

So, who are you?

Quick exercise.

Without overthinking, use the three lines below to describe who you are using nouns:

____

____

____

Now with *adjectives:*

____

____

____

Last one. Check both shoulders, then how you currently *feel* about the person you are:

____

____

____

Assuming you were honest, these three lists provide a clue to how you see yourself. A good clue, but still just a clue. After all, both pearls and great whites harbor below the surface.

. . . . .

SO, WHO'S IN THE MIRROR?

That's the question.

And it matters. A broken identity will result in splintered self-worth.

I've squeezed my chin on this one a good bit. From a glut of reflection, I'm convinced,

> *Identity isn't just a film around your heart; it creates the shape of it.*

Picture a cookie cutter—star, circle, square, you name it. Whatever confidence you foster through the truths of this book will only fit within the shape of that identity.

In this way, *identity is the container of your confidence.*

It's the shape, the vessel that holds your soul.

If you want to expand your confidence, you must expand the container. You must clarify the curves, erase the lies, and broaden the borders. Ensure it's healthy and whole.

Sounds lovely, but pumps out obvious questions.

If identity is the shape, what shape are *you*? What shape do you *want*? Can you *change* it? Is there a force in the universe strong enough to *reshape a soul?*

I'm convinced there is. I believe our identity is fashioned and refashioned by sonar power. By voice.

God spoke and galaxies spilled. He opened His mouth, and land and water divided like pastry. And this genetic wonder—the power of voice—was passed down to us. We get it honest from our Designer. Made in His image, Imago Dei.

From an active viewpoint, God created *the* world with *His* words, and we create *our* world with *our* words. From a passive viewpoint, our existence is spoken *by* God, our esteem then shaped *by* others, their words becoming the echo inside our own souls.

Think back through your life. I think you'll notice the contours of your confidence, the scars on your spirit, come from *voices,* good or bad.

It's true for me. Words have launched me into realms of possibility I never thought possible. And words have chipped away my self-belief and sent me shivering onto the sidelines.

People have taken their lives because of words. And people have chosen their lives because of words. Children have become hollow and violent because of words. And children have become leaders and savants because of words. People believed an outrageous dream about human equality from Martin Luther King Jr. because of words. And people followed Hitler into genocide and world chaos because of words.

Words. They kill and heal, reduce and shape.

Scripture says, "The power of life and death is in the tongue."[8]

We know it's true. Our days are ruined, weeks made, and lives haunted by the words of others.

Even war itself doesn't come from warplanes. It comes from words. The truth is, you and I have been going around with fingers on the nuke button since we were toddlers. Speaking life and death over each other, ourselves, and our future. It's too much power for a human being if you ask me.

. . . . .

THERE'S A LOT OF DEBATE RIGHT NOW in metaphysics on whether or not our words can impact matter[9] or help your favorite snake plant thrive. I have no expertise to offer on the matter. What I do know is what words do to the human spirit. I'm not sure if your voice can distort the crystallization of water, but I know what it's like for a sentence to mangle my heart.

It's fresh so it comes to mind, but yesterday someone made a comment that literally had a withering effect. I felt myself diminish from the words, the leaves of my soul browning. I had to take action before the night ended, had to pluck out the weeds, replace them with truth, and get the soil in sunlight.

I have to be that intentional. You probably do too.

And this gets tricky. After all, a dominant way God (*and* the enemy) speaks is through people. We just have to ensure the stories getting inside us are *true* and bring oxygen, not carbon. Even from the well-intentioned.

To be clear, God's voice won't always be fluffy and warm. Sometimes it'll encourage and sometimes it'll cut. But when it does slice us open, it's only for healing. Even the most challenging words, if God's voice is behind them, will help us. As I heard someone say the other day, God's Spirit only calls us *out* to call us *up*.

．．．．．

THE REAL TRAGEDY IN THE GARDEN?

It was the first time another voice entered the human story.

A malevolent voice replaced the benevolent Voice.

Did God really say . . .

The moment Adam and Eve metabolized the lie, God's heart was distorted and ours destroyed, the sonic fallout catastrophic.

So, what do we do with all this?

We take control of the words we *speak* and the words we *absorb*.

If we're to become whole, we must partner with the garden-Maker to do some reversal, allowing His voice to reshape our internal world.

How?

A few ways.

Pay attention to what we consume. *Thin out the noise* (less media, less content, less bombardment) and *improve the quality* (wiser voices, purer entertainment, faith-building podcasts/messages).[10]

Renew our minds with truth from Scripture, absorbing it into the bloodstream. Memorize it and contemplate it through the day. Think higher and more critically through culture's messages (cliches'll kill you). Encircle our lives with faith-filled people who echo God's voice most closely.

But mostly? Walk intimately, heel to heel, with the One in the garden, living in His Presence, learning the frequency of His whisper.

And this tango can get tricky.

We do have a choice over what internal and external voices get in. To an *extent*. Unfortunately, in the real world, people *do* say destructive things and toxic thoughts *do* enter our minds.

But—and here's the key—we have absolute control over *which voices we partner with*.

Every thought that comes—we can accept, reject, or redirect into God's truth and perspective for our lives.

This is the prescription for emotional well-being.

We get to choose the thoughts we think. We get to extract the ruinous voices that have fastened onto our inner walls. We get to decide who we'll listen to and who we won't.

We get to let another Voice reshape us.

And odd as it sounds, I have to tell you there's a voice in your life more important than other people.

Or even God.

That voice?

Yours.

Sounds blasphemous. More important than God's?

The reality is that it doesn't matter what anyone, even God, tries to whisper to you, if *you* don't receive it, believe it and speak it back.

You know this. People sit in church every week hearing life but never change because they keep rehearsing death.

We must learn to stand up to the bully inside our own souls. Carry shield and sword around our own brain. Refuse to tolerate destructive words from *ourselves* any more than we would from someone else. We should take stock of what we hear first thing in the morning inside the score of our mental movie. And if need be, snap records and put on new ones.

As Dr. Martin Lloyd-Jones said, we need to stop listening to ourselves and start talking to ourselves.[11] Intentionally.

Yes, if voice shapes identity, how are you using *your voice* to shape *your identity*?

This is where the power of self-declarations come in. "Confessions" in the church world, "affirmations" in the corporate.

For over a decade, some years more than others, I've made a practice each January of writing not just vision, but declarations. Then speaking those declarations over my life.

Too self-help or cheesy?

Well, if cheesy means I emulate the likes of Craig Groeschel, Oprah Winfrey, Tony Robbins, Arnold Schwarzenegger, and the other greats in every field, then break off the gouda.

As a person of faith, my "I am" statements aren't top-of-mind hopes but grounded-in-Scripture truths. That kind of radiation gets into the cells.

It's why when I led my small group through Ephesians this year, we plucked out every descriptive word from Chapter 1 and went to town, writing them down.

Chosen.

Holy.

Adopted.

Forgiven.

Destined.

Sealed.

Blessed.

Redeemed.

Then we began every class like a school pledge, standing up and chanting them over ourselves. They hated it. And their countenances changed (and their lives) as some of them began to speak atomic truth over their spirits for the first time. Some taped the list to their mirror or Bible.

See, I believe Scripture has a pulse, that it's alive.

And if it is . . . then what happens when you take the *intrinsic* power of your words, combine them with the *eternal* power of God's words, and speak that dynamic energy over your soul each day? Nuclear fission happens, light and explosion.

For a nice *Chili's* sampler, I've adapted a list you can try out.

If alone, muscle through some awkwardness and declare it over yourself. Out loud. Like you mean it.

If you've stepped into a life-changing relationship with Jesus, here's what's true of you:

> I am *chosen.*
> I am *complete.*
> I am *free* from guilt and condemnation.
> God is working both the good and bad in my life for
>   *good.*
> I am *confident* God will complete the work He started in
>   me.
> I am *significant*, God's own workmanship.
> I can *approach* God with freedom and confidence.
> I am fearfully and wonderfully *made.*
> I have been *established, anointed*, and *sealed* by God.
> I have not been given a spirit of fear, but of *power, love,*
>   and a *sound mind.*

A complete list is available in the Notes section in the back. Feel free to rip it out and tape it to your fridge or notebook.)

Eventually, your belief can change at a biological level. And that will change you on a biographical level.

We live out who we believe we are.

. . . . .

ABOUT A DECADE AGO, I DAMAGED MY life against a wall of heartbreak and self-medication. I had to take a break from ministry altogether.

As part of my restoration, I met with one of the elders in the basement of his home each week. A tall, eagle-eyed school administrator who gave vibes of closet prophet, he led me through a half-counseling, half-freedom-curriculum[4] experience.

We never talked about the fruits of my actions like I anticipated, only roots. Together we rubber-gloved some tumbleweeds out of noxious soil and went to work. I identified lies—several orbiting around insecurity—and molded truth statements as arsenal against the assault, taping those bullets to a mirror and building the case into my soul every day for a year.

Five years ago, I had the privilege to do the same with Jesse. When I moved to Columbus, I liked the guy immediately. He was kind and mature, rarely talked, and nursed wounds from childhood and unhealthy leaders.

After half a year, we began to slice away the layers and spoon out the lies. I gave him homework. I told him to search Scripture for truths that replaced those lies and craft them into portable statements He could speak over himself.

Then I told him to quit putting off making a counseling appointment. I told him if he didn't make a call by that Thursday, he had to give a coworker a hundred dollars. Looking back, I don't think I'm allowed to do that and I'm glad he didn't tell HR.

He completed both assignments.

It's been four years and he's a different man. What God has done in his heart and life is nothing short of miraculous. He's confident, bold, influential, a leader of leaders, has been given promotion after promotion, and, most importantly, is *healthy*.

With his permission (and acknowledgment he ripped a few of these off), here's some of what he wrote and spoke over his life every morning for a year:

THIS IS ME.

Jesus is first in my life; I exist to honor Him.

I don't have to be perfect, because His grace is.

Christ is in me; I am enough.

I love people and believe the best about them. They are my purpose.

I am anointed, empowered, equipped, and called to reach people who are far from God.

I am creative, innovative, driven, focused, and blessed beyond measure because the Spirit dwells within me.

I am a leader. It's not something I do, it's who I am.

I bring my best and then some.

I wake up with purpose, meaning, and direction every day of my life.

The world will be better because I served Jesus today.

Now. Your assignment. Hold the eye roll.

Take some time. Look back on lies that need replacing. Think through who you want to become. Reflect on the best version of yourself and virtues that matter to you. If you follow Jesus, find where these intersect with Scripture. Then, in the same "I am" vein as Jesse, write out your new personal code, one you'll speak over your life in the morning, one that will be the filter for your decisions and life.

THIS IS ME

____

____

____

____

____

A genius is the one most like himself.[1]
—Thelonius Monk

Let your love, God, shape my life.[2]
—David

Human beings will always act through whatever they associate themselves with. Your identity shapes your reality.[3]
—Todd Herman

10)

The Future You

"**J**UST DO YOU."

Ever heard that?

It feels so authentic. So *right*.

Like most cliches, it's got issues.

Do *me*? What if current me is a jerk? Should I *do* that?

And which *me* should I do? Some days I feel like I experience a thousand *mes*, how about you?

I can begin the morning a peaceful Zen me, enlightened like a Trappist monk brewed of green tea and wisdom. Then battle lustful thoughts and express mild road rage on the way to work. By midmorning express epitomal leadership, serving my team with inspiration and creativity. *And* catch myself being defensive and indecisive.

And I've been working hard. But feeling lazy. And today I'm disciplined with my diet. Or I've fallen off the wagon for the fourth day straight, muttering "I'll start back tomorrow" to myself under my breath as I reach for the third donut.

And this is all before lunch.

So which *me* should I do? And more importantly, am I doing *well* by doing *me*?

. . . . .

I WANTED TO BE A LOT OF PEOPLE growing up.

Greg Maddux. Indiana Jones. Bruce Lee.

And Zeke from *The Faculty*,[4] an angsty teen film in which parents and teachers were the enemy and aliens were taking over the school. Zeke and his friends were the trendy, moody anti-heroes.

Everything—soundtrack, clothes, dialogue—gushed *cool*.

Especially Zeke (Josh Hartnett). I immediately wanted to be Zeke. He just didn't care. I mean, I wish you could see how much he didn't care. Zeke oozed nonchalance and brooding, winsome moodiness like a country song oozes heartbreak.

I took on his persona. I grew out my hair, bought a lot of Tommy Hilfiger, wore black and white and combat boots and an *I don't care* attitude. I got myself in bad moods and listened to a lot of Creed. Even begged my parents to buy me Zeke's black '71 Pontiac GTO with two red racing stripes down the middle. They never caught the vision.

I suppose part of growing up is experimenting with your identity. Trying on different ones for size. All normal.

But getting older, I've noticed something. It seems the more confused we get on the *inside*, the more we tend to overcompensate on the *outside.*

Evidence for court: midlife crisis.

Unfortunately, the reason you *know* someone goes through a midlife crisis isn't because they "quietly mull a matter over" with God and counsel. No, they overspend on a motorcycle, sport decade-younger outfits, and run off with a flirty coworker their daughter's age.

They are screaming on the outside that something is screaming on the inside.

Of course, now we don't wait for midlife crises; we do *quarter-life crises.* It's getting wild out here.

Regardless, when we're broken in our internal identity, we tend to reach for extremes, outlandishness, and noisy colors to paint over an empty, desolate canvas. Or . . . give up altogether and resign to mere existence.

Ironically, that's why one of the keys to true self-discovery is not more external noise but quiet solitude. Reflection. Enough time alone with God and silence to let the demons surface, deal with them, and get to know our voice and God's voice in the stillness.

But screaming feels better than solitude.

It's why I used to have to talk myself out of new tattoos after tough breaks. No kidding. Not because I'm against tattoos. I have a couple and plan to get more. But I like them as markers, not medicine. I don't want permanent decisions out of temporary emotions.

I've long resonated with those achy, wanderlust lyrics:

> *Now that she's back in the atmosphere, with drops of Jupiter in her hair. She acts like summer and walks like rain, reminds me that there's a time to change, hey. Since the return of her stay on the moon, she listens like spring and she talks like June, hey.*[5]

Have you ever felt that urge? To move or return from a trip looking "new"? I wish I could tell you I never feel that anymore. But on trips, *part* of me still wants to return different. Better. A little exotic and cultured. A dark tan, an ancient-looking tattoo, and a far-off look of mystery in my eyes. Maybe a slight Italian accent.

There's just something forbidden and exciting about the idea of reinventing yourself, isn't there?

And, may surprise you, I think it can be a *good* thing.

I listened to Todd Herman the other day at a conference.[6] He's the performance consultant who helped Kobe Bryant when his career stalled. Kobe had gotten in his head, so Todd helped him develop his alter ego, "the black mamba." A ritual, uniform, and persona to express a manifestation of himself that needed to come out. Sure enough, it helped him break the rut, extract his potential, and express greatness.

An alter ego isn't fake, Todd argues. We all have fluid versions of ourselves. Why not picture the *best* version for the different moments that demand it, put on those particular capes, and practice stepping into it?

I also think there's power in leveraging moments and seasons of your life for change.

I did this when I returned from Buenos Aires. I thought long and hard about who I would be when I got back. My last six months, I worked out like a maniac and only ate protein and oranges. Then I experienced a God-awakening of sorts. My return was a near physical and spiritual reincarnation.

I leveraged my move to Atlanta for healing and a clean slate, to *become new*. My move to Columbus to elevate my leadership. And every new year and birthday to dream afresh the code of who I'm becoming.

If there's a transition in your life, why *not* springboard that to pivot? Grow and change. Go for it.

Or to level up, find a legend you look up to and move in that direction in a way that's true to you.

Here's my nuance. Reinventing yourself when you know who you want to be is admirable. It's renovation from the inside out.

On the other hand, a life crisis is when you try to reinvent yourself from the *outside in*. Or you *run away* from your problems (wherever you go, there you are . . .). Without a solid center, this is lipstick on a pig at best, untethered and destructive at worst.

One's true. The other is a panicky shortcut from the external when we don't want to address the internal.

It's another reason David inspires me, to be honest. Young, about to face Goliath, he's faced with a moment of personal distinction. Saul hoists his heavy armor onto David to prepare him for battle. And David tries. Slips on the large bronze helmet and coat of armor and straps himself with the heavy sword. Then finally says in essence, "Sorry, this isn't me," takes it all off, picks up some stones, and heads to battle.[7]

Somehow, he'd already developed a strong filter for his identity. And someone else's approach/style/opinion didn't fit it.

I can only imagine the courage it took a teenager to tell a king, "Not my color. This isn't how I'm wired. This isn't who I am."

It takes some chutzpah to brush off the armor pressured onto us by those we love—the agendas, mindsets, and convictions. It takes nerve to discover with God who we were authentically created to be and let every competing distraction fade away.

It takes vision to reinvent ourselves.

And I'm convinced—those few free souls who find the audacity to pursue their own path are the ones who cause the rest of us to stop and marvel.

· · · · ·

I'M A SMIDGE TIRED TODAY. IT'S MY fault. But I blame Tommy. The other night at the gym, he told me I just had to watch this Netflix show (just what I need) called *All the Light We Cannot See*.[8]

But he was right. It's a beautiful story in the starkest of settings. A blind girl living in Nazi-occupied France. It held me, kept me up, MacBook by pillow. Healthy, right?

I've always been drawn to WWII, tragic as it is. America found its role in it. My grandfather served in it. Oppenheimer developed the nuclear bomb through it. Hitler's evil brain fascinates us by it. Mass fear and hysteria instruct us from it.

And the most profound philosophers of modern history emerged out of it.

Austrian neurologist Sigmund Freud arguing that human beings are driven by *pleasure.*

German philosopher Axel Honneth arguing that human beings are driven by *status.*

And Austrian psychiatrist Viktor Frankl arguing that human beings are driven by *meaning.*

Frankl was deported to a Nazi concentration camp (he spent time in *four*). A coterie of misery, where hope was lost, family members had been murdered, and suicide rates were enormously high. Though forbidden, Viktor coaxed his fellow prisoners away from self-harm, whispering in their ears that they still had a *purpose,* that there was a reason they were still alive.[9] And it worked.

In fact, after the war, he was asked to lead the mental health division of the Viennese hospital system, with more than 30,000 suicidal patients under his watch. Incredibly, *not one of them chose to end their life.*

Unlike Freud and Axel, Frankl was convinced that man's

greatest search is a sense of purpose. That, "When a person can't find a deep sense of meaning, they distract themselves with pleasure."

Frankl is right.

He developed his ideas into what's called *logotherapy*, arguing three components make a meaningful life:

1.   A redemptive view of suffering.

2.   A purpose to pursue.

3.   A community to belong to.

One modern philosopher synthesized these into the *three human intrinsics*: a drive for meaning, progress, and intimacy. A need to believe, become, and belong.[10]

You may be wondering what any of this has to do with identity.

Everything.

How we connect to our story, our purpose, and our community is *integral* to identity, not *peripheral*.

In *community* we find out *what we're like* (our personality and personhood), in *purpose* we discover *who we are* (our character and talent), and in pursuit of our *meaning/beliefs* we discover our *why* (our reason and story).

One by one . . .

Community. The need to belong. Our identity forms meaningfully in the context of relationships because it's in relationships that we see ourselves. Integration occurs as we connect. That's why isolation is so unhealthy. It moves us toward disconnection and brokenness of identity.

Purpose. The intrinsic desire for a future, to move forward, toward something, anything. When we don't progress, we get depressed. That's why purpose is the true, holistic cure by every measurable study. And it can start small. As small as running a mile a day, serving coffee at church, or reading a chapter in a book.

Meaning. A reason we're here. A need to believe. A redemptive view of pain. Part of how we heal from pain is finding purpose in it. It's the *medicine* of meaning. But it's also more than that. It's mapping out a meta-narrative that takes you out of an all-engrossing chapter and into a larger novel for your life.

These three elements create the strength of your story and the health of your identity.

They are the three primary colors with which we paint the canvas of our life.

Do you have them on the brush?

. . . . .

SPEAKING OF THE POWER OF STORY.

The human heart was made for it. It's the universal tether, the language of humanity across every age and tribe, inked in us from the beginning.

It's also healing and empowering.

A vital part of increasing our mental fitness, not to mention building a healthy identity, is to pay attention to—and adjust—the stories we tell ourselves.

Exhibit A: "I can't believe I did that last night. I am a horrible person and will never change. Stupid, *stupid* Russ."

Or . . .

"Last night I didn't express the best version of myself. I need to deal with what I did, take responsibility, learn from it, and move on. That's not who I am, and with God's help, I will do better next time."

Which one of those *stories* I choose and repeat will determine the *character* I become and the *identity* I develop.

I have to break it to you, the wind's not at our back on this one. When we're not intentional with our inner narratives, we trend toward negative ones, not positive ones. We must get ruthless.

Like David.

When we pry open his diary in Psalms, we're virtually eating popcorn inside his mind, watching his self-talk. We see him vent and lament about how bad life is, then turn the corner and reframe his situation in light of God's goodness.

In fact, in perhaps the darkest moment of his life, when he led his men back from war to Ziklag, they discovered their homes burned, families killed, and wives kidnapped. To add disaster to disaster, his men blamed *him*, turning on him, threatening to kill him.

David's response?

He "encouraged himself in the Lord."[11]

Wait . . . *what*?

How does one rise to that level of Shaolin self-mastery?

I'm not sure, but I can tell you, at least for me, the most important messages I've ever preached have not been on stages to thousands but in cars to myself.

Same for all of us. You may not be called to preach publicly, but I hereby ordain you to preach privately. I commission you to tell yourself better stories. To master the mic inside your own ears.

Another sampling? In Psalm 42, David moans,

> "Day and night I weep for his help, and all the while my enemies taunt me."

Then point-guard pivots with,

> "Take courage, my soul! Do you remember those times (but how could you ever forget them!) when you led a great procession to the Temple . . . singing with joy, praising the Lord? Why then be downcast? Why be discouraged and sad? Hope in God! I shall yet praise him again . . ."

Oh, David. The OG of CBT.[12] (Cognitive Behavioral Therapy.)

Let's try again:

"My childhood left me broken. I never had the parents everyone else did. My abuse will leave me handicapped for life. My future will never be what it could have been."

Or . . .

"The pain I went through was real. I need to work through it. But my past doesn't have to determine my future. People have been through unimaginable tragedy and risen to profound greatness. I have the choice to make my past a platform through which I become resilient and serve the world."

I love Jamie Kern Lima's lines. Billionaire and co-founder of IT cosmetics, she endured a *messy* amount of hurt and prejudice throughout her life. In her book, *Worthy*, she walks the reader through a powerful process of embracing worth and redefining rejection. One statement she internalized:

"Rejection is not about what's wrong with me; it might be about what's right with me."[13]

This stuff isn't mere poetry; it's potency. And true. You know this. You know siblings who've come out of the same heartbreaking circumstances yet embraced two different narratives and became two different people.

In 2013, I hit a narrative crossroads myself. One that could've taken me out. I was living in Lexington and felt trapped by the dream of a church plant collapsing, the mantel resting on me, meanwhile feeling as spiritually disconnected and stained as I'd ever felt. Vice and grief were closing in. Sounds absurd, but it was also the first time I realized I'm mortal. All the fluid had been collecting inside, all the betrayal, church pain, relational pain, left alone to hold together a church that was falling apart while *I* was falling apart.

I remember days, pathetic to write now, where I'd sleep in, then sit outside the second-floor balcony of my apartment, stare outside, and weep. Before long, I couldn't recognize myself. I started losing weight and hair.

Then I heard a message from T.D. Jakes. He unpacked the story of David carrying the ark of God's Presence to Jerusalem. How David gravely miscalculated, not following God's instructions. How it led to a man's death. How all the partying turned to mourning. How for months David remained paralyzed, too grief-stricken, numb, and scared to move forward.[14]

Then, he talked about how David finally healed, understood his mistakes, gained perspective, summoned his strength, and kept going.

Bishop Jakes highlighted the following line from the previous chapter slowly, telling us to replace David's name with our own.

Here it is:

> "So David *went on,*
>
> and *became great,*
>
> and the Lord God of hosts *was with him.*"[15]

Something in me rose up, *I'm not dying in this apartment. And my calling is not dying in Lexington.*

I grabbed a piece of notebook paper, tore it in half, and through tears, scribbled:

> *And Russ went on,*
>
> *And grew great,*
>
> *And the Lord God of hosts was with him.*

I taped that terrible delusion to my mirror, looked at it with hollow eyes, and repeated it for months until it became true.

I don't know that I ever grew great.

But I did move on.

And the Lord God of hosts *is* with me.

The stories we tell ourselves matter.

. . . . .

YOU HAVE TO DETERMINE WHAT story you'll believe. Both the macro and micro.

Which can get dicey. Have you ever felt conflicted by what's true of you? A friend says one thing about you. An enemy says another. We must choose what stories we partner with. They must be *true* but informed by faith, not fear.

The long night may be real. God's promise to see me into the morning is even more real. The assessment of my current dysfunction may be true. God's vision and commitment to see me through to my most virtuous self is even more true.

And so . . .

Maybe even more important than,

> *Who you are*

is,

> *Who you're becoming.*

This is the golden ticket to golden identity right here.

And it's not easy. It's tough to see ourselves through God's eyes. It can be even tougher to see *the future us* through God's eyes. To see what's in us that hasn't yet been actualized. To see the side of us on the other side of the struggle. To see what "no eye has seen, and no ear has heard, no mind has imagined."[16]

When you're Abram and God changes your name to Abraham, "father of many nations," and you're still old and childless, what do you do with that?

This is the power of God speaking into your life.

And the importance of what we do with it.

Will we believe what God speaks over us, about us, and into us?

What if—like Abram, Jacob, and Simon—God wants to give you a new name? What if there's a new identity God's waiting for you to step into? A "black mamba" waiting for you on the court?

When we give our lives to Jesus, Scripture says we are made "new creations,"[17] that "the old has gone and the new is here."[18] And *then* we must "put off" the old and "put on" the new.[19]

What if your new identity and life have already come, and you simply need to step into it? It'd be a shame to keep wearing the same dirty clothes each day if a deep-pocket relative already bought you a new, stuffed walk-in closet.

So, God loves to remind us who we are. Even more, He loves to give us glimpses of who we can become.

He'll whisper your name. And that's beautiful. But He can also give you a *new name*. If you're Jacob, a cheater, He can make you Israel. The same God who created you can *re-create* you.

That's the Gospel, by the way. That's the good news of Jesus.

He can make Adam out of dirt and He can remake you out of whatever dirt you're in.

Your current *location* doesn't matter nearly as much as your current *trajectory*.

It's both a challenging and encouraging paradigm shift.

Challenging because it doesn't matter how great you think your life has been and how great you might think you are . . . right *now* when you look at the direction of your patterns and character, who are you becoming?

And encouraging because, well, who you've been doesn't have to determine who you'll be. Is there any more hopeful thought on this blue dot rotating in space? Tigers do change their stripes. And you can too.

To quote A.W. Tozer, "The great hope of this world is that a man can change."

. . . . .

A DANGEROUS STRATEGY IS TO ROOT your confidence in who you've been. A good strategy (if you're healthy) is to root your confidence in who you are. A *revolutionizing* strategy is to root your confidence in who you're becoming.

It's where the power of vision and identity collide.

The wisest people I know reverse engineer their life. They start with the end and who they want to become.

So, not to be tacky,

> but don't do *you*.

> And don't just do the *new you*.

> Do the *future you*.

Take some time to "Kobe Bryant" visualize the best version of yourself. Take all the splendid things people have said about who you truly are. Take the ways God has wired your personality and gifts and passions. Take what burns inside you. From there, dream up who you long to become. What does this person look like? How honest? How courageous? How creative? How humble? How kind? How pure? How disciplined? How joyful? How passionate? How close to God? How sacrificial?

Picture it.

Write it.

Then step into it. Today.

It really doesn't matter who you've been. Or even who you are. It only matters who you're becoming.

And you can make choices to move yourself in that direction *right now*.

Here's to the future you.

You get your confidence and intuition back by trusting yourself, by being militantly on your own side.[1]
—Anne Lamott

Insecurity comes when we find our identity in anything but God.[2]
—John Bevere

Sorry, Nate, you'll have to speak up. I have a real tricky time hearing folks that don't believe in themselves.[3]
—Ted Lasso

11)

Small in Your Own Eyes

D O YOU BELIEVE IN YOURSELF?

If you don't, no one will. You know that.

I listened to a "Summer Bucket List" episode on a leadership podcast the other day.[4]

Last year's summer episode was all about how this family grabbed posterboard and scribbled fifty spike-ballin,' road-trippin,' blueberry-ice-cream-tastin' ways to make the sunny season stand out.

But this year's went off the rails, an unleashing on *radical Self-belief.*

> "It's not about how much you know; it's about how much you believe in yourself . . . On the bucket list this summer is developing an insane, an exuberant, over-the-top amount of self-belief . . . If I could gift every leader one gift—I would give them the gift of confidence. It is the most underrated quality of a leader."

I love that.

How *is* your self-belief these days?

Bone deep? Paper thin?

What if it's more important than you know?

Self-belief isn't at war with God-belief, by the way. Christians get nervous here and start throwing out qualifiers and cliches like confetti. But healthy God-belief should *fuel* healthy self-belief. As I heard Jon Acuff say, "It's not arrogant to believe in what God has put in you unless you think you created yourself."

A lot of people possess God-belief but no self-belief and thus never step into the life available to them by the God they claim to believe in.

So, believe in God. But realize God made *you* and wants *you* here. *He* believes in you enough to create you, deposit gifts in you, and entrust you with tasks and other humans. And no matter how it feels, *others* believe in you.

The question is, do *you* believe in you?

. . . . .

WE FIND A POWERFUL DESCRIPTION OF Saul's insecurity the first time he's confronted by the prophet.

Samuel uses an interesting phrase:

> "'Although you were once *small in your own eyes*, did you
> not become the head of the tribes of Israel?
> The Lord anointed you king over Israel.'"[5]

Samuel said Saul was *small in his own eyes.*

A lot can make you feel small if you let it—a close friend becoming distant, a harsh word from a boss or loved one, even neglect.

Again, on the surface, "small in your own eyes" could lay on the table like humility. Until you thin-slice it and remember inferiority's a self-focused posture.

Yes, *Small in your own eyes* might sound noble.

Noble until it causes you to be unfaithful because you minimized what God entrusted. Noble until you're irresponsible in your role because you downplayed the person He called you to be. Noble until false humility causes you to be false before God and others.

God isn't impressed when we're unimpressed with what He's given us.

Saul kept self-sabotaging because of his self-optics. He felt small. So small he hid behind luggage when announced king. So small he didn't think it was a big deal to be negligent in what God placed in His life to carry out.

Small in his own eyes.

I want the phrase to haunt you.

It might sound familiar, by the way.

When the children of Israel camped in the wilderness, Moses sent spies to scout the promised land. The desert trek was to be brief and the scouting report informational only. Before long, the itinerary read: "Enter Canaan, conquer enemies, and settle down at a *Sandals* resort surrounded by God's Presence and Protection."

Unfortunately, on the scouting trip, ten spies became more impacted by the giants they saw than by the land God promised. They came back with an infectious report of negativity, fear spread through camp like influenza, and that entire generation (minus Joshua and Caleb) died out without ever seeing their dreams come to pass.

And here it is, notice the phrase:

> "We saw the Nephilim there . . . *We seemed like grasshoppers in our own eyes*, and we looked the same to them."[6]

You have to appreciate the honesty. They didn't just say they seemed small in the giants' eyes. They admitted they felt *small in their own eyes*.

And it literally cost them their destiny.

This has to drop deep into our hearts. They had the most epic future awaiting them, but because of the limiting way they viewed themselves, they never experienced it.

Likewise, Saul had it all, had been entrusted with so much, but his self-view vandalized the story that would be told of his life.

All that gifting. All that anointing. All that opportunity. And insecurity made him despise it all.

Wouldn't it be traumatizing to look back on your life and realize you had so much going for you, so much you could've experienced, only to discover you missed out simply because of how you chose to see yourself? That you never experienced what could've been ahead of you because you never believed what was inside of you?

I wonder what outdated lens we need to shatter and replace.

I journaled the following statements several years back as reminders for my heart anytime I let insecurity get the best of me or wave it off like it's not a big deal:

It is sinful to be small in my own eyes.

It is irresponsible to be small in my own eyes.

It is dangerous to be small in my own eyes.

It is joyless to be small in my own eyes.

It is powerless to be small in my own eyes.

It is ungrateful to be small in my own eyes.

Saul was small in his own eyes, and it destroyed him.

The children of Israel were small in their own eyes, not trusting God, and never crossed over to their future.

So how do you see yourself? Through the eyes of your giant problems and internal imperfections, or through the eyes of God?

Paul must have felt this same burden for his friends in Corinth:

"Dear, dear Corinthians, I can't tell you how much I long for you to enter this wide-open, spacious life. We didn't fence you in. *The smallness you feel comes from within you.* Your lives aren't small, but you're living them in a small way. I'm speaking as plainly as I can and with great affection. Open up your lives. Live openly and expansively!"[7]

Paul wanted them to rise into the incredible, epic space God intended for them.

If I can say it this way, He wanted them to live heroic lives. He wanted them to be fully human, fully alive, fully on fire.

But they were *thinking* small, so they were *living* small.

Paul reminds them, "The smallness you feel comes from within you."

Hey, if I can get in their face for a moment:

Scout on the edge of the promised land, it's not the giants making you cower; it's what's inside you. The external giants just expose your internal giants.

Saul, it wasn't your father's or Samuel's approval that determined your worth. It was never who was with or against you, Philistines or Moabites, friends or leaders. None of that mattered. It's the world inside you that you never mastered.

And you, reading these words. It doesn't matter who's rejected you. Your only issue may be that *you* have rejected you. And you may need to repent. To change your mind about it. And open yourself again to the boundless space inside you where God can do anything.

If I could be so bold . . .

Don't you *dare* let yourself be small in your own eyes.

God Himself sculpted you, arrayed you, and lives inside you.
Don't insult Him by minimizing the potential that soaks your
every cell.

Go ahead, give the Moses objections to why God can't do
amazing things through your life . . . *I can't speak well. . . I'm
not this . . . I'm not that . . .* and watch God's eyes light up
with fire as He answers you back with His question:

"Who do you think made the human mouth?"[8]

Listen, God made you. With real-time, eternal purpose.

So He doesn't call our self-loathing humble; He calls it an
insult to His workmanship. He doesn't call our minimization
godly; He calls it ungrateful. And He doesn't call our sideline
sitting noble; He calls it unbelief and disobedience.

None of our false humility and self-disdain honors God.

No, what honors God is when you're Gideon, trembling like a
coward inside a wine press and God whispers into your soul,
"Mighty man of valor" and you dare to believe Him.

What honors God is when you're Peter, a flimsy reed your
whole life, stumbling all over yourself, convinced you'll never
overcome your failures, and God says your new name is
"Rock" and that He's going to build a future on your life and
leadership, and you somehow find the grit to believe His words
over your own self-condemnation.

What honors God is when you feel forever stuck in the past, forever labeled by your worst moments, and God's Word declares you new, the old gone, your slate sparkling clean by Jesus's sacrifice, and you dig down and believe it.

In this way, the starting point of self-belief is choosing to believe what God says about you over what you think about you.

. . . . .

CAN I TELL YOU A SECRET?

If you perpetually walk around small in your own eyes, you'll eventually become small in everyone else's too.

And you'll do things that make you look small.

You'll subtly fish for compliments and it won't be so subtle. You'll lead from uncertainty instead of clarity and it'll be obvious. Little slights will master your emotions and you'll look weak. Your FOMO will scream louder than you think and make people uncomfortable. You'll find little ways to prop yourself up and people will see through it.

The good news is that the opposite is true too. If you walk around big—not cocky and strutting, but quietly confident on the inside—you'll come across big.

If you carry yourself well on the inside, you'll carry yourself well on the outside.

I'll never forget an incredibly surprising moment of this insight.

Anyone who knows me knows I'm not tall. Occasionally, I've wished I could change this. But I remember meeting a beautiful girl when I lived in Lexington, Kentucky and taking her home for Christmas. Over smoked sausages, my cousins whispered that I'd once again "overpunted my coverage." Whatever that means. Either way, we dated for a few New York minutes and months, and then one day, something odd occurred. She stopped and looked at me, puzzled.

"You're not six feet tall, are you?"

"Ummm . . ."

I thought she was being unkind. Or was going in and out of blindness.

"Uh, last time I checked, no. Why do you ask?"

She went on to explain, incredibly, that after months of watching me, she'd actually come to believe I was six feet tall.

Friends of mine are squinting their eyes to make sure they're reading this right.

But she was a *brutally* honest person, so I knew she was serious. She added something I never forgot: "Oh, I don't care. I like you as you are. I think because of your spirit and the way you carry yourself, I just always thought you were six feet."

That day I decided—and maintained—I'd rather have a six-foot-spirit than a six-foot-stature any day of the week. (But still, God, maybe in the next life?)

Listen, your spirit is the most important thing about you.

It's what people will notice more than anything else.

It's what will determine your destiny.

Your spirit is more important than your stature. Your spirit is more important than your success. And your spirit is more important than any other scorecard you think makes you bigger in this life.

In fact, alongside the ten small-in-their-own-eyes scouts who brought down the camp and died in the desert, there were two who saw themselves, their problems, and their futures through God's eyes.

Joshua, who led the children of Israel after Moses.

And Caleb.

I won't recap the whole Caleb section from my first book. But I will remind you this: When God decided to bring the hammer of judgment down on that ungrateful, fear-based, disobedient, doubt-filled, small-in-their-own-eyes generation, God gave an atomic asterisk for a gruff, dangerous man named Caleb:

> ". . . Not one of them will set eyes on the land I promised . . . But my servant Caleb—this is a different story. *He has a different spirit*; he follows me passionately. I'll bring him into the land . . . and his children will inherit it."[9]

Caleb had the same giants but a different spirit.

He saw the same thing a million others saw, but with different vision.

He wasn't small in his own eyes.

He figured God was with them, so they could do it. A can-do spirit filled him from head to toe like buzzing electricity. He was ready to charge life like a foaming pit bull.

If God's with you, why wouldn't you?

I don't care how small your bank account, social media numbers, or muscles. You'll only be as small or as large as you are on the inside. The only thing that will determine your future is the smallness or largeness of your spirit.

"The smallness you feel comes from within . . ."

Do you have limitless vision that tips life your way or self-limiting constructs that keep you trapped? Either way, therein lies your future.

. . . . .

REMEMBER THE GIRL THAT MADE ME so nervous I had to watch *Hitch* at night to relax? Well, there's something else I didn't tell you.

I met her while working retail and was bumbling from the beginning. My friend Matt worked freight in the back. Matt's smooth. Easy operator kind of confidence. And he watched graciously. Watched my cheeks turn to apples when the girl talked, heard me speak too eagerly when she came near, noticed my nerves gather like bundled wire before each date.

One day, he and I went to an Atlanta Braves game with friends. He was eating Dippin' Dots out of a plastic baseball helmet when he turned and smiled.

"Listen to me. You are Russell Freaking Moore. Do you hear me? Russell. *Freaking.* Moore. Don't you forget it."

He said my name like it meant something. Like one would say Michael Jordan. And I both hated and loved him for how it made me feel.

It became another phrase I tucked away. Sure enough, before that next date, I paused before I got out of the car and whispered to myself, "You're Russell Freaking Moore."

Now, what does that mean?

I don't really know.

It's definitely embarrassing to tell you. And if you were to ask me if I *still* feel the need to tell myself this from time to time, I would say it's none of your business.

But unless you're too cool, try it.

Say your first and last name with "freaking" in between it. (How am I a pastor?)

No?

I tried.

The point is, you need to hear your name like you believe it.

Better yet, when the noise of self-doubt begins to cloud over, you need to hear *God* whisper your name, saying,

This is who you are . . .

Gideon, mighty man of valor.

Esther, destined for such a time as this.

. . . . .

SPEAKING OF MICHAEL JORDAN...
what a Harvard case study on the power of self-belief.

He possessed extraordinary talent, bone-crunching discipline, tireless work ethic, and competitive fire. But the movie *Air*[10] gave us insight into the psyche that made Michael Jordan *Michael Jordan*.

His mom.

Deloris Jordan home-brewed a ruthless, unapologetic belief in her son and what he deserved. The belief transferred, settling deep into Michael's bones.

Look, I grew up on Jordan. I had all the tapes, read Shoe Dog, and watched *The Last Dance* alongside *Tiger King* when the world shut down. But until *Air*, I had no idea Jordan changed how the entire shoe franchise even worked. His shoe deal, signed when he was a rookie, not only skyrocketed Nike; it redefined how brands signed individual athletes, paving the way to make millions from sponsorships. And Nike sold *seventy million dollars* worth of Air Jordans within two months of the sneaker's release.

To be clear, other brands offered a lot of money. But his mom possessed such a belief in what he deserved that she held out, with the potential of losing *million-dollar opportunities,* meanwhile demanding a new paradigm be created in how athletes owned and generated income from their names. The rest, as they say, is history.

In this way, it wasn't Michael's *talent* that changed the entire industry; it was a defiantly stubborn *self-belief.* A self-belief that couldn't settle for what had been. A self-belief so intense it demanded he refuse the good to hold out for the great.

How we see ourselves affects us deeply. Our self-perception shapes how we engage the world. It informs how we serve people. It limits or expands how we step into God's mission for our lives.

Like Michael Jordan and the shoe industry, a strong, buoyant self-belief won't just open up a new universe to you; it will change the entire universe around you and of the people beside you.

It's why I want confidence to crawl into the marrow of your bones. Because I'm convinced if anyone should be confident, it's the sons and daughters of God walking the earth. His power inside them, knowing who they are, fire in their hands, vision in their eyes.

Last year, I had a heart-to-heart with my friend Jesse, who crafted the self-declarations. We slipped into a side lounge on the east side of our building. The sun was low, and through the glass-stained glare, I picked up moisture in his eyes. Jesse might just be the most emotionally steady person I know. But I could tell, like a cat in a box, he'd slipped back inside his thoughts and gotten stuck.

His ministry was doing well and so was he. But he could read the tea leaves. With God's help, our church had been growing in numbers, depth, influence, and caliber of employees and leaders. He had peered into the future and didn't know if he could see himself there. He didn't know if he could keep up. Didn't know if he had what it took.

So much went through my mind as he opened up. I thought about how much I believe in him. I thought about all the moments I struggle with the same feelings. I thought about how cruel a prison our minds can truly become. I thought about how TD Jakes said the hardest person to see is yourself. I thought, if only Jesse could see himself the way I see him, the way others see him, the way God sees him. If he could, he'd never doubt himself again.

I began to speak these things into him. Then, honestly, that scene of the spies flooded my soul. I couldn't shake the image. Twelve men representing their people, looking into the mouth-stopping dream that was their future. All ready for them, all promised by God. But then not stepping into it because they felt small. Dying in the sand of a desert instead of the space of their purpose.

I nearly got emotional. I painted the picture I saw of Jesse's future, described the things I saw inside him. And said:

"What a tragedy it would be to have that whole future in front of you but to never experience it. All because of how you choose to see yourself in this season. All because you got stuck in your head and stopped living in the confidence of who you are."

I told him it was time to make new declarations, this time not to heal from the past but to propel him into the future.

He did. It's been a year and he's thriving. Leaving us in the dust if you want to know the truth.

Right now, if you're in a place where all you see is your imperfections, rejections, worst moments, and most frustrating tendencies, will you have the courage to see yourself differently? Not just reinvent yourself, but redefine yourself in your own eyes? Will you have the courage to see yourself through the lens of your future instead of your failure?

I'm praying a heaven-descended Oculus comes over your internal field of vision in this moment, opening your mind and soul to see yourself in a whole new dimension.

Ceiling erased, ground lifted, mistakes wiped away, capacity bigger than you know. And the God of heaven longing to declare into your soul—right now—louder than words:

> *Stop being small in your own eyes. Silence the voices and listen to mine. Borrow my eyes. See yourself the way I see you.*

See yourself well.

Believe in yourself big.

Live from that space with courage.

ASSESSMENT

What stood out? What wounds have surfaced through this chapter? What questions of identity? What's your level of self-belief?

____

____

____

____

____

____

____

APPLICATION

What steps can you take this month, this week, and today to address where you are? Who can you call and what systems can you implement to keep you accountable?

____

____

____

____

____

____

____

Part 3

DEVELOPMENT OF CONFIDENCE

VALLEY OF ELAH.

1020 B.C.

"Tonight, the birds will gorge on your flesh."

Each syllable crashed into him like thunder. His senses grew acute, heightened as if plugged into voltage. The crunch of dirt beneath leather. The smell of campfire. The cold touch of stone against palm. The sight of grizzled beard and ruby-black eyes towering ahead. The coppery note of blood prickling the tongue.

The present image and moment twisted, then time slowed with a whoosh.

Suddenly, he was back in time.

A lone field. Dusk. Running a calloused hand through tussled wool, eyes trained ahead. With crook to neck, he'd collared another stray lamb.

But an odd sensation had washed over him. A knowing. He felt it before he saw it. Glancing south, he noticed the roast fires of his father and brothers in the distance. Peering back north, he squinted. Sure enough, in the darkness just up ahead, yellow eyes glowed at the tree line.

A limb snapped.

Bear.

A tremor passed through his knees then. Pins and needles

stabbed his heart. But then, like a breeze through the soul, a whisper came. Not to his physical ear. Deeper.

He'd learned that voice. Gentle and unmistakable. Words bubbling up like hot oil now in his spirit:

> *"I was with you when you faced the lion. I'll be with you as you face the bear."*

Thinking was over. The yellow eyes widened. Grunt moved to rustle and rustle moved to sprint.

The bear was charging. And he was too.

Then, without warning, whoosh. Back to the present.

Staring, squinting against the sun. This time, a giant. Again, he felt it—the fear, adrenaline, and anger.

More than anything . . . fire. Heat blazed through his belly.

He felt it all in his bones, felt the flames, felt the familiar moment, like a buried song. He felt like yesterday the metallic warmth of the lion's blood. The bear's blood. And now, here in the valley, he keenly felt the presence of the One who made the valley.

Then the familiar whisper . . .

> *"Just like with the lion and bear, I'm with you, David."*

That was all it took. Feet kicking dust, grin barely veiled, David was off, hurtling toward Goliath, stone flying.

Part 3: Preface

D AVID WAS A BEAST, THERE'S NO DOUBT.

Six-pack and tubular veins and scores of battlefield victories.

More impressively, he burned with *fierce confidence* no matter what came his way.

How do *we* do that? How do we *develop* that?

Well, we're punching numbers to open that safe. Everyone is.

We know confidence attracts the opposite sex and advances your career, so you can hear the click-clack search through TED talks, Instagram accounts, and YouTube influencers.

Even neuroscience.

I actually dove into Dr. Adam Kepecs' work studying rats[1] as I prepared for this book. True story. His research argues for a more statistical brand of confidence, one from certainty in decision-making based on experiments with decisive rodents.

NYT best-selling authors Katty Clay and Claire Shipman have even built a whole empire of books and tests based on his work to help women crack the code to become their more confident, capable selves.[2]

In any case, I hope *you* are starting to hear that sweet, opening *swish* of the safe. And we're about to bust it all the way open. I believe a holistic understanding of how we're wired is the key. That we crack the code by strengthening our core and building our muscles.

So we're about to take a slight turn.

In the last two parts, we've leaned heavily into scriptural theology and our internal psychology.

Now we go for the jugular.

We're about to get even more *practical.* We're going to deconstruct King David, not just studying his heart but teasing out the hacks and habits that helped produce such an extraordinary life. We'll look at things we tend to under-spiritualize even though they're integral to how God wired us.

I'm convinced it will transform us.

If we've just undergone surgery and rehab, now we enter a gym.

Wait a minute. You said in Chapter 1 we were just grabbing coffee . . .

I know. I promise not to work a whistle and clipboard. But we can't just sit with ideas; we must work them into our lives. So along the way, if my voice raises like a trainer, or God help us all, I sound like the life coach you didn't ask for, please don't throw the medicine ball at my throat. I promise I'm in the thick of this with you.

And I'm so expectant. I only preface because I know some of

our makeup and how easily dementors of shame waltz back into our real estate. So here's my gym waiver to sign: No matter where we are on the journey, we celebrate the progress for *where we are*, we recall that *our value isn't pegged to our performance*, and we remember *we're in it together*. No shame allowed.

But there *are* muscles to be developed, helpful techniques to walk out, and unavoidable ways God designed us in which our bodies, brains, and souls interact.

Ready?

We'll begin by addressing our core.

You always hear it. Fitness enthusiasts going on and on . . . "Gotta get the core strong, folks."

It might surprise you to hear that *character* is the core of your confidence—the center affecting everything else. If not strong, every corresponding muscle becomes destabilized. After all, confidence comes out of who you are, and character is the strength of who you are.

And I know. Character isn't thrilling. Speaking to adults about character feels like speaking to kids about flossing. But that's why plaque finds its way into our hearts.

So we'll bring this ethereal concept of "character" out of the clouds and break it down into *integrity*, *humility*, and *courage*, and how those actually funnel into the confidence we need in everyday life. Then, we'll grab kettlebells and have some real CrossFit fun.

Heart rate and highlighter ready? Okay, deep breath . . .

You don't rise to the level of your hopes and dreams; you fall
to the level of your self-worth.[1]
—Jamie Kern Lima

My heart is confident, God.[2]
—David

I may not face Goliath, but I've got my own giants.[3]
—Elevation Worship ("Same God")

12)

Puzzle Work

T HE WORD *INTEGRITY* MAKES ME FLINCH A LITTLE, HOW ABOUT you?

No? Yours must be impeccable. Like Michelangelo's flawless nude of David himself. For the rest of us mortals, integrity sounds noble, but also like something we instinctually feel we're falling short of, at least somewhere.

Yet for David, it was priority and central to his confidence.

> "I will live with a heart of integrity in my house," he wrote.[4]

And,

> "Because of my integrity you uphold me."[5]

In fact, in one of the first recorded acts of his life he risked his safety and hunted lions to defend sheep that weren't even his. I think I would've just counted my losses.

So, let's make it simple. It helps me to think of integrity in three ways. The first is the one that probably comes to mind.

Lifestyle or *moral actions*.

Staying above board in what you do. Not being devious, sexually promiscuous, financially conniving, or abusing substances or beating up grandmas, that kind of thing. These are obviously important. And if you claim to follow Jesus, you have a big Book full of how to live in a God-honoring manner.

The second is where the meat is.

Living a whole life instead of a divided one.

Here the etymology helps. The word integrity evolved from the Latin word *integer*. You may recognize that word from math class. It simply means a whole number. Doesn't matter if it's negative, zero, or positive. It just can't be a fraction. It can't be 2.5. Only 2 or even—2. Just complete. Whole.

And that's an *integrous* life. An integer individual, if you will. Not perfect. But not divided. Not *I'm this person here*, and *this person here*, and *this secretive thing at night* . . . no, it's living a whole life without division. It's being integrated in your character so you don't become disintegrated as a person.

Which is challenging but also encouraging. Integrity is about integration, not perfection. Being the same person in every room.

This doesn't mean there aren't different expressions of who you are and different places to display those. Some take this concept to the extreme. For example, instead of confessing their struggles or grievances in appropriate places, they spew them all over social media or to anyone who will listen. That's insanity, not integrity.

The point is to make sure you are always a *person* and never a *persona.*

The point is to live in the light and out of the shadows.

So I probably don't need to get all preachy. You and I know what's right. We just need to do it.

Again, one could argue David's sins were more egregious than Saul's. But his motives stayed true north even when he faceplanted catastrophically. He didn't paper over his mistakes, lie, or blame anyone else. He took ownership, learned, and moved forward.

As a mentor of mine says, "The difference between David and Saul isn't that David wasn't *faultless*; it's that he was *falseless.*"[6] He refused to live falsely before God and others.

If you want the truth, when I think of integrity, I picture Hugh Jackman doing a jigsaw puzzle.

I heard him on a podcast with Tim Ferris talking rhythms and routines. Apparently, when out of town, he stays grounded by returning to his hotel and working those end pieces.[7]

Only Hugh Jackman could make this sound nice. I picture a cup of hot, Earl Grey sitting on the left armchair, his right wolverine claw carefully placing the last missing piece before he grins a satisfied grin, leans back, and howls through the ceiling and to the moon.

Anyways, it's what I picture. The puzzle doesn't need to be polished, just whole. No pieces hidden or separated between this room and that.

Because here's the thing, and you know this . . .

Dishonesty will eat your confidence for breakfast.

But integrity will eat your *insecurity* for breakfast.

Insecurity gets you hiding behind baggage with shifty eyes and shifty feet. It is *exhausting* when your public life and private life don't match. You need a really good memory. And you perpetually nurse a bit of paranoia about what or who may find you out.

But when you have nothing to hide and you are at peace in your heart? That's a rolled-out carpet to a relaxed, confident life.

As the French proverb goes, *There's no pillow as soft as a clear conscience.*

Integrity helps you sleep better and live better, at ease and secure.

It's why Solomon, David's son, wrote,

> "The wicked flee though no one pursues, but the righteous are as bold as a lion."[8]

Want to be bold? Avoid duplicity and live true. Let the puzzle come together.

The final aspect is even more practical. And it's an internal muscle we can grow *today.*

It's the relationship of integrity to *the promises you keep.*[9]

Even now as I type this, I'm going to make you my priest. I confess I fell short yesterday. I told God I would do something and I didn't. If I were to tell you what it is, you wouldn't think it's a big deal. But it is to me. My word is my bond. My ability to keep my word is the strength of my integrity.

And God seems to take it seriously too:

> "If you make a promise to God, keep your promise. Don't be slow to do what you promised. God is not happy with fools. Give God what you promised. It is better to promise nothing than to promise something and not be able to do it." (Ecclesiastes 5.4–7)

That hurts.

Here's another:

> "The person who promises a gift but doesn't give it is like cloud and winds that bring no rain." (Proverbs 25.14)

When you say you're going to do something—pray, call, follow through, do lunch—are you cloud and winds? Or are you that rare, refreshing shower that actually comes?

It may be high time we become the kind of people who under-promise and over-deliver.

Of course, Jesus came along and simplified it even further. He told us to quit making all our fancy vows altogether. Simply let our yes be yes and our no be no.[10] That our plain word should be enough.

The problem is most of us know our plain word is not enough. So, we surround it with a lot of extra words, like verbal spotters under a shaky barbell. It's only a weak muscle of character that makes me want to undergird all my commitments with "I promise" and "I swear." The deeper my character grows, the more I'm able to just say yes and believe it and mean it.

So I have a very simple but life-changing challenge for you.

Over the next thirty days (the rest of your life, really, but let's start somewhere):

Keep your word no matter what.

Even in the small things. Scratch that. *Especially* in the small things.

If you put something on your to-do list today, *do it.*

If you make an appointment for next week, *keep it.*

If you said you'd call, *call.*

If you said you'd pray for them, *pray for them.*

If you have a coffee scheduled with a friend, *show up.* On time.

Less promises. More action.[12]

In an increasingly flaky world, revolt. Be someone with fiber of character, strength of resolve and reliability. Someone who's kept your word enough with the small things that when it comes time to keep your word with the big things, you'll have the internal musculature to do so.

You probably have some things bubbling up in your conscience like fizz in soda. Address them. Make a text or call before the next chapter. Don't put it off. The shape of your character is the shape of your future.

You'll soon realize that self-respect will grow inside you as you become the kind of person even *you* can trust. And this builds a powerful core of personal confidence.

In a way, integrity is the *strength* of your character.

And Scripture *abounds* with promises that the righteous (those who do right) will live solid and secure with a beautiful unaffectedness.

In Psalm 112 alone, David spends the first half illustrating the aspects of integrity and the second half listing the benefits of integrity:

> "He will never be shaken . . . He will not fear bad news; his heart is confident, trusting in the Lord. His heart is assured; he will not fear. In the end he will look in triumph . . ."[11]

Bad character just gets you stuck. I can tell you for me, when character breaches occur, anxiety and insecurity flood in through the cracks.

But. When I fix the fissures, peace and confidence return.

Don't spend time kicking yourself over the past. When you nurse regret, you live in reverse. So, no regret, just action.[12]

And what I've found is when you choose to live an overall life of integrity, the mistakes along the way don't get to define you.

I want to look life in the eye.[1]
—David

So, here's to my beautiful life that seems to leave me so unsatisfied. No sense of self but self–obsessed.[2]
—Lewis Capaldi ("How I'm feeling")

Angels can fly because they take themselves lightly.[3]
—G.K. Chesterton

13)

The Other Side of the Coin

I HAD LUNCH TODAY WITH HUNTER. THE GUY'S FLOURISHING.
Crushing it as youth director, adoring husband to high school sweetheart-turned-wife (pastor's daughter, brave man), and beaming father to a new baby boy stealing hearts in his onesie.

Over a posh salad, I jabbed a fork his way and thanked him. He's why I wrote this book. Honest.

I'd spent a couple of years on different projects. But one Sunday, I spoke about the "coin" of Saul's insecurity. Hunter passed me in the office with, "That's your next book." I knew in my bones he was right.

His life resonates with the message.

I told him five years ago he reminded me of David. That God had written His name across his heart like the young shepherd. That you could still smell the ink. Years before he was hired on staff, he spent all his discretionary time at church, taking students to Wendy's, setting up chairs, leading small groups, anything.

Along the way, I watched well-meaning people plant seeds of

discontent (*Why are you doing all this when they don't even pay you?!*). But he stayed humble and coachable. He walked with Jesus, kept his heart right and trusted God's timing.

That doesn't mean it was easy.

Those seeds of discontent tried to go *in*. In an entitlement-tempted, instant-fame, microwave moment in culture, Hunter had to *choose* faithfulness. He had to *choose* to *go through the process*.

Just like David knew his calling but spent years bringing cheese to the front lines for his brothers, Hunter knew his calling but spent years delivering *Pizza Hut* to pay bills and carry cheese pizzas to youth group.

Moreover, he had to deal with some chameleonic, people-pleasing tendencies of his personality structure. He had to allow a healthy "fear of God" to shatter a crippling "fear of man." Had to come clean when impatience made his spirit go sideways.

The process served him well.

He spent years learning to follow well.

Now he knows how to lead well.

He scraped some pimiento cheese that had fallen off his burger and I began to remind him. Told him I was proud. Watching him rise in influence and gifting was great. But watching him rise in confidence and health was even better. He's a different man.

I reminded him how he planted the seed for the book. He

finished his food and replayed the part of that Sunday message that hit him. That took him back to that thing he felt as a boy. The calling. The way God marked him as a kid.

His eyes got red as he talked.

"I'll tell you what changed it for me."

I leaned forward, secretly hoping it was something brilliant I'd said in my talk. It wasn't. He said the switch came when he realized he'd been praying the wrong prayer.

A tear slipped.

"For fifteen years I prayed every day for more confidence. But last year I changed that. I stopped praying for confidence and started praying for humility. That's when the confidence came."

. . . . .

" GOD, INCREASE MY HUMILITY."

What a prayer. And what a paradigm shift.

If integrity is the *muscle* of strong character, humility is the *posture*.

Humility grounds us, creating a center of gravity from which security can flow.

In fact, like Hunter, whatever you're hoping for in life, not only does a formational journey *develop* humility; you won't make it through the process *without it*.

You'll get frustrated and discouraged, so eager for a title or attention while God tries to develop your character and prepare you for what He has.

See,

Humility postures us for sustainable success.

By the way, we talked earlier in the book about living from the coin of calling instead of the coin of self. How *pride* and *insecurity* are two sides of the same coin. But the inverse is also true:

Humility and *confidence* are two sides of the same coin.

They go together.

The deeper your humility, the sturdier your confidence.

Confidence is an inner *security* held together by these two powers.

When I consider my faith heroes, I see this tandem correlation. Deep, deep humility and high, high confidence.

In fact, one of the things I admire most about David is he seemed to possess this magical mixture of being both a *kid* and a *king* on the inside. Full of awe *and* strength.

. . . . .

IN CHAPTER 1, I MENTIONED THAT confidence has been both a strength *and* struggle for me. A seesaw, if you will. I'm convinced the saboteur in it all is *pride*.

The *enemy* of humility.

Pride is the cardinal sin of us all. The core in the fruit Adam ate. The disease of self that insists on my way. The deception in my veins that I don't need God or others. The silly but destructive idol that puts me at the center. The lie of self-indulgence that robs my joy and freedom.

It's also the *root* that produces fragile and insecure *fruit*.

When Jesus calls men and women to pick up their cross, deny themselves, and follow Him, He's not calling us to masochistic, pleasureless conformity. Quite the opposite. He tells us to lose ourselves *in order to* find our true selves.[4]

He invites us to take an axe to pride so we can stop getting old, small, and insecure. He wants that old nature to die an early death so He can breathe fresh Spirit into us and help us really live.

As C.S. Lewis said, "The more we get what we now call 'ourselves' out of the way and let Him take us over, the more truly ourselves we become."[5]

But humility can be tricky.

The other day I listened to a faith-based performance coach discuss how dysfunctional we are in the sense that we *always personalize our failures* but, out of fear of being arrogant, *never integrate our wins . . .*[6]

Which results in a pretty low bucket of esteem.

Humility isn't constantly giving yourself a lousy grade as much as it is not hyper-focusing on your grade to begin with. If you're gifted at dance or math, it's not humble to pretend you're not. It's only humble to avoid losing your soul in self-focus and instead use those talents to serve the world.

On the other hand, I confess that I felt God whisper into my soul the other day,

"Stay low, Russ. Stay low."

The energy of confidence had begun inflating me a bit. I could feel it. I could feel my attention turning inward to self instead of outward to others.

Scriptures echoed between my ears.

> " . . . Humble yourselves under the mighty hand of God, that He may exalt you in due time . . . "[7]

> "When you are invited . . . don't sit in the place of honor . . ."[8]

> "Do nothing out of selfish ambition or conceit, but in humility consider others as more important than yourselves."[9]

> "Don't indulge your ego at the expense of your soul."[10]

I believe we should stay white-hot with passion and meat-eater-hungry for growth. We should strive for greatness in everything we do and serve with all the fiery excellence of a samurai.

But we should *not* expend a single drop of energy on who sees it or appreciates it.

This is the difference between pursuing greatness and pursuing fame.

Greatness, from Jesus's words, is about others. Fame is about you.

And—important to note—Jesus never told us *not* to desire greatness. That pseudo-humble, tall poppy, "mediocre is okay" syndrome never came from Christ.

Here's what He actually said:

> " . . . Whoever wants to become great among you must be your servant . . ."[11]

He didn't say, "If you want to be great . . . cut it out."

He said, "If you want to be great, here's how . . ."

If you want to be great . . . don't *shove* people around to show that *you're* important; *serve* people to show them *they're* important.

Don't sharpen your gifts so the world can clap. Sharpen your gifts so the world can be changed.

Be great. Become great. Develop greatness.

But don't do it with haughtiness. Do it with humility. Be a servant-leader.

The irony is it takes humble confidence to pursue greatness. It only takes fragile ego to pursue fame.

Now, if someone becomes famous, there's nothing wrong with

that. They might deserve it and the world might need more of what they have. Don't be one of the small souls that throws rocks at them to make yourself feel significant.

But at the end of the day? I'm convinced the world doesn't need more famous people; the world needs more great people.

. . . . .

ALRIGHT. IF HUMILITY IS THE posture of character, what chiropractic adjustments do we need?

Exposure, for starters. Exposure to beauty, the vastness of creation, others' greatness. These create marvelous tremors of humility.

Exposure to God. The bright light of God's presence has the same effect on my soul as the sun's rays do to shadows. It's a perspective-changer for a thousand reasons. Ever strutted around, thinking you were all that and a bag of chips until you got around someone at the top of their game?

To an infinite degree, this happens when you near God. It's healing. It's confidence-building. And it's humbling. In the best possible way.

Humble *action* is another pride-buster. The posture of serving others. When you make it a lifestyle, it gets in your blood. It's the key to happy days. View your life as a joyful opportunity to serve the people around you. It seems a well-kept secret that you can't make a confident servant feel insecure.

But the best spine adjustment might be *awareness*.

For starters, awareness of *the person you are.*

Not to contradict the self-belief chapter and all your awesomeness I've been trying to drill in, but a basic awareness of our humanity should breed some humility.

From the moment we're born, we're dependent and interdependent on others. And *utterly* dependent on air, food, sleep, the earth, all the systems inside our body—just to keep existing.

We are astonishing and fragile creatures.

And small. Have you ever drunk in the stars at night? Or basked in the immensity of the ocean's horizon? Or just considered our precarity as temporary, carbon and oxygen beings?

I've always been encouraged by David's words, "The Lord is like a father to his children, tender and compassionate to those who fear him. For he knows how weak we are; he remembers we are only dust."[12]

Thank God, in the dust of my failures, He remembers the dust I'm made of.

This is one of the many stabilizing aspects of Scripture, by the way. It has a magic mirror effect.[13]

Inside God's Word, the mirror emerges. In it, I see my value, potential, and inestimable worth. In it, I also see my blind spots, sins, and endless weaknesses. I am reminded of the mess I'd be apart from the grace of God.

As Timothy Keller said, "The gospel is that I am so sinful that

Jesus had to die for me, yet so loved and valued that Jesus was glad to die for me. This leads to deep humility and deep confidence at the same time. I can't feel superior to anyone, and yet I have nothing to prove to anyone."[14]

Beautiful.

Scripture constantly brings this healthy perspective to who I am. I can't read it and remain proud—not if I'm letting it read *me*.

Loving, honest community does this too. Friends unafraid to give each other kind, helpful feedback. Healthy relationships make us better, provide us confidence, *and* keep us humble.

Finally, an awareness that everything I have comes from God.

Small and big. That side-busting laugh I enjoyed this afternoon? God. The sunrise that warms my face by the sea? God. That last breath I just took? God.

Every person. Every talent. Even every penny.

In fact, I'd be lying to tell you there isn't a danger of pride as we grow in confidence and success. We must remember where it all comes from. We must keep watch.

"Guard your heart above all else," Solomon warns.[15]

In the Old Testament, we watch a constant *sin-seek-save* pattern with God's people. They'd *sin* themselves into a lot of trouble and pain, then *seek* God with all their hearts for help, and then God in mercy would *save* them and get them out of their trouble. And then apathy, spiritual amnesia, and pride would quickly set in, and the pattern start all over.

Feel familiar?

When the children of Israel were about to leave the wilderness to enter their future, look how God warned them:

> "Be careful that you do not forget the Lord . . . Otherwise, when you eat and are satisfied . . . build fine houses and settle down . . . flocks grow large . . . gold increases and all you have is multiplied . . . *your heart will become proud* and *you will forget* . . . your God, who brought you out of Egypt . . . He led you through the . . . wilderness . . . brought you water . . . gave you manna . . . You may say to yourself, "My *power* and the strength of *my hands* have produced this wealth for me." But remember the Lord . . . for *it is he who gives you the ability to produce wealth* . . ."[16]

The danger is real. With God's help, we grow in confidence and success. Then, we look at our hands instead of God's hand. Instead of our hearts becoming big toward the world, our hearts become big toward ourselves. We become the "build bigger barns guy"[17] Jesus warns about. The children of Israel. Nebuchadnezzar.[18]

We must remember: Even when we've worked hard, developed our skill, carved our own path, there are more people to thank than we remember. And every opportunity, every bit of health in our body, every ounce of raw talent and mental capacity, is a gift of grace from the One who made us.

My prayer is that the journey through this book will create a powerful tandem growth of both confidence and humility inside you. A *sustainable* power. A power that, as it increases, only further develops your character and fuels you to serve others.

I pray the people who read this book go on to lead the greatest companies, sing the most moving songs, raise the most incredible humans, and create the most breathtaking masterpieces. And that with every promotion, a humble, confident joy rises to say, "Thank you, God."

It's a joyful posture of open hands that realizes every gift is from God and for God and people. That everything we have is not a *possession to grasp* but a *gift to steward*.

That is a posture that will prosper you.

Also, this kind of posture-awareness triggers another superpower essential to confidence and a happy life:

Gratitude.

It's one of the few good trends making the rounds. Science and CEOs alike jabber on about its preternatural effects. How it raises state of mind, replaces worry, and brings joy.

When I'm sick with self-pity or flat out discouraged, a simple, five-minute gratitude walk is near magic. For every new pound of gratitude-muscle we build, we shed fear, entitlement, frustration, and greed.

Choosing every day to be grateful—through walks, lists, texts, calls, and thank-yous—is a king exercise that will better your heart and shave off pride.

A great reminder to hold before God:

Everything I have comes from You.

The person who is arrogant is simply the person who has lost awareness.

Oh, and along the way? Healthy awareness not only protects us from arrogance; it protects us from something equally unhealthy: *False* humility.

See, the problem is most of us instinctively know humility is a noble, attractive trait. So if we lack it, we do something even worse than not *being* humble; we *act* humble.

Humility is a lovely thing to practice but a dreadful thing to pretend.

And I'm not just referring to the "humble brag." I'm talking all our little nuanced feigns of humility. The timed words and tones we don't really mean. The fishing for compliments through self-degradation.

Especially in Christian circles. Christians get *weird* with this.

And if you've ever had to be around the "It's not me, it's Him" Christian, I just want to say I'm so sorry.

Some of you know what I'm talking about. Suzy sings a great song in church and gets paid a compliment afterward. Suzy kind of smile-frowns, tilts her head, looks through the ceiling, and says in a knowing, aw-shucks way, "It wasn't me; it was God."

No, I think that was Suzy. It looked and sounded like her. And with all respect to Suzy, I think if God had been singing, we might have all died instantly.

I've heard people say this about all kinds of things. Even books.

I didn't write this book. God did.

Yikes.

Look, I've prayed like crazy over this book because I want it to help us. But I hope you won't be disappointed to learn I wrote it.

Maybe you're not in that camp, but like me you tend to minimize and self-deprecate every time someone compliments you. I'm sure that can be annoying too.

I'm riffing a bit to tug a smile. I believe most of us mean well. But can we get practical? Not just with humility but with people skills?

When given a compliment, we don't have to fall into the ditch of arrogance *or* false humility.

We just need to memorize two very hard words:

Thank. You.

I don't know why it's so hard, but it is. Trust me, I've been practicing this over the last couple of years, and I keep falling off the bike every few blocks. Those two words might as well be Mandarin.

But from a secure man or woman, a simple "thank you" is all that's needed when someone says something kind.

. . . . .

HUMILITY IS A CHARACTER TRAIT
often developed slowly as we walk with God. But we can
expedite the process if we get intentional. We can develop
humility every day through:

1. *Cultivating awareness* by unrushed time in God's
Word and Presence.

2. *Expressing gratitude* by prayer walks, thank-you
texts and affirmations, time worshipping and thanking God.

3. *Practicing humility* through humble actions, i.e.,
finding ways to celebrate, help, and serve others daily.

These actions will produce a beautiful essence within us.

In Chapter 1, I mentioned David's awed posture toward God.

"When I consider your heavens, the work of your
fingers . . . what is mankind . . . that you care for them?"[19]
And, "Who am I, Sovereign Lord, and what is my family,
that you have brought me this far?"[20]

Unlike Saul, I would contend David's humble-sounding
statements were actually . . . *humble.*

The rest of his life proved it, coloring in the lines of those
words.

His years of desperately seeking God, his thankless service to
his brothers, all that sheep-watching, the soft give of his
conscience to the impact of conviction.

Even how he kept his heart tender toward authority, no matter how wrong the person in authority was.

In one particularly bizarre moment, on the run from Saul, waiting to be king, it appeared God finally granted David his moment on a silver platter. Saul snuck into a cave to relieve himself, unaware of David and his men.

This is your chance! They cried, quoting verses of vindication.

But David wouldn't dare. Instead, he crept over and sliced a swath of Saul's robe to prove his benevolence. From a distance, patch of robe in hand, he appealed to Saul's heart, asking why a great king would waste his time to hunt down a "dead dog? A flea?"[21] Then David rebuked his men for even suggesting he lay a hand on God's anointed.

His conscience was so warm, so responsive, it even smarted under the mere act of *cutting off a piece of Saul's robe* . . .

Is it any wonder God trusted David with His presence and the palace for all those decades?

"God *opposes* the *proud* but *gives grace* to the *humble*."[22]

Humility truly is a sneaky, underrated power. A rare-earth magnet that attracts unusual favor with God and people.

It also seems to be the one trait no one can resist. The one spice that makes every meal better.

Leadership. Relationships. Communication. Everything.

It's a posture that holds joy. A posture that triggers confidence. A posture that makes your character strong.

If you are filling yourself up by feeding your ego, then God
can't fill you. You are full but not fulfilled.[1]
—Jon Gordon

So be content with who you are, and don't put on airs. God's
strong hand is on you; he'll promote you at the right time.
Live carefree before God; he is most careful with you.
—1 Peter 5.7 MSG

Don't be the best; be the only.[2]
—Kevin Kelly

14)

Do Hard Things

I HAVE FELT IT LATELY.

Like spiders crawling across my skin, like poison entering my bloodstream, like guards cuffing my ankles and wrists.

Fear.

Especially the last couple of years for some reason. I have felt it in a unique, visceral way concerning my future, the world, people I love getting older, me getting older, and coming to grips with the very real possibility I might die one day.

I've also felt more acutely than ever the need to *destroy* any spirit of fear that gets in me before it destroys me, not to mention my confidence.

I *must* live a life of courage. I must live a full, boundless life in defiance of the small, trapped existence fear pulls me toward.

And I think you should too.

So far, we've discussed integrity as the *strength* of our character and humility as the *posture*. I view courage as the *expression*.

And perhaps the most important of all three.

To quote Lewis yet again, "Courage is not simply one of the virtues, but the form of every virtue at the testing point."[3]

Courage is what reinforces all our other desired traits. I cannot grow confidence if I do not grow courage. And harsh as it may sound, I cannot be a confident person if I choose to be a cowardly person. In fact, in many ways, confidence is the natural outflow of courage. But we must choose it. We must *fight* not to let fear's poison taint our hearts and shrink our borders.

One of the reasons "Don't be afraid" is one of the most repeated commands in Scripture is because God knows it will steal our life more than almost anything else.

Of course, I feel pinched inside even as I type this. I think of the appointment I keep putting off and another conversation I still need to have.

But we can do it. It starts with taking steps in the direction of our fear, even if small ones. It begins with assuming a posture of courage instead of convenience.

One practical way? I can develop the habit of *doing hard things*.

I think about my friend Brock. He runs ultramarathons for fun.

I'm still not sure what's wrong with him. But he's an incredible guy, suspiciously positive, and looks like a long-lost Marvel hero.

A while back he asked if I wanted to be the eighth runner in the Ragnar Relay Race in the mountains of Kentucky. I think he drugged me because I said yes. Before I knew it, I was on a Zoom call with nine men and Brock's wife, everyone going around introducing themselves and giving a snapshot of their fitness bio. One by one, with straight faces, they spoke of their seventy-five-mile races and how "Fitness is a way of life" and "There ain't nothing to it but to do it" and casually threw out the minor marathons they'd been knocking out. I just nodded along, trying to normalize it all.

Then it was my turn. My humor is dry and sometimes I forget people don't know my sarcasm.

"Well," I started. "My name is Russ, and I don't mean to make you all feel bad about yourselves, but this is my nineteenth Ragnar Relay Race in the last three years. Ran about twenty-three miles today before lunch, an ultramarathon last Tuesday, and next week I'm actually set to be the first North American to complete the Navajo 200-mile Ascent Volcano of Destruction Iron Super-Man of Doom."

They all stared at me, and it got really quiet on the call. No one said a word. Everyone even forgot how to blink.

Brock eventually cleared his throat, got involved, and tried to explain me.

When the weekend came, it was brutal but also romantic in all the best roughing-it kind of ways. We set up camp beside dozens of other tents in a clearing, ate elk burgers at night and sausage in the morning, and consumed protein energy balls and hydration packets throughout the day. In the morning, you'd take your thermos to a tent near the relay station where a Nordic man descended from the Vikings had coffee brewing strong enough to put hair on a kid's chin.

All in all, I found the trail-running community incredibly kind and interesting. Everyone had Androids and wore digital watches halfway down their arms and hats patched with trees and mountain symbols and they all donned colorful shoes and tattoos. And for some reason they all used military time, which I found infuriating.

Eventually our time came. We'd sharpied an itinerary on the dry side of torn-off cardboard. Each of us had three legs of the race, fifteen miles each.

Now here's the thing. I don't consider myself a runner, but I do run. Especially in warmer weather. A few times a week, a few miles at a time. *I'll be fine* . . .

However, I *severely* underestimated the difference between road miles and trail miles. I also took for granted the toll an entire weekend of not sleeping would take on my body. Oh, and the high after your first run fades quickly. Your muscles get cold and collectively say, "We're done" before your next leg.

Worse, none of us could have predicted what my last leg would entail.

I ran a four-and-a-half miler to start. Arduous but invigorating. Around midnight, legs like Jell-O, I ran my second leg, a cyclops-flashlight bobbing from my head like an amateur miner. It went okay. But the *moment* I completed it, the skies opened. The clouds had prepared a second Noahic flood that would go on for nine hours. I eventually managed twenty minutes of sleep before Brock nudged me awake at 5:00 a.m.

"Hey man, I have to level with you," he started, slight alarm in his voice. "Your last leg begins soon, and the trails are completely washed out. Every incoming runner says it's treacherous out there. Take your time and be careful. It's your longest leg, by the way. Seven miles."

I got up, brushed my teeth, found a parka to slip over my running gear, clicked the third eye on my forehead, and downed some of the Viking's caffeine. When I got to the trail, I realized they weren't exaggerating. To this day, it may have been one of the most mentally demanding things I've done. And it *was* treacherous. I found out the next morning someone actually slid off the cliff and into the river. What should've taken me an hour took me three and my camp grew concerned.

But I was just putting one foot in front of the other in the dark and rain, footslogging through mile after muddy mile, repeating to myself a mantra that came up from somewhere inside me: "Just muck through it, Russ. Just muck through it."

As I finished the last lap, the sun was coming up like a ribbon, like earth itself was happy for me. There was a delirious, rowdy celebration from the team, and I felt weary and filthy and amazing. I grabbed one of those nonalcoholic Athletic Brews floating in the tub of ice by the entrance and downed it like water.

The rest of the day Brock kept asking if I'd ever do it again. I kept lying in a high-pitched voice, "Maybe!"

But the next day, I was struck by several things.

One, I immediately wanted to do it again.

Two, I walked around the church with an unusual lightness

and confidence that surprised even me.

And three, when it came time to leave church and head home for my dream Sunday nap, my car turned toward the park instead.

Before I knew it, I was running another five miles for fun.

What am I saying?

I'm saying don't ever trust Brock.

And I'm also saying doing hard things builds your resilience.

Doing hard things builds your courage.

Doing hard things builds your confidence.

I'm saying I don't want to gravitate toward comfort. I want to gravitate toward courageous choices. And I've noticed: The courage or cowardice I build in one area of life trickles into the others.

Brock, who might be one of the biggest encouragers I know, leaned in close after I finished that last hellish lap and said, "Russ, runners who've done this for years said that leg may be the most brutal they've ever seen. But for the rest of your life, you can carry with you the confidence that *if I can face that, I can face anything.*"

I knew he was being kind. It's not like I'd pulled off an Olympic back twist or been to war or done hell week with the Marines. But the principle is true.

It may sound corny, but a great phrase has invigorated me the last couple of years. Maybe you can holster it in your arsenal:

I do hard things.

Write it down somewhere as a declaration, perhaps at the top of next week's calendar.

Develop the habit of doing hard things. Even if it's small. A difficult workout, a step outside your comfort zone, a challenging conversation, sharing your faith, or one of those crazy cold plunges. The habit of regularly doing hard things will *change you.*

And one of the best ways to encourage yourself to do hard things is to remind yourself of the hard things you've already done.

Remind yourself like Brock did me, if I can do *that*, I can do *this*.

In fact, jot down three hard things you've done/endured recently or over the course of your life:

____

____

____

From now on, remind your soul: If I can do *that*, I can do *this*.

You have what it takes.

You can face your fears.

You can do hard things.

You really can. And gently, with self-encouragement, not self-critique, hold yourself accountable to do them.

There are other small exercises too.

One leader I respect encourages people to start with food.[4] That it's the smallest, safest way to practically face fear. Pick a food this week you wouldn't usually try and go nuts.

I selfishly love this idea because I *love* trying new foods. But if you don't, start there. Worst thing that can happen is you don't like it. I guess you could throw up, but that won't kill you.

Another exercise is to lean into human interactions, especially ones that make you uncomfortable. If calling someone instead of texting them terrifies you, call them.

On that note, it builds our courage (and relational health) when we commit to not avoiding tough conversations or worse, having them over text. Let's reserve difficult conversations for in-person or over the phone. And let's ghost the idea of ghosting people. That's the weak, easy path when we lack the courage to have a conversation. And that's not who we are. We're strong, confident, respectful people who do hard things.

Yes, let's be people who lean forward, not back.

> "But my righteous one will live by faith. And I take no pleasure in the one who shrinks back."[5]

   CONFIDENCE

If nothing else from David's imperfect but inspiring life, notice he moved *toward* Goliath, not *away*.

Sure, some of our moments will end in failure. But it's better than living in fear.

Freedom is found on the other side of fear. Meanwhile, our comfort zones are creating comas inside us. I say we violate them regularly in order to live fully awake. To taste things that only exist in our imagination.

On that note . . .

What's *one decision or action* you've been putting off? If you'll allow me to push you:

- Put down the book.
- Give yourself a date this week to complete it.
- Text a friend promising them a painful amount of money if you don't.

We're not getting younger. But our dreams are getting older.

Personally, I've found it shocking how much healing, breakthrough, and help I've experienced when I finally just made *one call*, scheduled *one appointment*, initiated *one conversation*.

All because I finally took a step I feared.

When *overwhelmed* with fear, I find it helps to think of the smallest first step I can take toward the scary waters and just move that left foot.

God told Joshua a dozen times to be strong and not afraid. He knew Joshua needed a considerable measure of courage to step into a land as large as Canaan. But He didn't tell Joshua *where* to put his foot; He simply told Joshua He would be with him *wherever* he put his foot. The important thing wasn't the specificity; the important thing was the step. Take a step and just keep stepping.

When we're afraid, we need to step faster and harder. Look fear in the face and charge *through it* anyway in the power of God, knowing He's with us to back us and catch us and help us through His grace.

And on *that* note, to develop courage, don't just step through *fea*r; run toward *love*.

It's the petri dish of courage.

Intuitively, you know this. If you've ever fallen in love, you feel like you can take on the world. If you're a parent, you know you could die for your child.

Why?

Someone said it brilliantly the other day, "Courage is not the absence of fear; it's the absence of self."[6]

Love is the most dominant force in the universe. It's the driving energy behind all God is and does. It's why the Presence of God melts away anxiety like sun to ice.

"Perfect love drives out fear,"[7] John wrote.

I don't know about you, but when I feel loved, I feel secure. I feel the robust Psalm 23 ocean of peace and security that,

> "The Lord is my shepherd. I have what I need. He lets me lie down in green pastures . . . and prepares a table before me in the presence of my enemies . . ."[8]

I'm telling you, a secure man or woman is a powerful thing. And that's what the love of God does. It *breaks fear* and *brings security*.

What would it do to your mental health if you began to live like the Supreme Creator was your soul's Shepherd, watching over you, protecting you, caring for you, loving you?

Maybe you'd walk with less of the fear that haunts you.

Maybe you'd walk like David, even when, as he wrote, "I go through the darkest valley . . . I fear no danger . . . for You are with me . . ."[9]

I know this much: When we begin to embrace God's *unconditional love for us* and express *sacrificial love for others*, we begin to experience a *life uncontrolled by fear*.

And that's where actual life is waiting.

Insecure people need more and settle for less. Secure people need less and expect more.[1]
—Craig Groeschel

Haven't I commanded you? Strength! Courage! Don't be timid; don't get discouraged. God, your God, is with you every step you take.[2]
—God to Joshua

It's not the length of your life but the strength of your life that matters.[3]
—Clint Claypoole

15)

So Much More

I THINK EVERYONE SHOULD WAIT TABLES BEFORE THEY DIE.

I do. I think everyone should know the blissful madness of bussing, running, and remembering orders. Everyone should also know what it's like on the other side of our cheap tips, bad attitudes, and dehumanizing orders without eye contact.

But I digress.

For a few years, I served at Saul Good restaurant in Lexington, Kentucky. I was intimidated at first. I saw a guy named Todd balance six plates across his wingspan, a dozen mustard bottles on his knees, and a cheese fondue on his head. At least that's how I remember it. It was magic or Velcro.

I remember thinking, *I'll never be able to carry more than a plate, a coffee cup, and maybe a napkin.*

Fast forward a few months and I was balancing all that tableware with the best of them, plates situated on arms like they belonged there, glasses palmed, condiments secured under arms, briskly spinning through the restaurant like a "laughing peasant of Italy."[4]

Moreover, I noticed this newfound skill spill over into other areas. I realized, unless stocking up, I no longer used carts at the grocery store. No kidding. Without thinking, I tucked jars and bottles under each arm, maneuvered multiple packages between hands, interlaced bag after bag between each finger. I caught a few stares, come to think of it. *Look at that strange man . . .*

But you know what had happened without me realizing it?

I had *stretched my capacity*.

The process I embraced in one season enabled me to— literally—*carry more* and *do more* for the rest of my life.

Crazy, huh?

Nearly every scientific assessment shows that when we think we've reached our absolute physical capacity, we're only around fifty to sixty percent.[5]

Just imagine mentally, emotionally, and spiritually.

We all have far more capacity than we know. It just needs to be grown.

And we can begin to grow it *now*.

. . . . .

I LOVE WHAT CRAIG GROESCHEL SAYS: "The pain you endure today is the strength you enjoy tomorrow."

This is definitely a visible element in David's biography. All those years of pain prepared him for all those years in the palace.

Capacity, in general, is an important conversation for our current culture. A culture obsessed with boundaries and rest. I'm all about those things, for the record. I discuss in length in my first book about how Sabbath changed my life. Wise pace and rhythms are essential for a healthy soul.

But if we want to grow, we can't just ask, *Where do I need grace and space?* But also, *Where do I need to increase my capacity?*

This is true in the small and big.

My last year in Atlanta was a mixed bag. My time was done. I was eager to get away from a room with one too many painful pictures hanging on the wall. But I also felt grateful for my time there. And I *loved* the city. I relished my leisurely weekends walking the beltline, comparing breakfast tacos, letting sushi dissolve on my tongue over cityscape views, grabbing vanilla lattes from Octane (R.I.P.).

One week, a friend flew out from Dallas and we caught up over dinner. He's a great time. A deep, old soul who carries maturity beyond his years. Also—I'm not quite sure how to language this—he's so filled with God's Spirit he flows prophetically in everyday, jokes-over-cheese-fries conversations.

All that to say, I was opening up over cheese fries. Reminding him how discouraged I felt while I waited for what was next. Lightning struck his eyes. He put a palm on the table and pointed my way.

"Russ. Enjoy this season. This time of driving into Atlanta whenever you want and relaxing in your current ministry is coming to an end. Mark my words because I feel this strongly: The time's soon when the new assignment will dwarf anything you experience now."

His words became flesh. Within months, I'd moved to Columbus, Ohio. And the role was *demanding*.

I won't play martyr about it, but it's been said in the church world that few roles are as complex and grueling as campus pastor. The hours are long, the weight is heavy, and you have to navigate facility overseer, leader, boss, central staff liaison, hire-and-fire man, Sunday host, vision-castor, spiritual staff pastor, occasional preacher, and church location pastor all in one. It's a lot.

Oh, and the meetings here were *intense*.

I was used to gathering for staff prayer, an hour-long meeting, and lunch, then tinkering away at a to-do list the rest of the afternoon.

Mondays here were an unrelenting marathon of focused super-meeting after focused super-meeting. I began to hallucinate each day around 2:30. As the new guy, I couldn't say anything, but occasionally coworkers asked if I was okay. I'd blink and wipe drool from my mouth and mutter, "Yeah, what's up?"

I had a decision to make. Would I complain and get discouraged? Or would I grow my capacity?

I'm happy to report meetings barely faze me now. Please be impressed.

Super lighthearted example to illustrate we shouldn't automatically avoid or cut out things God might be using to grow our capacity.

There are seasons you need to pay attention to your soul and handle *less*. Other seasons the answer is to handle it *differently* (work smarter, not harder). And sometimes the answer is to grow your capacity so you can handle *more*.

I've often been haunted by God's challenging question to Jeremiah:

> "If you have raced with men on foot and they have worn you out, how can you compete with horses? If you stumble in safe country, how will you manage in the thickets by the Jordan?"[6]

The implication is obvious.

If I can't handle *this*, how am I going to handle *that*?

And am I really going to ask God for more *blessing* but refuse to grow my ability to handle the corresponding *burden*?

Spiritually, this is how New Testament writers encouraged their churches. To embrace the process of spiritual development. That the trials we face put steel in our spine, develop callouses on our hands, put size on our triceps. All so we can endure and become all we were destined to become.

I'm just curious. What process can you embrace *right now* to stretch your capacity? Your capacity for endurance. Pressure. Character. Time management. To carry and handle more.

In an odd way, how quickly you move toward the stretch is

connected to how much you operate from a sense of calling. If you live from the coin of self, you tend to avoid challenges and gravitate toward convenience. When you live from the coin of calling, you stop gravitating toward *comfort* and start growing your *capacity*.

On a practical, societal level—and I'll try not to get on a soap box here—I'm concerned for our growing fragility as people.

In the breakout scholarly work, *Coddling of the American Mind*,[7] we see some of the paths that led us where we are. How out-of-control safetyism, helicopter parenting, political polarization, safe spaces in universities, and more have resulted in charred and brittle psychological muscles. In this new cultural ground, we're scared of ideas that might "trigger" us, we're susceptible to fear-based tribalism, and there is an alarming uptick in anxiety and depression. Not to mention a growing inability to address issues, engage in uncomfortable conversations, or bear up under difficulty.

It's not a faith book. But it is a prophetic, insightful, and needed one.

I sound like an angry talking head on your uncle's favorite news show. I'm not trying to be critical. But so many of us are becoming increasingly fear-driven and insulated. It's trickled into parenting and schools and politics and life in general. I just know we need bigger muscles to endure the times we're in, not smaller ones. We need arenas to toughen our souls, not holes to climb inside.

And this is a *crucial* part of confidence—not just the ability to do hard things but to face the future, a strength to *endure* whatever may come.

We took our faith community through a ten-week mental health campaign a while back. It was beautiful. For the last portion, we flew out a clinical psychologist from LA. I made our reservations at a bougie brunch spot in the city, and we ate our cracked eggs and avocado outside under the midmorning sun. He leaned in and poured wisdom through his perfectly manicured grey facial hair and Australian accent. I felt lifted. For a moment transported to my childhood in an Indiana Jones movie, a more attractive Sean Connery telling us out loud the secrets to the universe.

I asked him what he saw in this cultural moment—about the tendencies to isolate instead of socialize, hide instead of face, protect instead of confront.

"As a therapist, my goal is to get my clients to actually expose themselves to their fears, not avoid them."[8]

I was taken aback. That's not what you usually hear on TikTok.

He unpacked *exposure therapy* versus *avoidance therapy*.

He said the goal is to incrementally get people to expose themselves to the fears keeping them captive.

Exposure therapy helps you conquer your fears and grow strong. Avoidance therapy grows your fear and makes you weak.

Exposure helps us grow our capacity.

I know easy is well . . . easier.

But if I'm going to be a confident person, I can't just be a convenience person. Eventually, that'll turn me into a cowardly person. I already have enough real battles with fear as it is, how about you?

The truth is, we need to expose ourselves consistently to things that challenge us and grow us.

. . . . .

THERE'S A LOT WE CAN EMBRACE TO expand the world inside us.

Enduring trials expands us. Reading and curiosity expands us. Befriending people with different backgrounds and perspectives expands us.

The one I'm most passionate about?

Travel.

Seriously. Studies abound regarding what it does for your brain, happiness, health, and open-mindedness.[9] And yes, capacity.

Time spent away from familiarity, in general—be that a mountain to hike, a state to see, a city to explore, especially experiencing new perspectives and cultures overseas—builds something inside us. It enlarges us.

I know travel isn't everybody's thing. And it may not be in everyone's budget, or for that matter, feasible with young kids.

I'm aware of that. I know people saving up a lot of paychecks to finally kick back their tired feet at Myrtle Beach and eat shrimp tacos by the pier, and when you do, I'll be jealous.

Wherever we find ourselves, my challenge is just to get out there a bit more, past our usual borders, whatever that looks like.

And if you do have a desire to see the world one day, then if it's any consolation, it may be more accessible than you think.

I'm in ministry and my dad's a retired educator. We're not floating on yachts. We find deals so absurd people don't believe us.[10] It feels like highway robbery to see ancient pyramids piercing an Arabian sky for what I make. In today's world of discount travel sites and Airbnbs, one can probably cover a heavy chunk of the map if they get scrappy.

All that to say, it made my day last week when my friend on staff asked for help so he and his new bride could traverse the Greek Isles for their one-year anniversary. I sent them links. They couldn't believe it. By the end of the next day, they'd booked a week-long adventure in the Mediterranean.

Bravo, Tucker and Anna. Bring me back some feta and baklava.

I want to incite your inner child. Imagine an adventure that fills you head to toe with anticipation. And move toward it.

I'm only sharing my perspective, don't throw that medicine ball, but I do get concerned when people *never* venture into nature or *never* venture into the city. I don't think this timidity and avoidance build resilience, broad-mindedness, or mental tenacity. It might just reinforce internal limits.

So, even if it's starting small, perhaps a brief escapade to another side of town, consider taking incremental steps out of your comfort zone. Stretch and risk a little. Start saying yes if you usually say no.

Collect some experiences. They will enrich your life and expand your mind. Surprising moments of joy and serendipity will delight you. And you might just find the world around you *and* inside you begin to open up in the most beautiful and unexpected of ways.

Anthony Bourdain once said, "Travel is not a reward for working. It is an education for living."[11]

. . . . .

SOMETIMES STRETCHING OUR capacity is exploring a new city. Other times, it's learning a new role, exercising a new muscle, breaking an old habit, or gaining a new perspective.

Other times, it's staying planted and committed when everything inside us screams to bail. Finishing the project when we want to quit. Working through community when things get wonky instead of running for shiny new hills. After all, *resilience* comes from *roots*. That's when the branches stretch. Just ask that tree in your front yard.

The more we grow our capacity, the more we'll experience that resilience. That super force that postures us to endure hardship and take on the world. The inner fortitude that prepares us for any room and any season.

After all, it doesn't matter how much confidence you build in a singular moment. If you're not resilient, you'll be . . . well, fragile. You'll learn tricks to make your emotional balloon fly high but one little prick and *pop, there you go.*

I've met people with skin as thin as a matzo cracker, consequently breaking with every sideways glance or perceived slight. I've been there myself. Overthinking interactions and reading into things that aren't there. Glorious, Pauline devotions in the morning, then knocked back on my heels for the rest of the afternoon by one remark that didn't sit well. God wants to grow me beyond that. Maybe you too.

I once heard Shelley Giglio remark that in ministry you need the mixture of "tender heart and thick skin." I think it's true for life in general. We must cultivate hearts that are gentle and affected yet lined with steel of nerve and resolve.

So, let's not avoid the gyms that life offers to build our muscles, grow our capacity and deepen our resilience.

You have so much more in you than you know.

> "Consider it a sheer gift, friends, when tests and challenges come at you from all sides. You know that under pressure, your faith life is forced into the open and shows its true colors. So don't try to get out of anything prematurely. Let it do its work so you become mature and well-developed, not deficient in any way." (James 1.2–4 MSG)

Embrace the gym.

Do things that stretch you.

Stand firm when you want to run.

A strong, confident life will be the result.

Self–esteem comes from the outside in; self–worth comes
from the inside out.[1]
—Tim Moore

Exercise daily in God – no spiritual flabbiness, please!
Workouts in the gymnasium are useful, but a disciplined life in
God is far more so, making you fit both today and forever.[2]
—Paul to Timothy

Be brave. Take risks. Nothing can substitute experience.[3]
—Paula Coehlo

16)

Walk like It

Time to get granular.

Magic happens when faith mixes with function and we begin to walk it all out.

This takes many forms, and we'll hit a few rapid fire at the end of the chapter, but here's the big one:

To *walk in confidence*, we must *live with discipline*.

Discipline. Not a sexy word, I know. And you may wonder what discipline has to do with any of this.

A lot.

Disciplines are how we take ownership of our lives. And when our ownership increases, our confidence increases.

When we have a plan for our money and take control of our budget, our confidence rises. When we increase our EQ and maintain healthy relationships, our confidence rises. When we have a vision for our lives and habits moving us there . . . you can guess what happens.

Also, healthy habits reap the kind of rewards that aid natural confidence. Regular time with God produces peace and spiritual vitality. Regular exercise and nutrition boost energy, physical exuberance, and increased capacity. Regular reading and learning result in knowledge and insight. And so on.

But mostly?

Disciplines are a *declaration that you are worthy.*

See, so much of our confidence emanates out of our sense of worth. And while you *possess* intrinsic worth no matter what you do (see Part 2), disciplines *express* that worth. They declare to your brain that you matter. That you deserve to be invested in.

God can speak worth over your life in a thousand ways, but if you don't communicate it back to yourself in gritty, everyday life, the runway runs out. Yet every time you invest in your health, passions, and future, you make an internal statement that you're worth the time and energy. And you are.

I don't know about you, but I've also experienced the inverse. At times, when I've had a slashed heart and felt unworthy of love, I began living like it. A low state where I underslept or overslept, pulled back from projects, shrunk back in leadership, didn't shower as much, you know, that kind of thing.

Why? I didn't feel worthy. The unspoken narrative below the surface was, *Well, I'm obviously not worthy of love, so why does it even matter if I . . .*

You could apply this to your career. If you feel inadequate or underappreciated long enough, what's the natural recoil? You give less energy and output to both the company and yourself.

The problem is, when we give in to this self-defeating cycle, we perpetuate the narrative and exacerbate the problem.

It's worth underscoring: When you *shake hands with discipline*, you *hug your esteem*.

Altruism aside, the greatest investment we'll ever make is not real estate or stocks but our own lives. Our character, development, and well-being.

We'll continue to onboard the internals we've discussed. But let's take the next step and build into our discipline.

. . . . .

THIS IS AN OFTEN OVERLOOKED KEY to David's life. He applied bone-crunching discipline, not only to sword and string but to his spiritual sharpness. In Psalm 119, we discover his practice of worship (seven times a day) and his practice of prayer (three times a day). Sheesh.[4]

No wonder he felt he could pray bold, third-person prayers like, "Lord remember David and all his self-denial . . ."[5]

The man was serious.

If you've always struggled in this area, don't be discouraged. And don't do the foolish thing that brand-new-to-disciple people who do. You know . . .

"Dang, I suck. So, starting tomorrow, I'm getting up at 5:00 a.m., praying two hours a day, changing everything I eat, doing

75 Hard[6] workouts, and completing ten office projects."

I probably don't need to tell you what'll happen. You'll fail and then feel like a failure. And be less confident than before.

Quick replay: Your value isn't hitched to performance. Your value is a word already spoken. Spoken by the One voice that matters. Inflation isn't on the table.

But while your worth is forever settled, there *are* things you can do to increase your "sense" of worth, not to mention quality of life. Like discipline.

The good news is you don't need to move the needle a lot to see big changes. Sometimes if I'm in an emotional funk, a thirty-minute run does the trick.

To grow muscle here, *start small, stay consistent*, and when (not if) you fall off the wagon, *show yourself grace* since you're human, and *keep going*.

Easier said than done, but those are the basic ingredients. Add in the protein of people, accountability, enjoyable routines and rewards, and you've got yourself a recipe for success.

Here's the real secret: Pick *one* area at a time. Just one.

It could be as simple as "I'm going to start showing up on time and put a system in place to make it happen." Or "I'm going to get up half an hour earlier." Or "I want to start going to the gym every day, but for now I'll walk twenty minutes a day, three times a week." Or "I'm going to cut out sodas and drink water."

Start *singular*, start *small*, and start *specific*. Then stay *steady*.

That's it.

Discipline is usually built one block at a time, not given by birth as a whole set.

Apart from James Clear's phenom, *Atomic Habits*,[7] I can't recommend the book *One Thing* by Gary Keller strongly enough.[8] As the name suggests, Keller argues that the power of the most successful individuals and companies in the world is laser-like focus. A whittling down to the few things that matter and doing them most and first.

He also gives brilliant insight into discipline development. In fact, he makes a somewhat controversial claim: *There's really no such thing as a disciplined person.*

He contends that a "disciplined person" is simply someone who took one habit at a time and integrated it into their life until autopilot, then moved to the next. Eventually, after enough of these habits have been stacked (maybe you've heard of "habit stacking"), people look on from the outside, impressed to the point of drooling.

I'm convinced it's true. At least for me. Half the time I still feel *very* undisciplined. I beat myself up about it too. I'm getting better at my self-talk, but I'm on a journey.

Here's what's funny, though. People tell me I seem *highly* disciplined. In some respects, *maybe*.

I exercise six days a week.

I pray and study Scripture each morning.

I've gone to church every Sunday unless sick or out of town for the last twenty-something years.

I read and write on a regular basis.

I eat healthy.

Dang, I'm disciplined. Gold stars for me.

Not really.

First off, I could walk you through plenty of ways I'm *inconsistent* and perpetually fall short. (Budget, sleep, work receipts, phone hygiene, thought life, cleaning, habit changes, let's move on.)

Second, back to Keller's argument: Those things I'm "disciplined" at are things simply built into my patterns over the years. They're subconscious. I'm not gritting my teeth and quoting Gary V to make them happen. I do them like I put on shoes.

What looks like *deep disciplines* to some are *daily defaults* to me. They're ingrained. You have things like this too, I'm sure.

I'm not saying there aren't days I'm not feeling it and have to make the choice (especially with the gym after long, cold days in Ohio winter).

But for instance, I've been having morning devotions for twenty years. I can't imagine not. It's my sanity and highlight. When I get up, it's what I do. Someone clapping for that would feel like someone clapping because I brush my teeth.

Same with the gym. I have playlists. I go to a gym I enjoy and have community there. It's my reprieve after a long day.

Without thinking, my car turns that way as I leave the office.

When I fell in love with Jesus as a teenager, I took the decision-making out of church and decided it wasn't an option each week any more than showing up to work each day.

On and on. You get the gist.

Add all that up and I could trick a few people into thinking I'm disciplined.

Point is, you pick a habit and ingrain it into your life until it's like breathing. Then another.

Before you know it, people will ask you "how you're so disciplined."

Just sigh, point up, and say, *It's not me, It's Him . . .*

Kidding.

More importantly, you'll reap the external benefits of your disciplines and the internal benefits of your self-respect.

I've long loved the quote by Brutus Hamilton, "It is one of the strange ironies of this strange life that those who work the hardest, those who subject themselves to the strictest discipline, who give up certain pleasurable things in order to achieve a goal, are the happiest people."

. . . . .

THE EXCITING PART?

Disciplines build compound momentum once they become consistent. The winds of life start blowing your way and excellence gets in your blood. And you start getting *wins*.

And wins build your confidence.

By the way, when you do the *small things* consistently, it becomes *diligence*.

I feel like that's one of my biggest downfalls, to be honest. At least with things I'm not passionate about. Who has time for it? Who has time to make every dentist appointment, pay and renew car tags (what a rip off), rotate your tires, keep everything clean, and respond to texts for crying out loud?

But that's where we get a plan and live with intention so we don't get stressed. Because you know what'll really stress you? The end result of negligence instead of diligence.

Scripture tells us plainly that the diligent will prosper.[9]

Dave Ramsey defines it like this: "Work is doing it. Discipline is doing it every day. Diligence is doing it well every day."

It's when you make the important *urgent* so that it doesn't become a *detriment*.

It's when you realize the more you care, the less careless mistakes you make.

It's the *details*.

Recently, I felt sucker punched. In the span of two weeks, I heard *three different people*—a leadership guru, a sports and CEO coach, *and* the author of a new book on unicorns in the

workplace[10]—discuss one of the most telling signs of the health
and relational hygiene of a person: how quickly they respond
to texts.

Gulp.

God, are you telling me something?

Last chapter we wrote down an item we keep putting off out of
fear. A diligence blind spot may be something we keep putting
off out of *apathy*, out of *I don't feel like it*.

Quick, powerful exercise. Take inventory of your "diligence
blindspots" and then calendar one action each day this week.

The way we can know a blind spot is serious? The trajectory.
A diligence blind spot is something that's not a big deal *now*
but will be a big deal *later*. Let's give ourselves the gift of a
mental spa by taking care of it.

. . . . .

WHEN WE INTEGRATE DISCIPLINES
into our life, we don't just grow in confidence; we begin to
walk it out.

It's the neuromuscular work.

That's why I titled the chapter how I did.

To walk in confidence, at some point we must do just that. We
can't ignore the weird kinship between attributes and action,
body posture and heart posture. We must sync up. There are
things we must *express* in order to *experience*.

I want to be oh so careful here. I'm not saying, "Fake it 'til you make it."

But I am saying *be it* as you *become it.*

I'm saying it's not fake to exercise faith, regardless of emotions. It's not false to remain faithful, even when void of motivation. I like to remind my *Enneagram Four* friends—*being faithful isn't being fake.*

Some of us need to let that sink in.

Faithful isn't fake.

When you *feel* like isolating but know it's healthy to get yourself in community and go anyway—that's not fake; that's faithful.

When all your burning chemicals *feel* like making love to someone else, but you resist temptation and pour the affection onto your spouse—that's not fake; that's faithful.

And when you *feel* disappointed but choose to lift your hands in worship through the tears to God anyway—well, I think you get the point.

I was talking to an accomplished psychologist friend the other day, sharing these thoughts. He responded in trademark bluntness:

"Well, yeah, Russ. Plenty of people in prison today followed their emotions. I suppose you could say they were being 'true' to themselves. But the people who grow as human beings and experience success in life are the ones who mature into being principle-driven instead of emotion-driven."[10]

It's a good thing feelings are being given more value in our current psychological ecosystem. Feelings shouldn't be ignored, minimized, repressed, or unevaluated. Feelings matter.

But while feelings are helpful indicators, they're terrible idols; great mirrors but crippling masters.

Perpetual feelings can be a great odometer, letting us know how the engine is doing and how empty the tank is. But they should never be the hands on the wheel.

All that digression to say, as we work out the spiritual and emotional core muscles of confidence, we need to begin to activate them externally, regardless of feelings. This, in turn, builds internal momentum.

To break it down?

As your character goes up, let your chin go up. As God returns the sparkle to your eyes, practice looking people in theirs. As you steady your spiritual walk, put a pep back in your step. As joy returns to your soul, harness the power of a smile.

I guess what I'm saying is *If God is with you, act like it.*

If Jesus is for you, live like it.

If the King is in you, walk like it.

These things matter.

Preachers get corny about it, but Scripture does teach that for sons and daughters of God, a divine, spiritual kind of royalty enters the bloodstream. Let's move and shake hands as if it's true. Not as haughty, spoiled heirs but as fiercely secure, humble servant leaders.

We *have* to get this stuff into our central nervous system. For practice, sit up straight and take a deep breath. Lift your chin.

Think of how loved and secure you are. Take another deep breath and let a grin slip across your face and a gleam sneak into your eyes.

Get in the habit of living from *there.*

Science has much to say about body posture. The emotional effect of unclenching our fists, opening our palms, lifting our hands, unfolding our arms, unpocketing our thumbs.

Even how we sit in chairs—slouched, tall and attentive, or forward and leaned in—these all not only communicate something to those outside us, but they communicate something *inside* us.

Jesse, the one I've told you about? We had a check-in the other day. Nowadays, we do walking meetings. Trying to get our steps in, you know.

Jesse's an introverted, quietly confident leader who's always working to leverage his strengths and shore up his weaknesses. So I asked him what he was learning, and he mentioned a fascinating book by Leil Lowndes called *How To Talk To Anyone: 92 Little Tricks for Big Success in Relationships.*[12]

He said one chapter encourages you to imagine a horse bit on the doorframes of every room you walk into. To imagine you are a horse catching it on the way in, lifting your head and pulling back your cheeks into a smile.

I thought that was so wild and weird.

And clever and worth trying.

I don't want to get you overthinking your every move. But paying attention and making slight changes could have major psychological impact.

I can just tell you there've been seasons I've felt sad and dejected for an unhealthy length of time. And sometimes, before I knew it, I developed the habit of walking with my head down, slumping my shoulders, sighing more than smiling, and engaging people behind counters with less enthusiasm. The moment it dawned on me these new habits were becoming ingrained, an alarm surfaced inside. I realized my new counter-productive physical response was actually affecting the way others interacted with me and the way *I* was interacting with me.

As my friend's dad likes to say, "You see yourself the way you carry yourself."

It's okay not to be okay. And it's okay to permit yourself to feel what you feel.

But *beware of ceasing to bring the best version of yourself to life.*

Beware of developing the habit of not actually showing up. Don't tolerate the persistent cancer of not bringing the full *you*. And what you'll find is that when you bring your full self, your *self* usually fills up.

You could oversimplify *Part 2* to "Sometimes you won't feel better until you believe better."

But this *Part 3* contains a parallel truth: "Sometimes you won't feel better until you *do* better."

Honestly, I envy people who aren't in their head. They seem happier. And often more successful, truth be told. They don't overthink. They do.

I want to be more like this.

Not overthinking.

Picking a direction. And *doing*.

It's why I love the counselor advice to "Get out of your head and into your body." Sometimes when I'm in a funk or feel foggy, I need to transition my thoughts to paper, go for a walk, serve someone else, complete a task, or lift some weights. Just get moving. Get *out of my head* and *into my body*.

After all, one of the most lethal blows to being in your head, overthinking, or even insecurity in general is pure, old-fashioned action.

And action compounds.

I heard Rob Kaple from Grace Midtown Atlanta say something in passing about a decade ago, a little hidden gem I've palmed like Copperfield:

"Confident moments lead to confident lives."

Simple but profound. That's why it's important to bring the full expression of yourself into your interactions and tasks, whether you feel like it or not. Because *moments* become *momentum*. And the best way to create momentum is to bring your best *into your moments.*

Every time you choose to look people in the eye, use the fullness of your voice, and fully engage in conversation, you're creating momentum. You're becoming someone. And you're not just communicating something to others; you're communicating something to yourself. Your self-respect grows as you fully engage the world.

So try it.

Before the hour ends.

Lean into some confident moments and watch the immediate effect it has.

Confidence is what happens when you have done the hard
work that entitles you to succeed.[1]
—Pat Summitt

Beginning empty-handed and alone frightens the best of men.
It also speaks volumes of just how sure they are that God is
with them.[2]
—Gene Edwards

"I'll live my life if it kills me."[3]
—E.E. Cummings

17)

Sheep & Stones

WHEN IT COMES TO PRACTICAL CONFIDENCE–BUILDING, here's another lever to pull:

Grow your *confidence* by growing your *competence*.

It's the reason parents put kids in activities. Starting something new, sticking with it, building skill, eventually gaining success—these are rudimentary building blocks of confidence.

As my friend Steve said yesterday, "Success breeds confidence."

And success comes through sharpened skills.

We see this dynamic in 1 Samuel 17 when David takes on Goliath.

It's a story we could unpack for days.

David's faithfulness. Goliath's defeat. Theological foreshadowing. The creative, pragmatic battle strategy.[4]

But what leaps off the page to me is David's shimmering, unassailable confidence. It shines out of his every word and move.

Roll the scene in your head like a 70mm. Philistines versus Israelites. Forty days of taunting over the valley of Elah. David transporting thermos and cheese to commanders and brothers. And one tense, epic gridlock, soldiers scampering whenever this giant named Goliath approached.

One day on his errands, David heard rumblings. Not just the roar of the giant but the talk of the town. Rumors of the king's promised reward to whoever slays the behemoth: wealth, king's daughter in marriage, and lifelong tax exemption for his family.

The taxes thing must have got him. David's ears perked and he began to ask questions.

Much to the chagrin of his brothers. They scoffed in annoyance and told him to mind his business. How could a forgotten runt like David defeat a dragon like Goliath? Who'd he think he was?

In fact,

> "When . . . David's oldest brother . . . heard him speaking . . . he burned with anger . . . and asked, 'Why have you come down here? And with whom did you leave those few sheep in the wilderness? I know how conceited you are and how wicked your heart is; you came down only to watch the battle.'"[5]

The hostility.

David, the kid in the field watching sheep. The errand boy rising early to rush charcuterie to his brothers before their important battle. David, the forgotten of the litter.

That David . . . *conceited*? Instead of being thankful, they're resentful?

We don't know the family dynamic or whether they were all just chaffing under the announcement of David's future kingship. But it might be worth slipping this reminder into your pocket:

Insecurity often interprets *confidence* as *arrogance*. And becomes offended by it.

Even healthy confidence can be misunderstood. Also, it's worth reviewing David's dialogue with his brothers here and how firm he stood. He was humble but savage, kind but direct.

Skipping forward, Saul overhears David's inquiry and tries to talk him out of it, reminding David this guy's been a warrior since youth. But David was unfazed, his confidence a soaring kite not to be brought down by the fickle weather of his brothers' immaturity or even a king's fear.

I see two layers of confidence in his response.

The first, a spiritual boldness. David walked with God. He knew God was with him. That's jet fuel for the pack right there. Didn't matter how big the giant; with God, David was bigger.

So, he was confident because of his *connection to God*.

But I see another layer.

He was also confident because of his *competence and skill*.

He tells Saul:

"... 'Your servant has been keeping his father's sheep. When a lion or a bear came and carried off a sheep from the flock, I went after it, struck it and rescued the sheep from its mouth. When it turned on me, I seized it by its hair, struck it and killed it. *Your servant has killed both the lion and the bear; this uncircumcised Philistine will be like one of them* ... The Lord who rescued me from the paw of the lion and the paw of the bear will rescue me from the hand of this Philistine.'"[6]

All those decked-out soldiers looked dangerous. But David *was* dangerous. And the reason he was *dangerous* was because he *developed* his skill. His confidence didn't come from presumption; it came from practice.

Long before the spotlight shown on him in that valley, he'd developed himself in secret. Steadily practicing with sling and stone. Steadily rehearsing combat. Steadily watching sheep and practicing faithfulness. Steadily walking with God and learning to hear His voice. Steadily confronting one obstacle after another, graduating with each test.

Sheep.

Lion.

Bear.

Now giant.

Not to get all sermonic, but in an era where we glamorize big, quick wins, I fear many of us drown in the sea of wasted potential because we simply refuse to go through the process. Obscure years. Years of diligence, faithfulness, and work.

When others chose casualness and complacency, David was working and crafting, grinding and refining.

> "If the axe is dull and its edge unsharpened, more strength is needed, but *skill will bring success.*"[7]

You have edges to sharpen. I promise you do, even if it doesn't seem like it. Gifts and aptitudes. Personality traits, inclinations toward arts, handiwork, design, marketing, calculating, problem-solving, whatever. Those gifts are *talents*. When you take the time to develop them, they become *skills*. And those skills can open doors, expand opportunities, and improve other's lives.

Also, the more you tap into your design, into the things you were uniquely made to do, the more your confidence will rise. There's a groove, a sweet spot in your sense of self, when you align with your intention and design.

As for David, it's obvious he viewed every opportunity and ounce of talent as a stewardship. He developed his talents into skills. He wasn't an "overnight success," though I'm sure many saw it that way. No, he put in the hours for a long time when no one was looking and no one cared. He had been "faithful with little" and now was ready to be "faithful with much."

. . . . .

DAVID HAD HEART *AND* HUSTLE.

He was an incredible musician and songsmith, a captivating and charismatic leader, a gifted poet and writer, and a bad, bad man with a sword.

We honor David for the authenticity of his heart, and we should. But let's not get so theologically in the clouds that we forget he worked his butt off to be great. He paid the price to excel in everything he stepped into.

I love this description of David's leadership from Psalm 78.72:

> "He cared for them with a *true heart* and *skillful hands*."[8]

I've adopted this as a prayer over myself and the leaders I lead.

True heart. Skillful hands.

I don't know about you, but I want both.

I want character *and* craft. I want to cultivate godliness *and* greatness.

One day Jesus told that famous parable about the talents. A rich man left on a trip and entrusted money to employees. Each received differing amounts. And each did different things with it.

One hid it in the ground out of fear. The other two invested and multiplied it. When the master returned, he called the one who played it safe "wicked and lazy" and the ones who invested it "good and faithful."

It doesn't honor God to hide our potential in the ground out of self-focus, apathy, or fear of what others think. And it doesn't honor God to undervalue the hard work of sharpening our axe, spiritualizing away our laziness with, "All I need is the anointing," or, "Just waiting for the right door."

It also won't help our personal esteem. In fact, I know this will be unpopular to say, but there have been times I've given half-hearted effort at work and felt insecure about it. And I *should* have felt insecure about it. Perfectionism is unhealthy, absolutely. But why should I pretend to be proud of poor effort?

Scripture warns, "Slack habits and sloppy work are as bad as vandalism."[9]

To flip it to the positive, I heard a high-caliber leader say something a couple of years ago that put an IV of motivation in my blood:

"Don't rationalize away the joy, the thrill, of bringing God your best in everything you do."[10]

I *love* that. What an exhilarating feeling to bring the full force of your energy and intellect into the jobs, talents, and opportunities before you.

Bottom line, to become distinguished, we must be dedicated. We must make good friends with *hard work*.

If we want God to do something extraordinary through our lives, we have to stop crossing our fingers for opportunities and start giving our all where we are. God doesn't look for *wishers*; He looks for *workers*. And if we labor wholeheartedly in every season of life, I promise whatever ceiling we think we have will break and sky will pierce through.

Ten years ago, at a conference, I heard the hurricane-preacher

Christine Caine remark that God tends to *work through those who are already working.*

Elijah threw the mantle on Elisha *while* he was plowing land. God spoke to Gideon *while* he was threshing wheat. Samuel called David from the field *while* He was tending sheep.

Self-promotion isn't the way to our best future; sacrifice is. Getting in the dark and mixing our dreams with some blood, sweat, and self-denial.

Not to mention . . . working hard in your lane and on your craft is another antidote to the comparison and inferiority trap. I love the Message paraphrase of Paul's words to the Galatians:

> "Make a careful exploration of who you are and the work you've been given, and then sink yourself into that. Don't be impressed with yourself. Don't compare yourself with others. Each of you must take responsibility for doing the creative best you can with your own life."[11]

Comparison is crushed by concentration.

Find your lane and go hard in the paint *there*. Develop your skills at night instead of doom-scrolling others' success. Become aware (and content) of the unique person you are called to be and the unique contribution you are called to make and focus on *that*.

Who has God called you to be in this season, and what has He called you to do?

Whatever it is, in the words of Paul, *sink yourself into that.*

That'll help sink insecurity.

I know I sound old-school, but whatever character trait we grow in this season, let's add work ethic. God doesn't anoint lazy. God doesn't honor shoddy work or half effort. God doesn't commiserate with us while we cut corners in the boring years just praying for our big break.

If I have one screaming regret, it's that I didn't figure this out sooner in the areas I wasn't excited about. I romanticized the call of God in my high school years, so I considered learning math or the saxophone beneath me, an irrelevant waste of time.

I didn't connect the dots between my present and my future. I didn't draw the line between current patterns and future potential. Because of this, I had to wrestle through parts of my character as I got older.

I want you to be first-class in the arenas God has called you to, be that manufacturing, communication, engineering, or developing software. So excellent in skill and character, people *have* to ask what's different about you.

This may be too practical for some (I warned you). But I just think it's sad how many of us have the Spirit of the Creator inside us and yet somehow think sloppy and unoriginal is okay. That status quo is acceptable. Content to fossilize fifty years in the past instead of blaze the way in innovation. Fine to settle for mediocre effort and haphazard presentation.

Where are the Daniels of today "possessing an excellent spirit" so extraordinary that pagan Babylonian cultures seek us out for our wisdom and expertise?

Where are the Bezalels of today anointed for craft and beauty so stunning, the world emulates *us* in artistry instead of the other way around?

Where are the followers of Jesus today who do the hard work to shine in every room and sector they inhabit, in both spirit and skill?

Where are those who refuse to settle for the lowest baseline?

Where are those who nurture their genius?

Where are those who choose to be great?

. . . . .

IF YOU CAN'T TELL, I BELIEVE EACH of us has an exciting but serious responsibility to *grow our gifts.*

Paul told Timothy not to "neglect the gift that is in you . . ."[12]

A deposit was there. A measure of anointing, a speaking gift, a mantel of leadership. We don't really know. All we know is Paul reminded Timothy that what was inside him could *remain dormant* or *become dynamite.* And that *the choice was up to him.*

When it comes to our gifts, are we hiding them or honing them? Are we decommissioned on the sidelines by discouragement or knocked down but getting back up and sharpening the blade again? Are we entitled and asking why someone won't give us an opportunity, or are we developing ourselves in the darkness, trusting God to shake that polaroid in the light when He so chooses?

Let's get even more tactile.

I don't want to be a good writer. I want to be a phenomenal writer. I admit it.

By default, I've invested in this my whole life. I've been reading and writing like a maniac since first grade, nearly thirty years.

But as I got serious about finishing my first book? I invested in my craft.

Great writing comes from great reading, so I set aside modern favorites and dove back into old classics. I'm talking the legends. Fitzgerald, Steinbeck, Hemingway. I took in their words like truffles on the tongue, absorbing their genius.

I bought books on writing. Anne Lamott, Steven Pressfield, one by the master himself, Stephen King. He recommended certain academic grammar books to perfect literary mechanics with militant form. I bought those as well.

Donald Miller promoted an all-day writer's conference online during Covid for a few hundred bucks. I joined.

I sent the draft to peers with an uber-specific feedback form inviting them to be brutal. Then I sent it to professional editors, paying thousands of dollars that squeezed my budget. Then I spent months applying edits, weeks blue-taping every square inch and idle word to make it shine as brightly as possible.

All that effort and I am still *so far* from where I want to be. But I *am* committed to developing any raw talent inside, be it small or large.

We've done this in our staff with preaching. In addition to studying and praying, we prepare, practice, give feedback, and spend a great deal of money and time going through masterclasses on the art of communication.[13]

The point is, you and I need an absolute belief in the calling God has put in us. A burning vision with a corresponding desire to step up and fulfill that vision. Intentionality to practically pursue improvement. An ability and willingness to receive feedback so we can become our best.

. . . . .

MAYBE YOU'R THINKING, *I'M actually one of the few born without any talents . . .*

Not true.

If you don't know what you're gifted at, that's okay. Ask those who know you what they see in you. Ask yourself what you enjoy and what comes naturally. Find those things that when you work hard, you accelerate and self-replenish. And if you're not currently doing what you love full-time, make it your side hustle and develop yourself off the clock.

In the meantime, don't treat anything in your current season as unimportant. Speak over every menial task and job you have:

> *This matters.*

"Whether you eat or drink or whatever you do, do it all for the glory of God."[14]

Looking back, I can tell you I took something with me from

every job I ever had. The grocery store, the moving company, the clothing retails, the foreign ranch, my one day at a pharmacy, all of it. When you bring intention to your job, it translates to future jobs. I guarantee you David was not passionate about sheep. But the resilience from him bringing his whole heart into that responsibility translated into his next role and the role after that.

"The way you do one thing is the way you do everything."

So, if you are, say, a barista (out of obligation, not passion for the artistry), it might be tempting to phone it in and pray big, idealized prayers about "the big thing God has in store."

I believe He has those. But right now, the "big thing" He has in store is the kind of person you're becoming. The way you reflect Jesus and change the atmosphere where you are. The way you express excellence and integrity in the small, mundane tasks in front of you.

Just like with David, forever remember: Sheep become lions. Lions become bears. Bears become giants. Giants become nations.

Zechariah 4.10 warns us not to despise the day of small beginnings.

I would tell you, especially if you're younger and not connecting the dots of *life right now* to *destiny one day when*—don't despise the small beginnings. Don't despise the sucky starts. Don't despise the uncomfortable, embarrassing learning curves. Don't despise the unglamorous roles.

Don't dare despise "the sheep." Not if you want God to give you people-sheep to shepherd one day. Not if you want Him to take you to the heights of your calling.

I feel this in my gut as I type, so I'm going to hit the keyboard a little harder:

You might be dreaming of being king; God is looking at how you watch sheep. You might be waiting for someone to hand you a mic; God is watching how you will handle a mop.

Don't despise or minimize what's in your hands.

In fact, amuse me if you will and hold out your hand. Both if you can balance the book.

Here's my question: What's in those hands? Seriously. Go through the catalog of everything in your life right now—tasks and assignments, no matter how big or small; relationships, no matter how great or frustrating; money, no matter how minimal or overflowing.

Now, whatever you see invisibly floating there above the lines of your palms, take in Paul's words:

> "Whatever your hand finds to do, do it with all your might."[15]

Steward it. Grow it. Multiply it.

Maybe one day they'll say of you what they said of David: that you lived and led with a "true heart and skillful hands."

My hair is thin and falling out in all the wrong places. I am
a little insecure. My eyes are crossed but they're still blue.[1]
—Ed Sheeran ("Best Part of Me")

". . . He rekindles burned-out lives with fresh hope,
restoring dignity and respect to their lives—a place in the
sun![2]
—1 Samuel 2 MSG

I suppose the best brand is being yourself.[3]
—Leslie Higgins (Ted Lasso)

18)

Dress the Part

Samuel went to assign the next king, and Jesse brought forth his sons.

The tall one, the handsome one, the healthy one, the strong one. Even Samuel eyed them with mere physical observation, thinking, *That's the one. No, that's the one . . .*

Before highlighting David, God adjusted the prophet's perspective:

> "But the Lord said to Samuel, 'Do not consider his appearance or his height, for I have rejected him. The Lord does not look at the things people look at. People look at the outward appearance, but the Lord looks at the heart.'"[4]

People look at the outside. God looks at the inside. At this, we nod and clap.

Several years ago, a visiting leader suggested an accompanying insight.

"Yes, God looks at the heart, and that's what matters most.

But we always ignore the first part of the verse and miss the wisdom in its parallel truth: *Man looks at the outside.*"[5]

This leader argued that God wasn't just making an indictment but also stating a reality. We humans *do* look on the outside, and therefore to an extent it *does* matter.

Stay with me.

When someone walks into a church, they look on the outside. In part, to know if they belong.

If a homeless person walks in and only sees Louis Vuitton, it communicates something. If a young person walks in and only sees grey hairs, it communicates something. If a person of color walks in and only sees Caucasians, it communicates something.

Every time someone walks into a room, even subconsciously, they note the general age, personality, dress, and skin color of the people there. We all walk into spaces *looking on the outside* to see ourselves reflected somewhere in the story. It's human nature.

That is why it's important, when possible, to have diverse representation on platforms, in companies, and leadership.

Excellence is another example. It's the inside, the heart and culture of an organization, that matters most. Absolutely. But if you don't think excellence on the outside—how clear a website is or how clean a building is—matters at all, you may not be living in the real world. Walk into a McDonald's restroom and tell me you don't *look on the outside.*

In fact, sometimes the *outside* speaks to what's on the *inside.*

It all goes back to the danger of extremes, doesn't it?

Like God with Samuel, Scripture goes to great lengths to communicate how much more the internal matters. Especially—important clarification—*in comparison*.

Take 1 Timothy 4.8:

> "For physical training is of some value, but godliness has value for all things, holding promise for both the present life and the life to come."

The classic KJV says, "bodily exercise profiteth little."

Well, there you have it. Ditch the gym bag for the Cheetos bag. Doesn't matter!

Except it does. I don't think you need me to list all the ways exercise affects your quality of life and the body God gave you. But if their ancient culture was *anything* like ours, the reminder's needed. Today, millions worship at the altar of physical appearance for hours a day, giving minutes or less to their souls

Paul isn't saying bodily exercise doesn't matter; just that *in comparison* to eternal things—your prayer life, character, divine purpose—there hardly *is* a comparison.

Just because something doesn't matter *as much* doesn't mean it doesn't matter *at all*.

Whether we're talking physical exercise, spending, food, or digital media, moderation is the key.

And so—God looks at the inside. That matters most.

But man looks at the outside. And that matters some.

All that to say, I was having a dull day the other day. I wasn't feeling super inspired about life or great about myself.

Then something happened. Something that shifted things. Something that made my day and filled my confidence back up.

I got a haircut.

I mean, a *good* one.

There's just nothing like a fresh cut, is there? (Or hat or Vin Diesel shine.)

I know, I know. I'm supposed to tell you I read Ephesians. But it's true. I got a haircut and felt like a new man.

It's easy to forget the basic power of basic things, isn't it? We teach kids the importance of flossing, smelling nice, wearing clean clothes, that kind of thing. But even as adults, it can be easy to neglect ourselves, to not care for our skin, eat well, rest, or move our bodies.

Last summer I cracked open Tony Robbins's new book.[6] An encyclopedic manual on all the latest breakthroughs in health, energy, and longevity.

On a flight to Daytona, my eyes landed on a chapter about appearance. Cutting-edge technology on skin enhancement, hair regrowth, complexion and glow, fat loss and muscle growth, everything. All of a sudden, I was freshman Russ back in BI-LO, scanning for secrets.

And Tony, a man zealous to transform people on the *inside,* made some common-sense statements about the *outside*:

> "... A better reason to care about how you look is that it can strongly affect how you feel about yourself. You radiate confidence when you look and feel your best. That sense of physical well-being is the serotonin of self-esteem. I'm not arguing that you should obsess about your appearance, since there are so many things that matter more. But why *wouldn't* you want to look your best as much as possible, so you can relish that vibrant sense of well-being on every level, both inside and out?"

I think it's a fair question.

Narcissism needs the reminder that "beauty is fleeting,"[7] but *negligence* needs the reminder to,

> "Seize life! ... Oh yes—God takes pleasure in your pleasure! Dress festively every morning. Don't skimp on colors and scarves. Relish ... your precarious life. Each day is God's gift. Make the most of each one!"[8]

Life is short and beautiful, Solomon says. So dress colorfully and live fully! (Most of my wardrobe is black, so I guess I should work on this.)

. . . . .

WHEN IT COMES TO APPEARANCE, maybe you're like me and don't always feel like you have much to work with. Well, you know the saying: Work what you got!

Leadership guru John Maxwell felt early in his public leadership that he wasn't particularly pleasing to the eye. That it might even hurt him. So he worked what he had. Beyond a positive attitude (which makes anyone more attractive), he came across a study on how smiling increases attractiveness. He decided he'd spend the rest of his life cheesing big.

There are dozens of ways to put our best foot forward. Recently, on *Diaries of a CEO*, Steve Bartlett talked with an expert about the different *colors* that make you attractive. Who knew? I *do* remember that *Men's Health* magazine saying, "When in doubt, match your eye color." I better flash those blues and hope for the sky.

And speaking of fit . . .

There's as much science on that as there is on body posture.

Most of us subconsciously dress based on mood, anyway. Cozy day? Throw on sweats. Relaxing weekend with friends? Something loose and fun. Date? Something that accentuates our best features. Corporate world? Something sharp.

The hoodie is a *fascinating* example of this.

I love hoodies. But last time I was in LA, I couldn't help but notice how many there were . . . in *eighty-degree* weather.

I understand skin concerns, but still. I even googled: *Why on earth do people wear hoodies in the blazing sun?* Lo and behold, article after article on the psychology of clothing. Hoodies are emotionally comforting, plain and simple.

And here we have a hidden inverse truth. Instead of just reaching for clothes based on current mood, we can *choose clothes based on the mood we're going for.*

Psychologists call it "dopamine dressing"—choosing fabrics, colors, and fits that intentionally lift our spirits.[9]

Why not?

A few years ago, we threw a "Hope Day" event close to Christmas. It was a Saturday filled with outreach and compassion all over the city. We held one particular portion in a corridor of our campus where we'd recruited beauticians and hairdressers willing to volunteer their skills.

We were in a part of the city near low-income families. People who didn't have a lot of money and many who didn't feel worthy to sit down in a chair and let another human bestow care onto them. I can't express the joy of watching people walk in, beat down in life, then walk out beaming, looking and feeling like a million bucks.

Can you imagine me telling them on the way out, "Wipe that smile off your face! Don't you know it's what's on the inside that counts!"

They experienced our joy in sharing the hope of Jesus, providing food and clothing, praying for them, and speaking life over their souls. But they also saw us care enough to minister to the *dignity of their humanity*, to honor every arena of who they are and communicate that all of them matters.

All of you matters too.

So embrace the coin of your calling. Kill off self-focus. Serve others.

But also.

Splurge on a haircut. Pick out some killer clothes. Use some extra mouthwash (at least for the rest of us). It's amazing sometimes what a trivial, physical act can symbolize and declare.

It's funny. My late southern grandma would even dress up for the grocery store. "Well, they're people too, aren't they?"

You know what, *Mema*, you're right.

So, dress enjoyably. Bring your full expression. Be you.

And don't just dress *for* confidence; dress *with* confidence.

When I entered retail, I wanted to try funky new outfits but felt self-conscious. Then a friend challenged me, "Don't you know fashion is just twenty percent clothes and eighty percent confidence?" I don't know where he pulled that from, but it rings true. (Now, if I ever get so confident that I dress up like a Christmas octopus like people do at awards shows, please pull me aside and have a gentle conversation.)

If you want to try something new but feel lost, recruit a well-dressed friend (a tad younger). Go shopping and buy them lunch. Find things that stretch you a bit but that you feel comfortable in and wear them with confidence as you step into the amazing adventure that is your life.

Or do the Steve Jobs thing and wear the same thing every day. Just as long as it's sharp.

Look, you may obsess over what you wear in an unhealthy way. Or you have a passion for the artistry and beauty of fashion. Or you're like me and you've just loved it since watching Zach Morris steal hearts in his cotton sweaters in

Saved By the Bell.

Or you couldn't care less. Whatever. Do your thing.

All I know is caring how you present yourself isn't superficial; it's a sign of self-respect. An appropriate investment into each aspect of your life is *healthy*. And taking intentionality up a notch could have a greater return on investment than you think, especially if you're reinventing.

If we're to live heroic lives, I say let's pick our capes accordingly.

. . . . .

"MAN LOOKS ON THE OUTSIDE."

Okay, how about this aspect?

The spaces of your life—your car, home, and office.

What are they like? Cluttered or clean?

Uh oh.

We won't spend long here. Mainly because it's painful.

Years ago, at that retail store, a college girl walked in for her shift, saw the messy register, took a deep breath, and declared with a sigh and sass, "I feel like my life is a mess because this *place* is a mess."

Her statement might be more profound than she knew. Honestly, it's the first time I'd considered that kind of effect.

But it's true, isn't it? A clean house can't cure depression. But peace in our outer spaces can elevate at least a little peace in our inner space, even if marginal.

Mm-hmm, some of you uber-clean people are nodding with a smug, thin-lipped smile.

Maybe you're on the other extreme. One step away from being on *Hoarders*. And you need a little kick in the pants. Come on, man.

Personally, I value clean, aesthetic, decluttered spaces. And even though part of me is getting more introverted, I'm an environmental extrovert. I love to be alone in vibey coffee shops, stimulating restaurants, and cities and atmospheres intentionally designed and inspiring.

However, my personal execution doesn't always live up to my values. For much of my life, some spaces will be great, some okay, and at least one so horrible I hope even Jesus can't see it. It's felt like a big, terrible game of whack-a-mole, to be honest.

Maybe you can relate.

Or you feel shame at the topic. I hate that. You're a single mom or dad just trying to keep a thousand plates spinning for crying out loud. The last thing you need is a dollop of guilt spooned onto your anxiety. When you already feel like you're not doing enough, you don't need another reminder you're not doing enough.

So, deep breath. *Part 2* reminder: We don't need to do anything else to be loved or be enough.

But there *are* ways we can get innovative and take daily micro steps toward dignifying the spaces in our lives. And doing so might sweep some added peace and confidence under our need-to-be-dusted doors.

We should start a Marie Kondo tidying club, get some strong espresso, and just begin *somewhere.*

Someone once bought me the book *Make Your Bed.* It's by a famous military commander about how the way you start your day sets the order for the rest, which begins with making your bed. Currently, the book's on my bedside. By my unmade bed.

But small things do matter.

"Peer into someone's car and you peer into their soul."[10]

Honestly, my car *is* the worst offender. One of the most horrifying, embarrassing moments of my life happened in it if you want to know the truth.

A well-known leader decided to invest in our church plant in Lexington, Kentucky. Who knows why. He spent a lot of time with me, though, challenging me, encouraging me, mentoring me. And he was *huge* on excellence.

One day, before I was on staff full time, we met somewhere to talk life and church. After breakfast, he uttered some terrifying words:

"Would you mind giving me a lift back to my hotel?"

"Uhhh . . ."

"Is there a problem?"

"Oh, no, Sir. I, uh . . . well, no. No, Pastor _______, there's no problem. Just one minute."

He looked at me. A knowing look. An amused look, like I was a young puppy who'd just been caught having an accident in his cage.

I hurried over to the passenger side. I'm not just saying this, I promise I'm not, but it was *the worst* my car had ever been.

I tossed pile of clothes after pile of clothes into the back. Empty food bags and Starbucks cups and a dozen items I didn't know existed.

He folded his arms and stood there, grinning. A sadistic, cruel grin.

"This is embarrassing for you, isn't it?"

"Um, yes, Sir," I replied. "Yes, it is."

I followed up, regrettably, with,

"You know, it stinks. My apartment and office are spotless. I just haven't gotten around to my car because I've been traveling . . ."

"Yeah," he started without skipping a beat. "Usually when we have disobedience in one area, we like to point out other areas to make ourselves feel better."

I moaned audibly like an elbow had been shoved in my rib.

"Yes, Sir."

Now he was just a tiger playing with his food.

Anyways. I've gotten better. Mostly.

The point is, we shouldn't neglect the inner corners of our souls. And we shouldn't neglect the unseen spaces of our lives. It all adds up.

It breeds calm and confidence when we experience it. And the discipline of tending the gardens of our life well brings an inner self-respect.

Along with the respect of others.

After all, man looks on the outside.

I can still hear the pushback through the page. "Well, I don't *care* what anyone thinks."

I get that.

However, I'd argue we should care, at least a little, how we represent *our* world to *the* world. Our "testimony," if we want to get churchy about it.

We know in the faith world that the environment a person enters is the sermon before the sermon. Our spaces preach our stories. Our design tells our narratives. And not just to the world *around* us; our environment echoes into the world *inside* us.

That's what I really want you to catch: "Man looking on the outside" includes *you*.

These small, "on the surface" things affect your confidence

perhaps more than you know.

So, yes. God looks at the heart. Focus the lump of your attention there. The outward flows from the inward. It comes last, not first. "Clean the inside of the cup," Jesus says. Don't be a hypocrite cup: All glossy on the outside and filthy on the inside. Cleanse the interior and make it glisten.[11]

But that doesn't mean you should never polish the glass.

. . . . .

DAVID HAD SOME HORRIFIC
moments, no way around it.

None lower than the dark beginning with Bathsheba. Lies, affair, manipulated homicide. For a season, his life a British murder mystery.

When all was said and done, David had to look himself in the mirror, racked with guilt, and watch the child of the affair become gravely ill.

He buried himself in repentance and went on a bender of a fast. He prayed and prayed, lying all night on the ground, refusing to eat. Believing maybe, just maybe, the child might survive.

This went on for a week. Then David heard muttering from those around him. The child had passed, and no one knew how to break the news.

"Just tell me," David said.[12]

They told him.

And braced for his reaction. An explosion of anger? An even greater meltdown? No showering or eating for weeks?

But David did something unexpected.

> "Then David got up from the ground, washed himself, put on lotions, and changed his clothes. He went to the Tabernacle and worshiped the Lord. After that, he Returned to the palace and was served food and ate."[13]

Wait, what?

His attendants were perplexed. For David it was simple. He'd fasted and done what he could. But now that what happened *happened*, what use was there to wallow? He must move forward.

There's so much here.

In fact, it may be jarring to read that if you've just experienced loss. And if you have, I'm so sorry. Depression and grief have a way to sucker punch our confidence and hope. If you're hurting right now, I hope you grieve on your timeline and with loving people surrounding you, knowing you will eventually make it through to life on the other side.

But while David may not have shown us the best way to grieve, I do want to take a page from him when it comes to moving past shame and becoming unstuck.

David had made the worst mistake—scratch that—*mistakes,*

plural of his life. On top of that, the worst possible consequences had descended. And word was out. The Netflix documentary about his toxic leadership would be leaked in weeks. Life's over for Dave.

But he decided it wasn't.

And because of the penitent, humble posture of his heart, God gave more mercy than judgment.

Oh, the consequences would continue. Division in the family, split of the kingdom, regret, chipped confidence in a future season, and more.

But you know what's beautiful?

Before that chapter ends, David does two things. He makes love to Bathsheba, resulting in Solomon, the wisest king that ever lived and from whom the lineage of Jesus would lead. And he returns to battle.

Big sidenote: If we don't process our pain and allow God to heal our wounds, we'll *stop loving* and *stop fighting*.

Even bigger sidenote: God is so good and so big, He can even use our worst moments to fulfill His plan through our lives.

But back to David's *first steps*.

David did the opposite of what I do. Often when life has broken my heart, feelings of sadness cause me to care for myself less, shave less, dress up less. But David chose to move forward powerfully, even externally. Almost as a symbol to himself that,

I will not smell like the past. I will not keep my head down. I will not drag myself in the shame and dirty clothes of yesterday . . .

So, what'd he do?

He got up.

He washed his face.

He changed his clothes.

He entered God's Presence.

He went back to work.

What a simple but powerful strategy for life.

What a simple, powerful strategy for each morning . . .

Get up with purpose. Moisturize that money maker. *Anoint yourself with oil and lotions,* as some translations phrase it. Pick your heroic uniform. Get into God's presence. Head into your day with intention.

How you treat your outside might matter more than you know. Not because the outside matters. Because *you* matter.

I don't know what you've been through. And I don't know what you may be carrying. The truth is, maybe you've been lying in some dirt, guilt, or dysfunction for a while.

Consider this a permission slip.[14]

You can get back up.

You can wash yesterday off your face.

You can exchange the dirty robes of the past for a new wardrobe in Christ decked out with kindness, strength, joy, and courage.

And you can dress to the nines while you're at it.

You can enter God's presence and receive mercy, lifting your chin and letting Him anoint your face with fresh oil.

You can move forward.

I have an undying belief that the future is bright.
—Simon Sinek

I'm ready to face any challenge foolish enough to face me.[1]
—Dwight Schrute, The Office

Creating means living.[2]
—Dejan Stojanovic, The Shape

19)

A Tale of Two Men

A FEW YEARS BACK, I TOOK A BOAT FROM CAPE TOWN TO ROBBEN Island, South Africa's version of Alcatraz. It's been a floating land of banishment for centuries, now famous for a former prisoner.

Nelson Mandela.

A man who changed the world.

His name alone is synonymous with courage, nobility, and sacrifice.

In the early 1940s, as a young lawyer and former boxer, he joined the struggle against apartheid—one of the cruelest, most unjust systems of oppression in modern times. MLK Jr. called it "home to the worst racism in the world."

For his efforts, Mandela was arrested and sentenced to life imprisonment. He served this at Pollsmoor Prison and Victor Verster Prison, and here, where we were about to safely tour and take iPhone pictures on Robben Island.

Upon docking, they bussed us all around, eventually stopping at Section B. I looked into the two-by-two-meter cell where Mandela—the then-imminent President of South Africa and Nobel Laureate—eked out an existence for eighteen years of his life. Away from his kids. Denied permission to attend his own mother's funeral or even that of one of his sons. Twenty-one years unable to hold his wife.

I remember stepping into one of the larger rooms. Our guide, a man in a wheelchair with eyes that seemed to bore into another time, began to speak slowly. When he opened his mouth, ours dropped, all sound and breath sucked away into some black hole. The passion and pain that came out of him got onto me.

He had been Nelson's roommate and close friend.

He regaled us with tales of Nelson's brilliance, his lawyerly wit that infuriated the guards. His integrity and discipline, all his daily push-ups. "Is *this* many against the law?" he'd tease the prison wards when they got nervous. He told sad tales of the torture and racism inside these chipped walls. Tales of Mandela finally negotiating the guards into a cot to sleep on instead of a cold floor. But when he realized they would only give *him* a cot, he refused. He'd sleep on the floor until *everyone* could have a cot. Throughout his life, even in prison, Mandela didn't just advocate for the rights of himself or even Black people, but all people.

I felt the immensity of this room. I felt the self-mastery these men developed in themselves. I felt the pain and heroism.

He showed us all around and described the fateful day. How after twenty-seven years, the fax came—Mandela was to be free.

It was funny to hear his old roommate's side, how slow and

unrushed Mandela was the day he received the news. They wanted to whisk him away to give an address to the nation. But he lingered, wanting time to collect his thoughts. In the end, he consented to leave the next day, and together, before he left to speak to the world, he and his jailer shared a glass of whiskey.

It's no exaggeration to say this speech would—and did—affect the course of the nation. For three decades, many Black people held him as a symbol of hope for their emancipation. Many white people feared he would unleash violent rhetoric that would incite civil war.[3]

What would he say?

You have to wonder . . . what would *you* say? What would *your* next words be?

After your life has been ripped from you. After decades of torture and unjust treatment and the murder of friends and family. With power shifting your way, and the nation on tiptoe to hear your every syllable.

Will you let out a roar of retribution and divisiveness?

With a raucous crowd of over 100,000 gathered and the world watching, he opened his mouth and started with,

> ". . . I greet you all in the name of peace, democracy and freedom. I stand before you not as a prophet, but as a humble servant . . ."

From his lips, flowing from his heart, poured words of hope and healing.

He didn't speak as an embittered victim. He spoke as a "wounded healer."

He cast a vision worth creating. One of equality and prosperity. And then together, the country created that dream.

Sure enough, he went on to lead peaceful talks to end apartheid in South Africa and turn it into a nonracial democracy. Through his example, democracy even began to spread across the whole continent.

Before we left the island, they walked us over, down below the cliffs, to a rock pile at the lime quarry. An unimpressive, nondescript hill of rocks. A hill that's reached into history like the piles of rocks God told His people to build to remember His faithful acts in the time of Moses.

After Mandela's release, a reunion of sorts took place as he and other former prisoners returned to Robbin Island. They discussed and reminisced. Then they all walked to this clearing, grabbed stones, and dropped them here to memorialize their time.

The way I look at it, stones had been thrown at them their whole life. And now they would decide—do they spend the rest of their lives throwing stones back? Or do they use those stones to build a different future?

. . . . .

I N T H E S A M E W A Y S O U T H A F R I C A
waited breathlessly for Mandela's words when he emerged from exile, Israel waited for David's words.

David had also waited a long time to lead his nation. Fifteen years, in fact. He'd spent the last seven years living as a fugitive in a small countryside, unable to move freely in the very nation he was destined to reign. And he'd spent thirteen years of his life hunted down by Saul, narrowly avoiding assassination attempts.

Like Mandela, his day eventually arrived. The stars fell into place, clearing the way for him to rise to power.

And like Mandela's, the nation awaited his words.

To set the stage, David had left his stronghold and was out at battle, unleashing a devastating victory against the Amalekites.

Which is striking to me.

David kept fighting even when he was a fugitive.

Just as an aside . . . I wonder how many of us are waiting for a role, a title, acknowledgment, or permission to finally start living the kind of life and fighting the kind of battles that matter?

David did not.

Upon returning from battle, he spent time in Ziklag. A couple of days in, a soldier pulled up breathless, bringing him the evening report.

Saul had been killed.

David would now assume the throne.

What will he say? What speech will he give? What actions will he take?

Finally vindicated, would he, as kings did, hunt down all of Saul's lineage, erasing any potential threat of uprising? Would he give a victorious speech about how justice finally came to evil, jealous, murderous Saul?

His reaction:

> "David and his men tore their clothes in sorrow when they heard the news . . ."[4]

Are we reading this correctly?

> ". . .They mourned and wept and fasted all day for Saul and his son Jonathan, and for the Lord's army and the nation of Israel, because they had died by the sword that day."[5]

Hmm.

And then David executed the soldier who had killed Saul and brought the news.

And then,

> ". . . David composed a funeral song for Saul and Jonathan, and he commanded that it be taught to the people of Judah . . ."[6]

And *then* . . .

David found anyone left of Saul's family to whom he could bless and show kindness.

What's going on here?

What's going on here is David is a better man than me. His every bone was soaked in honor. As I've heard it said, "David was a servant when he was a shepherd, a servant when he was a warrior, and a servant when he was a king."[7]

David had spent thirteen years dodging spears, and now that he was in power, he had to decide . . . Do I throw them back?

This is why what we do with our spirit and "in-between seasons" matters.

Whatever we build *inside* us will eventually become what we build *around* us. Whatever paintbox we let form inside will determine the colors we paint with going forward, be they dark or light.

David never let the spears get inside him. He didn't let hate, fear, and bitterness take hold in his soul. He kept all that loamy soil inside fertile with honor, love, courage, hope, and the presence of God. And all that became the material he used to create the next four decades.

Like Mandela and David, we each decide what we do with the spears and stones life and people have thrown at us. Will we throw them back? Or will we create something beautiful?

. . . . .

AS WE ESCAPE *INSECURITY*,

And grow a healthy *identity*,

And develop *confidence*,

We get to decide . . .

What will we spend our energy building? What kind of future will we construct?

We've talked David and Saul's differences. Their motives. Their reactions to failure. The different coins they lived from. How David had an incredible sense of destiny and Saul just a messy sense of self. How David led as a shepherd, Saul mainly a supervisor.

But as we get close to the bone in our time together, our second and third cups of coffee rumbling in our stomachs, I'd like to lay out one last difference on the table.

Because of what was inside them,

Saul *contained*.

David *created*.

Because Saul lived in insecurity, he spent his time merely *containing*—defending, excusing, comparing, guarding, worrying.

Because David lived in confidence, he spent his time *creating*—designing, crafting, risking, building, dreaming.

As we break insecurity and rise in confidence, we must choose what we do with our freedom. We must determine what we build.

And honestly, in Saul's life, we don't see him build much of anything.

He *secured* some good for his nation, we conceded that. But the primary thing I remember him *creating* is that statue of himself. When you live in scarcity, you live in self-service. Saul was so busy *comparing* that he was rarely *creating*.

It reminds me of Paul's strange words to his friends in Corinth:

> ". . .While there is jealousy and strife among you, are you not of the flesh and behaving only in a human way? For when one says, 'I follow Paul,' and another, 'I follow Apollos,' are you not being merely human? . . . According to the grace of God given to me, like a skilled master builder I laid a foundation . . ."
> (1Corinthians 3.3, 10 ESV)

I love that phrase, "Are you not being merely human?"

When we compare, we're barely human.

When we create, we're being like God.

God didn't put you on the earth to compare; He put you on the earth to create.

Paul said, as for me, like a "skilled master builder . . ."

I don't know if you've ever considered this truth, but *God put you on this earth to build something meaningful.*

That church planter who punched me in the gut over lunch with his "orphan spirit" comment? He said something else that day I haven't forgotten . . .

"A spirit of self-preservation will never give birth to something new."

When we're closed in, defensive posture, protecting and comparing, our hands aren't free for paint brushes and pens to lean forward in joy and create.

You can't construct a house or design a blueprint with folded arms.

You can't create with a contracted spirit.

But it's what we were made to do.

Erwin McManus has famously said:

"We are both works of art and artists at work. We were created to create and imagined to imagine."[8]

Perhaps the greatest tragedy of Saul's life wasn't in the wrongs that he *did* but in the wasted potential of all the good that he *didn't*.

Even in David's life, we see both the beauty of when he was creating for others and the disaster of when he was indulging himself.

We rushed briefly past his painful dark moment last chapter. The affair and subsequent murder. But the context of that adulterous scene opens ominously:

> "In the spring . . . when kings normally go out to war . . . David stayed behind . . ."[9]

David was supposed to be out fighting and advancing. But he

stayed home to chill. And then saw a woman bathing from his rooftop. And then decided to give a second glance. And then got a little curious and started asking about her . . .

You know the old wisdom that nothing good ever happens after midnight?

Same here. Nothing good ever comes when you're idle instead of intentional. Nothing good happens when you avoid responsibility and let your mind wander into trouble.

David was supposed to be on the battleground but he chose the playground. And invited a war into his soul.

And here's the thing. My whole life, whenever I read this, I pictured David as a young, immature man making a horrible but youthful mistake. Great guy but shouldn't have gone to Panama City for spring break, that kind of thing.

Except that isn't true.

When David, King David, wise David, man after God's own heart David, made this mistake, he was around *fifty years old*.

In a season of apathy, David gave into a moment of weakness. He decided to indulge himself instead of work and create. Precisely what Paul warns us not to do.

> "Don't use your freedom to indulge the flesh; rather serve one another humbly in love."[10]

There is a positive inverse principle: One of the best ways to beat your *cravings* is to spend your life *creating*.

When you get busy doing good, serving others, and creating

the future, you run out of time for lesser things. Especially stupid or destructive things.

Serve one another in love.

This is the posture of freedom, power, and confidence.

Fortunately, aside from some grave mistakes, David spent *most* of his life creating.

Unlike Saul, who lived with clenched fists, David lived open and forward. And his humble, confident posture before God propelled him to build masterpieces with his life.

Music. Poetry. Combat techniques. Worship anthems. Teams of fiercely loyal leaders. Protection for Israel. Strategies to bring God's Presence back to Israel through the Ark of the Covenant.

The more he built, the more he expanded. All the way to his Sistine Chapel. His *pièce de résistance.*

David decided He wanted to create a house for God.

Well. That's ambitious.

I've heard old, romantic lores of men building castles for their muse. But a house for the One who made the known universe? That's David for you.

Saul built himself a house of cards, but David said,

> "Everyone else has a house. But God has no temple, no place to dwell. I want to build this . . ."[11]

David wasn't so small and self-focused that he wasted his life merely building his own house. He wanted to give his life building God's house.

We must see this principle of measure: The largeness we allow inside our souls will become the largeness we build with our lives.

. . . . .

CONFIDENCE ISN'T JUST A POWER that helps you become free; it's a power that helps you build a future.

A spirit of confidence multiplies the potential inside of you instead of just managing the pain inside of you. This is where we begin to soar. This is where fire begins to fill up our eyes.

St. Ignatius once said, "The glory of God is man fully alive."[12]

I can tell you, at least for me, the moments I'm fully alive are the moments I'm creating. A friend from across the country called last year as I really began to dive into this book. Somewhere along the way, it got brought up.

"I can always tell when you're writing," he said. "I can hear it in your voice."

You and I were born to imagine, craft, and build.

So what will it be? That looks different for all of us, of course.

It could be as grandiose as a new business or as gritty as using our pain to serve others who have suffered like us in loss or addiction. It could be enlarging the tent of our hospitality if we're empty nesters or new homeowners, creating space for the lonely and confused.

For business leaders it might be to make money but with purpose attached. Moving past mere income to a vision of "I'm creating a future. I'm creating legacy for my great-grandchildren. I'm creating wealth to fund God's kingdom, be ridiculously generous, fuel my passions, provide jobs, and create memorable experiences with people."

Sometimes for me it, ethereal as it may sound, it means creating space inside my own soul—a decluttering of disappointment and fear. A permission to dream again. To open the windows inside, do some spring cleaning, and let imagination out of its fencing.

To clear out cynicism and unforgiveness and create in my soul the possibility of new love. To forge new space inside my mind to learn and explore or even broaden my life for more people.

I think of my parents. They've lived beautiful, simple, consistent lives where they've educated the next generation by being elementary and high school teachers. They've experienced wonderful things. And, perhaps without ever thinking of it this way, they created a home of spacious love and hope, where people like me and my sister—both admittedly touched with a dab of madness—have felt the permission and confidence to dream wildly about our lives.

Our every choice and our very lives—all a creative act. Let's make it stunning.

. . . . .

HERE'S WHAT I WANT YOU TO KNOW.

You begin to create confidence as you begin to create the future.

And your soul comes alive in the process.

And here's what's *really* exciting.

Many of you, as you begin to imagine a new future, are going to shatter paradigms holding other people captive.

In fact, quick trivia. I'm going to throw out four names and see if you can tell me who they are:

Lahmi. Ishbi-Benob. Sippai. Exadactylus.

Any guesses?

Those were Goliath's *brothers.*

And they were *also* defeated.

Funny that we never hear of them. Especially since all of them were even *bigger* and *taller* than Goliath. No kidding. One of them even had six fingers on each hand.

See, from what we know, David was the first mortal to defeat a giant. But he wouldn't be the last. After him, it became the norm.

When you create a new future, you break glass ceilings.

Some of you are going to break ceilings and redefine what's possible for your family, your race, your gender, your profession. You're going to be the first person out of your family line to graduate college, stay married, buy a house, or break that addictive pattern. You will show what can be accomplished. You will show your children a new path. You will show people at your work a new way to be human.

. . . . .

THE FUTURE IS OUR CANVAS.

Will we dream with God again despite failure and pain?

Back to that phrase used to describe Mandela: "wounded healer."

I love that distinguishment. I love that choice. We can use our wounds to remain victims. Or we can use our wounds to become healers.

Even self-inflicted wounds.

In my first book, *Hope for the Wilderness: Through All the Pain to All the Promise*, I described a few difficult seasons for me personally, including a rather shameful, volitional one involving heartbreak and handcuffs.

It always shocks people when they find out I never intended to put that story in the book. Part of the reason at the time was wisdom. The book was a five-year journey, and that part of my story was still fresh as I began to put ink on paper. But also, the shame of it simply made me cringe.

But I *knew* and *felt* something was missing the closer I got to submission and publishing. A few wise people began to nudge me that it was time to divulge that part of my story. Peer reviewers said it was obvious something was missing, something integral to the story arc. And then, without any subtlety whatsoever, my Pastor looked at me one day and said, "You know you have to put that in the book, right?"

I stood there and stared at him for a long, uncomfortable time, extremely irritated.

That Friday, I wrote the chapter faster than I've dribbled off any chapter before or since and told myself, *I will never print this, but just in case . . .*

Then, I e-mailed it to my friend, Amanda, who knew my story, saying, "This isn't going in the book, but just read it and give me your thoughts."

An hour later, I received a novella of a text. She'd been weeping. Though she's walked with God for years and is in ministry herself, a few pages into the chapter, she'd experienced her most intense encounter with God's presence in a long time.

And then—I don't know how to describe it—she said she saw something. Something undeniable. A vision of sorts. An image of countless people walking with their heads down in shame, but then reading that chapter, rain falling from the sky and wiping away the mud and shame from their faces, their heads lifting back up in healing and confidence.

I texted back.

"So . . . are you *also* saying I have to put it in?"

Again, I was irritated.

But as I write, I can tell you her words became life. I can't tell you how many people have come out of the hills and said in essence, "Me too." How many people—by allowing my stupidity and failures to become a bridge—have told me through tears how God has used my stumbling words and life stories to heal their hearts and change their lives.

We can use our wounds to stay stuck in the past, or we can use our wounds to paint new colors for the days ahead. Days where we take responsibility for the past so we can take ownership of the future. Days where our pain turns into purpose.

. . . . .

GOD'S REACTION TO DAVID'S request was interesting.

He seemed to get a little snarky. He asked David when He had ever asked anyone to build Him a residence made of wood.

It's a solid question.

After giving David some humbling perspective, He told David there *would* be a temple but that *he* wouldn't build it. David's hands were too bloody with war to build such a house. His son, Solomon, would be the one to complete it.

But then God flipped the script in the conversation.

Using the same Hebrew word for house, "bayat," God said that even though God wasn't going to allow David to build a house for him, God was going to build a house for David.

He would build a legacy and lineage through him. One day,

through the "house of David," a Messiah would come. A Man who would use His scars to save us. The ultimate "wounded Healer."

Isn't God the most masterful storyteller?

Doesn't it breathe wind into your sails to think of the alchemy God can weave even out of our worst pain and mistakes?

So. As you escape the lies of insecurity, develop your identity, and build the structures of functional confidence into your life . . .

I hope you begin to dream again.

But I also hope your dreams are bigger than you.

I hope your dreams make the world a better place. I hope your dreams make more space and life for people. I hope your dreams partner to see God's dreams come to pass on earth.

And as you do . . .

Don't be too surprised . . .

When God flips the script.

That as you build His House, He builds *your* house.

That as you advance His dreams, He exceeds *your* dreams.

And in the process, He might just do more than you could have ever anticipated in your wildest thoughts or hopes.

Part 3 // Reflection

ASSESSMENT

What stood out? How would you assess the three areas of character in your life – integrity, humility, and courage? How about your discipline, competence, or how you carry yourself? Are you creating the future or holding on to the past?

____

____

____

____

____

____

____

APPLICATION

What steps can you take this month, this week, and today? Who can you call and what systems can you implement to keep you accountable?

You are the instrument, not the gift.
—Brooke Lighterwood

Strength is for service, not status.[1]
—Paul

Now I see all that I have. Oh, I've got my confidence back.[2]
—Elevation Worship ("More Than Able")

PROLOGUE

Give It Away

IN THE SECOND CHAPTER, I TOLD YOU a story about a negative word spoken over me that stuck. That I had a horrible nose. My sophomore year, someone else spoke a word that stuck. But this word didn't steal self-esteem; it pumped liquid confidence into it.

French class, second period. Mrs. Girardeau. One day, I asked permission to slip out for water from the hallway fountain. She responded in classic French witticisms of which I couldn't comprehend a word. I muttered something witty in reply. She laughed and I smiled. When I smiled, she looked at me seriously, stopped me with her finger in the air and said, "Russ, you have the most beautiful smile. Don't ever lose it."

I blushed at the compliment and went outside for water. But somehow her words watered my spirit. I never forgot them. I'm still not sure why they meant so much. But once a year, something will happen, or I'll go through a season where my smile begins to fade, and I'll remember her words. And obey them.

That is the power of encouragement. The power of *giving* confidence.

Of course, there are more significant examples. One kind

moment has stopped people from ending their lives. One small gesture has redirected someone from a self-destructive path. One affirmation in youth has rocket-fueled the world's greatest writers, artists, and athletes. As Bob Goff once said, "Words don't just shape us; they launch us."

And here's what I'm getting at. Whether through words or actions, the greatest thing about developing more confidence is that *we get to give it away*. It's kind of like money in that way. The healthiest thing to do is spend it on others.

In fact, if you're anything like me, sometimes I overthink or feel guilty when I experience confidence. But the litmus test is simple: Am I focusing more on me or more on others? I've noticed when it's healthy confidence, I actually become *less* fixated on myself and have more energy to pour out. It's how I can know whether I'm *full in soul* or just *full of myself*.

And, thankfully, you don't have to *feel* full and confident in order to give it away. In fact, when you're feeling low and navel-gazing for too long, one of the best things you can do is step out and lift up someone else. There's almost no better antidote to getting out of your head than to get outside it by *serving other people*. And that's when we experience the principle Solomon laid out:

"Those who refresh others will themselves be refreshed."[3]

It's ironic and powerful.

See, a beautiful life isn't just a life where we *have* confidence; it's one where we *give* confidence. So, as you grow into a person of confidence, can I offer this final charge?

Be someone who *imparts* it.

Let's use our words to build others up, to speak life into them. Let's be less sarcastic and biting. Let's make it a habit to smile when people approach. Let's get creative in telling others how good they look, how good a job they're doing, how much they mean. Let's say *thank you* and *I'm sorry* often. Let's look for the lonely and overlooked, build into people's self-belief, and give away our platforms so others can flourish.

When we do these things, life becomes fun. It just does.

It's an irony, perhaps: If you want a confidence that soars, live a life that serves.

Full circle to David, don't forget the words etched over his life's biography thousands of years after he passed:

> "When David had *served* God's purpose in his own
> generation . . ."[4]

David refused to live from the coin of self. He lived from the coin of calling. He lived a life of service.

Thousands of years later, a Man from David's lineage did the same.

God, wrapped in human flesh, Jesus, stepped out of eternity and into the mess of time and humanity.

He didn't come to impress, prove, or defend. He stayed silent and secure against accusation, took the humble, high road against betrayal and hostility, and when He stepped into a room as the most important person there, He grabbed a towel, got on his knees, and began washing people's filthy feet.

Paul expanded on this in his letter to his friends at Philippi when he said that Jesus,

> "Who, being in very nature God, did not consider equality
> with God something to be used to his own advantage;
> rather, he made himself nothing by taking the very nature
> of a servant, being made in human likeness. And being
> found in appearance as a man, he humbled himself by
> becoming obedient to death—even death on a cross!"[5]

The result?

> "Therefore God exalted him to the highest place and gave
> him the name that is above every name, that at the name
> of Jesus every knee should bow, in heaven and on earth
> and under the earth, and every tongue acknowledge that
> Jesus Christ is Lord, to the glory of God the Father."[6]

Paul now encourages us to do the same:

> "Therefore, humble yourselves under the mighty hand of
> God, that He may exalt you in due time."[6]

It may sound counterintuitive to the American way, but if you
want to be great? If you want to soar in confidence? Don't
reach for titles; reach for towels. Serve your way into the stars.

I want you to know I'm rooting you on. I'm not naïve enough
to think just because you read this book, all your insecurities
have melted away and your confidence is eagle-soaring 24/7.

But I do hope healing and courage have seeped into you. I do
hope there's been some practical and spiritual lightbulbs go off.
I do hope it's revealed steps for you to take on the journey to
regain your confidence.

By the way, long shot, but . . . Do you still have that coin? If so, take it out.

Hold it. Stare at it. And decide: What coin will you live from?

Will you use your past and pain to justify a life of self-focus? Or will you live fully, creating a future so large that people find healing, strength, and confidence inside the walls?

In an odd sense, the spirit of Saul will always call, always whisper. But so will the spirit of David.

And, if we listen carefully, so will the Spirit of David's great—to the 28th degree—grandson who bore agony deeper than any man ever has. A Man who created an entirely new paradigm from His pain. A man who is still changing the world through His scars.

I just want you to know as we end this cup of coffee together, trite as it may sound:

You are doing so much better than you think. Whatever baggage you have, God can heal it. Whatever hang-ups you have, with God's help, you can grow through it. You are more valuable and loved than you've dared imagine. And you have more inside you and for you than you've ever let yourself hope or dream.

Grab ahold of this like a rope on a cliff: God is with you. God is in you. God is for you.

So, as the writer of Hebrews said, "Do not throw away your confidence."[8]

In it is great reward. It will open the door to the life you were meant to live.

I'm confident about it.

> "May God our Father himself and our Master Jesus clear
> the road to you! And may the Master pour on the love so
> it fills your lives and splashes over on everyone around
> you, just as it does from us to you. May you be infused
> with strength and purity, filled with confidence in the
> presence of God our Father when our Master Jesus arrives
> with all his followers."

(1 Thessalonians 3.11–13 MSG)

Dear Reader

Thank you. I'm so grateful. It's meaningful to me that you would purchase this book and take the time to read these words. To me, it's a shared experience. I hope it's had an impact.

If the content was helpful and you believe it could serve others, let's get the message out. It'd mean the world to me and could change the world for someone else.

Here are three ways:

1. Leave an Amazon review. This weirdly makes a big difference.

2. Post a paragraph/line from the book that stood out on Instagram with a purchase link to the book and tag me @mooreruss.

3. Buy a second book and give it to someone it would encourage.

Believe it or not, those three simple steps go a long way.

I'm convinced a healthy, humbly confident world is a better world.

Grateful,
Russ

Acknowledgments

I am indebted so much to so many.

My parents. Your unconditional love and ardent support gave me an unfair starting place and foundation for confidence. I hit the lottery with you two.

My friends. I often think of Lewis's words from *The Four Loves* after waxing poetic about friendship . . . "Life—natural life—has no better gift to give. Who could have deserved it?" I for one do not. You all enrich my life.

My book crew. The peer review team for their tireless review— Alana, Zach, Tim, Sara, Chloe, Codi. Editors from Gatekeeper Press, you were terrific. Dr. Wes, Kay, and Kim, thank you for your clinical oversight as psychologists and counselors. Thank you, Logan, for the gracious foreword and all those kind enough to write endorsements. And sheer gratitude for my custom creative team—Tucker, Christi, Logan, Seth, Hannah, and others—you are rare talents.

My faith community. X Church—you are my people. You allow me to both serve you and be part of you. Thank you for letting me be me and for teaching and molding me while allowing me to share any gems I find along the way. And Pastor Tim, thank you for the generous trust you give me, for opportunities to lead and teach and share, not to mention for the rare Pastor and friend you are.

Jesus. Your love has changed my life. I don't know who I am or where I'd be apart from You. And I don't want to. I can't wait to be in your immediate presence, healed and unashamed. No longer naked. Confident.

And you. For taking time to read my words. I hope this humble offering has brought nourishment and spice. Life is nothing if not a meaningful journey to share together. Thanks for having coffee with me. Next one's on me.

About the Author

Russ is a pastor at X Church in Columbus, Ohio, where he leads, teaches, writes, and hosts a weekly podcast. He is also the best-selling author of HOPE FOR THE WILDERNESS: Through all the Pain to All the Promise.

He loves to travel, discuss culture and life and philosophy, try foods he can't pronounce and take long walks around German Village.

You can connect with him on Instagram at @mooreruss or check out his website - www.russmoore.co to check out messages, podcasts, and blogs or book him to speak.

Notes

PREFACE
1.Hebrews 10.35.
2. 1 Samuel 13.14.

PART 1 PRELUDE
1. Should be obvious, but I'm taking creative liberties in the preludes.

CHAPTER 1
1. Wilkerson Jr., Rich. *"The Secret to a Confident Life."* Published by WaterBrook, 2017.
2. Deuteronomy 31.6 MSG.
3. Goff, Bob. *"Love Does: Discover a Secretly Incredible Life in an Ordinary World."* Published by Thomas Nelson, 2012.
4. This is what I remember from over twenty years ago. I confess I did not bother school officials for old numbers to cross these t's.
5. Same as above.
6. For any theological purists, I want to clarify I am not projecting fault onto God or how He made us. He's a perfect Potter and we're fearfully and wonderfully made. I'm simply writing honestly from the POV of the clay and how we often *feel.*
7. Avett Brothers, *"I and Love and You."* Album: *I and Love and You, 2009.*
8. 1 Samuel 8.
9. This scene and its verses from 1 Samuel 9.
10. 1 Samuel 9.21.
11. 2 Samuel 7.18.
12. 1 Samuel 10.1.
13. 1 Samuel 10.22.

CHAPTER 2
1. Jay Shetty, *Think Like a Monk: Train Your Mind for Peace and Purpose Every Day* (New York: Gallery Books, 2020), p. 142.
2. Romans 12.5 MSG.
3. Angels & Airwaves, "Saturday Love". *Love: Part Two,* To The Stars Records, 2011.
4. 1 Samuel 18.6.
5. This whole next scene is all taken from 1 Samuel 18.
6. 2 Corinthians 10.12 NKJV.
7. Information gleaned from https://www.investopedia.com/terms/z/zero-sumgame.
8. *The Shallows* by Nicholas Carr, *Together Alone* by Sherry Turkle, and *Coddling of the American Mind* by Greg Lukianoff and Jonathan Haidt.
9. "The Social Dilemma" on Netflix.
10. Following information taken from https://mitsloan.mit.edu/ideas-made-to-matter/study-social-media-use-linked-to-decline-mental-health .

11. "When We Were Young" music festival. You should go!

12. David Copperfield and David Blaine. The best!

13. *WSJ* Article, "Stop Telling Everyone What You Do for a Living" (4.10.2023) by Rachel Feintzeig.

CHAPTER 3

1.William Penn, *Some Fruits of Solitude* (Philadelphia: William Penn Press, 1709), 45.

2. Bill Johnson, Senior Leader of Bethel Church, Redding, CA.

3. Gary Allan, "Every Storm (Runs Out of Rain)," *Set You Free* (MCA Nashville, 2013).

4. Lawrence Durrell, *Justine* (London: Faber & Faber, 1957), 72.

5. Proverbs 27.4 NLT.

6. ESV.

7. *The Count of Monte Cristo*, directed by Kevin Reynolds (Walt Disney Pictures, 2002), Adaptation from the eponymous novel by Alexandre Dumas serialized between 1844-1846. I understand for the purists that the book came out first, so the baby metaphor is backwards.

8. Andy Stanley, *Enemies of the Heart* (Atlanta: Multnomah Books, 2010), 102.

9. 1 Samuel 18.8-9.

10. The term "ASMR" stands for Autonomous Sensory Meridian Response, a tingling sensation often experienced in response to certain sounds, popular in social media and YouTube.

11. While this is not a new concept, I want to give credit to the teachings of Erwin McManus for really drilling this into me. I need to give him *a lot* of credit for his impact on my thinking.

12. Goethe, Johann Wolfgang von. *Maxims and Reflections*. Translated by Elisabeth Stopp. London: Penguin Classics, 1998, p. 35.

13. Philippians 4.8.

14. Rauch, Steve. *Hugology: The Study of Hugs*. Self-published, 2021.

15. Speaking of Erwin McManus… This is his story and one he has told a few different times on the Battle Ready / Mind Shift podcast.

16. Mark 9.40, paraphrase.

CHAPTER 4

1. Lewis, C. S. *A Grief Observed*. New York: HarperCollins, 1961.

2. Stroup, Amy. "As Long as You're with Me." *The Other Side of Love Sessions*, Milkglass Creative, 2015.

3. In conversation with my former pastor and mentor.

4. McConaughey, Matthew. Interview by Ed Mylett. *The Ed Mylett Show*. Podcast audio, January 18, 2021.

5. Ecclesiasts 1.14.

6. 1 Samuel 10.22.

7. 1 Samuel 10.22 NLT.

8. 1 Samuel 9.1.

9.1 Samuel 10.16 (*Interestingly, he didn't tell his uncle *everything*…).

10. TLB.

11. *Emotionally Healthy Spirituality* by Pete Scazzero, *The Gift of Being Yourself* by Richard

Rhor, *The Burden is Light* by Jon Tyson, *Changes that Heal* by Dr. Henry Cloud, *Ordering Your Private World* by Gordon MacDonald.

12. A great analogy from Donald Miller in *Father Fiction*.

13. Dr. Wes Beavis taught me this one.

14. 2 Chronicles 25 MSG is one example of this simple phrase.

15. Lamentations 2.19 NLT.

CHAPTER 5

1. Ed Mylett, *The Ed Mylett Show* podcast, episode titled "The Power of Your Inner Circle," (June 23, 2022).

2. Luke 16 MSG.

3. Lauv, "Modern Loneliness," ~how i'm feeling (BMG Rights Management, 2020).

4. https://www.history.com/news/napoleon-bonaparte-downfall-reasons-personality-traits

5. https://reasonabletheology.org/napoleon-bonapartes-view-of-jesus/.

6. 1 Samuel 14.

7. 1 Samuel 13 NLT.

8. 1 Samuel 15 MSG.

9. 1 Samuel 15.27-28 paraphrase.

CHAPTER 6

1. Gaslight Anthem, "Positive Charge." *History Books*, Rich Mahogany Recordings, 2023.

2. John 12.43.

3. Thoreau, Henry David. *Walden; or, Life in the Woods*. Boston: Ticknor and Fields, 1854, p. 224.

4. Commonly attributed to Lewis, though not in his specific works. The spirit of it is from *Mere Christianity*. It's very possible the quote was taken from a lecture or letter.

5. Forbidden census taking, ego-bruised vengeance, affair, murder…

6. 1 Samuel 15.30.

7. My summation/paraphrase of Psalm 51.10-11.

8. 1 Samuel 17.

9. Acts 13.36.

10. 2 Chronicles 20.15.

11. Romans 11.29.

12. Hebrews 10.35.

13. Psalm 63.8 NKJV.

14. Psalm 42.1.

15. Jeremiah 1.6.

16. Exodus 4.10.

17. Isaiah 6.5.

18. Genesis 17.17.

19. I heard Steven Furtick say something similar at *Inside Elevation* 2017.

PART 2 PRELUDE

NA

CHAPTER 7

1. Erwin McManus' message, "A Place Called Sent."

2.Isaiah 24.5-6 MSG.

3. Fleetwood Mac, "Landslide," *Fleetwood Mac* (London: Reprise Records, 1975).

4. I had to drop an Easter egg in here for Mandy Moore, who I mentioned in my first.

5. Donald Miller, *Searching for God Knows What* (Nashville: Thomas Nelson, 2004), 95–97.

6. Donald Miller's summary of the report in the same section as above.

7. The book I'm referring to here is *Wild at Heart* by John Eldredge. People seem to have visceral reactions to this book, good or bad, some even being triggered by it in a pretty harmful way. Personally, I tend to find most of Eldredge's newest works very helpful in dealing with the soul. Regardless, what I remember—and found helpful—from this book centered around father wounds, not gender roles.

8. In addition to several males, I submitted this book in advance to seven females and three clinical psychologists, all varying ages and beliefs and places in life in hopes for the most helpful representation, balance, insight, and benefit. Having said that, as mentioned in the chapter, I know gender is a very controversial subject. My aim is only to help advance the conversation, not hurt it. Grace requested.

9. *Embodied* by Preston Sprinkle, *Love Thy Body* and *The Toxic War on Masculinity* by Nancy Pearcey, *The Intentional Father* by Jon Tyson.

10. www.afathersplace.org/why-it-matters/fathers/.

11. 1 Corinthians 6 MSG.

12. Oxygen tank illustration, Francis and Lisa Chan teaching on relationships.

13. Phillips, Michael. *A God to Call Father*. Minneapolis: Bethany House Publishers, 1995.

14. Johnson, S. M., & Coan, J. A. "The Role of Oxytocin in the Therapeutic Effects of Loving Relationships." *Journal of Neuropsychiatry and Clinical Neurosciences*, vol. 24, no. 4, 2012, pp. 413-419. Or for insights on relational dynamics and neuroplasticity, see Dan Siegel, *The Interpersonal Neurobiology of Trauma* (New York: Norton & Company, 2006). (These are just two that explore this. Many other articles and books elaborate on and unpack this idea).

CHAPTER 8

1. McConaughey, Matthew, *The Ed Mylett Show* podcast.

2. Isaiah 55.1 NLT.

3. Lewis, Quinn. "Everyone But Me." *Everyone But Me - Single*, Self-released, 2018. John 15.5 ESV.

4. John 15.5 NLT.

5. Nieuwhof, Carey. *The Carey Nieuwhof Leadership Podcast*, circa 2020.

6. https://www.dripdrop.com/blog/health-wellness/6-dehydration-facts-may-surprise.

7. Jeremiah 2.13.

8. John 4.10 MSG.

9. John 4.13-14 MSG.

10. There is a lot of complexity and nuance to this story. I tried to nuance that dysfunctional love *may* have been the issue. It's also just as possible from the context of this sexist society that she was victimized by the system. Either way, she needed real love

and healing.

11. John 4.11 MSG.

12. https://www.businessinsider.com/us-surgeon-general-compares-loneliness-epidemic-to-smoking-2023-5#:~:text=A%20report%20from%20US%20Surgeon,a%20dozen%20cigarettes%20a%20day.

13. Philippians 2.7.

14. Matthew 3.16.

15. Matthew 3.17.

16. Matthew 11.28,30.

17. Ephesians 1.6 NKJV.

18. Chandler, Matt quote.

19. *Hitch*. Columbia Pictures, 2005.

20. Angels & Airwaves. "Sirens." *I-Empire*, Geffen Records, 2007.

21. John 14.18.

22. Romans 8.15-17 NLT.

23. Hebrews 12.1.

24. Ephesians 3.14,18 NLT.

CHAPTER 9

1. "Hawn, Goldie. *The First Time I Was Single*. Penguin Books, 2022.

2. *Stranger Things*. Created by the Duffer Brothers. Netflix, 2022.

3. Ackerman, Gary. *Identity Crisis: The Search for Meaning in a Modern World*. HarperCollins, 2019.

4. Directed by Frank Darabont. Warner Bros., 2001.

5. I want to again credit Erwin McManus and several Arena sessions in which he taught on this.

6. Hamp, Bob. *Think Differently, Live Differently: Keys to Developing a New Mindset*. Franklin, TN: Nelson Books, 2010.

7. Proverbs 23.7.

8. Proverbs 18.21.

9. https://thewellnessenterprise.com/emoto/.

10. The "thin out the noise" concept and juxtaposition is a known concept, but while writing this book, the phrasing and approach of this was influenced by an incredible book by Strahan Coleman. *Beholding: Deepening Our Experience in God*. Colorado Springs: David C Cook, 2023.

11. Lloyd-Jones, Martyn. *Spiritual Depression: Its Causes and Cure*. Grand Rapids: Eerdmans, 1965.

CHAPTER 10

1. As quoted in *Thelonious Monk: The Life and Times of an American Original* by Robin D.G. Kelley. New York: Free Press, 2009.

2. Psalm 119:41 MSG.

3. This quote is derived from his work on performance and identity, specifically from his book *The Alter Ego Effect: The Power of Secret Identities to Transform Your Life*.

4. *The Faculty*. Directed by Robert Rodriguez, 1998.

5. Train. "Drops of Jupiter." *Drops of Jupiter*, Columbia Records, 2001.

6. Arena Conference, Los Angeles, California, 2023.

7. 1 Samuel 17.39.

8. Netflix Show: *All the Light We Cannot See*: All the Light We Cannot See. Directed by Shawn Levy, 2024.

9. https://www.simplypsychology.org/logotherapy.html.

10. Human Intrinsics from "Art of Communication." Erwin McManus.

11. Psalm 42, TLB (Story from 1 Samuel 30.6).

12. Cognitive Behavioral Therapy, now-famous therapeutic approach to addressing negative self-talk and self-image.

13. Lima, Jamie Kern. *Worthy: How to Believe You Are Enough and Transform Your Life*. New York: Gallery Books, 2023.

14. "Potholes" message by Bishop T.D. Jakes, discussing 2 Samuel 6.

15. 2 Samuel 5.10 NKJV.

16. 1 Coritnthians 2.9 NLT.

17. 2 Corinthians 5.17.

18. Same as above.

19. Ephesians 4.22-23.

20. Roman 8.38.

21. Ephesians 3.17-19 TLB.

CHAPTER 11

1. Anne Lamott, *Bird by Bird: Some Instructions on Writing and Life* (New York: Pantheon Books, 1994), 215.

2. John Bevere, *Insecurity: Understanding the Roots and Overcoming the Fear* (Nashville: Thomas Nelson, 2017), 82.

3. Ted Lasso, "Episode 7: Make Rebecca Great Again," *Ted Lasso*, Season 1, Episode 7, Apple TV+, August 14, 2020.

4. Chad Veach, "Summer Bucket List," *Leadership Podcast,* episode aired July 2023.

5. 1 Samuel 15.7.

6. Numbers 13.33.

7. 2 Corinthians 6.11-13 MSG.

8. Exodus 4.11 MSG.

9. Numbers 14.23-24 MSG.

10. *Air*, Warner Bros., 2023.

PART 3 PRELUDE
NA

PART 3 PREFACE

1. Dr. Adam Kepecs, "Statistical Decision-Making and Confidence: A Study of Rodents," *Journal of Neuroscience Research* 28, no. 3 (2015): 111-122.

2. Katty Kay and Claire Shipman, *The Confidence Code: The Science and Art of Self-Assurance — What Women Should Know* (New York: HarperCollins, 2014).

CHAPTER 12

1. Jamie Kern Lima, *Believe It: How to Go from Underestimated to Unstoppable* (New York: HarperCollins, 2021), 210.

2. Psalm 108.1 CSB.

3. Elevation Worship. "Same God." *LION*, Elevation Worship Records, 2022.

4. Psalm 101.2 CSB.

5. Psalm 41.12.

6. Pastor Clint Claypoole.

7. Tim Ferriss, "Hugh Jackman — Building the Mental Fortress of a Champion," *The Tim Ferriss Show* podcast, episode 515, October 16, 2018.

8. Proverbs 28.1.

9. Another concept I've heard Erwin McManus talk about in length.

10. Matthew 5.37.

11. CSB.

12. *Arena* call advice from Erwin McManus.

CHAPTER 13

1. Psalm 13.3 MSG.

2. Capaldi, Lewis. "How I'm Feeling." *Divinely Uninspired to a Hellish Extent*, Vertigo Records, 2019.

3. Chesterton, G.K. *Orthodoxy*. New York: John Lane Company, 1908.

4. Matthew 16.24-26 MSG.

5. C.S. Lewis, *Mere Christianity*, pg. 190.

6. Burchard, Brendan, interview with Steven Furtick.

7. 1 Peter 5.6 NKJV.

8. Luke 14.8 CSB.

9. Philippians 2.3 CSB.

10. 1 Peter 2.11 MSG.

11. Matthew 20.26 CSB.

12. Psalm 103.13-14 NLT.
13. James 1.23.
14. Keller, Timothy. *The Reason for God: Belief in an Age of Skepticism*. New York: Dutton, 2008.
15. Proverbs 4.23 NLT.
16. Deuteronomy 8.11-18 (bits and pieces).
17. Luke 12.18.
18. Daniel 4.
19. Psalm 8.3-4.
20. 2 Samuel 7.18.
21. 1 Samuel 24.14.
22. James 4v.6 NLT.

CHAPTER 14
1. Gordon, Jon. *The One Truth: Elevate Your Mind, Unlock Your Power, Heal your Soul*. Wiley, 2023.
2. Kelly, Kevin. *The Inevitable: Understanding the 12 Technological Forces That Will Shape Our Future*. Viking, 2016.
3. Lewis, C.S. *The Abolition of Man*. HarperOne, 2001. Original work published 1943.
4. Take a guess. Erwin McManus in multiple podcasts.
5. Hebrews 10.38.
6. Erwin strikes again.
7. 1 John 4.18.
8. Psalm 23.1-5 CSB (broken up, "prepare" changed to "prepares").9. Psalm 23.4 CSB.

CHAPTER 15

1.Craig Groeschel: Groeschel, Craig. *Fight: Winning the Battles That Matter Most.*
Zondervan, 2013. p. 84.
2. Joshua 1.7-9 MSG.
3. Claypoole, Clint.
4. Borrowed phrase from Chesterton, G.K. (1905). *Heretics.* New York: The John Lane
Company.
5. https://www.bbc.com/future/article/20160501-how-its-possible-for-an-ordinary
person-to-lift-a-car#.
6. Jeremiah 12.5.
7. Haidt, Jonathan, and Lukianoff, Greg. *The Coddling of the American Mind: How Good
Intentions and Bad Ideas Are Setting Up a Generation for Failure.* Penguin Books, 2018.
8. Concerning avoidance therapy, I'm not giving psychological advice. Especially
want to be delicate with those facing severe abuse, trauma, addiction, PTSD, or
suicidal ideation. See a professional. Help is available.
9. www.wypr.org/show/clearpath-your-roadmap-to-health-wealth/2023-01-17/
traveling-for-health-happiness.
10. www.affordabletours.com and *Gate1.* You're welcome.
11. Bourdain, Anthony. *No Reservations: Around the World on an Empty Stomach.*
Bloomsbury USA, 2007. p. 95.

CHAPTER 16

1. Moore, Tim. Sermon Series, "Sound Mind" at X Church, Ohio.
2. 1 Timothy 4.9 MSG.
3. Coelho, Paulo. *The Devil and Miss Prym.* (2000). HarperCollins.
4. Psalm 55.17.
5. Psalm 132.1.
6. Intense, popular program designed to transform you both mentally and physically.
7. Clear, James. *Atomic Habits: An Easy & Proven Way to Build Good Habits & Break Bad
Ones.* (2018). Avery.
8. Keller, Gary, and Jay Papasan. *The One Thing: The Surprisingly Simple Truth Behind
      Extraordinary Results.* Austin: Bard Press, 2013.
9. Proverbs 10.4.

10. Vanderbloemen, W. (2022). *Be the Unicorn: 12 Data-Driven Habits that Separate the Best
Leaders from the Rest.* Lioncrest Publishing.
11. Dr. Wes Beavis strikes again.
12. Lowndes, Leil. *How to Talk to Anyone: 92 Little Tricks for Big Success in Relationships.*
      (2008). McGraw-Hill.

CHAPTER 17

1. Summitt, Pat, and Sally Jenkins. *Reach for the Summit: The Definite Dozen System for
Succeeding at Whatever You Do.* Broadway Books, 1998.
2. Edwards, Gene. *A Tale of Three Kings: A Study in Brokenness.* Tyndale House Publishers,
1993.
3. Cummings, E.E. *Complete Poems, 1904 – 1962.* Edited by George James Firmage,
Liveright Publishing Corporation, 1991.
4. First chapter of *David and Goliath* by Malcom Gladwell is eye-opening on this.
Gladwell, M. (2013). *David and Goliath: Underdogs, Misfits, and the Art of Battling Giants.*
Little, Brown and Company.
5. 1 Samuel 17.28.
6. 1 Samuel 17.34-37.
7. Ecclesiastes 10.10.
8. CSB.
9. Proverbs 18.9 MSG.
10. Craig Groeschel, Sermon Series 2022.
11. Galatians 6.4-5 MSG.
12. 1 Timothy 4.14 NKJV.
13. "Art of Communication" Masterclass by Erwin Rafael McManus.
14. 1 Corinthians 10.31.
15. Ecclesiastes 9.10.

CHAPTER 18
1. Sheeran, E., & McDaid, J. (2019). *Best Part of Me*. On *No.6 Collaborations Project*. Atlantic Records.
2. 1 Samuel 2.7-8ish MSG.
3. Sudeikis, J. (Executive Producer). (2020). Ted Lasso. Season 2, Episode 5. Apple TV.
4. 1 Samuel 16.7.
5. Pastor Ed Funderburk, Former Executive Pastor, Church Consultant.
6. Robbins, T., Diamandis, P., & Hairi, R. (2022). *Life Force: How New Breakthroughs in Precision Medicine Can Transform the Quality of Your Life & Those You Love*. Simon & Schuster.
7. Proverbs 31.30.
8. Ecclesiastes 9.7-8 MSG.
9. https://fashionjournal.com.au/fashion/fashion-mood-psychologist/#:~:text=According%20to%20Michelle%2C%20there%20is, our%20mood%2C"%20she%20says.
10. Erwin McManus, *Battle Ready Podcast*, and this one about made me wreck.
11. Matthew 23.26.
12. 2 Samuel 12.19, my paraphrase.
13. 2 Samuel 12.20 NLT.
14. Pastor Steven Furtick once preached a sermon series called "Permission Slip" or something like that and talked about this story, circa 2012. This is my little nod/easter egg.

CHAPTER 19
1. "The Office." Season 5, episode 10, "The Surplus." Directed by Paul Feig, written by Gene Stupnitsky and Lee Eisenberg, featuring Rainn Wilson as Dwight Schrute. NBC, originally aired December 4, 2008.
2. Stojanovic, Dejan. *The Shape*. Belgrade: Dajla, 2000.
3. https://www.npr.org/sections/parallels/2013/06/11/190671704/the-day-nelson-mandela-walked-out-of-prison.
4. 2 Samuel 1.11 NLT.
5. 2 Samuel 1.12 NLT.
6. 2 Samuel 1.17-18 NLT.
7. Erwin Rafael McManus.
8. McManus, Erwin Raphael. *The Artisan Soul: Crafting Your Life into a Work of Art*. New York: HarperOne, 2014.
9. 2 Samuel 11.1 NLT.
10. Galatians 5.13.
11. My paraphrase, 2 Samuel 7.
12. Irenaeus. *Against Heresies*. Book 4, Chapter 20, Section 7. In *The Ante-Nicene Fathers*, edited by Alexander Roberts and James Donaldson, translated by A. Cleveland Coxe, vol. 1, Buffalo: Christian Literature Publishing Co., 1885.

CONCLUSION
1. Romans 15.1-2 MSG.
2. Elevation Worship. "More Than Able." Lyrics: "Now I see all that I have. Oh, I've got my confidence back." [Elevation Worship, "More Than Able," 2021.]
3. Proverbs 11.25 NLT.
4. Acts 13.36.
5. Philippians 2.6-8.
6. Philippians 2.9-11.
7. 1 Peter 5.6 NKJV.
8. Hebrews 10.35.

Full List from Chapter 9

I am *chosen*, chosen and adopted by God.
I am *complete* in Christ.
I am *free* from guilt and condemnation.
I am a *friend* of Jesus. He calls me friend.
I am *justified* before God, my legal debt of wrongdoings paid for
in full.
I have been bought with a price and my life and body *belong* to
God.
I am God's *child*.
God is working both the good and bad in my life for *good*.
I am *confident* God will complete the work He started in me.
I am *significant*. God's own workmanship.
I am God's *temple*.
I can *approach* God with freedom and confidence.
I am a *citizen* of heaven.
I am fearfully and wonderfully *made*.
I have been *established, anointed,* and *sealed* by God.
I have not been given a spirit of fear, but of *power, love,* and a
sound mind.
I have the same *power* inside me that raised Jesus from the
dead.
I am *accepted*.

Also Available by Russ

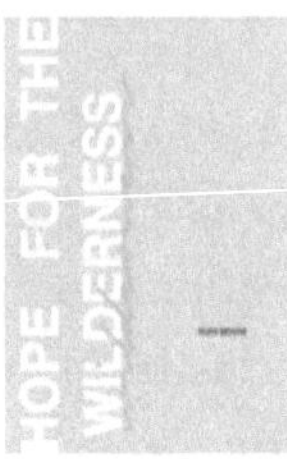

Hope for the Wilderness: *Through all the Pain to all the Promise*

"Survive this season, thrive in the next. Everyone goes through a wilderness. Not everyone makes it to the promised land. We all know what it's like to feel trapped in a difficult place. But hope is available. Inside the pages of this book, you will find strength for your heart, fire for your eyes, and a map to get you through the other side and into a flourishing future."

The No Girlfriend Rule

Pineview University

DB Jacobson

Copyright © 2026 DB Jacobson

ISBN-13: 9798994214831
ISBN-10: 1477123456

Cover design by: DB Jacobson
Library of Congress Control Number: 2018675309
Printed in the United States of America

Thank you to AC. Your enthusiasm for this series brought
me so much joy.

To all those that wanted a fuckboy to grow into his
potential, this is for you.

Contents

Welcome to
Pineview University

Congratulations on your acceptance to Boulder's own D1 school. We are so pleased you have decided to join us in furthering your studies and education!

As a student at Pineview, you may enjoy the firsthand account experiences from several of our best and brightest student athletes.

We hope you enjoy your time spent at Pineview and with all her students.

The No Girlfriend Rule focuses on two Pineview's favorite students: Rhys Goodman and Tama Bulris.

Rhys has spent his entire life working towards one goal: playing in the MLB. Tireless hours practicing, improving, and grinding to meet his goal. He's made plenty of sacrifices along the way. The biggest one? No girlfriend until he makes it to the big leagues. He's enjoyed his years at Pineview as an eligible bachelor with fans to spare. That sacrifice is made easy with best friends like Tama Bulris at his side.

Tama was homeschooled and sheltered making her feel like she hasn't experienced normal things, like having a boyfriend. Her first experience with being around people her own age only happened when she started college at twenty. Wanting to harness all the things she feels like she has missed in life, she follows the leads of all her friends. But with friends like Rhys means one thing: heart break is inevitable.

The No Girlfriend Rule takes place over ten years where Rhys and Tama grow and mature in their friendships, careers, and who they are at their core.

Trigger Warnings

Some scenes include:
Strong sexual content, depression, death of a parent, alcohol use, bullying, and cheating

Tropes:

Second chance, found family, small town, college romcom, sports romance, baseball romance, friends to lovers, bed sharing, unrequited love

Chapter 1

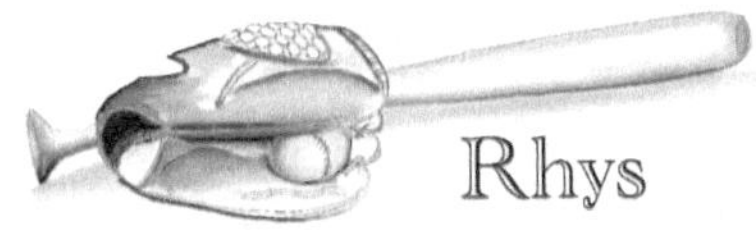

Rhys

Girlfriends are overrated. My personal goals were more important than a romantic relationship. All my spare time was dedicated to graduating on-time and being draft ready.

Playing in the MLB had been a dream since I was a child, and no one was going to derail my progress.

Girlfriends demand time and when things start to sour because my focus is elsewhere or bat bunnies surround me constantly, girlfriends mean drama. I hate drama, jealousy, and all the other things that pull my focus.

However, girls that are your friend, are extremely underrated. Especially if that girl is Tama Bulris. She is arguably the smartest, kindest, and funniest person I have ever met. I adore her and becoming her friend made my junior year incredible. She is the best friend I had ever had.

I spotted her at the party before I had fully walked into the front door. I didn't see her the entire summer, which sucked. I missed her even though we talked multiple times a week. We shared the same online summer course and would compare notes via email. The first two weeks of the semester had been too busy to hang out, but that ended tonight.

Tama's smile spread across her beautiful face as she delicately tossed the ping pong ball across the table, sinking it with ease into the cup.

She was one of a kind. Never jealous of other women that would approach me while I hung out with her. She was funny as fuck with a dry sense of humor and a sneaky sarcasm that made you question whether she was joking or naïve. It was a toss-up half the time.

Being homeschooled and not leaving her small community until she was twenty when she started at Pineview, made some pop culture references go over her head. I had no idea when I met her that she was technically a freshman, but she was two years older than most incoming first years.

Her mom guilted her into staying in their little town until her uncle finally convinced her mom to let her leave the nest. Because of her nontraditional schooling, she was insatiable to learn about anything and everything.

She was compassionate and supportive of my baseball aspirations. She went to every home game and streamed most of my away games. It always gave me a thrill when I would get a message from her after an away game letting me know she was cheering me on from afar.

Admittedly, I had been problematic about sharing her with the rest of the male population. I loved hugging her. Her skin was always silky smooth and warm. And she gave the best hugs. Every party we would meet up at I would wrap her in my arms.

I wasn't consciously cockblocking her, but when my teammates Reiser and Foust pointed it out I decided I needed to chill out.

Will Reiser and Matt Foust lived next door to Tama, so they knew her almost as well as I knew her. The only person that could rival me in their friendship with my girl was Henry, Matt's cousin. Henry Foust lived next door to Tama last year and much to my dismay was her actual roommate after Will and Matt coupled up with Tama's roommates.

I groaned when I saw Henry standing next to Tama. I didn't hate him, per se, but I didn't like him either. She was the nicest person I had ever met, and Henry was a dick. I wasn't jealous of their friendship, but I didn't want him to corrupt her either.

When I had a bad day, she was the first person that would try to cheer me up. When I was sick, she made me homemade soup and nursed me back to health. She never asked anything from me. And never once did I get the vibe that she was sexually interested in me, so it kept temptation at bay. So far, my experiment on whether men and women could be friends despite attraction seemed to be working out for me. While I was very attracted to her, my desire to keep her friendship at all costs overrode every twitch of my dick that I had for her.

She floated another ball into her opponent's cup. She was weirdly good at all drinking games. Beer Pong, she ran the table; flip cup was too easy for her; cage match, put her opponents to shame. She even kicked me and my roommates' asses in poker.

The irony was she wasn't competitive. She didn't play sports growing up. As far as I know the only sporting events she watched were to cheer on someone she personally knew. There's also the fact that she was extremely unathletic.

She and I had walked from campus to my house on a few occasions, and she would huff and puff attempting to keep up with my longer strides. At one point I was worried she was going to have an asthma attack. I had to give her a piggie back ride to my house. She refused to walk in the snow, said it hurt her lungs to attempt to keep up with me. Not that I minded one damn bit. Having her wrap her legs around my waist was like having a warm, giggling backpack on.

I made a few strides over to the beer pong table. "There's my girl." I pulled Tama away from Henry's side and wrapped her in my arms. My fingers stroked the warm smooth skin of her back that was exposed when I lifted her off her feet in a bear hug.

Henry scowled in my direction before his expression lifted into a chilly smile that didn't reach his eyes. I grinned over to him.

"Henry," I said with the same cool tone he gave me time and time again. My smile was forced. I didn't want to fight with Henry or even show Tama there was tension between the two of us. I didn't want her to ever feel like she needed to choose between us.

"Rhys, how was your summer?" Henry asked me. He looked like he was also trying to be on his best behavior.

"Fine. I missed my best friend." And to drive the point home I buried my nose into Tama's neck.

She always smelled so fucking good. Uniquely her like someone baked an apple pie while jasmine bloomed in the summertime. Sweet but earthy. I inhaled deeply. My fingers flexed around her waist. My thumbs touched across her stomach and my middle fingers touched across her back.

She squealed as I accidentally tickled her and elbowed me playfully when I set her down. I had forgotten she was so ticklish.

"Don't try to distract me. Henry and I are trying to run the table."

She was well on her way to winning. Their opponents were losing badly. I tipped my chin to Bennet who was playing against my girl. He tossed the ping pong ball and overshot the table. I wasn't surprised he missed considering his eyes hadn't left Tama's tits. Which I deduced were real, and she was genetically blessed. I never asked but after a thousand hugs and a few sleepovers, I knew.

I wrapped my arms around her waist and pulled her against my chest. It was a claiming move that I had promised myself I would chill with, but Bennet's blatant staring was annoying me. I rested my chin against her shoulder. "I can't believe I didn't get to see you all summer. Tell me about your road trip you've been mentioning for weeks."

Tama wiggled her ass against my thighs. She wasn't trying to rub against me. It was what she did when she was loosening up to make her shot. The ball sailed into her target before she answered me. "It was an epic road trip with Henry. We hit up a bunch of national parks and Vegas."

Henry rolled his lips in to hide a smile. Annoyance rippled through me. She had always maintained that they were just friends, but a fucking road trip with only the two of them was some intimate shit. My jaw clicked as I schooled my reaction.

"That sounds like fun. Why wasn't I invited, again?" I was going for playful, but I was annoyed as fuck.

My eyes flicked back over to Henry who was looking around, not paying the slightest attention to Tama. His eyes raked the party as his mouth grew into a tight line.

"Well, for one, we left when you still had two finals to take. Second, it was supposed to be an all-girls trip with Nicole and Lily, but I can never say no to Hen."

My jaw relaxed. It wasn't some romantic getaway where he was trying to stake his claim.

Henry's eyes continued to rove over the crowd before he excused himself to get a drink. I pulled my body around to Tama's side, keeping her close with an arm looped around her shoulder.

"Well, I fucking missed you."

She turned to me as I gave her my best impression of puppy eyes. She rolled hers and elbowed my ribs. "You're so dramatic."

I grinned down at her as Henry came back. He passed her a beer and whispered something in her ear. She glanced over her shoulder before squinting at him and nodding.

"Be right back. Henry, Rhys, play nice." She turned away from the table before lightly tossing the ball into Bennet's last cup. It sank in dead center, and the crowd surrounding the table erupted in cheers.

"Fuck, she's awesome," I whispered, but Henry was close enough to hear me.

He agreed with me before his eyes tracked to where Tama was ascending the steps to the bedrooms.

A swirl of anxiety made my stomach clench. If she was going upstairs, then it was to check out if there was a free bedroom. Since I knew she wasn't checking for my benefit, it meant she was checking for Henry's. The last person I wanted her in a relationship with was Henry. He would try to limit my friendship with her.

I gripped the stack of used cups and reset the triangle as calmly as possible. "What's going on with the two of you?"

Henry's lip curled in disgust as he shook his head. His reaction calmed me down. It was not how I would have reacted.

"She's my roommate and friend. What's going on with the two of you?"

This fucking question again.

I had to justify my friendship to my former and current teammates as well as my roommates on more than one occasion.

Nate Winthrop, AKA Whinny, and Nathan Thomas had been my teammates and roommates for a few years. They knew Tama and asked me several times last year. I don't know why it was unfathomable that we were just friends, but it was always met with skeptical looks.

I braced. "She's my friend too."

Henry was looking worriedly over his shoulder and back to the stairs. Which made me second guess his lip curl from earlier.

"So, there's nothing romantic going on between the two of you?"

He rolled his eyes. The look of disgust was back. Shaking his head, he said, "No, there isn't. If you want something to happen between the two of you, you better piss or get off the pot. You're stringing her along, and it's fucking shitty."

I saw red at the insinuation. We were friends. I was so fucking sick and tired of everyone assuming I was the one that didn't want her. If anything, it was the other way around. Given the chance to have no-strings-attached sex with Tama knowing it wouldn't affect our friendship, I would every day that ends in Y.

Swallowing down the bitter pill, I held my hands up. "I'm not stringing her along. She's my friend, nothing more. Actually, I told her I was going to help find someone suitable for this year."

We talked about it after class. She mentioned how both her roommates last year are now in relationships, and it made her want to see what the big deal was. It was a surprise to me. I had assumed she was like me with her drive to succeed and stay single.

She took a heavy school load, didn't take a break in the summer, opting for online courses. I figured she saw relationships as distractions she didn't want to deal with.

Henry made another shitty comment like he didn't believe me. Thankfully Tama came back before the conversation could escalate to throwing fists. Henry's jaw tightened as he had another whispered conversation with Tama and then turned on his heel to storm upstairs.

Tama cut her warm brown eyes to me and squinted. "Why do you look annoyed?"

I shrugged and took a gulp from her beer and passed it back to her. She rolled her eyes and sipped after me.

"Your friend doesn't like me."

She smirked and shook her head. She lightly tossed the ball, and it landed dead center again in the middle of the triangle of cups. "My friend is recovering from a concussion. He's probably grumpy because he has a headache."

My stomach twisted. Henry had been attacked in an alley last semester. His cousin Matt and roommate Will, my former teammates, intercepted to keep the guys from killing Henry. Matt's arm was too fucked up to draft which was a bummer for him. But now he's an assistant coach and the scout for our baseball team so not all was lost. Henry was hospitalized and placed in a medically induced coma for a few days. Tama was a wreck about it.

The night of his attack she ended up sleeping in my bed. She was too emotional and worried to be by herself. Her cop uncle kept her up to date on the case, so she knew while Henry was still in the hospital that he was targeted and attacked with the intent of causing serious harm. I held her until she fell asleep three nights in a row before she felt ready to sleep in her own bed again.

Guilt niggled at me. Tama's eyes moved to look beyond my shoulder. Her jaw loosened as her eyes widened. I glanced behind me to see Henry marching towards us with a cute brunette clutching his hand. She was as small as Tama and had the type of pretty face that made you certain someone had already claimed her. My brow perked at the way Henry's fingers had laced into the brunette's.

I tried to get a gauge on the situation. Introductions were made as I assessed Ava (the brunette) and Henry. I came to the easy conclusion that Ava was Henry's. She may not have known it, but it was blatantly obvious that he wanted her, and he wasn't going to let anyone else near her. It was how he kept her close, constantly touching her. He arranged how she was standing so his body blocked her from the rest of the party. It was possessive.

I chuckled to myself. Fifteen minutes ago, I was positive that Henry wanted to fuck Tama, and now after seeing him with Ava, I understood. He saw Tama as more of a sister. I didn't have to worry about him trying to keep her away from me.

The four of us played together for the rest of the night before Henry decided it was time to go. I wanted Tama to come home with me and spend the night. Not for anything sexual to happen, but I missed her. We had a lot of catching up to do and my favorite way to fall asleep was talking to her.

Begrudgingly hugging my friend goodbye, I asked her to call me when she got home. Attempting to leave shortly after them, I was stopped by a few girls that called out my name and wanted my dick. Any other night I would have been more than ready to oblige, but I was too tired to take them up on their offers for a threesome.

It was my senior year. My last season to buckle down and prove to the baseball world that I was ready to play professionally. It meant I needed to stop fucking around. Even the end of my friends with benefits situation with Lydia was more dramatic than I cared for. She dated Henry after me, possibly during.

I wasn't going to go on a sex ban, per se, but I was going to be a hell of a lot more selective. One thing I noticed last year was even the most 'low drama' girl I chose for a quick hookup had issues with my friendship with Tama. They'd be dismissive of her, rude, or act like jealous children. I had no patience for that shit this year.

"Call me," Lydia mouthed to me as I was leaving.

Not fucking likely.

Been there, done that. Too much drama. First, she was shitty to Tama, which I ignored for far too long. Then she flaunted Henry around to make me jealous. She told me that she didn't want anything serious, that we were like-minded. And I believed her until she started showing up to my place unannounced. She complained about my lack of availability. I had baseball practice and workouts. Then she friended my mom on social media.

Maybe Henry did me a favor.

My place was a two-block walk from the party. Whinny (Nate) was drunk as fuck in the kitchen with a girl making a mess. It looked like she was trying to make fried rice if the spilled eggs and rice kernels all over the counter were any indication.

Whinny gave me a lazy grin and saluted me as I took the stairs. Nathan's door was propped open. He was at his desk, headphones on. It looked like he was finishing his homework.

My shoes were kicked off as I walked into my room and pulled my shirt overhead. Pausing as the chest went over my nose, Tama's apple jasmine scent had etched into the cotton. A satisfied hum came out as I sniffed it again and tossed my clothes into the corner. I walked into my attached bathroom. I won a bet between my roommates and was given the bedroom with an ensuite; a perk I had no interest in ever giving up.

My shower was quick as I washed the stench of the party from me. My phone pinged with a text as I wrapped the towel around my waist. Tama's name made my lips hitch into a smile.

I debated on whether to send Rhys a message that I had gotten home. A fair amount of longing looks his way and scowls at me throughout the night made me pause. My friend was a hot commodity, and the clamoring female population did *not* like that I was in their way. It was the second reason why I wasn't always comfortable with his affections. The first being, it's confusing. I knew he wasn't interested in me *like that*. But his body language told a different story.

It made me public enemy number one in the eyes of all the Rhys Goodman fans. I had endured enough sneers in my direction to last a lifetime from being his friend. But he was worth the momentary discomfort of seeing his fan's hateful side.

He was the best. Mostly. Behind Henry, he was the best. I guess he was the second best, but I didn't have any romantic feelings towards Henry, so maybe they were in two very different categories.

I typed out a message, erased it, and tossed my phone. It was likely he was in the process of hooking up with one of his many fans. The moment I left the hyenas would swarm, and he would be busy with choosing who was going to see his penis.

I tried to not be jealous of the lucky girl. He had made it clear he didn't want that with me. He had too many opportunities to seal the deal and never did. And I was happy to be his friend. It was rewarding. He was kind and funny. There was a tenderness about him that he didn't let a lot of people see. I may not have been around a lot of men in my life, but I recognized Rhys's tendency to soften when it was just the two of us.

I grew up in a retirement community and my mother homeschooled me. My first experience with people my own age was after I turned twenty. My mom and I lived where she worked as the activity director and taught a sewing and knitting class to the senior citizens of Hemet's Friendly Village Retirement Community. The youngest male I interacted with was my Uncle Beckett, and he was still twenty-five years older than me. He's my dad's brother. He became the male figure in my life.

My dad was a teacher who protected his students before launching himself on a shooter. He was the only one who perished, and he died a hero. I was four, so my memories of him are murky at best.

After his death, my mom snapped, and my safety became her number one priority. No public school for me, and since I lived in a retirement center no young people to interact with until I left for college at twenty. Without Uncle Beckett's support I wouldn't have been able to move away from home. Beckett and my mom married over the summer.

They admitted to me that they had been romantically involved for the better part of ten years. First it was about grieving together after losing my dad. Then it turned into real romantic feelings that they fought out of guilt. Next was the realization that they couldn't fight it anymore. And finally coming clean to me that they loved each other and wanted to get married.

He had already spent the night most nights so not much had changed in that regard. And had my mom not skimmed over the sex education chapters of my homeschooling (and threatened my neighbors not to teach me about sex) I would have been able to put together on my own that they were having intercourse nightly; however, I didn't know what human copulation was until last year when my roommates and Will explained the birds and bees to me.

We watched porn and Will showed me his penis. None of it was sexual for me at the time. I was too embarrassed to have been so naïve, so it wasn't erotic.

I went down a rabbit hole on attraction after that night. Up to that point in my life I hadn't experienced true attraction. Don't get me wrong, my neighbors, Will, Matt, and Henry, are attractive men, but I never felt that stomach-tightening tingle. Then I met Rhys, and it was unexpected and confusing.

By the time I got home from my class, my thighs were damp to the point where I worried I started my period. Which would have been unfortunate as the only times I wore underwear was during my menses. It was a practice my mother had taught me. Good vaginal health meant fresh air and natural fibers when under garments were necessary.

I was certain the sticky residue that coated my thighs was blood. Nope it was arousal, straight up chemical reactions to procreate. It was fascinating.

Since that moment only a few men had pulled that reaction out of me. I chalked it up to pheromones and my body's ability to sense the right amount of testosterone. At the end of the day, that is all that sexual attraction is, chemical reactions to stimuli. My stimuli came in the form of a certain 6'3 first baseman with brown hair, blue eyes, and a square jawline that made him look like a young Henry Cavil.

I whimpered at my phone. Rhys asked me to call him when I got home. I couldn't bring myself to do that. If he answered and I heard a girl in the background my heart would crack a little more at the knowledge that he didn't want me like that. Or worse, he didn't answer at all because he was too distracted by whatever the girl was giving him.

Procrastinating, I took a quick shower. My apartment was built for roommates. Every bedroom had its own private bathroom. They were small, but efficient. And after the horror stories my roommates Lily and Nicole had shared about getting athlete's foot from the communal shower, I was grateful to not have to share my space.

My phone sat innocently on my bed before I scooped it up. If I didn't send Rhys some sort of message he might worry, and I didn't want him to do that.

> *Me: I'm home. Sorry I didn't text sooner. I needed to shower.*

There. Short and to the point. If he didn't respond, no big deal. It was late. The party was loud and crowded. He probably wouldn't even feel his phone buzz in his pocket.

My cell vibrated in my hand. I bit into my smiling lips as Rhys's handsome face flashed across my screen. He was Face Timing me. I took a deep breath and settled against my pillows.

"Hey." He had sleepy eyes and a smiling face before his brows pinched. "Are you naked?"

I glanced down and cringed. "Not really. I'm in a towel." I squinted at him. "But you aren't wearing much more."

He chuckled, his bare chest flexed. "That's fair."

The video jostled as he turned on his side and propped his phone on his nightstand, freeing his hands. I did the same thing. We video chatted most nights.

"Do you want to put your pajamas on?"

I looked back down at my towel. "Give me a minute. Tell me about your day while I get dressed." He chuckled as I stood up. I listened to his deep voice rumble.

I heard a little clatter as I dropped my towel and figured it was Ava in her room. Rhys's voice cracked and got deeper as I bent over to rifle my pajama drawer. Giggling to myself, *he must be very tired if he was losing his voice.* Still bent over, I pulled my wet hair into a knot.

"Uh Tama?" Rhys said after a quiet moment. His voice sounded strained.

"I'm still here."

My long hair was heavy and stubborn as I twisted it around itself and looked at my bare toes while still bent over.

I wonder if Ava would get pedicures with me.

The t-shirt that Rhys had let me borrow went over my head. It was huge on me, gathering the fabric to find the head hole was proving difficult. I wiggled my body and blindly spun around towards my bed.

"Yeah, I know," he drew out the last word before sucking his breath in through his teeth. "I think your phone fell over. I can see you."

I whipped my head into the collar of the shirt. Sure enough my phone had dropped from my nightstand and into my shoe. It was standing up and filming me from the floor. It took a moment of stunned silence for me to gather what happened. My cheeks heated as I yanked the hem of the shirt over my chest and covered my bare body. I had no doubt he had an uninterrupted view of my naked self.

"Oh my god, Rhys. I am so sorry. It was an accident."

His pupils nearly took over the light blue of his eyes. He shook his head and cleared his throat. "No need to apologize for an accident. I didn't want you to… uhhh…." He swallowed thickly. "Think I was watching you without your consent."

My brows pinched together. I could feel my embarrassment from the tips of my ears to my toes. No one had ever seen me naked as an adult before. I covered my face with both of my hands.

Oh god, I had bent over.

He probably had a straight view right into my vagina as I pulled my hair into a bun. *At least Lily had insisted on those Brazilian waxes.*

I whimpered into my palms.

"It's not a big deal, Tama. It's not like you were trying to seduce me. And it's not like I haven't seen a naked woman before."

I peeked at him from my fingers. His pupils were still huge as he licked his bottom lip over and over again.

"If it's any consolation prize your tits are perfect. Way perkier than I thought they would be braless. Also do you always sleep without panties? Wait, don't answer that."

He sounded flustered so I dropped my hands and took a deep breath. "Thank you for the compliment, and no I don't sleep in underwear. I rarely wear them."

Rhys's eyes widened as his lips parted in a quick intake of air. Then he puffed his cheeks out. "We have to change the subject," he said abruptly.

I rolled my eyes to the ceiling and agreed. "I think Henry has a crush on Ava."

My assessment did the trick to get my mind off the fact that I had not only flashed my friend, but I'm also pretty sure he saw my insides when I bent over.

I crawled under my quilt and nestled around until my covers surrounded me. Henry called me a cover hog. Rhys didn't share the sentiment. Every time I woke up next to him, he was sharing as many covers as I had.

Henry and I had shared a few beds during our road trip over the summer. One thing I had learned about Henry was that he ran hot and turned the AC way down in all the hotels we had stayed in. That meant that I bundled to survive. He referred to me as a human burrito.

Our conversation flowed away from Henry and Ava and into how hard we thought Advanced Human Anatomy was going to be. His voice became deeper and rumblier until he fell asleep. I liked looking at him while he slept. His face was relaxed and handsome. There was a sweet innocence about him that didn't show when he was awake.

Letting myself stare at him for another minute, I disconnected our call. This is what we did most nights when we were both available to talk.

I flipped on my back and sighed, embarrassment heating my cheeks again.

I can't believe he saw me naked.

I felt confident it was a moment that would haunt me the rest of my life.

Chapter 2

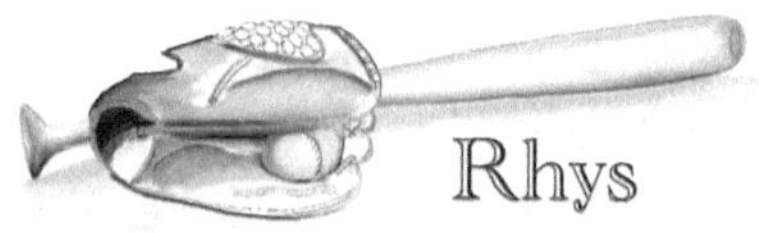

Rhys

What the fuck do you do when you see your best friend naked and now every time you close your eyes you see her perfect tits and pink nipples before being gifted with the bent-over view of her perfect bare pussy from behind?

I had woken up with a painfully hard boner that had started to leak precum into my belly button.

My dreams were erotic tributes to every filthy thing I would have done to her if I were in her bedroom. I hadn't had a wet dream in years but she damn near inspired one.

The cold tile of my shower bit into my arm as I fucked my fist.

Tama in my shirt.

Tama's tits jiggled as she pulled my shirt over her head.

The view of her pussy from behind.

A groan echoed as my orgasm took over. My hips snapped forward as my grip tightened before my release coated the tile.

My lungs heaved as the shower poured down my back. "Fuck."

I turned my face into the water.

Fantasizing about fucking your best friend is not normal.

Those thoughts needed out of my head. She didn't want me like that. She apologized for flashing me. I should have thanked her, but I was too busy squeezing my dick and trying to remember to breathe when her towel dropped. She was fucking perfect, and the image of her perfection was seared into my memory.

The valve squeaked as I twisted the water off. I couldn't fuck Tama. One, she's my best friend and I'd never want to jeopardize what we have. I *loved* being friends with her. She put things in perspective, made me happy, and gave me a sense that I had someone who cared about me for more than my ability to play ball.

Two, and this is a big one, she doesn't see me like that. I wasn't in a friendship with her in hopes that she would change her mind. She never discussed sex of any kind with me. It was like she didn't want to affiliate me with sex, so she never talked about it. I had tried to broach the subject a few times; she'd dismiss it and move on to a new topic.

I slipped my boxers on and flopped onto my bed.

Tama was off limits, but it seemed like I needed to explain that to the trouser snake that refused to believe that. I puffed out my cheeks and blew out a harsh breath.

If Tama was dating someone, it would shove her right back into the untouchable friend box. I had already told her I would help her, now this solidified it. I'd hook her up with someone.

It had to be someone that could handle my friendship with her. I wasn't going to give that up no matter who she was with, so they needed to be on board before I let them get involved. It made me itchy thinking about some schmuck trying to convince Tama to pick him or me.

It needed to be someone that would treat her with respect. I wouldn't handle it very well if I heard locker room gossip about my friend. I'd break my fist on someone's face if they spread rumors about what she's like in the sack. That would be counterproductive to my batting average.

It needed to be someone who could handle her quirks. She was sheltered and homeschooled. She's crazy fucking smart but naïve about enough things that someone could find it endearing or weird.

In a perfect world that person would be me, but it's a flawed system. I was steadfast in my commitment to no relationship until I made it. And once again, Tama doesn't want me like that.

Even if she did and I went for it, and it fucked with my friendship… I could kiss my chances of making it to the MLB goodbye. Losing her would fuck my head. Tama was the type of woman that you married. She wasn't some bat bunny wanting to get her rocks off. She was the woman that I met five years too early, but at least I could keep her friendship.

Speaking of which, I don't think I would like it if the guy I set her up with was my close friend. I don't know how I would handle it if I was the third wheel in hanging out with them. Seeing anyone snuggling with my girl would annoy me. So, I would need to find a friend of a friend. And he needed to be cool, not some dick like Henry Foust in case we did hang out.

Someone knocked on my door.

"It's open."

I expected Whinny to stroll in, so I was surprised to see Tama standing in the doorway. Her eyes were wide as she looked over to me on my bed. Her gaze flicked to my bare chest before glancing up to the ceiling with a sigh. She had seen me in my boxers on many occasions, so I wasn't sure what her reaction meant.

I sat up quickly. "What's up?"

A whimpered sigh came from her throat as she stalked over to my bed. She knee-crawled and sat in front of me. The deep purple dress she was wearing hit above the knee, but on my bed the skirt of the dress rose higher on the thigh.

And she's not wearing panties.

I pulled my knee up to rest my chin on so I could hide the semi the thought had caused.

"I'm so sorry about last night. I wanted to see you today to make sure we were still okay. I know you said we were last night after it happened, but I needed to see you for myself."

I smirked as I reached for her. My hand gripped the back of her neck as I pulled her to me for a hug. Her face collapsed into my bare chest, ass in the air. My eyes glanced in front of me, and I had to look away from the mirror that reflected what she had confirmed last night, nothing under the dress.

She giggled as I released her.

I looked into her caramel eyes. "Don't apologize. It wasn't a big deal. Would it make you feel better if I flashed you?" I was joking, sort of. Knowing she was only wearing a dress was making my dick pulse. If I flashed her….

She grimaced into a whimper at the suggestion.

Okay then.

I scoffed. "I don't know whether I should be offended by your reaction or not."

A small smile cracked from her lips. "I don't think seeing your penis would take my embarrassment away."

I tipped my head back in a laugh at her comment. "Don't be embarrassed. It's not a big deal. I hardly remember it anyway. It was late, I had been drinking."

While it was late, I wasn't even tipsy by the time I had gotten home. I remembered every fucking detail. But my little white lie seemed to put her at ease. Her shoulders relaxed away from her ears as she let out a breath of relief.

"What are we doing today?" Now that she was here it seemed like a given that we would be spending the day together.

She settled next to me. "I was going to confront Henry about his crush on Ava, but after he avoided me at breakfast, I know he's not going to leave his room today. So, no plans. What do you have going on?"

"You're not upset that he likes your roommate?"

I had to know. She had told me on several occasions that she didn't like Henry like that, but I needed to make sure.

She shook her head. "No, Ava's great. She's so sweet and pretty and a fantastic cook. I don't think I could pick a better match for Henry. She's exactly his type. I'm a little concerned about how Will might react, but I'll give him the benefit of the doubt that he'll be mature and let Ava and Henry be together."

I didn't sense a moment of jealousy. She seemed genuinely happy for Henry and Ava.

"Another one bites the dust, huh?"

She grinned and rolled her eyes. "I don't know whether there is something in the pipes of my apartment, but my roommates are all coupled up and so blissfully in love. A year ago, everyone was single and now I'm the lone wolf."

I hummed and nudged her with my foot. "We'll find someone for you. I was thinking about it this morning. I'm going to set you up on some blind dates. I'll be your match maker." I waggled my brows at her.

She groaned and collapsed onto my pillows next to me.

"Would this be a good time to tell you that no one has ever taken me on a date before?" Her plump lip was pinned between her teeth as she looked up to the ceiling.

I turned on my side to look directly at her.

How was it possible that no one had ever taken her out before?

"Never?"

She shook her head. "Not a lot of opportunities at home school high."

I hummed. "Well, that's not a big deal. There are tons of people that have never been on a date. I mean realistically our generation is more about group hangs anyway."

"That's all I know." She chewed her lip. "But what if I screw up the blind date?"

I scoffed. "How in the hell could you screw it up?"

Her puffed cheeks blew out a breath. "I could flash him my goods. I could say something offensive. Or I could turn him off with my body language."

I laughed. "Bully," I started. It was a nickname from her last name, Bulris. The irony was in no world could she be a bully.

"The guy would feel lucky if you flashed him and you are the least offensive person I have ever met. As far as body language, I have no problem taking you on a mock date and critiquing you if it will make you feel better."

"How magnanimous of you," she deadpanned.

I grinned at her. She was so sarcastic. I fucking loved it.

I shook her shoulder. "I'm serious. I'll pretend that I don't know you, and we will go on a date. You'll get feedback and then by the time I set up your first blind date you'll feel ready."

"First blind date? How many do you think I'll need to have?" Her eyes were wide with shock and a little bit of apprehension.

I chuckled. "I don't know, three maybe? How many do you think you'll need before you meet the love of your life?"

She snorted. "I'm *not* looking for the love of my life. That is way too much pressure."

"Then what do you want?"

She chewed her lip. "I want to have sex with someone that will not want to do it with other people. I want to be able to talk to him about serious things, be his friend and then when the lights go out..." She wagged her brows.

I had frozen my face after she said the word 'sex'. It may have been the first time I heard her say the word. Maybe the knowledge that I had seen her completely naked had made her ready to talk about it with me. Then I thought about what she was describing.

"You want a friend with benefits?"

Oh, the possibilities.

I loved having a FWB, but I recognized it would be different with Tama than it was with Lydia. For one, I only talked to Lydia when one of us was horny. There was also no spending the night. And I sure as fuck didn't cuddle with her. All those things I didn't want to give up with Tama.

She quickly shook her head. "No, I want something more serious than that. I don't want the ambiguity of that situation. I want to be able to tell people, 'this is my boyfriend' and not have to explain a situationship to my friends."

I swallowed the lump in my throat. What I had to offer her wasn't going to work.

"You want a traditional boyfriend/girlfriend exclusive, relationship?"

She nodded.

"But if you aren't looking for the love of your life then you are guaranteeing that you'll have to deal with the bullshit of a breakup," I argued. I was advocating for myself a little, but I also wanted her to consider all sides of being in a committed relationship.

She shrugged. "That's life. I'm not afraid of a little heart break. Will it hurt when it happens? Sure, but that's fine. I'll learn and take away the positives from the relationship and be on my way."

I hummed. "That's an overly simplistic view of a breakup. I went through one and it sucked. It's a head fuck that you gotta be prepared for."

She shrugged again. "I'm also not going into a relationship assuming it's going to end. For all I know the first date I go on *will* be with the mysterious 'one'. It's a long shot, but since I haven't honed my psychic abilities yet, all expectations and bets are off."

"Will you be disappointed if your blind date is a dud?"

She grinned at me. "My expectations are low. But the beauty of that means I *can't* be disappointed. I'm going with the flow. Treat it like an experiment and see what I can learn."

Someone else knocked on my door. Whinny popped his head in.

"Sup, Bully," he said to Tama and turned to me. "Can I borrow your truck? I need to head to the store. I'm out of toilet paper and the girl at the front desk of the gym has been directed to search my bag after I walked out with the big rolls last semester."

I rolled my eyes. Whinny wasn't sly with his toilet paper thievery. He walked out with two huge rolls, one of which had started to unravel. He walked to our house with a thirty-foot trail of toilet paper behind him.

"Sure, get me some sour gummies while you're out."

Tama rolled her eyes and poked me in the ribs. "You need to eat some vegetables with your gummies."

I grinned at her and rubbed the spot she had jabbed with her missile-like finger. My fingers clasped around the one that poked me.

"You offering to make me dinner, Bully?"

She shrugged and yanked her finger from me. "I can. No one makes dinner at home on Sunday nights. I can make you something if you promise to eat your greens."

I waggled my brows at Whinny and turned to Tama. "Tell Whinny what groceries you want him to grab for dinner tonight."

My friend pumped his fist. "I love it when Bully makes us food. Do you think she'll make us those apple turnovers again?"

She giggled at Whinny. "I'll text you a list to get. Any other requests?"

Nathan walked through my open door that Whinny hadn't closed.

"Hey Nathan, I'm making dinner for you guys tonight. Any requests?"

He grinned broadly. "I heard. It's why I timed my grand entrance into this weird orgy now."

I scoffed and turned my head over to Tama to see her reaction.

She rolled her eyes. "If you think this is an orgy you need to take the parental lock off your searches."

Whinny snorted and leaned against my desk. Nathan had a point. I was in my boxers, Whinny was only wearing a pair of basketball shorts, Nathan was wearing a pair of sweatpants, and Tama was in a dress with nothing on underneath. Though I was positive that Whinny and Nathan weren't privy to that fact.

Nathan tilted his head. "Orgies aren't my kink. Anyway, I second the apple turnovers, but I also want to vote for the green bean casserole and fried chicken you made last year. Maybe those yeast rolls." Nathan rubbed his stomach.

"Ohhh yeah, that all sounds good," Whinny said and turned his hopeful eyes over to my best friend.

She shrugged. "Sure, that's easy. I'll send you my list. It's probably $30 worth of ingredients. I don't trust your butter and unless you bought flour in the past few months, I doubt you have that."

"Bully, I'd pay a hundred for that meal," Nathan said. Whinny nodded as I chuckled and looked back over to Tama.

She read a text on her phone and frowned before typing back to whoever had messaged her. She glanced up at the three of us. "That's not necessary." She went to scoot off the bed. "Would it be easier if I went shopping with you?"

I reached over and grabbed her arm. "You're staying with me, Bully. Whinny is a big boy and can follow your list. We are going to have a movie marathon."

She rolled her head over to me. "Are we?"

Her bicep was silky smooth and warm. My thumb glided over the protruding vein before I let go. "Yep, what else would we do today?"

She sighed and scooted back. "I have no other plans. I didn't want you to feel obligated to hang out with me. I have no problem heading home."

I shook my head. "Absolutely not. I need my Bully-fill after a summer without."

She smiled softly and rested against my headboard. "You drive a hard bargain, Goodman."

Satisfied, I turned to my two other roommates who were watching me and Tama together like they always did. They were skeptical about our friendship. It was annoying.

"Hey, do either of you know someone I could hook Tama up with? We are looking for some blind dates."

Tama groaned and cupped her cheeks with her palms.

Nathan leaned against the door frame and crossed his arms. He scowled at me before grinning at Tama. "I'll date you, Bully. You're hot as fuck and can cook."

My jaw clicked as I shook my head. "No. My friends are off-limits. I don't want to hear the post-mortem about the date from either side. I don't need to hear my best friend complain about how tiny your dick is the next day."

Nathan scoffed and cupped himself. "I'm well above average and you fucking know it. We've all seen each other naked, so stop talking shit to impress your woman."

"I don't think you actually want to go on a date with me. You want to annoy Rhys so that won't work for me. I'm not someone's weird petty payback or revenge."

He held his hands up. "That's fair, if that's what I was doing. Seriously, Bully, you're a fucking catch. But since Goodman has beaten his caveman chest, I'll withdraw my bid to take you out. The offer stands if *you* want to take me up on it."

She twisted her lips to the side. "Very generous, Nathan."

"My keys are in the kitchen." I didn't want Tama to seriously consider Nathan on his offer. God help me if I heard them fucking one night. My brain would melt, and it had potential of fucking with the team dynamics.

It was a no for me.

"Thanks, man." Whinny checked Nathan's shoulder on his way out of my room.

Nathan was still standing against my door frame. I scowled and tipped my chin at him, letting him know I wanted him to go. One brow perked as a shit-eating grin spread across his face.

"I'm heading to the gym so you guys will have the house to yourselves."

I rolled my eyes at the innuendo.

"Let me know if you need any help with dinner." He tapped the doorframe with his thumb.

A smug, punch-able smile etched deeper as he walked back over to his room. He left my door open, which was annoying, but it wasn't like Tama and I were going to hook up.

"I'm going to make some popcorn. Do you want anything else?"

She shook her head.

"Get comfortable, Bully, I'll be right back."

She grinned at me as she peeled back my covers. "When was the last time you washed your sheets?"

I chortled. "Yesterday, you germaphobe."

She shrugged unapologetically. "You are a very promiscuous boy. I must be careful."

I rolled my eyes. "Be right back."

Reminding her that I was going to be more selective this year was tempting. Some may even consider what I was going through was a drought. Three months was the longest I had gone since I was fifteen when I started having sex. I could have defended myself, but I didn't see the point. Tama was the type of woman that needed to see something to believe it.

The popcorn had just started to pop when Nathan came down from his room. I scowled at him.

He grinned. "Don't look at me like that. I couldn't resist fucking with you."

I rolled my eyes. "Don't fuck with Tama. She's serious about wanting a boyfriend, and I am going to do my part in making sure she isn't with some fuckface."

Nathan snorted. "I thought she was anti-relationship like you are."

I shrugged. "I thought so too, but all her roommates are coupled up or in the process of coupling, so she's interested in seeing what the big deal is."

Nathan leaned against the counter. "And you're going to be okay with her not being at your every beck and call?"

My brow furrowed. "She's not at my beck and call. We are friends. Neither of us want more from the other. And besides, that is why I am putting myself in charge of finding her a boyfriend. I'm not losing her to some bro who is insecure about my friendship with her."

"I don't think some bro will be insecure about the friendship aspect of what you two have. I think he'll have issues with the sexual tension."

I scoffed. "There isn't sexual tension. She's my friend, I'm hers. She's never hinted that she wanted as much as a kiss from me. Tension implies it's two ways, which is not the case."

"Huh, I didn't think you'd ever admit to wanting to fuck her. That was much easier than I thought it would be."

I whipped around. "What are you talking about? I didn't say I wanted to fuck her."

He tilted his head. "Not directly, but your message was clear. You want her, she doesn't want you. Must be a humbling experience, but I digress. I'm not trying to fuck with you about this. I'm checking in to make sure you're okay with it. I don't know if you have thought this through."

I huffed as the microwave beeped. The steam singed my fingertips as I dropped the bag in the waiting bowl. "I'm good.

And I have thought this through. There's a mental checklist of aspects of who I am looking for. As long as he checks off my list, we should be good."

"If you say so." He pushed off the counter and snatched his water bottle out of the fridge. "But if it gets too much for you, there is no shame in telling her you don't feel comfortable in helping her get laid on the regular."

He strolled out of the kitchen before I could respond or process the boulder he dropped into my stomach. I took the stairs two at a time and nudged my door open with my elbow. Tama was snuggled on her side of the bed, looking through her phone. She grinned at me and sat up. Her hair was pulled up into a bun on the top of her head. She was perfect like that, pretty with messy hair in my bed.

I kicked the door shut with my heel. She maneuvered around me, so her head was on my chest as I scrolled through the streaming app to find a movie to watch. We snuggled up and watched movies for hours. Between movie one and two she went down to the kitchen to make the yeast roll dough.

Her dinner was awesome and reinforced my thoughts that she was wife material. And I met her five years too early.

Four Weeks Later

I had coerced Henry into giving Ava and me a blowjob lesson using cucumbers. It was easy to manipulate him considering I knew he liked Ava, and he didn't want her to know it. So, I used that to my advantage.

I had been asking Henry for months to show me and up until I had a little leverage he wouldn't budge. It was way more awkward than I thought it was going to be. Maybe had Henry tried harder to hide his attraction to Ava and Ava did not try to swallow the cucumber whole, I would have found less humor in the lesson.

At least I had some know-how on that action if I was given the opportunity to test my oral skills. I found it ironic that I had learned how to perform a fellatio before I learned how to kiss, but all were skillsets I wanted to learn and hone.

One thing I had been practicing since the lesson was my jaw strength and my gag reflex. I had zero stamina, and my gag reflex was laughably bad. Henry gave some decent tips during the entire awkward encounter. One big takeaway was I needed to find a lip balm without menthol. My previous balm had a cinnamon flavoring, but I figured the spice of the cinnamon would be as burning as the menthol.

Another big change on the home front was that Henry and Ava were in a secret relationship. So secret that neither had mentioned anything to me about it directly. When I asked Henry, he gave me a grin that confirmed my suspicions.

Ava was a virgin at the beginning of the semester, and I'd bet a million dollars she wasn't any more. And since she was the closest to the experience, I would be able to ask her what first-time sex was like. I'd done plenty of research, but personal anecdotal experience was my preferred way to learn.

My sheltered life meant I was safe from everything. It also meant that I lacked certain exposures and more importantly

40

friends to relate to about it. I couldn't exactly ask Thelma who lived in the bungalow next door what it was like for her to lose her virginity or her first kiss. I doubted she remembered her first kiss, and the thought of Thelma having sex made my skin crawl. And god forbid I asked my mom, she'd fly to Boulder and personally pull me home by the ear.

I smoothed my hand over the skirt of my dress and turned around to make sure it looked good from behind. The weather was starting to change in Boulder, but it was a warm day for the beginning of October.

With my Vans on, I pulled my long hair back. I had been contemplating cutting it all off. I had long hair for as long as I could remember, and a part of me was curious on what it would be like to have a chin-length bob. I'd need to ask Lily and Nicole their opinions about it. They were both far more fashionable than I was and would steer me in the right direction.

Contacts next. I was still getting used to sticking my finger in my eye, but I liked how I looked without my glasses. My uncle had insisted I go to the eye doctor before moving away from home. He said it was important for me to have an option to not wear glasses. It did make it easier to apply makeup, which was also a new experience for me.

My mom never wore any and never taught me how to apply it. Lily, once again, showed me the way. She was a true friend, and I was so grateful that I had met her and Nicole.

I coated my eyelashes in mascara and smudged my new menthol-free vanilla balm across my lips. My pits started to sweat when I thought about why I was fussing so much about my appearance.

Rhys was taking me on a date. A fake date, but it was a date, nonetheless. I was nervous.

What if he kissed me?

A new wave of anxiety made my stomach twist.

I had watched countless tutorials about how to kiss, but none of them answered my very specific questions. I wanted to ask Henry, but I didn't want to tread on Ava's toes. I had gotten the sense that she was concerned that Henry and I were more than friends and asking him to kiss me would not build her confidence that I saw him like a brother.

My fingers pulled my hair into a braid. It was windy and the last thing I wanted was for my hair to stick to my lip balm. With my phone and some cash in my pocket, I headed for the door.

It was a twenty-minute walk to Rhys's house which was good. I needed a moment to calm down. It wasn't like it was a real date. Case in point, he wasn't picking me up. I was meeting him at his house, and we were driving from there. One thing I had learned from the copious amounts of research I had performed, i.e. reading Lily's supply of romance novels, the man was supposed to pick the woman up if it were a proper date.

The wind rippled my skirt around my thighs before a gust attempted to make me do my best Marilyn impression. Rhys was waiting in his living room watching a football game with Whinny and Nathan. Rhys's gaze flicked down my body before he grinned at me. "Ready, Bully?"

I fought the blush from his smile. Looking down at my shoes and sticking my hands in my dress's pockets. "As I'll ever be."

He stepped over Whinny's legs that were propped up on the coffee table.

Nathan wagged his brows at me. "You look hot. Don't tell me you put in any effort to look good for this fool's dating lesson."

Shooting Rhys a look, I was unaware he was telling people that he was taking me on a fake date. Apparently so. It shouldn't have been a surprise. Rhys didn't want anyone to think what we had was anything other than platonic friendship.

I chewed into my cheek and shrugged. "This is one of my favorite dresses and it's probably the last warm day of the year. I wanted to take advantage."

Nathan's brow perked up as Rhys scowled over to his roommate. He walked over to me and slipped his hand to the small of my back, guiding me out of the living room making my goodbyes to his roommates hasty.

Rhys opened the passenger door to his truck and helped me up by gripping my waist and setting me onto the too tall seat. I was grateful for the assistance. The first time I had attempted to get into the lifted cab I had to scramble onto the floorboards and use my forearms to pull myself onto the seat. It was mortifying and awkward. At least I was wearing jeans that day otherwise I would have accidentally flashed Rhys ten months prior.

Loud music boomed from the speakers before he quickly slicked the volume down. "Sorry, Nathan borrowed my truck this morning and apparently he was hoping to blow his ear drums out."

I rubbed my ears. "No worries. So, where are we going?"

"Maria Bella in Broomfield. You like Italian, right?"

I nodded. I was surprised he was taking us to a restaurant thirty minutes away, but then I remembered that in no way would he want anyone in Boulder to see us together on a romantic date and assume we were a couple. It would seriously mess up his hookup schedule he kept and thought I didn't know about.

The last thing I wanted was to interfere with his roster of bat bunnies, nor did I want them to be nasty towards me for thinking I was better than them because he took me out on a date. And I would never want them to know it wasn't a real. That would be mortifying.

"Love it." My throat knotted in my personal reminder that this was not real. Swallowing my disappointment, I focused on the positive. He was doing me a favor, nothing more. He was preparing me for when he set me up on a real blind date. And I was grateful for it. He was a good friend, and I needed to take his observations and use them as a learning experience.

We chatted about school and the class we had together. It was a fast drive that calmed down my nerves. He pulled into a parking spot and turned to me. "The fake date starts," he looked down at his watch, "now."

He looped out of his side of the truck and over to mine. My door swung open as he helped me down.

"Actually, starting now. You should not let your date touch you like this." He emphasized what he meant by squeezing my sides before releasing me to my toes. Our hands brushed as he walked next to me and gave his name to the hostess.

He pulled my chair out and sat across from me as the waitress poured us both some water. She gave Rhys a flirty smile before walking off to grab our drink order. My eyes pinched in an unimpressed stare before rolling my shoulders back and looking directly at Rhys. He was grinning at me, no doubt catching my glare to our flirtatious waitress.

"What? She doesn't know this isn't real. Flirting with you in front of me is rude."

He held up his hands. "That's fair, but as long as your date doesn't flirt back, you're good. You don't want to look jealous off the bat. I know from experience that you aren't jealous, but someone else won't know that."

"Good tip. So, tell me about yourself, Rhys?"

"I'm a senior from Seattle. I play baseball at Pineview, and I plan on drafting in July."

I tilted my head and chewed on my lip. I felt dumb asking questions I already knew the answers to, but it was what he had directed me to do. "What position do you play?"

"First base. Did you play any sports growing up?"

I snorted. "God, no. I was home schooled and lived in a retirement community. The most competitive league around was the Mahjong Mimis, and you had to be at least sixty-five and a grandmother to join. I was a part of the Poker Pals, but my mom found out we were gambling real money instead of butterscotch candies, and she freaked out."

Rhys bit his lip to hide his laughter. He didn't ask me often about living in Friendly Village, so I knew this anecdote was new to him.

"What was it like growing up in a retirement community?"

I blew out a breath and looked over to the approaching waitress. She set down Rhys's beer and my seltzer. I waited for her to walk away again, but she started flirting with Rhys.

"Why do you look familiar?" she cooed.

Rhys's brows furrowed as he shook his head. "I play baseball at Pineview, maybe it's that."

Her eyes grew wide. "Goodman, right? I went to the last home game last semester. You were incredible." She pulled a chair out and sat down.

I stared over to her at the sheer audacity, but I kept my face as neutral as possible.

"I heard you are planning on drafting. Is there a certain team you are hoping to join?"

Rhys glanced over to me before turning back to our waitress with a smirk. "My goal is to play professionally, so I'm not picky.

I'll take whatever opportunity comes my way and use it to learn and become as valuable as possible."

It was a nice, practiced answer.

Pippa, our waitress, continued, "But like, what's your team?"

Rhys's smile grew wider. "Seattle, but I'd be happy anywhere. Playing baseball is the goal, and the location changes almost daily."

She gave him a coy grin. She was a beautiful girl, the sort of girl that Rhys always went for. I shrank in my seat. She was tall, blonde, with striking hazel eyes and looked fit and confident.

My molars dug into the inside of my cheek and listened to them banter back and forth while focusing on my hands in my lap. I didn't want to appear to be a jealous girl, but when I had enough, I excused myself from the table, stating I needed to go to the bathroom. Pippa barely acknowledged me as I left.

I walked over to the bar, just out of sight from Rhys. The bartender raised his brow at me.

I smiled. "Hi, can you help me with something?"

He set down the glass he was polishing and walked over to me, leaning on his forearms. "Absolutely, Beautiful."

My face flushed. "My waitress is being extremely inappropriate. She's flirting with my date in front of me. She even sat down at our table. Now, trust me when I say I'll talk to my date about it later, but I need her to stop. Is there any way I can get a different server?"

His eyes widened as he chuckled. "Good for you. You must be talking about Pippa. Your boyfriend is sort of famous, at least he will be. She was gloating about how she was going to score his number."

Rhys would give it to her too.

"Yeah, I can tell." I bit hard into my lip. The stinging pain shifted my focus from disappointment.

The bartender grinned at me. His lip ring twinkled in the low bar lighting. "I'll take care of it, but if you want some unsolicited advice; if he didn't turn her away, you can do better. Fuck, I get off in three hours. I'd show you what you deserve."

My stomach fluttered. No one, and I mean no one had seriously asked me out before. I rolled my lips in to hide my smile.

"Let's focus on getting Pippa away from my date. If he ends up being a dud, I'll let you know."

He saluted me as I walked into the bathroom. I checked myself in the mirror and took a few deep breaths before I walked back to my table. Rhys was looking around the restaurant. The tension in his forehead relaxed when he saw me walking towards him.

"I thought you ditched me."

I shook my head and adjusted my napkin back on my lap. "No, sorry, I had to wait for a stall." I hid behind the menu and started to figure out what I wanted to order.

Rhys's finger appeared at the top of the menu and nudged it down. "Are you mad?"

I licked my lips and gave him a forced smile. "Why would I be mad? You are an attractive man. I'm used to women dismissing me and flirting with you."

His brow furrow was back. "I'm sorry. I should have asked her to go away sooner. I did remind her that I was on a date, but you had already left to go to the restroom."

I shrugged and gave him another smile that didn't reach my eyes. "Nothing to be sorry about. It's not real. I don't want to stand in your way of finding someone to warm your bed."

His jaw clicked as he gave me a curt nod.

I swallowed. "What are you going to get?"

He glanced down at the menu. "Haven't decided. Just to be clear, even though this is pretend, I would never disrespect you and give her my number. I shouldn't have let it get to the point where she felt comfortable asking."

I chewed my lip.

"Good evening, I'm Griffin, I'm taking over for Pippa for the rest of your dining experience. Can I get you an appetizer?" The bartender winked at me.

Rhys caught it and scowled. "Calamari," he answered briskly.

I tried to hide my smile. Apparently, Rhys did not like the shoe being on the other foot.

"Excellent choice. I'll put that in. Do you need any other recommendations for your entrée?" Griffin had only spared Rhys a glance before focusing back on me.

Rhys glowered. "Got it. Pretty standard Italian fare, but thanks."

Griffin continued to ignore Rhys to watch me. His gaze was soft and sweeping over my face in a way that was giving me butterflies. He bit his lip before a smirk hitched one cheek higher. "Has anyone told you that you look like Anya Taylor-Joy?"

I blushed and shook my head. "I can't say that anyone has, no."

Griffin flicked his lip ring with his tongue. "Well, you do. I'm going to put your order for calamari in. I'll check back in a few minutes after you have had time to look over the menu."

I didn't watch Griffin leave, even though he was attractive. He was tall, a bit wiry, hair pulled back into a top knot with the sides of his head shaved and had more of a hipster vibe. I appreciated that he was flirting with me.

Rhys watched him walk away with a narrowed gaze before turning back to me. I looked over to him through my lashes.

"What were we talking about before I got up to go to the bathroom?"

Rhys worked his jaw back and forth a few times before forcing a smile. "You were going to tell me what it was like growing up in a retirement village."

I tipped my head back in a smile. "Quiet, but full of drama. My mom plans all the activities and teaches sewing and knitting. The knitting circles were where you learned all the gossip. Most of it was about the success and failures of various grandchildren. It was fascinating. I made some great friends, and I learned at a pretty young age how to deal with death.

"I essentially have forty grandparents who treat me like their own. My old neighbor, Thelma made me a quilt when she found out I was moving to Boulder. To one up Thelma, her frenemy Yolanda, who lives across the street, added me to her will and set up a spending account for me to use while I am here. She pays for all my groceries. Any more than that and I would feel terrible for taking advantage, even though she insists her ex-husband was an oil baron. My other neighbor Gertie taught me the ins and outs of all things related to gambling."

His smile took over his face, straight white teeth gleaming, eyes crinkling in the corners. The tension that Pippa and Griffin had brought out melted away. I ducked my head down as my cheeks flushed and butterflies swarmed my belly. I didn't know what to do when he looked at me like that. It felt way too real.

Griffin dropped off the calamari. "What can I get you?" His focus remained on me.

Rhys cleared his throat. "Pork osso buco."

Griffin's eyes flicked in his direction before settling back on me.

"What about you?" His voice had lowered, his words slowed like he was asking me to tell him a secret.

Unnerved by his fake intensity I glanced quickly down at my menu again. Some hair that had fallen out of my braid tangled with my eyelashes. I looked up to Griffin to answer and batted my hair from my eyes. "Chicken Milanese," I squeaked.

"Here, let me." Griffin delicately plucked the stuck hair from my lashes and swept it behind my ear. He rolled his lips in to hide his laughter when Rhys's jaw audibly clicked.

"I'll put your orders in," Griffin said. He briskly walked away, but stayed within my line of sight, so I didn't miss the unmistakable bounce in his shoulders from laughing. He turned around with a red face and huge smile before disappearing in the kitchen.

Rhys was giving me a flat smile, and his fist was clenched on the table. I winced and took a swig of my drink to calm my nerves.

After another bout of silence I asked, "Are you close with your grandparents?"

Rhys shrugged and unclenched his hand. "My mom's family lived too far away to visit very often. I have cousins that I wouldn't recognize if I passed them on the street. Her parents both died over the past four years.

"My dad's parents are still alive. My grandpa has Alzheimer's, so he doesn't remember me. My grandma doesn't leave the assisted living center they live in because she doesn't want my grandpa to be alone. He remembers her most days, but she's basically the only person he does remember. So, I don't see her often."

I twisted my lips to the side. "That's a shame, but I get it. My dad's parents got depressed when my dad died and sort of stopped taking care of themselves. They both died when I was ten. My uncle was pretty upset but at least he had my mom and me.

"My mom's parents didn't like my dad because he was only a teacher and not religious. My maternal grandparents are strict Mormons, and my mom is more spiritual than religious, so they don't see eye to eye. The only thing they supported my mom with was me being homeschooled. I only see them every few years, they've sort of become radicalized and don't socialize with non-Mormons."

"This is a heavy topic for a first date," Rhys said.

My eyes widened. "You're right. Okay, change of topic. Do you have any hobbies?"

Rhys grinned and took a swig of beer. "Baseball takes up the majority of my time. Even in the off season I coach little leaguers. But my dad and I fix up cars during the summer. We rebuilt the engine of a 1987 Ford Mustang GT this past July. When we are done, he sells them and uses that money to pay for whatever baseball things I need."

I chewed on my cheek. "That's really cool." I didn't know that. It seemed strange that he never brought it up in the many conversations we shared over the past year.

He shrugged. "It's useful. I can handle most car related things, which is a good skill to have in the long run. What about you, what are your hobbies?"

I ate a few calamari before answering. "I love to read. My new roommate, Ava, moved in and brought around a hundred novels with her. We made a little book swap between Lily, Ava, and me. Their tastes are a little different, so it's been fun reading more fantasies. Lily's books are smutty, but easy reads and there is always a happily ever after."

Rhys perked his brow. "You read smut for fun?"

I blushed. I read it for more educational reasons, but he didn't need to know that. I shrugged. "I read romance for fun. Lily's books are eighty percent plot, twenty percent smut.

Though she had me read one book about a throuple, that was fifty-fifty, plot to smut. Ava's books are ninety percent plot, ten percent explicit content. Some of the content happens during inopportune times. Like sailing across the ocean where the sailors are battling sea monsters, getting sweaty and talking about the lack of bathing and then the female main character gets rescued and blows her hero as a thank you. At no point has the author mentioned the last time he bathed."

Rhys chuckled and rubbed his finger across his lips. "Yeah, I'd feel pretty gross if I let a girl blow me while I was sweaty straight from the field."

I held my hand out. "Exactly, it's already salty, we don't need to add to it."

Okay, realistically I had never touched a penis in my life, but every single book description mentioned how salty a blow job is. And I was hedging my bets that Rhys had no idea what a penis tasted like, so it felt like a safe comment to make.

Rhys rolled his lips in to stop himself from smiling again. "Any other hobbies?" he choked out and then started laughing.

I grinned at him. "I love to bake. Yolanda makes the best pie and Thelma's chocolate chip cookies are life changing. That's another thing I love about living where I grew up, I've become privy to every secret family recipe at Friendly Village.

"Did you know some people will put a coveted recipe on their gravestone. It's pretty cheeky considering you know those people had told everyone they would give them the recipe 'over their dead body'. I think it's healthy to have a sense of humor about death."

"I didn't know that about the gravestones." He forked a bite of calamari for himself. "What's your favorite thing to bake?"

I looked up to the ceiling. "My favorite things to bake are things that make people happy. I love the look of excitement on people's faces when they see their favorite treat. Right now, I'd say I love making cinnamon rolls. They are Henry's second favorite. His first favorite would be lemon bars, but I don't have a good recipe for that. Ava does though, and hers are," I kissed my fingers, "chef's kiss."

Rhys's brows furrowed again before he smoothed them out.

Griffin came by to check on us and brought me another seltzer before he dropped off our food. He kept his lingering looks to a minimum.

I dug into my chicken before swirling the side spaghetti into my fork and slurping up a bite. Rhys gave me a half-smile and started eating his pork.

"What's your favorite dessert?"

He licked his bottom lip a few times. "My favorite dessert is not appropriate to say in public, but my favorite baked good would probably be those pumpkin muffins you made last year during our study session for our first test together."

I leaned forward. "Why didn't you say something earlier? Those are easy to bake. It's pumpkin season so I can make them with fresh pumpkin too." The prospect of baking him something that he'd enjoy made my shoulders shimmy. He was always so verbose when he liked my food.

"You don't have to do that," he said quietly.

I waved a dismissive hand. "You can't stop me now. I love baking, so it's going to happen."

He chuckled and used the side of his fork to pull the pork apart. "Okay, Tama, tell me about your life goals."

Oh, back to the fake date.

"I want to be a sex therapist. I think there is too much misinformation about kinks and sexual proclivities. It should be destigmatized. Also, I think women don't have a true outlet to discuss their relationship with sex. Which is very complicated from the chemical reactions that happen during an orgasm and of course societal purity culture. But if sex therapy isn't in the cards, then I want to do something in the psychiatry or psychology fields."

Rhys blinked at me with his lips parted.

I guess I never went into detail about what I wanted to do.

He shook his head as if to clear it. "How's your chicken?"

I cut into another bite. "Great, thanks. How's the pork?"

"Falling off the bone." He licked his lips again.

We fell into a companionable silence while we finished eating. Griffin checked on us a few times. Rhys ordered us a salted caramel budino to share.

Pippa was at the bar when we passed by it. She scowled at me as Griffin winked. Rhys guided me to his car with his palm on the small of my back. He lifted me into his truck and grinned broadly at me.

His hands lingered on my hips as his eyes darted to my mouth. Air froze in my lungs as he leaned forward. His warm lips brushed against my cheek before he let go of me and ducked away.

I swallowed my disappointment and schooled my face before he got behind the wheel.

"That was fun. How did I do?" I tucked my hands under my thighs. The sun had set, and the air was a little too crisp for my dress. Rhys looked over to me before flicking on the heater. He was silent for a moment.

"You look pretty. Your dress was a good choice, but it is going to be colder when you go on your first real date, so you'll have to think about that."

I tamped down the butterflies his compliment had caused, of course him reminding me that today was fake helped.

"When we sat down it was clear you were a little jealous of the first waitress, but after I mentioned it, you reacted better. I want to apologize again. It was shitty, and I should have shut her flirting down faster."

I bit into my lip to keep my actions that removed Pippa as our server to myself. "It is what it is. What else could I have done better?"

He tilted his head. "You have great posture, but it can be a little intimidating. You look so confident and almost no nonsense."

I scowled. I wasn't going to slouch to make a man feel better. He chuckled at me. "But you can combat that by smiling."

I snorted and then frowned. "You did not tell me to smile more, did you?"

He chuckled. "No, I'm saying it'll counterbalance your severe posture, making you seem more approachable."

"And they say women are the more sensitive sex. Who would have thought my posture would be dangerous to a fragile ego?" I teased.

Rhys growled. "It's not about having a fragile ego. It's about changing the dynamic by smiling. You have a great smile, and you lit up when you started talking about your neighbors."

He blew out a breath before he continued. "Now some of your childhood was unconventional so gauge his reactions before you go into too many details."

My teeth gnashed my lip. I did have a weird childhood, and he was right. But he made me feel comfortable enough to share my little stories with him. He was past judging me.

"You mentioned Henry a few times, which is a little off-putting because you live with him. I know he's your friend, but the next guy may not. Henry may be seen as competition or that you aren't taking the date seriously."

"Don't mention other men, got it. What else?"

He rubbed the back of his neck. "You mentioned sex a few times which is fine, but you have to understand that talking so freely about sex during a first date is going to send the vibe that you are DTF. Just be careful about that. I don't want you to be put into a shitty situation because he thought you were sending mixed signals."

My mouth opened and closed a few times.

Did he think I was DTF with him?

I mean, I am, but I don't want him to know that. "Noted."

"Other than that, you kept the conversation flowing. You asked engaging questions, and you ate your food. I'm not going to set you up with any fucker that judges what you eat, but some dudes will. If he asks you to order a salad, fucking leave. Your body is perfect as is and no one should make suggestions or share their opinions of how you look unless you ask directly."

I chewed my cheek to control those pesky butterflies again.

With the pressure of the date over we slipped into an easy silence. I expected him to take me home, but he didn't. Nathan was eating chips on the couch. Whinny wasn't around, but it was Friday night, he was probably at a party.

Nathan wagged his brows at me. "How was your date?"

"Fine, except for our second server who kept flirting with Tama," Rhys answered.

Nathan snorted and turned to me. "Get it, Bully. What did you think? Of the three years I've known Goodman, he's never taken a girl on a date. How'd he do?"

I looked up to the ceiling. "He took me to a nice restaurant, made nice conversation, and paid, even though I came with my own money." I twisted my lips to the side. "But he failed to mention he also had a waitress flirting with him. She went so hardcore she sat down at our table. All in all, it was a nice date. I'd say if it was real I'd be hoping for a second."

"Ahh, sounds like a love connection," Nathan said.

Rhys scowled at his roommate and gripped both my shoulders to steer me to the steps. "Good night, fucker," Rhys called over his shoulder.

"Damn, Bully, you put out on the first date. Maybe I will ask you out for real," Nathan said.

"Ignore him," Rhys whispered as he pushed me up the steps. *I guess I'm spending the night.*

He passed me at the door and sat down roughly on his bed. "You can take the bathroom first. Your toothbrush is in the drawer. I'll get you a shirt to wear."

I walked woodenly over to his bathroom. It was bigger than mine. He did a decent job of keeping it clean. It was far tidier than Henry's and don't get me started on how gross Matt's bathroom was when I moved into his old room. Granted he hadn't been there most of the summer and prior to the end of the semester his broken arm prohibited him from properly cleaning.

I flicked on the shower and calmed myself down. Rhys and I had a few sleepovers before so there was no reason for me to be nervous, but this felt different. Maybe because it was at the end of our date, he didn't ask where I expected to sleep, and he had seen me naked recently. It was all confusing and I was trying to not get my hopes up that I might get my first kiss tonight.

I quickly rinsed my body and brushed my teeth. Rhys was typing on his phone. He stood when he saw me in a towel, passed me a t-shirt, and went into the bathroom, shutting the door. His shirt slid over my head. I inhaled deeply. It smelled like him and was soft and warm. I hung the towel on the back of his desk chair. Goosebumps pebbled my legs as I slipped into the cool sheets and snuggled down to my side of the bed.

My nose buried into the pillow that also smelled like Rhys. There was something about his warm heady scent that made me feel like I was home. It was a little woodsy without being too strong. I listened to the shower turn on and leaned over to the nightstand where my phone was sitting. I didn't have any messages from Henry, not that I was surprised. He was going to be busy with Ava and was probably taking advantage of an empty apartment.

I checked my emails and responded to a few from Yolanda and Thelma. They kept me up to date on all the village gossip and occasionally sent me recipes for new things they had tried out. My mom hadn't messaged me in a few days. Since marrying Beckett her communication with me was a little less frequent. It went from every day to every few days. I was happy she had someone else to talk to about her day-to-day life.

Rhys stepped out of the bathroom in his towel. I averted my gaze away from his perfect six pack and thick muscular chest. Out of the corner of my eye I saw that he had dropped his towel and walked back into the bathroom to hang it up. He grabbed mine and did the same thing. I froze, desperately wanting to turn my head and see what he looked like naked, but I resisted temptation.

I could see from my periphery when he slipped his boxers on. The discarded shoes were put in his closet, my dress was hung up, and the overhead light was flipped off, all while he walked around brushing his teeth. When he was finished in the bathroom he prowled over to the bed and pulled the covers back. He licked his bottom lip a few passes, staring at my legs before sliding in next to me. I glanced down to see what he had been looking at. The borrowed shirt had risen on one side over my hip bone and made the rest of the hem barely covering the apex of my thighs.

I wiggled my body to fix the shirt as he flipped on his side to face me. "I forgot to ask if you wanted to spend the night. Is this okay?"

Butterflies started wildly flapping. "Of course. Why wouldn't I be okay with this?"

He let out a soft chuckle and leaned forward. His eyes were focused on my lips as he braced his weight on one hand. The other glided towards my face. He reached past me and turned the light off that was on the nightstand.

His warm chest rubbed against my cheek making me giggle. "You could have asked me to turn it off. My voice was muffled as he smothered me into his body. The vibrations of his laugh against my cheek make me realize he was smothering me on purpose. I bit his chest.

He jerked back on a yelp and rubbed the spot next to his nipple where I had nipped him. His obstinate face made me laugh harder.

"Serves you right."

He shook his head. "If you think I won't bite you back you are sorely mistaken, Bully."

"You'd never dare to bite my boob." I laughed at his surprised expression.

"Are you calling my very masculine pec a boob?"

My eyes widened as I held back my laugh but failed when I nodded. He lunged for me, rolling me to my back. His knees bracketed my hips and pinned my hands down. A look of triumph crossed his face.

I tried to move my legs, but all I accomplished was pushing the shirt higher up and the blanket to slip lower. I was grateful he was sitting on my pelvis. He hadn't noticed that the shirt was bunched up and my entire lower half was exposed. All he would have to do was glance behind him and he'd see me live and in 3D.

"I'd never bite your tit, huh?" he challenged. His smile was broad and teasing.

I wiggled again, feeling the shirt bunch higher up my back. Cool air shivered my naked skin as more of my stomach was exposed. He wagged his brows at me and quickly dipped his head down and bit the side of my boob. His butt slid down, I could feel the weight and heat of his manhood resting on my mound before the sting of his teeth nipping the side of my breast. I yelped and thrashed while I laughed.

He chuckled, letting his eyes drag down my body. His stare stopped at my exposed abdomen. I could practically see the moment he realized he was sitting on my naked lower half. His nostrils flared as the muscle in his temple bounced. It took a moment for him to recover before his eyes flicked back up to mine.

"I'll get off you, if and only if you tell me I'm the greatest baseball player of all time and you promise to make me breakfast in the morning."

I rolled my lips in, considering it. I didn't want him to get off me. Him on top of me could lead to me finally losing my virginity and he was so warm. I could feel his pulse pounding against my lower belly and it made my blood rush there in response. But the thought of blood stopped me. All my research said there would be blood after the hymen tore.

I swallowed thickly. I couldn't let Rhys have sex with me without telling him about my hymen status. I was extremely positive he would shut it completely down. He had made more than one comment about not wanting to be the one to take a virginity. He called himself temporary and said that losing it should be with someone that was at least willing to date them.

"You, Rhys Goodman, are the greatest baseball player of all time and I promise to make you breakfast in the morning." My voice shook as I said it. A sly grin crossed his face as he leaned forward. He kissed my cheek again, but this time was dangerously close to my lips.

He eased off me, rolling to his side, keeping me covered enough with his thigh that I was able to yank my shirt down before he had settled back on his side and saw my naked lower half.

"What are your plans tomorrow?"

I turned on my shoulder and looked at him. He was on his back, looking at the ceiling. One knee was bent up. He turned his face in my direction when I didn't answer right away. Dealing with the abrupt topic change, I chewed my cheek.

"Nicole and Lily have a volleyball game. Normally we all go and then hit up a pub of some sort. You want to come?"

He hummed, as if weighing the pros and cons of going. He shook his head after a moment. "Nah, I told Whinny I'd go to the Kappa party. He's trying to hook up with some girl in Phi Mu, and she's supposed to be there."

He probably was relieved I wasn't going to be at the party. It meant he would be able to hook up with whoever he wanted without me cramping his style. "I've never known Whinny to need to chase a girl."

Rhys chuckled and agreed with me. "Yeah, I guess she's lowkey mean to him so he's in love. I think it's a bit dramatic, but what do I know?"

"I can't help you either. The male brain is a complete mystery to me."

Rhys swayed his propped-up leg a few times. "You seem to understand me pretty well."

I chortled. He was a complete mystery to me, too. Minutes ago, I could have sworn he was going to kiss me and try to take things further and then the next thing I know he's talking about going to a party where I know he'll hook up with someone.

We talked until he fell asleep midsentence. I wanted to lean forward and kiss him, but consent is important, so I shuffled around to face the wall, refusing to stare at his perfect face any longer.

Chapter 3

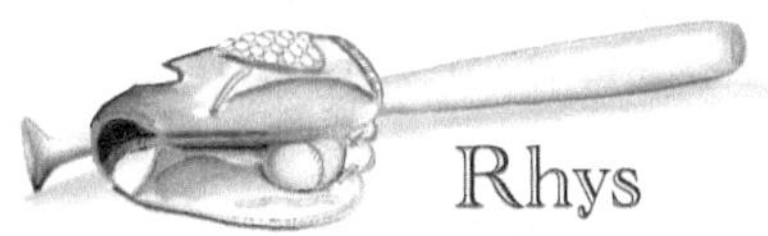

Rhys

I woke up with my bare dickhead, hard as a rock, nestled into Tama's naked ass cheeks and back the morning after our mock date. Thank fuck she was asleep. It gave me a moment to slip my boxers back over my exposed head and pull my hips away gently, so I didn't wake her up. My movements were slow as I eased out of the bed and tiptoed to my bathroom. I jerked off like my life depended on it. She was still sleeping by the time I got back in bed. I tipped my head to the ceiling and tried to ignore my disappointment from last night.

When she told me I was the greatest baseball player of all time it made me want to laugh and groan. It was a small test to see if she was interested in more with me. I was so fucking tempted even before I realized she was practically naked under my hips.

After I saw her bare stomach, the heat from her exposed pussy radiated up to my ball sack. It took me a moment to calm down enough to move off her, but my dick didn't get the message and went full salute by the time I had gotten to my side of the bed. I knew my uncontrollable hormones had everything to do with the fact that it had been months since I had sex.

Maybe the Kappa party was the perfect place to change that.

Tama wouldn't be there so I wouldn't have to worry about some bunny being rude to her. I could disassociate and get my rocks off.

Tama yawned next to me and pulled me out of my thoughts.

Damnit she is cute when she first wakes up.

She blinked up to me with a shy smile across her face.

"Morning," she murmured.

I grinned at her and pulled her against my chest in a hug. She was always so warm and compliant first thing in the morning.

"What do you want for breakfast?"

She giggled as she pulled away when I squeezed her harder.

"Dealer's choice."

She kicked the covers off. I averted my eyes away from her exposed thighs and rubbed my face when she disappeared in the bathroom. When she emerged a few minutes later, her hair was unbraided and falling to her waist in blonde waves. She was still only in my t-shirt, looking sexy as fuck.

I swallowed back a groan as she opened my bedroom door and took a few minutes to calm down.

My phone buzzed from my nightstand. My mom was giving me her weekly update on the goings on in our neighborhood. I had another message on my socials from a new follower. It was the waitress from the restaurant. I shuddered at the weird stalker move. It was tempting to ignore it, but I knew if I left her on read it would leave a more definite nonanswer.

Hey Rhys,

It's Pippa from Maria Bella. I was hoping to give you my number, but your weird friend was too intimidated by me to allow me to continue serving you. She complained to the manager and had me removed. I'm only sorry I didn't get to spend a little more time with you. I felt a connection, and I feel extremely confident that I can make you cum harder than your friend ever could. Call me.

Pippa

What the fuck? The whole message made me pissed the fuck off. One, Tama wasn't weird and two, Tama had made me cum hard several times since I saw her naked and she hadn't even touched me. I blocked Pippa and tossed my phone against the mattress.

Then I chuckled to myself. It wasn't totally unbelievable that she complained about our waitress. I'm sure had I not told her she was acting jealous before she would have confronted her directly, but after my comment she decided to take matters into her own hands without giving her frustration away. It was slick as fuck and made me proud that she figured out a solution without looking like a jealous child.

Though was she jealous or just thought the waitress was being rude? The waitress was being rude. She interrupted our date and dismissed the fact that I'd be on a date with Tama in the first place. When she sat down, she acted like Tama didn't exist.

I should have put a stop to it, but I didn't. I viewed it as practice for when I was famous. Each of those experiences was a way to figure out how I was going to treat people and act when those situations became more frequent. But I fucked up by not considering my date.

As soon as Tama pushed her chair away I knew that she was upset. Her rigid posture had rounded, and her head was tipped down. I half expected her to call a ride share and leave. What I had done and not done was shitty. But she didn't, she took matters into her own hands and let me spend the rest of the evening with her.

No wonder she didn't want to fuck me.

She didn't think I'd pick her over a stranger. She would have a point. How many parties did I let bunnies treat her like shit, then let the bunnies suck me off? Too many to count. *What the fuck is wrong with me?*

I call her my best friend and yet I let people treat her like that. Yeah, not anymore.

I rolled out of bed and snagged a pair of sweatpants from my drawer. Tama was busy mixing something by hand. She grinned at me before setting the bowl down and grabbing something from the fridge. She bent over to grab a few lemons, showing me the bottom curve of her ass in the process. I bit into my lip, knowing she was unaware of what she just did.

"What's for breakfast, Bully?" I pulled myself to sit on the only free space on the counter.

She beamed at me. "Buttermilk pancakes, but you don't have buttermilk, so I am making my own. I'm also making a hashbrown casserole with the potatoes that were on their last leg that I found in the pantry. And finally, your standard scrambled eggs."

An amused smile took over my face as she started mixing milk and lemon juice together. She set it aside and put the grated potatoes in ice water. Her weight shifted from leg to leg.

"I need to wait a few minutes before I can go on. Do you want me to make you some coffee?"

I wanted to reach out to her and bury my nose in her neck, so I sat on my hands instead to keep the temptation at bay.

"I can make it." I swung my legs down and busied myself with the coffee maker.

"So Bully, what is your type?"

"What do you mean?" Her wide eyes were staring up to me.

"Type of guy. I'm going to set you up, and I realized I have no idea what kind of guy you are into."

Her cheeks flushed. "I don't know if I have a type. It's more of a gut feeling, you know? Obviously, he needs to be nice. I don't think I'd handle an actual bully very well. Attraction is important, but I won't know if I am attracted to him until I meet him. For example, Will, Matt, and Henry are attractive men, but I am not attracted to them."

Interesting.

"So, who are you attracted to?" I pushed. Heavy footsteps distracted me from watching her face.

"Good morning, Bully." Whinny sauntered into the kitchen.

I looked over to Tama. Her cheeks were pink.

Fuck does that mean she's attracted to Whinny?

"Please tell me you are making enough for me too."

Tama grinned at my roommate like he was the funniest fucker alive. "Of course. I'm making enough for everyone plus a little extra in case you have a guest."

Whinny walked over to her and kissed her temple. "You are the fucking best, and no I don't have a guest. So more for me."

She chuckled and rolled her eyes as her cheeks went crimson.

"How was the date?" Whinny asked me. Before I could answer he kept going. "I mean, Bully is still here, so I assume it went okay. But I didn't hear a peep from your room last night. Tell me Tama, does Rhys not do it for you?"

The blush spread from her cheeks to her chest before she cleared her throat. "Noise from the bedroom is not a foolproof method to indicate whether an orgasm was achieved. I have a friend that is into silent play. He has engaged in sub/dom relationships where the sub gets punished for being louder than a whisper."

What the fuck?

"Nothing happened between me and Tama. We are friends. But if you spent the night with your ear to my door it seems that you also didn't score last night." As soon as the words left my mouth, I registered that it sounded like I wanted to score last night. *I did.* But I didn't need everyone in the kitchen to know about it.

"Riiight, anyway. I was thinking about who we can set Bully up with, and I might have someone."

I perked up as my stomach tightened. "Tell me about it later. I don't want Tama to look him up on her own."

She scoffed and resumed stirring the milk mix into the batter. Pulling the potatoes from the ice water, she dried them off and turned a burner on under the skillet with a healthy douse of oil to heat.

Nathan strolled into the kitchen. He too kissed Tama's face, her forehead specifically, and then poured himself some coffee. I wasn't sure why my roommates thought kissing my friend was now acceptable, but I wasn't impressed.

"You coming to the Kappa party tonight?" Whinny asked Tama.

Her eyes flicked over to me. I winced the smallest amount knowing if she showed up it would ruin my pre-emptive plans to hook up with someone tonight.

She looked down at the bowl in her hands before answering.
"No, I'm going to the volleyball game and then probably the pub
with my roommates."

"Oh! I love going to the volleyball games. Remember last
year when we went to almost all of them? That shit was fun."
Whinny harrumphed a moment and then shrugged. "Oh well, I
have big plans tonight and the volleyball game is at the same time
as those, so I guess it is what it is."

Nathan sipped his coffee. "I'll go to the match tonight. Are
Reiser and Foust going to be there?"

Tama smiled. "Yeah, Matt is dating Nicole Winters, and Will
is dating Lily Young, so they go to all the home games."

"When did Will seal the deal with Lily?" Nathan asked.
"He'd been pining for a while."

Tama snickered. "It happened over the summer. And he got
into law school here so he's still on campus. They live together
now. It's sweet seeing them."

"Lucky fucker. Lily is perfect."

Tama smiled. "She's the best. If you decide to go to the
match, come and find me." Her back was to us now as she
worked on frying the potatoes. Nathan looked me dead in the
eye with a shit-eating grin on his face. "It's a date."

Motherfucker.

Tama walked up the steps to her building. I made sure she got
into the apartment before I pulled away. We had spent the entire
day together and it was a little bit of torture and a lot of fun. It

made me horny as fuck, but I was with her, and she makes everything better.

I pulled back into my driveway five minutes later. Nathan was in the living room playing his Xbox. "Wanna play before you go to the party?"

I huffed and yanked the spare controller into my hand. "What was that about earlier anyway?"

Nathan frowned before he flicked his eyes over to me. "What do you mean?"

I flexed my jaw. "With Tama. Why are you all the sudden interested in her?"

He chortled. "When you made a public announcement that you were going to hook her up with a blind date. Why do you have a problem with it?"

I scowled at him. "I already told you. I don't want to hear a post-mortem from either of you about a date. Just back off, okay?"

He set his controller down and turned his body towards me. "So let me get this straight. You don't want her. I'm not allowed to have her. And only someone of your choosing will get a shot at her? Do I have that correct?"

My eyes rolled, but I didn't answer.

He laughed without humor. "She doesn't get a choice at all?" he pushed.

I licked my lips. "It's easier for all parties involved if her boyfriend isn't my friend."

He scoffed. "If she has a boyfriend then you shouldn't *be* involved, bro."

I gritted my teeth making my temple bounce. My jaw was starting to hurt. "She's my best friend. I only want the best for her."

"And that's not you?"

I rolled my eyes. "Not this again. She doesn't want me like that."

"Bull. Shit. You are fucking blind, man. You two talk every day. She made you breakfast after spending the night. I can tell by your shitty mood you didn't get laid, but tell me, did you cuddle her in bed?"

A scowl formed before I relaxed my face. "I don't see how that's relevant."

Nathan threw his head back and laughed. "Don't tell me you haven't figured it out yet."

My glare burned towards him. "Figured what out?"

He squinted at me, stood up, and took a few steps away, just out of punching reach. "You're in a relationship with Tama. She is your girlfriend without the title and sexual benefits."

I shook my head. "No, I am in a *friendship* with Tama, nothing more."

"Sure, next time I have a hard time falling asleep I expect you to spoon me while you whisper sweet nothings about not letting the boogeyman get me. We are friends. The same as you and Bully, right? She gets that, I get that."

My eyes cut to him, but I didn't say anything.

"Yeah, that's what I thought."

"I don't need to justify my friendship to you."

He held up his hands. "Didn't say you did, but I'm telling you; if you set her up on a date, you need to mentally prepare yourself that all those friend benefits like talking until you fall asleep, snuggling all night, and having her as your emergency contact, that all changes. You will have to accept the back seat. If you can't, then you need to reflect on that."

"I have no problem with that," I lied.

Nathan's brow perked up. "Prove it."

Tama

My fingertips tingled as I pulled my hunter green sweater on. I shook my trembling hands out. My jeans made a jerky path up my legs before I slipped on the knee-high boots Lily had gotten me for Christmas.

Rhys made good on his promise to set me up on a blind date. It had been two weeks since my first mock date. He had taken me out on another one but didn't give me any more tips. The biggest difference between the first and second date was the fact that he took me home when it was over.

I hadn't spent the night at his place since that night. After he dropped me off, he pulled away. Which was fine, I was fine, perfect even. Great.

Whinny told me that Rhys was busy 'trying to get his dick wet' the night of the volleyball match. Whinny drunk texted me and asked if I was willing to come over to bake some cookies for him since he had struck out. I declined for numerous reasons. One being that Henry's ex went a little crazy and Ava was upset and two, I didn't want to be in Rhys's house while he was having sex with another woman.

Nathan had text messaged me a few times too asking for a dinner invite, but I was trying to give Rhys the space he clearly needed. A week after our date he reached out to take me out again and told me he had missed me that week. It was confusing, but I missed him too, so I didn't remind him it was his choice to ice me out.

We had a fun date, so I had forgotten about it not being real. I had assumed he wasn't going to set me up. I guess I had read one too many romance novels to convince me that Rhys was going to come to his senses and decide that he wanted me for himself.

Ava tapped on my door before letting herself in.

"You look pretty."

I gave her a shaky nod. "I wanted to check in on you before we head out. We will be back Sunday night. But you can call me if you need anything, okay?"

She and Henry were flying down to Baylor to continue her alibi that she was a student at the Waco school. They were meeting with her family because her mom wanted to meet Henry. He had been on cloud nine for the past week. Last weekend because he was able to be out about his affections towards Ava with her dad's surprise visit and this week because he was going to have an entire weekend where they didn't have to pretend they weren't together. I still maintained that they needed to tell Will and rip the bandage off, but it wasn't my call.

"Do you need to talk anything through?"

I licked my lips and shook my head. "Nope, I'm sure it'll be okay. If it's not, then it's not." I shrugged, acting far calmer than I was feeling.

She chewed her lip. "Do you think that you'll get your first kiss tonight?"

A shaky breath buffeted my hair. "No idea. I'm going to go with the flow."

Ava twisted her lips to the side as Henry walked into my room. He wrapped his arms around Ava and pulled her into his chest. "You good, Tama?"

I gave another shaky nod.

He frowned. "You'll be fine. If he doesn't like you, he's missing out."

I slipped my phone into my back pocket.

"Do you want us to drop you off? We are on the way to the airport now, it's no trouble," Ava asked.

I twisted my lips to the side. "Yeah, I was going to get a rideshare but dropping me off will save me a few bucks."

As they pulled away, I tucked my hands into my coat pockets. The weather had turned to winter practically overnight. There was snow on the ground, but none currently falling. I burrowed my nose into my scarf and looked around the parking lot. After a few more minutes I stepped into the restaurant to see if Grant, my blind date, had already arrived. I doubted it as I was still ten minutes early.

I took a seat at the bar and ordered a seltzer while I waited. The restaurant was a few steps above a pub but not fancy in the least. American fare, decent prices, all-in-all a good choice for a neutral blind date.

Ten minutes came and went, then another ten minutes. I checked my phone to see if I had any missed messages. My nerves started to ratchet up when another ten minutes passed. I wished I had Grant's phone number so I could ask him if I had gotten the time and date wrong, but since everything was set up through Rhys, I had nothing.

Forty minutes after my date was supposed to meet me, I decided to call it. I had officially been stood up.

He probably saw me and decided not to go through with it.

I numbly paid for my seltzers and ordered a rideshare.

My apartment was silent when I got home. The quiet had never bothered me, but after my night it was lonely.

Nicole and Lily were away for a volleyball tournament. Matt and Will flew with. Will had a small break in his law school studies, and Matt was scouting a kid in the next town over from the tournament. It was just me.

I wasn't sure what I was feeling. Sad? Certainly. Mad? Of course. Disappointed? Yeah, that too. But there was more. There was shame mixed in there even though I had nothing to feel ashamed about. There was also a sense of remorse. I knew that was weird. I hadn't done anything wrong.

The only regret I could think of to date was not escalating things with Rhys weeks ago when I was in his bed. It would have been so easy, but I stopped it from happening. I didn't want him to see me bleed. I didn't want him to know I was a virgin, an inexperienced freak, someone he didn't want to be friends with anymore.

I had a few conversations about what having sex felt like. Ava's was the most reliable account: It hurt until it didn't and there was blood.

I sat on my bed and stared at my nightstand drawer. Lily bought me my first vibrator a year ago. I thought it was a joke, but it was not. It was small and harmless and only for clitoral stimulation. Next to my discreet vibrator was a less discreet dildo made to pack a punch. I hadn't used it. Nothing bigger than a tampon had been in me and that purple monster was bigger than a thin cotton roll.

I tapped my foot on the floor a few beats and tried to calm my breathing down.

I'm going to do it.

I kicked my boots off, grabbed a towel, and Barney, my purple dildo.

This is going to hurt.

I wasn't the least bit turned on so when the pinching made me wince, I pulled it out and sat it down on my bed.

My hands shook as I rubbed my face. Decision made, I dashed over to Henry's room. He had a safe under his sink full of his condoms and sex toys. I tried the same code he used to unlock his computer and the safe clicked open. My teeth gnashed my lip at the idea that I was going to steal lube from Henry, but I knew if he were here, he'd give it freely.

I darted back across to my room and poured a little too much onto Barney. I wasn't sure if it was a more the merrier scenario or a little goes a long way. I gathered quickly that a little went a long way when it started to puddle on the towel beneath me.

I counted down like I was about to sky dive. My legs flexed in nervous energy, causing my muscles to burn and tremble.

Just get it over with.

Barney stabbed me. Tears leaked down my face as I yelped out. *Pinch of pain? Lies!* It was terrible. I let out a choppy breath and pulled Barney out. My eyes were squeezed closed as I rolled onto my side in the fetal position.

I wasn't sure if it was lube or blood that was coating my towel, but it didn't matter. It was over, done. Physically I no longer possessed a hymen.

Ten minutes passed before I was able to pull my knees away from my stomach. I took a shower to clean up what I could, rinsed my bloody towel, and replaced Henry's lube. When all evidence of what I had done was gone and the cramping had stopped, I folded in on myself and cried to sleep.

Loud hunger pangs woke up at 2am. In all the scattered emotions from the evening I had forgotten to eat dinner. I warmed some leftover Chinese food and sat at the dining room table to wait for the microwave. A light thumping on my front door made me freeze. I was hardly breathing, listening for the thumping to start again. There was no reason for anyone to be on my floor.

Thump, thump, thump.

I squeaked and clapped my hand over my mouth. My heart pounded frantically when I tiptoed over to the door and pressed my ear against it. A low rumbling noise burbled out and then a light thump, thump, thump. I was too short to see through the peephole. I slowly backed away and grabbed a dining room chair to stand on and checked the breezeway from the safety of my locked apartment.

All I could see from the fish-eyed view was the top of a hoodie-covered head and legs sticking out. Someone was leaning against my door. I let out a whimper and backed away to my bedroom, abandoning my Chinese food. I yelped and clapped my hand over my mouth again when the microwave loudly beeped.

The thumping quickly turned into knocking. I couldn't catch my breath. *This was how I died.* I reached for my phone on my nightstand, preparing to call the police. Rhys had left dozens of messages. The last message snagged my attention.

Rhys: I'm outside, let me in.

It was from ten minutes ago. The relief that pulled through me was swift as I grabbed the chair to check the peephole again. Sure enough, a disheveled Rhys was leaning against my door.

I pushed the chair aside and swung the door open. Rhys stumbled in, tripped on the chair and ungracefully fell to the floor. He laid there for a moment, giggling before propping himself up on his elbows.

"I fell down," he whispered.

Oh, he was drunk.

"You did. Do you want some help, or are you going to lie on the floor the rest of the night?"

He hummed and attempted to swing his body up, nearly headbutting me in the process. He settled himself by grabbing my shoulders.

"I fucked up," he slurred.

I rolled my lips in, waiting for him to finish.

"I told you that your date was tonight, but you know what," he shook his head, "it wasn't. Grant told me last week that he had a football game tonight and needed to reschedule for tomorrow, but I didn't see the message until tonight."

I chewed my lips.

"But I was already getting drunk because what if you like Grant? Then he won't let me snuggle with you anymore. And you're my best friend. So, guess what? I needed to drink to get my head ready for you to break up with me. But it turns out, I'm a shit. You thought you were stood up, right?"

I didn't speak, not wanting him to stop his drunk babbling.

He groaned. "Your eyes are red which means you cried. It's all my fault because I didn't double check my messages and you thought he didn't want you. But everyone wants you, you're the best."

The pressure on my mouth was becoming painful, so I let my lips go. The microwave beeped again, reminding me that I had food waiting.

Rhys whipped his body around. "Are you making food?" he whispered. I nodded.

A child-like grin spread across his face. "I'll be your best friend if you share with me."

I rolled my eyes and grabbed his hand so he'd follow me into the kitchen. I filled two plates with tangerine chicken and rice. His smile stayed on his face the entire time he ate. When he attempted to steal a piece of my chicken from my plate he missed, making a horrible screeching noise as his fork slid against the stoneware.

"Party foul, my bad, baby." He wrapped his arms around my head as if to shield my ears from the screech.

I wiggled to free myself and looked up to him. He gazed down at me and then dipped his face.

His lips were warm against mine. I was too shocked to move at first when I realized he was kissing me. He turned his head to deepen the kiss and licked the seam of my lips. I delicately opened as his hands slid from around my head to down to my waist. He picked me up and placed me on the counter, next to our plates. Without breaking the kiss, he stepped between my spread thighs and thrashed his tongue against mine.

My knuckles ached from how hard I was gripping the counter's edge. I was afraid to move a muscle, worried it would break the spell, and he'd realize he was kissing me. He let out a satisfied hum and pulled his lips away from mine.

"We taste like Chinese food," he slurred.

An embarrassed blush heated my cheeks as he backed up.

"Can I sleep here tonight?" He walked away from the kitchen as if he hadn't kissed the life out of me. I stared blankly at the cabinets before easing off the counter.

"Sure," I finally answered.

He dramatically pumped his fist. "I'm going to take a shower," he announced and started stripping his clothes in my living room.

I grabbed his hoodie, shirt, socks, and jeans as he left a trail to my room. I sucked in a sharp breath as he dropped his boxers and passed them to me with a smile on his face.

I tried, oh how I tried to keep my eyes above his belly button, but it became impossible when he said, "You can look at me."

Still clutching his discarded clothes, I let my eyes trail down his perfect body right down to his penis. It was pointing down and flaccid, but good lord he was big. He put Barney to shame, and he wasn't even hard.

"Do you want me to wash these?" I held his clothes up.

He shrugged. "I'd rather you helped wash me."

I bit my lip as he grabbed my hand. "Come on, Bully, it's only a shower. I can't get it up if I tried, so you don't have to worry about me trying to fuck you. I know you don't want me like that."

I let out a harsh breath as I laughed at how ridiculous his statement was, but he was too drunk for me to argue with him. "Give me a second to start these." I motioned towards his clothes.

His smile was back as I rushed out of my room.

Oh my god!

I quickly shoved his clothes into the washer where the bloody towel was waiting for me to start the load. I cringed and ran into Henry's bathroom, yanking the menstrual pad away and thanking my lucky stars that I had stopped bleeding. I knew I wasn't going to have sex, but nothing is less sexy than blood running down a thigh.

Rhys was standing in my bathroom, shower on, leaning against the counter, still butt naked. He wagged his brows at me. "Can I do the honors?" He motioned to the hem of my pajamas.

I gave him a quick, nervous nod before he pulled it away from my body. He cursed under his breath as my bare chest came into view. He curled his fingers into the waistband of the shorts I was wearing and tugged them down.

"Perfect," he murmured to himself when he stood back from my naked body. He grabbed my hand and led me to my small shower.

80

It was not built for two. It was hardly built for one, which made me giggle when he realized that we were going to have to basically hug the entire time.

"Can I touch you?" he whispered in my ear.

I sucked in a shaky breath and closed my eyes as his hands followed the water's flow down to my butt where he squeezed tightly. He pulled one leg up to wrap around his hip as his fingers teased my lower lips. I whimpered against his chest. My mouth dropped open in a gasp as he swirled his fingertip around my clit.

His chest rumbled against my ear as I started to shake. He was barely touching me, but I was already on edge. A few more flicks and my hips were chasing after his caress. Chuckling, he pulled his hand away, leaving me without an orgasm. He licked his fingers clean and then reach for the soap to lather our bodies. The suds swirled around the drain as he turned the water off and picked me up.

"I know you didn't cum." He wrapped me in a towel. My knees were shaking and my legs felt heavy. Scooping me up, he carried me to my bed. My back hit the mattress as he pulled the towel away. "I decided that I wanted you to cum on my tongue, not my fingers."

Oh my.

Like a predator, his strides were slow and confident as he stalked over to me. Pulling my hips to the edge of the bed, he kneeled on the floor. His lips surrounded my clit before his hot tongue slid up and down my cleft. I moaned and bit into my hand to stifle the sounds bubbling from my mouth.

"God, you taste good. You asked me what my favorite dessert is. It's this." He dove back in.

I grinded my pelvis into his face as he greedily ate me out. My stomach started to hollow as his tongue flicked rapidly against my clit. My body jerked forward as he shoved two fingers inside me. With his free hand he pushed my lower belly down.

My head was thrashing against the mattress as his lips surrounded my clit again and sucked while his two fingers continued to scissor inside me. The most intense pleasure of my life took over. It was a warm tingle that turned into a wave of euphoria as my thighs shook against Rhys's cheeks. My walls clenched and fluttered as I moaned and gasped, my hot orgasm left my body. Rhys licked and sucked until my tremors stopped.

Relaxing as I caught my breath, Rhys kissed my thighs and stood up. His dick was no longer flaccid as he walked back over to the bathroom. He washed his face and winked at me from the mirror.

"I'm never washing my hand again." To emphasize he sniffed his fingers, making his eyes roll back as he groaned.

My cheeks grew hot.

He giggled. "You're so fucking perfect."

My heart was still drumming in my chest when he walked back over to me. I sat up and looked up to him from my lashes. He rubbed my lip with his thumb and bent down to kiss me.

Feeling bold I reached forward and wrapped my hand around his erection. His hips jerked back as he gasped in my mouth. What I wasn't expecting was how hot and smooth his penis was.

Way better than the cucumber.

He pulled his lips away from mine. "I'm drunk," he repeated.

I swallowed hard. "I know, do you want me to stop?"

He shook his head. "Fuck no, but I may not be able to cum, baby."

The saliva pooled in my mouth. "I understand. I'm not very good at giving head."

He chuckled and tipped my chin up. "I doubt that."

I glanced back down at his dick, and I swear to god it got bigger and twitched. I let out a shaky breath and thought back to the awkward blowjob lesson. Gazing at Rhys from his thighs, I licked my palm before giving him the same attention. I lavished him like a dripping ice cream cone, covering his shaft in my saliva before I grasped him at the root.

Here goes nothing.

My lips surrounded his head and started to work down. He did taste a little salty, but it was from the precum that had gathered at his tip. Otherwise, his skin tasted like skin and a hint of my soap. My cheeks hollowed and pulled back up, my tongue flicking the crown before sucking him down further. A gag came on but breathed through my nose and backed off. I brought my hand to my lips and twisted my fist as I worked him back down my throat.

My eyes caught his. He was watching me with wide eyes, licking his bottom lip as his breathing became choppy. He cursed under his breath. Closing my eyes, I started to work my mouth and hand together. I sucked harder and tightened my grip, which made his thighs shake. He didn't tell me I was hurting him, so I took it as a win.

My free hand snaked to his sack and my thumb ran down the seam. I had done a fair amount of research on perineum stimulation and figured he was too drunk to stop me. I decided on the external massage versus the internal. My thumb gently pressed and rubbed his sensitive spot. He gasped above me as his stomach hollowed out. I slowly increased the pressure on my thumb while I sped up my mouth and hand. His hips had started to rut into me, causing me to gag, but I kept going.

He tightly gripped my hair. "Fuck, baby. Don't. Stop. Any. Thing," he gasped between each word. "I'm going to cum, fuuuccck," he gritted out.

I braced myself as I kept sucking and massaging. His release coated my tongue and made me squeeze my eyes as I attempted to swallow it down. The grip he had on my hair loosened.

"Holy fuck," he hissed.

After my last swallow I popped off him and stood up on shaking legs. I needed to drink some water. He leaned in and kissed me again. His tongue was lazy against mine before he pulled away with a series of pecks to my cheeks and eyelids.

"You're incredible. No one has ever…" He groaned and dropped another kiss to my lips, "touched my p-spot."

I giggled as I walked over to my dresser and pulled out a pair of basketball shorts that was left in my room. I had asked Matt if they were his and he said they weren't.

I passed the mystery shorts over to Rhys who had sat hard on the bed. He had a lazy grin on his face. I excused myself to rotate his laundry. I brushed my teeth before checking the locks to my apartment and gulping back a glass of water.

By the time I got back in my room Rhys was passed out on the top of the covers. He had managed to put the shorts on, but that was the extent. His legs were still hanging off the bed. I giggled to myself and turned off the light.

Rhys had unknowingly marked a lot of firsts off my list. It was too bad he was drunk. I wondered what would have been different if he were sober.

Chapter 4

Rhys

My legs hurt, my brain felt like it was trying to squeeze through my eye socket, and my stomach lurched. It was too bright for it to be my bedroom, and the bed was too firm.

Where the fuck am I?

I shivered and reached around myself for a blanket. The ache in my arms made me wince, but it was nothing compared to the burning in my calves. I peered an eye open.

How the fuck did I get to Tama's?

She was sound asleep on her side of the bed. I glanced down. I had no clue whose shorts I was wearing. My clothes were nowhere in sight. I winced as I shuffled to the head of the bed and pulled her quilt down so I could go back to sleep. Tama mumbled something. I was too hungover to catch it. I would have smiled that she was talking in her sleep again, but everything hurt too much for that.

I rubbed my face and scowled when my fingers smelled like pussy. Cringing, I had obviously hooked up with someone last night then came to Tama's. My drunk brain likes snuggling with her. I had promised myself I'd cut that shit out after our first fake date. I didn't want a relationship and according to Nathan everyone assumed I was in one with Tama. Which wasn't fair to her. She deserved to be in something real.

Oh fuck, the date.

I remembered why I got so drunk. Nathan got in my head about how if Grant and her were a love match, I could kiss my 'relationship' with Tama goodbye.

Whinny and I got shit faced. I remember blurs of making out with some chick. Clearly, I did more than make out if my favorite smell in the world still coated my fingers. My stomach churned as I remembered. Grant was there making out with some girl. I asked him where Tama was and he told me… *Oh shit.*

Guilt swarmed my stomach as I remembered Tama accidentally getting stood up. Obviously, I came over, but I have no idea how I got here. I don't remember anything past talking to Grant. I don't remember hooking up with the blonde at the party. Kissing her, yes, fingering her, not so much.

I'm a piece of shit.

My best friend was being stood up while I was hooking up with a random instead of being there for her. I squeezed my eyes shut. I was the worst friend. Why the hell did she put up with me?

"Just like that," Tama whimpered in her sleep.

My face jerked over to her, causing my head to spin at the sudden movement. She was still sleeping, but it sounded like she was having a sex dream.

"Please don't stop," she whispered.

Fuck. She whimpered as her chest started to rise and fall rapidly. Her eyes were still closed as her lips parted in a gasp. She moaned and tipped her head back. I watched in fascination as my friend orgasmed while she slept. I squeezed my dick to keep myself from blowing my load in a stranger's shorts.

My cock was in my hand before I had latched the bathroom door. I replayed the sounds she had made, her breathy whimpers, and then my imagination gifted me with a real dream. Tama spread on her bed as I ate her pussy. Then Tama sucking the soul from my body giving me the best blow job of my life. It had to be a dream with how hungover I was, there is no way I was able to properly use my dick. It didn't matter that only I had touched my dick in months, I knew my body. Getting it up *and* cumming wouldn't happen under normal circumstances. My brain was showing me the ultimate fantasy between me and my best friend.

I grunted as my cum shot out of me. The pounding in my head intensified as my breathing leveled out. I grabbed some medicine from her cabinet and drank some water directly from the sink. A few more hours of sleep and I'd be right as rain, and then I could apologize for last night.

I woke up the second time to the smell of bacon in the air and my clothes from last night neatly folded on the desk. I stretched my arms and legs, grateful my headache was gone, but I was starving.

I pulled off the borrowed shorts and tugged on my clean boxers and jeans. My shirt smelled like Tama which made me inhale deeply as I pulled it on. She was in the kitchen. Biscuits were cooling on a rack, gravy was bubbling in a pot, bacon was crisping in the oven. She beamed at me.

"I was wondering when you'd wake up," she said and turned back to the oven.

"I'm so sorry about last night," I started. I figured if I ripped the bandage off, we could get right back on track.

Her back straightened as she paused.

"Apparently, Grant told me last week he had a game last night and I missed the message. I should have caught it, and I feel terrible."

Her shoulders rounded as she looked down at the counter. Her back was to me. She nodded to herself once before she turned around. "Yeah, I know you explained last night when you got here at 2am."

I cringed. "Did I wake you up?"

She shook her head, not looking at me. "Nope, I was warming up Chinese food. You don't remember eating when you got here?" Her eyes looked a little shrink wrapped.

I shook my head. "I don't remember anything past seeing Grant at the party I was at. I was hooking up with someone and I saw Grant with a girl that wasn't you."

She blinked rapidly. Her chest heaved a few breaths as she licked her lips. "It's fine. It is what it is. You don't have to explain."

I chewed on my lip, not sure why she was upset when she seemed content a minute ago. Her eyes darted around the kitchen before settling on the fridge magnets to my right.

"I shouldn't have mentioned anything about Grant hooking up with someone, if that's what you are upset about."

She shook her head, forcing a smile to her face. Her eyes looked too bright. "It's fine. I don't know anything about Grant, so he has no loyalty towards me. It's fine, I'm great." She turned back around and stirred the gravy before grabbing a plate.

"How long did you wait at the restaurant?" I held my breath. I already felt like shit, and her answer had the potential to guilt me.

"Not quite an hour," she answered without turning around. I cursed and went to hug her from behind. She went stiff in my arms, not the soft melting she normally did. She was clearly upset with my fuckup.

"I'm so sorry. Why didn't you text me?"

She shook her head. "It's mortifying to be forgotten about." Her voice cracked as she said it. I let her catch her breath.

"Breakfast smells good."

Her posture was still rigid against me.

I sighed. "Listen, if you want to cancel tonight, I'll let Grant know. This was all my fault anyway. I'll take the heat."

She shook her head quickly and stepped out of my embrace with a wince. "No, you want me to go out with Grant, so I will. I won't hold it against him about last night. He didn't do anything wrong. It was a failure to communicate. It happens, right?" Her tone was lifeless. I felt like hot garbage as guilt swarmed me.

"Whatever you want," I tried to reassure her.

She blinked rapidly to clear the tears and grabbed her plate from the counter. "Biscuits and gravy with candied bacon. It's good if you crumble it on top. You get salty, savory, sweet, creamy, crunchy, and chewy all in one bite."

There was a quiet devastation about her that made my stomach clench in guilt.

"Sounds good."

She wouldn't meet my eye the entire time we ate, always darting around the room or to her plate.

"I regret everything about last night. I'm fucking sorry," I repeated quietly. I hated seeing her like this.

Her brows furrowed as her eyes shimmered before she blinked rapidly again. "It is what it is." She cleared her throat. "What are you doing today?" Her voice cracked. She cleared her throat again and gave me a smile that didn't reach her eyes.

"Whinny and Nathan need to go grocery shopping. I have a paper I need to finish. What about you?"

She licked her lips. "All my roommates are out of town, so it's just me until my date tonight."

A fresh wave of guilt pummeled me again. She was stood up and didn't have anyone to console her last night. I looked up to the ceiling and swallowed thickly. She grabbed her plate and rushed to the kitchen.

"Um, I have a headache. You can stay as long as you want, but I am going to go lie down."

My heart pounded and my stomach sank at her dismissal. She was clearly upset by my failures. I fucked up so bad by not double checking the time and date. She was embarrassed, no, mortified, and I came here a drunk bumbling idiot. She didn't have a headache; she wanted to be alone. Or at least not around me.

Tama's head was down and back slumped as she closed her bedroom door. I washed the dishes from breakfast and grabbed my phone which was on the floor by the couch. I had no idea how it got there. I pulled up my truck's location and rolled my eyes. I had walked from the party. Which was probably the most responsible thing I could have done, but my truck was still parked at Kappa House.

I shoved my phone in my hoodie pocket and walked home.

Whinny was sprawled across the sofa with a frozen bag of popcorn kernels on his forehead. "You look how I feel," I said.

He winced. "How's Tama?"

I grimaced. "She waited an hour before she left. All her roommates are out of town, so she's pretty bummed about being stood up. I fucked up by telling her I saw Grant hooking up with someone. She's upset."

"That sucks. Probably shouldn't have mentioned that last bit for sure."

I slumped down on the sofa. "I'm an idiot. My best friend was stood up, and it was all my fault. And then I rubbed salt in the wound by telling her about Grant."

Whinny nodded. "A certified idiot."

Nathan strolled into the living room. "Thanks for the almost sloppy seconds, bro," he said with a grin.

"I have no idea what you are talking about," I admitted.

He chuckled and sat down on the loveseat and propped his feet up on the coffee table. "That girl who was sucking on your neck last night, Yazmin. I appreciate the hand off."

My brows furrowed. "I hate to break it to you but if you hooked up with the blonde last night, then it was definitely sloppy seconds."

Nathan chortled. "How powerful do you think your neck skin is? Because it's not sexy enough to make a girl cum, bro. I did that twice."

I squinted at him. "My neck skin? What the fuck is wrong with you. I'm talking about my fingers smelling like pussy this morning."

Nathan snorted. "Well, it wasn't Yazmin's pussy. Those orgasms belong to me."

I looked over to Whinny. "You saw me hooking up with a blonde last night, right?"

Whinny shrugged. "I saw Yazmin suck your neck and you pushed her off when you saw Grant, and you told me you needed to get to Tama. But I probably missed something. Dakota told me to go fuck myself with a fist full of glass shards. It was a bummer, so I sort of blacked out after you left."

I sniffed my fingers again. "Who the fuck did I finger?"

Nathan threw his head back in a laugh. "Don't tell me you sealed the deal with Tama, and you don't even remember."

I shook my head. "I told you, she doesn't want me like that."

"Then who else did you finger fuck?"

I forced a bright smile on my face as the hostess showed us to our table. Grant pulled my chair out and then sat across from me. He had a soft smile on his face as he tilted his head.

"You weren't who I was expecting."

I rolled my lips in, unsure how to take it. I had already had one of the most heartbreaking days of my life. I was normally an optimistic person, but after having the man I was pretty sure I was madly in love with forget we had *sexual relations* I was feeling down in the dumps.

"Oh, sorry to disappoint. I brought money to pay my own way."

Grant shook his head. "Not like that. You're beautiful, I was expecting the tall brunette that Ava lives with."

I forced another smile. "Right, that would be Nicole and I am physically her opposite. I'm sorry she's dating Matt Foust."

He made a face that said, 'yeah makes sense' and reached for his glass of water.

"You know Ava?"

He waved his head back and forth. "Not really, we exchanged phone numbers about a month ago, but she kept dodging my invites out."

My cheeks hurt from forcing my smile. "She's also involved with someone."

He nodded sagely. "Yeah, I gathered that when, Henry is it?"

I chewed my lip and nodded.

"Yeah, Henry told me that I should take Rhys up on his offer and take you off his hands."

I swallowed hard and looked down to the table. My stomach swirled in the knowledge this date was born from pity. "I didn't know Henry spoke to you."

"Yeah, it's not a big deal. Rhys had been talking you up for a few weeks. I just have a thing for brunettes, but like I said you're really pretty."

I faked another smile. "Thank you," I murmured.

"Also, I'm sorry about the miscommunication last night. I sent Rhys a message last week reminding him I had a game. I play football for the school, so he should have known, but you know, sorry. It sucks that you thought you were stood up."

I let out a shaky breath. "It's fine. Accidents happen. Tell me about yourself. You play football, what's your major?"

I was surprised my voice didn't shake. Though it may have been something to do with the fact that there was zero chemistry between me and Grant. He was attractive, but after the day I had I didn't have the energy to force anything.

"Poli Sci, you?"

"Psychology and Biology."

His brows shot up. "That's a heavy load. No wonder you look a little tense."

I tried to relax my shoulders. "I'm nervous," I admitted.

He gave me a soft smile. "No reason to be nervous. This is a practice date, right?"

My stomach swooped again. Of course, he thought this was another fake date.

"Right, it's not real," I forced out.

"You know Rhys is going to be blowing my phone up the minute this date is over. Should I lie to him and tell him you took me to the bathroom and had your wicked way with me?"

I laughed. At least Grant had a sense of humor. I shrugged. "Who said you'd have to lie to him?"

Grant's mouth gaped, mulling over my joke like it was a real offer.

I shook my head. "That was a joke, sorry."

He leaned back in his chair. "Cool. So how long has Ava been seeing Henry?"

Love connection it was not. Grant was nice enough and if he were my friend I probably would have had more fun, but he made it clear I was not his type.

I stashed my change from dinner in the little water jug on the floor of my closet. Grant said he was happy to pay but didn't put up a fight when I asked for two checks. And why would he? It was all fake to him. I was a pity date.

A few tears leaked from my eyes. All of it hurt, every single bit since I woke up, hurt. My phone buzzed next to me.

I had no interest in telling Rhys about what a pathetic loser I was. Besides, it sounded as if Grant was more than happy to regale Rhys on my subpar dating skills. Grant was probably hitting up the same party that I was positive that Rhys was at.

With my phone on silent, I took a shower. I didn't want the world to bother me for the rest of the weekend. I wanted to wallow alone like I was always meant to be. It was silly of me to assume anyone would take me seriously enough to date me.

Sunday was spent in a stupor as I did my laundry and cleaned the apartment. I didn't touch my phone all day. I wanted to be left alone. It was moments like this that made me mad that I didn't have a driver's license. I would have liked to go on a mountain drive and be in nature. It was way too cold to be outside for more than twenty minutes, but the drive would have been pleasant.

I looked up driver's ed classes for when I went home for the winter. Beckett always told me that as soon as I had my license, he'd get me a car. Not that I had a parking spot to bring it to campus. And the drive from Hemet to Boulder was way too daunting for a new driver to tackle, but it would be nice to have the option to drive somewhere.

Ava and Henry's flight was landing later in the evening, so I knew that I wasn't going to see them if I didn't want to. When Nicole and Lily got in, I was too mentally exhausted to leave my bed to go see how their tournament went.

I turned my bedroom light off twenty minutes before my roommates got home. Ava's giggle and Henry's growl sounded through the hallway, letting me know they arrived safely home. I turned to face the wall and tried to sleep. In all my life I had never felt this numb before. It was weird. I was feeling a lot of things, I didn't understand why my brain was buffering, not picking one emotion to feel.

Avoiding Rhys on Monday was tough. We had Human Anatomy together. I ended up skipping the class and walking home. I emailed the professor that I had a migraine, and she sent me the class slides so I could take my notes from them.

Henry barged in my bedroom two hours before dinner. "What's going on?"

My blank stare made his forehead furrow. "What happened?" His head tilted as he gave me a sympathetic frown.

I twisted my lips to the side as the numb veil finally lifted. Tears poured down my face as I told Henry everything. I could tell he was upset for me when I told him about being stood up and then how embarrassing it was that Grant clearly didn't want to go on the date with me.

"I feel so fucking bad. I'd have never told him to take you out if he was going to be such a fucking tool about it."

I swallowed thickly. He pulled me against his chest and kissed the top of my head. My body rocked back and forth a few passes before he let me go. "As far as Rhys forgetting," he shrugged. "Did you cum?"

I nodded. He grinned. "Then whatever. It's his loss he was too drunk to remember. Though, now is a good time to remind you that consent matters even when someone is drunk."

I scoffed. "He stripped down and told me to touch him."

Henry snorted. "Well, that sounds like a green light. I'm sorry if you're hurting about it but seriously fuck that guy."

My teeth pressed firmly into my cheek. He grunted. "Look, I know you two have a weird friendship thing going on, but when it starts feeling shitty, it is okay to draw boundaries."

I nodded into his chest as he hugged me again.

"Uh, Tama, there is someone here to see you," Ava said from the doorway.

Her pretty face was soft with concern. She knew I was feeling blue. She clocked it on the ride to school this morning. She's probably the one who told Henry to check on me.

"If it's Rhys, tell him he can suck a bag of dicks," Henry said loudly.

"I'd prefer not," Rhys responded.

I glanced up at my door. It looked like Ava was trying to bar him from my room, but he was shoulders and head taller than her. His expression pinched in concern when he saw me.

Henry rose up from my bed and stood in front of me, arms crossed. They were more comparable in height. Rhys didn't look impressed by my calvary.

"It's fine," I murmured.

Henry turned to stare at me. "I'm across the hall if you need anything." He leaned forward and kissed my forehead.

He checked Rhys's shoulder before tugging on Ava's arm. She was glaring at Rhys. She had no idea why I was upset or who I was upset with, but she was on my side no matter what.

Rhys shut the door when we were alone and leaned against the wall. I kept my eyes glued to the quilt on my bed. There was a short loose thread that I twirled between my fingers. After a moment of silence Rhys said, "I talked to Grant Saturday night."

I nodded slowly, still looking down. It confirmed my theory that Rhys went to the same party. He probably hooked up with another girl, but he probably remembered her. *Unlike me.*

"I swear to you I didn't say anything about it being a pretend date. When he told me that I wanted to punch him. It turns out Finn, his roommate is my teammate, told him how I took you on a mock date. I guess Whinny was talking about it and Finn assumed all the blind dates were going to be fake. Believe it or not it was more talking shit about me and my inability to commit then about you."

I rolled my lips in and bit down.

"Fuck, I keep fucking up," his voice cracked which made me glance up at him. He looked like he had run his fingers through his hair dozens of times. He had dark circles under his eyes.

I swallowed the burning salt in my throat. "Is that why you're here?"

"No, I'm here because you stopped reading your messages. You didn't come to class. I haven't heard from you since Saturday morning and I've been worried as fuck."

"I didn't mean to make you worry. I wanted to be left alone. Sorry." My tone was still flat.

Rhys approached the bed slowly and then sat in front of me. He delicately pulled my hand away from the thread and laced our fingers together. I didn't fight it, but I didn't reciprocate either. His rough fingers were warm against my cool skin.

He squeezed. "I'm sorry," he whispered again. "Tell me what I can do to make it better?"

Go back in time and be sober enough to remember our time together.

The lump in my throat was thick and unrelenting. "What's done is done. I need to get over my pity party."

He clicked his tongue and reached for me, pulling me against his chest. "I hate that you are feeling bad about yourself. You are the best and so gorgeous, it's Grant's loss."

But not Rhys's loss.

"Do you want me to beat him up?"

I shook my head. "I'm not upset about Grant," I murmured.

Rhys let go of me enough that he was able to look into my eyes. "Then what is it?"

"It's all of it. It's being forgotten about and dismissed and treated like I'm someone to pity."

My treacherous eyes watered up as I looked up hoping to keep the tears from rolling down my cheeks.

Rhys looked like I had gutted him as I cried silently. He swiped my tears away with the backs of his fingers and pulled me back against his chest.

"I just want to go to bed."

"Okay, Bully, but it's only 6pm. So maybe eat dinner first."

Right.

"Do you want me to go get you something? I can order you food."

I shook my head. "No, it's Ava's night to cook. I can't miss it. She ate alone one time after cooking dinner, and I'll never do that to her again."

He kissed the top of my head. "Okay, I'll check to see when dinner is going to be ready." He kissed my hair again before getting up.

Henry slipped back into my room. "Do you want me to ask him to leave?"

I shook my head.

He sighed. "Okay," he whispered. "Can I tell Ava what happened? She's sharpening the knives right now, getting ready to gut Rhys."

I snorted. "Sure, maybe leave out some of it until our company is gone." Like the part about being forgotten about after giving and receiving oral sex. *Maybe my performance was so bad he blocked it out.*

"You got it."

Rhys walked briskly back into the room, shut the door, and locked it for good measure. "Ava is scary as shit when she's angry." His blue eyes were wide as he walked back over to the bed. "But dinner will be ready in thirty minutes. Do you want me to stay?"

I shrugged. He groaned. "Can I stay? I don't want to leave you like this."

I looked into his crystal eyes. His brows were puckered in the center. Tension bracketed his mouth.

"Sure," I answered back.

He relaxed as he moved to sit next to me. "You missed out on a thrilling lecture today," he started. "We learned about the elbow. Professor Langley had probably twenty slides of elbows. Just pictures of elbows, not labeled, just every size, shape, ethnicity of elbow."

I snorted and rolled my eyes over to Rhys. He chuckled. "Want me to tell you about my wenis?"

I bit back a smile.

"I'd rather you showed me," I joked.

His eyebrows wagged. "Prepare yourself." Pretending to adjust his belt, he popped his arm a few inches away from my nose.

"Oh shit, I almost elbowed you in the face." He tittered a laugh and hugged my head. The position was familiar from how he had me before he kissed me. He loosened his grip as I stared up to him. His eyes narrowed for a moment, his lips parted. "I'm having the craziest deja vu."

I wiggled away from him. "You have a lot of dreams about hugging my head?"

"That's what triggered it, but it felt like a memory of something that never happened."

I hummed, wanting to tell him it *did* happen, but then the mortification of being that forgettable stopped me. "Maybe you dream about suffocating me."

Rhys snorted. "Not likely."

I shrugged, not wanting to talk about it anymore.

He took a deep breath. "Fuck that smells good. Do you think if I make you a heaping big plate Ava will assume it's all for you?"

I rolled my eyes. "Ava is harmless. Henry's telling her what happened now. You can eat dinner with us if you want. I promise she won't stab you."

Rhys snorted. "Henry, the dude that said I should suck a bag of dicks? I'm not certain he's going to share an unbiased version of events."

Dinner was awkward. In keeping with the ruse that Henry and Ava were not a couple, he ate away from the dining room, opting to sit next to Matt and Nicole. Rhys sat next to me and talked to Will about law school. Will asked Ava about Texas. Ava glared daggers at Rhys. Lily looked between everyone but stayed relatively silent. Her gaze sliding between Ava and Henry. I was positive she had made the connection that Ava and Henry were dating last weekend, but she hadn't mentioned anything to me directly.

It was clear to anyone that knew Henry, the way he gazed at Ava left no doubt they were together. Add that to his ability to snuggle into her and touch her constantly to convince Mr. Reiser of their relationship, it was blatantly obvious.

I expected Rhys to leave when dinner was over, but he didn't. He followed me to my room and turned the shower on for me. By the time I had gotten out he was already under the covers on his side of the bed. His backpack and gym bag were open next to the desk.

"Come here, Bully, let's go to sleep."

Chapter 5

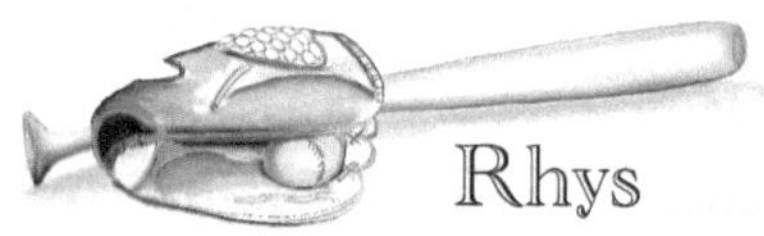

Rhys

I glanced over to Tama while we took our test before Thanksgiving. She was chewing on the end of her pen and squinting at the test. Her shoulders wiggled as a smile spread across her face and she hunched over the paper to write her answer.

She was so fucking cute.

Concentrating back on my work, I tried to remember the mnemonic Tama and I came up with for the ligaments of the knee. She finished before me. She's a smarty pants, but I knew she'd wait for me. I drove her to school today, and it was too cold for her to walk home.

I passed my exam to Professor Langley with a nod and headed to the hallway where my girl was resting against the brick wall. Her eyes lit up when she saw me, a smile stretched across her cheeks, making her doe eyes squint.

It had been a month since *the Grant situation* and things were starting to fall back into their familiar groove with Tama. We were talking every night again. She would spend the night at my place a few nights a week. We would either be out at parties until late or studying and she'd crash with me. I loved it. Pillow talk with her always allowed me to sleep well. Plus, she was all warm and snuggling and never got upset about me not having time to hang out if I was busy.

Worrying about starting my final season of baseball twisted my stomach. I didn't want her to feel like I was ignoring her when the schedule got busy. But so far, she'd been resilient and understanding. She didn't guilt me when I needed to be alone and didn't question me when I was MIA. Granted, I still hadn't broken my celibacy yet so my days of being MIA had more to do with a rampant hangover or taking care of my hungover roommates than anything else.

"How'd you do?"

I shrugged. "Fine. I'm glad it's over. When are you leaving for SoCal?"

This was the week I had been dreading. It meant that I couldn't be around her whenever I wanted. At least at school I had the distraction of friends and schoolwork. When I was home, I was bored, and Tama always kept me occupied.

She twisted her lips to the side. "Two days. Thelma and Yolanda are arguing about who gets to host this year. Gerty got all the Poker Pals to wager bets on who wins. I was thinking about mixing it up and hosting to stop their weird competition, but mom and Beckett don't want everyone over. The last time we hosted, Yolanda and Thelma got in an argument that ended with Thelma driving Yolanda's motorized scooter into the front wall of the house. Then Yolanda threw Thelma's walker into the window. It didn't shatter, thank goodness, but it did crack."

"Grannies gone wild, huh?" I laughed. She had the best stories about her upbringing.

"They are wild."

"Why doesn't Gerty host?"

She blew out a breath. "Terrible cook. She's a poker shark and can make the best mixed drinks of anyone I have ever met, but she doesn't mess with the oven."

"Gerty sounds like my kind of woman," I joked.

She chortled. "If you ever meet her, keep that to yourself. She was patient-zero on spreading the clap to the single male residents of Friendly Village last year.

"She knitted a ball cozy for Harald Beechem. According to her 'his nuts hang so low he sits on them and then he can't get up on his own.'"

Silent laughter rumbled my chest.

"She showed me it before she gave it to him. Horrifying. It was like a stirrup that looped into the button of his boxers. My point is, if you tell her that, she will flirt with you and she's pretty convincing. Don't play poker for favors either. I lost a big pot to her and now I must name my first child after her."

I looped my arm around her shoulder, laughing as we walked out of the science building. "What are your plans for the rest of the day?"

She shrugged. "No plans, nothing to study for. Only turning in a paper tomorrow that I have already finished."

"Then I have a suggestion. You can say no, but you mentioned something about wanting to learn how to drive." I paused and waited for her reaction.

She chewed her lip and looked around the quad. "Yeah, I did."

I grinned. "Well, I want to teach you."

Her brows furrowed as she blew out a breath. "In your truck?"

"Yep, it's practically indestructible, so no worries if you hit a curb."

"I'm more worried about hitting a human." Her cheeks flushed a beautiful crimson.

I snorted. "If you let me teach you, I promise that there won't be humans around to hit."

"Are you sure?" She licked her lips before rolling the bottom into her mouth and biting down.

"Absolutely. But I'm going to be honest. I'm not being completely altruistic. If you have a license and I get too shitcanned to drive, then I'll have you as backup since you don't drink."

She rolled her eyes at me as a small smile tugged at her lips. "Okay."

The drive was ten minutes away at a series of rec league baseball fields. It wasn't in-season, so the parking lot for the fields was completely empty. It was recently plowed so there was plenty of space to drive and maneuver around the snow piles. I parked and turned to her, keeping the truck on so we had the heat blasting. She was habitually cold.

"What do you know about driving?"

She blew out a breath. "The dynamics of driving I studied a while ago. It's drag and rotate. The engines are combustible with typical gasoline fuel. I also know the gas is on the right and the general rules of the road. I did study for my learner's permit, but I never took it."

"Good enough for me."

The truck idled as I walked to her side. She had opened her door and was sliding down to the ground. I grabbed her waist to assist her, so she didn't fall from the last foot. Her arm was warm in my palm as she made her way over to the driver's side. I lifted her up and grinned at her. She looked like a child behind the wheel. Her legs were nowhere near reaching the pedals. I pulled the seat as far forward as it could go.

My lips turned down in a frown when her eyes barely went over my steering wheel. I notched it down. "Can you see all the way to the front of the hood?"

She shook her head. I chuckled, reached behind the seat and grabbed my backpack. "Lift." I shoved two textbooks in the seat to boost her up.

"This is so embarrassing," she muttered.

I grinned. "How about now? Can you see the front of the hood?"

"Yes." Her cheeks tinted red. I went through mirror and seat adjustment, and I described exactly what she would need to do before I got in on the passenger side.

"Ok Bully, I need you to push your foot down on the break." The engine revved. I chuckled. "That's the gas. Remember it's on the right. Press down on the break."

I craned my head around to watch her hit the right pedal. "Now we are going to shift out of park and into drive. Are you ready?"

Her wide eyes stared at me as she shook her head. "I'm nervous."

I smirked at her. "It's okay to be nervous. It means you're taking it seriously and being cautious. Now hold down this button and move the gear shift from P to D." She let out a shaky breath and followed my instructions. "Now very gently ease your foot off the break. Don't touch the gas. There is nothing in front of us for three hundred feet, so you can't hit anything. Ease off the break."

The next hour was spent with me holding back laughter as she quietly narrated what she was going to do next. She didn't ease off the break the first time. It was a jerky start, stop, start, stop, that was testing the wear of my seatbelts, but she got the hang of it fast enough. By the end she felt comfortable circling the lot and pulling into parking spaces. We didn't touch parallel parking, but I promised her we would next time we went out. I suggested the weekend we got back from Thanksgiving break. It was a tentative date.

As a thank you she made my favorite muffins before I flew to Seattle to see my mom and dad. We spoke every night on video call. My day didn't feel complete unless I was able to share with her the mundane things my parents and I did. I went into too much detail about the latest car my dad and I were fixing up. I caught her nodding off a few times, but she insisted it was because Thelma kept her up late going through old photo albums.

I missed her so much after Thanksgiving that I ended up sleeping next to her for the following week whether it was in her bed or mine. Obviously, I preferred my bed. It was bigger, but her apartment was quieter as Ava was busy preparing for some ballet audition and Henry followed her wherever she went.

I walked up to my house after dropping Tama off at the airport. I wasn't flying out for another day.

"Hey Tama, settle a bet for us," Whinny called from the living room.

"Not Tama, she's on her way to southern California for the break. What's the bet?"

A shit-eating grin spread across Nathan's face as I kicked my shoes off and slumped onto the sofa where they were playing video games.

"That you would take her to the airport without her having to ask. Whinny said that she would take a ride share or coordinate with Lily. I said that you would volunteer," Nathan said.

I rolled my eyes. "What is the point of this bet? She's my friend. Of course I took her to the airport."

Whinny chuckled lowly while covering his mouth.

"Did she ask for a ride, or did you tell her you are taking her?" Nathan clarified.

My nose wrinkled. "What does it matter?"

Whinny groaned and slapped a twenty on the table. Nathan wagged his brows and pocketed the money. "It matters because that is some boyfriend behavior, bro."

My jaw clenched. "You are acting like I don't drive you two around whenever you need a ride."

Nathan chortled. "Nah man, you volunteer to take us to convenient places you are also going to. Or you let us borrow your truck. I can't think of a time where you told me you were going to drive me to a place an hour away that only I needed to go to out of the goodness of your heart."

"You are acting like I'm not driving you to the airport tomorrow. It's not a big deal."

Whinny snickered. I shot a glare at him as Nathan rebutted. "I coordinated my flight with yours so I could catch a ride. It is not the same thing."

"What's your point?"

"My point is that you are doing a lot of boyfriend things without the benefits."

I shook my head. "No, I am doing friendship things."

"Bro you are in an open relationship with no titles, and neither of you is getting laid. Make it official and cut this bullshit out."

"Not this conversation again." I glared at Nathan.

"He has a point." Whinny tossed a baseball in the air and caught it while lounging on the sofa.

"No, he doesn't. Just because neither of you know how to maintain a friendship with a woman doesn't mean I don't. Besides, I'm not having a girlfriend my senior year and not going into the draft."

"You already have a girlfriend, bro," Nathan insisted. "I just won twenty bucks as proof."

I shook my head. "You don't know what you are talking about. Besides, even if I wasn't completely against having a girlfriend, she doesn't like me like that."

Nathan rolled his eyes. "Have you ever pointblank asked her if she would ever be interested in a relationship with you?"

My jaw clicked shut. I hadn't. It was a weird question to ask. It wouldn't change how I felt about being tied down during a time in my life where I was going to be influx.

"Yeah, that's what I thought. Another question that is completely unrelated. When you draft do you plan on talking to Tama occasionally, maybe even seeing her every once in a while?"

My lip pulled into an uneven grimace. "What kind of question is that? Of course. It'll suck to not see her every day, but we'll still talk. My friendship with her isn't going to go away because I can't physically be near her."

Nathan rolled his eyes, tilted his head and flung his arm out. "Point made."

I shook my head. "That's not the same thing. There's no such thing as a long-distance friendship. There is no pressure with a friendship. Besides when I draft, I'm not going to put myself into the situation where I'll cheat. I know there will be temptations that I won't want to say no to."

Whinny scowled at me. "That's fucked."

"How?" I challenged. "I'll never cheat on a person. I'd rather be single for the rest of my life than cheat. I'm trying to do the right thing."

"Bro, the right thing is *not* allowing yourself to be tempted. Now I understand you wanting to sow your wild oats or whatever bullshit you are trying to spew, but do you think that you'd ever cheat on Tama?"

I blew out a breath, frustrated by the conversation.

"If she were fucking you regularly, would you cheat?"

I shook my head. "No, but there wouldn't be a *regular* with me traveling. And I'll be tempted. I know what it's like to be cheated on, and I won't do that to her."

"So, you mean to tell me that you'd rather fuck random mediocre women that you won't remember than attempt to be faithful to the woman you are in love with?" Nathan asked.

"I'm not in love with Tama," I insisted. My chest ached when I said that, and my ears burned.

"Then how come you only let her go on one shitty date with a guy that treated her like it was a joke? Why can't she date whoever she wants?"

I tipped my head back not answering.

Nathan shook his head. Whinny's eyes bounced between the two of us.

"If this is about you wanting to date her—"

"What if it is?" Nathan challenged. "What if I like her a lot? What if I could make her happy but you are preventing it from happening?"

"Tama's off limits."

Whinny scoffed. "I don't think he'd get the point if it smacked him in the face."

"What's the point?"

Nathan rolled his eyes. "That you are in love with her. You don't want to share her with anyone. You are treating her like your favorite toy that no one else is allowed to look at. You are possessive as fuck about her. You want to know why no guy on campus is crazy enough to ask her out?" His voice was loud, almost yelling.

"*Everyone* knows she's yours. But the fucked-up thing: the women that vie for your attention sees Tama as an obstacle to get around so they can get the attention you give her. You've made her untouchable amongst the men and a target amongst the women. She told you that she wants a real relationship. She didn't want to explain her situation to anyone. Be an actual friend to her and give her that." Nathan strode into the kitchen to grab a beer, slamming the fridge door and then taking the steps two at a time to his bedroom.

"Easy around this corner, Bully."

My hands squeezed the steering wheel as I navigated the icy roads. I had spent the three-week winter break going to driver's ed and obtaining my license. All the practice sessions with Rhys helped me not look completely clueless when I started drivers' ed. Beckett and my mom were thrilled. I told Beckett to hold off buying me a car until I had a place to park it.

"It's still mortifying that I need a booster seat to drive your truck." I pulled into the parking lot of the grocery store.

Rhys chuckled. "You won't need one with a smaller car. You should ask to borrow Ava's car when she gets back and see how you like it."

"But I like being able to be so high up," I said.

Rhys laughed. "Yeah, it's nice. There are smaller SUV options you can look into. I'll help you pick something out that will be perfect for you."

I chewed my lip. Rhys grabbed my reusable shopping bags and a shopping cart. His house and my apartment were completely barren of food, so we were grabbing essentials. The rest of my roommates were going to go shopping in two days.

"What should we have for dinner tonight?" Rhys stepped on the bottom shelf of the cart and let it carry him down the aisle like a child.

"What do you want?"

He shrugged and stopped in front of the cereal. A few boxes were tossed in the cart, and we kept going.

"You know what I would love to try?" he said when we made it to the rice/pasta aisle.

I hummed to him.

"Your meatloaf. When I first met you, you made it for your roommates, and I was so jealous."

Jasmine rice and spices were added to my cart. "That's easy. What do you want on the side?"

"You made this potato dish once that was like lasagna but with potatoes." He groaned and patted his taut stomach.

A smile hitched. "Au gratin, okay, what else?"

"I haven't had your cookies in a long time."

My eyes cut over to him to see if he was making a sexual joke. He looked innocently back to me, so I guess it was only my mind in the gutter. "Who all is going to be having dinner with us?"

He grunted. "Can we eat at your place? Nathan and Whinny pissed me off before break."

I frowned. "Anything you want to talk about? I hear I'm a good listener."

"Nah, it was stupid guy bullshit. They were talking shit about something they didn't understand." His eyes had a pleading edge asking me to drop it.

Turning towards the canned tomatoes, I snagged a few, not looking at him. He never fought with his roommates. He hated fighting in general, so whatever they disagreed about must have been a big deal that he is still hung up on it three weeks later.

"Are you ready to start your season?"

He blew out another breath. "I am. It's a lot of travel and I'm taking one additional class than I would prefer so I can graduate on time, but it'll be worth it. Coach Daniels and Foust are getting the catchers and pitchers ready starting next week. Then the week after we have practice five days a week with an hour of lifting every other day and cardio in between."

"Exercise is gross." A grimace wrinkled my nose.

He chuckled and pulled me against his chest in a squeezing hug. I looked up to him from his pecs. He had the softest smile on his face. His blue eyes twinkled as he licked his bottom lip a few times. "I want to talk to you about something tonight, if that's okay."

My molars bit into my cheek. I wasn't sure what he wanted to say, but it had to be important if it required a preamble.

Maybe he's ready to admit his undying love.

I choked that thought down. The undying love was in an unreciprocating arrow pointing from me to him, and not the other way around. "Sure. You know you can talk to me about anything."

He grinned at me and kissed my forehead before letting me go.

My whole body started to shake with nerves as I served dinner. As requested, meatloaf with au gratin potatoes was served with a side of pan roasted green beans and corn bread. I made enough chocolate chip cookies for him to take home and share, but he informed me that Nathan and Whinny didn't deserve my cooking yet.

Rhys helped me wash the dishes and wipe down the counters before following me to my bedroom. He still had his luggage from winter break with him seeing as how he drove straight over from the airport to me. "Do you want to shower first?"

I let out a shaky breath. "Yeah, I'd like to get the grime from the plane off me."

He chuckled and turned the shower on. I landed two hours before him, making it inconvenient to wait so I used a rideshare to get home.

The water was unsuccessful in calming my heart that was beating wildly out of control.

What if he wants to take our friendship to the next level?

I was ready this time. He'd take my virginity. He'd own all my firsts. I *wanted* him to have all my firsts.

Rhys was waiting at my desk, his laptop open when I got out. His brows rose when he saw my smaller than normal towel. I hadn't washed my linens yet, so I grabbed what was clean and left him the larger one. I didn't say anything as I walked past him and to my dresser. My back was to him, but I was feeling bold. I dropped my towel and bent down to my pajama drawer. It was suspiciously quiet behind me, so I schooled my face for a coy look. Rhys was already in the bathroom with the door shut.

I sighed through my disappointment and pulled on my flannel button up and matching shorts. I grabbed my laptop and cued up the show we had been streaming together. It was becoming a part of our bedtime routine, whether in person or over video, we'd watch an episode together, chat, and fall asleep.

Rhys came out of the bathroom with his sweatpants already on, rubbing the excess water from his tresses as he strolled towards me. He grinned at my cued-up laptop. "You read my mind."

My lips twitched into a smile. He pulled back the covers and snuggled into me. His head was touching mine as we curled our bodies around the laptop. We watched the show together and discussed theories on what we thought was going on and what next episode was going to entail.

I set the laptop on my nightstand and snuggled back down against the pillows before turning on my side. Rhys slipped in behind me, like was our routine. He kissed the back of my head and sighed. It was silent for a moment before I got the courage to ask him what he wanted to talk to me about.

"Oh, shit, you're right. I totally forgot." His arms squeezed around me. "Sorry, if you've been stressed. It's not a big deal. I wanted to let you know that I set up a dating profile for you."

My breath held to not betray my lungs that wanted to gasp.

"Since I know you better than anyone, I filled everything out. I used my favorite picture of you. You know, the one where you are looking to the side, in your blue dress, the sun is hitting your eyes." He had taken the picture of me last year. His team had just won, and I was waiting for him outside the locker room on a bench surrounded by black-eyed-susans.

I swallowed. "My contact picture?" I whispered. My throat was way too thick for me to speak at full volume.

"That's the one. Anyway, I know I said I'd set you up on a blind date, but I don't like any of the guys on campus for you.

I'm picky. You're my girl so I need someone for you that is as perfect as you are."

My lungs burned as I slowly exhaled.

"You've already gotten a few solid matches too. I'm not catfishing them or anything. I haven't responded, but it's all set up and ready when you are."

"I'll look at it sometime soon."

My heart was pounding in my stomach. I thought he'd given up on trying to find me a date. I hoped he realized he didn't *want* me to date anyone. It was toxic, but I had hope he'd realize his feelings for me and then we'd have a Hollywood moment.

"Awesome. I have one ask. Can you not have your first date with someone while I am at an away game? I want to be close in case he ends up being a creep. No one is going to be a dismissive fucker around you if I can help it."

"Yeah, I can do that," I said, my voice barely above a whisper. He squeezed my ribs again and changed the subject back to the show we had watched. I listened numbly, reacting when I thought was correct until he stopped talking. His grip loosened on my torso as he fell asleep.

My chin quivered as I let silent tears drip onto my pillow.

It was the reminder I needed. Rhys Goodman wasn't mine. He'll never be mine, and I needed to remember that.

Chapter 6

Tama

"**Y**ou look gorgeous." Lily applied some lipstick on me to 'finish the look'.

I smiled at her. I was trying so hard to not focus on the fact that I was going on a date with a relative stranger because Rhys couldn't commit. It wasn't his fault that I had gotten my hopes up. He had been upfront about how he felt, but I let my pesky positive thinking override what he had been telling me for a year. No girlfriend until he makes it.

Lily and Ava had helped me pick out my outfit. Nicole had helped me with all my 'flirtations' online, and Ava and Henry were going to be at the same restaurant on a date of their own to make sure I was safe. I was glad their relationship was out in the open finally. Will didn't like it, but he wasn't terrible about it anymore.

"Thanks, my arm pits are sweating," I admitted.

Nicole snorted from my bed. "Happens to the best of us. But if you want to cancel you can at any point."

I blew out a breath. "I need to do this so I can have the experience. I'm not always going to have my friends a few tables away to ensure I'm safe. Besides, maybe I'll like this guy, and it'll help me get over Rhys."

Lily frowned. "Maybe, but even if it's not a love connection it doesn't mean it's a waste."

"Just go, have fun. If the guy sucks, make an excuse and leave early. It's as simple as that," Nicole said.

I puffed my cheeks out and tipped my head back. "Okay, let's do this," I whispered to myself.

Henry drove as Ava gushed about her dance classes she was taking for her major. She was so happy and gabbing about a secret performing arts society at the school.

"I know I said I didn't want to be a part of a sorority, but if the Broken Leg Society comes calling, I'm going to answer. Rumors abound on the connections you have when you become a member."

My hands trembled as I attempted to steady my breathing. It had only been three weeks since Rhys told me about the dating profile he had set up for me. I had mentioned that I was going on a date but refused to tell him where and when. I let him know that Henry was going to be there and he scoffed. But I knew I wouldn't be able to concentrate on my date if Rhys was around.

Henry parked and looked back at me. "Ready?"

"Yeah, it's not a total blind date. I sort of met him before so at least he isn't going to think I'm someone else and make me feel bad for not being tall and brunette."

Henry shook his head. "I fucking knew Grant was a tool bag." He gripped Ava's hand. "See, you thought I was pissing on your leg, I was helping you out."

"Whatever caveman let's go. I'm starving," Ava said dramatically.

I let them walk in ahead of me before stopping at the hostess stand. Before I could utter a word, my date tapped me on the shoulder. I turned around and smiled up at him. Griffin looked more handsome than I remembered from the first time I had met him. One brow perked as he looked over his shoulder.

"Our table is this way." He motioned past the hostess stand.

I glanced around at Henry who was squinting in our direction. He sat down slowly and adjusted his chair to see my booth easier.

Griffin grinned at me. His longer hair was pulled back in a stubby bun. He was taller than I remembered with a different lip ring. He also looked more muscular out of his uniform. His biceps stretched the fabric of his green V-neck sweater.

"You look beautiful. I wasn't sure if you were going to show up. I know it was a little weird matching with me, but I couldn't resist."

I wasn't sure how to take that comment. "Well, you seemed nice over chat, and I knew you weren't a catfish. You look the same as in your profile picture, so win for you."

He chuckled. "I was surprised to see you online. The guy I saw you with last year seemed into you and a little possessive."

My nose wrinkled as I shook my head. "Rhys is a friend. He's not possessive of me per se, he just doesn't want anything bad to happen to me."

Griffin grabbed his menu.

"I was surprised to see you online, too. I'd think a guy like you would have no problems meeting someone the old fashion way."

He chuckled. "The old fashion way, huh? Well, I keep my options open. My world can get a little small, and I don't want to miss out on someone better because I didn't look hard enough."

I hummed. "What's your goal for the dating app?"

He rolled his eyes up to the ceiling and flicked his lip ring with his tongue. "I don't know. I'm not using it as some avenue to only hook up. I guess I want to connect with another person. If friendship is the connection, that's great. If it's more, that's great too."

I smiled at him. He was refreshingly honest. His hazel eyes twinkled in the candlelight of the dining room. "Tell me two truths and a lie, Tama."

I tapped my chin, thinking. "I grew up in a retirement community, my middle name is Bama, and I've never been kissed by a sober person."

His eyes widened as he leaned forward. He rolled his bottom lip in for a moment before popping it back out. His lip ring caught the light, drawing my attention to his full lips. "Those are some stellar options, but I am going to say the lie is about kissing."

I smirked at him. "My middle name is Isla."

He perked a brow. "Who do you hang out with that they have to get wasted before they kiss you? Seriously, I'm not trying to be a creep, but that red lipstick is making me have all sorts of thoughts. And I'm going to change the subject. My turn." He sipped his water, mulling over his answer.

"I'm the lead singer of a band that just signed on with a record label two days ago. My grandma raised me. And I have a twin sister."

I puffed my cheeks out. "You look like a singer, so I think that's a possibility. If that's true, that's amazing, congrats."

"Thank you." He gave me a shy smile and fiddled with his silverware.

"I'm sure you've been working your whole life for it, and it hasn't even sunk in yet. Hence why you are on a date with me."

He frowned at me. "I don't agree with the last part. When I met you last year, I thought you were beautiful, and you let me troll your date as payback for flirting with Pippa. I knew your sense of humor was as off as mine is." He squinted. "Anyway, what's the lie?"

I twisted my lips. "You do give me granny-baby vibes. Remember, I grew up in a retirement community. I'm going to say you're not a twin."

He wagged his brows at me. "You'd be correct."

I grinned at him. "Is your grandma so proud of you?"

His smile stretched. "She's over the moon. She's asked to go on tour with my band when the time comes, but that is putting the cart before the horse."

"What kind of music do you sing?"

"Alternative rock mostly, but we have a little bit of a Mumford vibe with some of our songs."

My brows rose. "That's really cool." I looked around and leaned forward. "Should I get your autograph now?"

He chuckled. "Probably, just to be safe. But who is to say we don't hit it off after tonight."

I licked my lips and shrugged. "You're right."

The server came and took our order. Henry kept glancing at our table, but he didn't come over. Even Ava turned around a few times and wagged her brows at me.

Griffin looked over his shoulder. "Friends of yours?"

I cringed. "They wanted to make sure you're not crazy."

He chuckled. "Good friends. To be clear, I am a little crazy, but it's in the weird way, not in the harbor organs sort of way. So, tell me, what was it like growing up in a retirement center?"

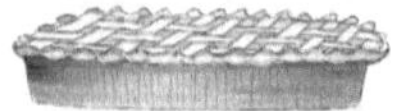

"How's it going?" Ava hissed at me from the bathroom sink.

I grinned at her. "It's going well. I think I'm going to take a rideshare home.

Ava's brows furrowed. "Are you sure?"

I nodded, feeling my cheeks flush for wanting to prolong my date.

"Hand me your phone." She motioned with grabby hands.

I passed it off to her. "You know you have like four messages from Rhys. Anyway," she sighed and passed my phone back, "I've activated your location for me to track. If you go anywhere but home let me know." I licked my lips and nodded rapidly.

"You look beautiful. Good luck." She stepped out of the bathroom.

I smoothed my hands over my shirt and adjusted my cleavage like Lily taught me. Griffin was talking to our server when I slipped back in my chair.

"Do you want to get dessert? Or can I interest you in a place a block away? It specializes in mini pies."

My smile stretched. "I love pie."

"We'll take the check."

"Can you split it?"

"No, he can't." Griffin turned back to the server and passed him his card. "One bill is perfect."

My blush heated my cheeks. As soon as the server walked away, I said, "I didn't want you to feel obligated to pay."

He shrugged. "And I want to pay. You are the best date I have had in a long time."

My blush deepened. The waiter came back with the bill book, Griffin's card hanging out of the top.

"Ready?" He pocketed his wallet and started to stand with his hand outstretched to me.

Guiding me from the restaurant, his palm warmed the small of my back. Ava gave me a thumbs up as Henry perked a brow, watching us leave. He leaned forward to say something to Ava as she pulled her phone out and showed him.

"Do you want me to drive or walk?"

The wind gusts intensified. "Nature just answered, but I'll defer to you," Griffin said.

I looked back to the restaurant and then to Ava's car. The weight of my phone in my pocket brought me courage. "Let's drive."

He grinned at me and led me to a 4Runner.

The drive was short, and he parked right in front of the pie shop. The frilly store smelled amazing. We stood behind four other couples, waiting our turn. Griffin talked about the weather before we both ordered.

We ate our warm pie at a small pink table in the corner of the shop. I moaned lightly. "I love to bake, and this pie crust is next level good."

He smirked at me. "Is it better than Yolanda's?"

I loved that he remembered which of my neighbors made the better pie.

I crinkled my nose. "It's a toss-up."

We finished our dessert. He sucked in a breath through his teeth. "It's almost time to turn into a pumpkin, Tama."

I nodded.

"Do you want me to drive you home or are your friends still waiting around for you?"

I looked up to the clear navy sky. "They went home, but I can call a rideshare."

"You could, but it'll make trying to kiss you that much more awkward if a stranger is waiting for you to get into their car."

I bit my lip to hide my smile. "You're going to try to kiss me?"

He licked his lip ring. "Can't have you walking around not knowing what it's like to kiss a sober person."

"This is true."

His hand slipped behind my neck as he pulled me gently to his face. His lips were warm against mine. Even the metal of his jewelry was hot. His tongue swiped lightly across the seam of my lips. I tilted my head to give him better access to kiss me deeper. He pulled away and rested his forehead against mine.

"I need to take you home before I try to get more than a kiss from you."

A nervous giggle broke free.

I gave him the turn-by-turn directions to my apartment. He double parked behind Ava's car and turned towards me. "I want to kiss you again, but I want to be honest about something."

I braced.

"I don't have time for a girlfriend right now. The beginning of a relationship deserves time to nurture it. Maybe if we would have started this four months ago, we'd have a solid base for a relationship. But with the record deal and then the touring that we will have to go on." He paused and looked at me. "I don't want to lead you on. I don't want to offer you something that I can't properly follow through."

At least he had the balls to admit it.

It could have been a huge excuse, but he was attempting to placate me. Unlike Rhys who had blinders up towards anything related to being with me.

"I understand. You can still kiss me, but we should probably stop there."

He leaned forward and captured my lips again. His warm hand cupped my cheek, as the calluses on his fingertips dragged along my jaw. We made out for ten minutes before the rumble of a truck pulled me away from his lips. I turned around and cringed when I saw Rhys parking on the street. Griffin pulled me in for another kiss before cupping my cheek and resting his forehead against mine again.

Griffin hummed. "He is possessive of you. Are you sure you two are just friends?" He glanced towards the steps of my building where Rhys was taking them two at a time.

My phone vibrated in my pocket again. I licked my lips, still tasting Griffin on my mouth. "He doesn't want a girlfriend and only sees me as a friend."

Griffin snorted. "Friends don't show up to their apartment uninvited at midnight knowing they are on a date."

I blew out a breath and shrugged. My phone buzzed again.

He leaned forward and kissed me one more time. "Let's keep our chat open, yeah?"

I reached for the handle of the door. "Of course."

I was walking up my steps as Rhys was walking down. He stopped at the top and looked beyond me as Griffin turned around and pulled away. He let out a gush of air and winced. His throat bobbed as he looked at me. "Date went well so I take it."

Going for nonchalance I shrugged. "He's nice. Dinner was pleasant. We had pie and he drove me home."

Brow furrowed, his jaw worked back and forth a few times. "Are you going to see him again?"

I shook my head. "Probably not. He signed a record deal and will be traveling soon."

He rolled his eyes. "Bullshit."

My head snapped back like he had slapped me.

He shook his head at me. "Don't look at me like that. He fed you an excuse to let you down easy, and you still kissed him. He wanted a one-night stand. He isn't going to call you and his 'record deal' is the perfect excuse to blow you off to save your feelings."

All the air had been sucked from my lungs from his cruel words. "That may be how you function, but it doesn't mean everyone acts like that. You are being mean. I didn't do anything to deserve that. I know you don't see me as someone worthy of a relationship, but I am."

He huffed and shook his head. "That is not what I meant. That all came out wrong, I'm sorry."

"Why are you here?" I was on the verge of tears but fought the quiver in my voice.

"I was making sure you were still alive. You weren't answering my text messages. I've been fucking climbing the walls of my house worried sick about you, and you went radio silent again. The last time you iced me out was after a bad date. I didn't want you to be alone tonight."

"Well, you can check this off your to-do list. I'm alive and well. And I had a decent date. Sorry I made you worry, but it's late. I'm tired and I want to go to bed."

"Then let's go to bed." Rhys turned on his heel and stormed back up the stairs.

My brain buzzed in confusion and anger as I followed him to my apartment. I unlocked as he pushed the door open.

Henry and Ava were watching tv on the couch. Henry scowled. "When'd you switch the hipster out for the douchebag?"

Rhys flicked him the bird and marched to my bedroom.

"Be nice," I hissed. Henry shrugged and went back to the movie.

Ava launched off the couch and pulled me into the kitchen. "What's going on?" she hissed.

I shrugged. "I have no idea. I'll tell you in the morning."

Rhys was already in the shower with the bathroom door completely swung open. I could see him in the reflection of the mirror. I was frustrated with him, so I leaned against the bathroom door frame so we could talk it out.

He glanced back at me and turned back to the wall, washing his chest.

"Are you mad at me?"

He sighed and leaned his head against the tile. He shook his head. "No, I was worried."

I backed away from the bathroom. My willpower to not join him was dwindling to zero. He turned the water off and walked into my room with the towel knotted around his waist. I kept the bathroom door open as I stripped my clothes off and showered.

The silence stretched between us, but he didn't avoid me. He brushed his teeth in the sink and shaved his face. When I turned the water off, he passed me my towel before he stepped back into the bedroom.

I finished getting ready to sleep and slipped on one of the shirts he had let me borrow. He was already in bed, laptop out and cued up. His demeanor was calmer than when he confronted me on the steps.

When the episode was over, he snapped my laptop shut and rearranged my body for him to spoon into me. He kissed my shoulder and head. "I'm sorry."

I wanted him to explain exactly what he was sorry for so it would clue me in to why he was so mad when he got here, but instead I nestled my back further into his chest. He held me close most of the night. I woke up to an empty bed and a head full of questions.

"He was jealous." Ava forked a piece of watermelon in her mouth and went back to mixing the clay mask.

I shook my head.

One brow rose high into her hairline. "He was jealous. He saw you kissing another guy and had a meltdown, that's why he lashed out and said shitty things."

I groaned and cupped my cheeks. "Why would he be jealous again?"

"He's in love with you," Nicole said from the living room.

Lily and Nicole were painting each other's toenails while Ava and I gave each other facials.

"No, he isn't."

Nicole shrugged and Lily torqued her body around to face me. "They're right. He may be in massive denial about it, but he's in love with you, and he was jealous when he saw you kissing Griffin. You're too close to the situation to see it, but trust me, it's gutting to see someone you like kissing someone else."

She would know. Lily and Will circled each other for almost a year, flirting with other people in front of each other, making out and more because they were convinced the other didn't like them.

I huffed a breath. "It doesn't make sense though."

"It makes perfect sense to me. Think about it. He text messaged you six times while you were on a date. He *knew* you were on a date, and he continued to blow up your phone. Then he shows up at your apartment ten minutes after you get home. I know you share your location with him after the Grant situation so he would know if you were home and safe and wanting to be alone. He stayed up until midnight, tracked your phone, came over expecting you to be alone and was woefully mistaken. Then he lashed out. He was jealous. And to prove that he's in love with you, exhibit A-Z he spent the night, snuggling you after a pseudo fight."

I whimpered.

"Listen, I get it. You don't want to get your hopes up, but you need to think it's a possibility that he is in love with you and is in denial about it. Will was in love with me for a long time before he admitted it and vice versa. It happens. I don't want you to dismiss it as possible."

I sighed. "But he set up my dating profile. He *wants* me to have a boyfriend."

"He's in denial about it. But I'm thinking by your empty bed this morning he may be getting clued in."

Chapter 7

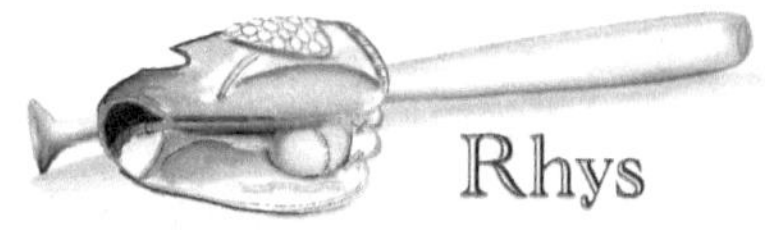

Rhys

Nathan and Whinny may have a point about my friendship with Tama. After her date with the hipster, I woke up with her in my arms and the image of her profile kissing another man in my head.

I didn't know it at the time when I saw it. I figured it was some random couple having a little fun in a car at midnight. I remember thinking 'get it' to the guy. And then the horror of realizing it was my Tama kissing him… I didn't think it was possible to feel my heart break and sink to my ass in five seconds.

I said shitty things that I shouldn't have said, but she's the best person I know. She forgave me. I was too angry to reflect on the emotions I was feeling when I marched us through our bedtime routine. I didn't calm down until I was in the shower and she asked me if I was mad at her. It took me until I turned the water off to realize she was standing in the bathroom watching me shower, completely naked, like it was totally normal. I mean, it's not like I turned around and stroked my dick in front of her, but she saw my naked ass.

I was even more calmed down by the fact that she kept the bathroom door open when she showered. I had zero reasons to shave, but I wasn't going to pass up the opportunity to be in the bathroom while she was naked, also feigning normality. It was like we crossed a level of friendship that I wasn't aware existed. So, I guess we are friends that are comfortable seeing each other naked.

The problem is, seeing her bare drives me wild. I've seen almost all my friends from sharing a locker room, but never once had I thought about staring at my naked friend and jerking off. Which meant I had to confront a lot of things while she slept in my arms.

Confrontation number one, I was more than attracted to her. I wanted her. I wanted to fuck her and keep her for only myself. Which was very unfriend-like. And while I had always known I was attracted to her this felt different than that. I had accepted she wasn't attracted to me and that had been fine until she established us as naked friends. I was going to have a hard time controlling myself around her. I didn't want to make her feel awkward. I didn't want to give her a reason to push me away by making the wrong move and turning our friendship physical.

Confrontation number two, I *was* possessive of her. I had been telling my friends that they didn't understand my friendship. It turns out it was me that didn't understand what they saw so easily. My possession clicked when I realized the hipster kissed her and my brain said, *but she's mine.*

That thought kept me up. How could I think of her as mine and not allow her to think of me as hers? I was steadfast in not having a relationship. I knew that I was putting her in a shitty situation, but I didn't want to lose her. She was mine, and it would kill me to give her up.

Confrontation number three, I loved her differently than I loved my male friends. I am not afraid of the concept of love. I have no issues telling my parents that I love them. In a few drunken rants I've told my teammates that I love them. I know when the time is right, while I am in a real relationship, I will be able to tell the girl I love her without being some toxic macho fucker. But if I told Tama how I felt, it would mean something significant. It would start something that would be unfair to both of us. The fact that I had *that* reservation meant that Nathan and Whinny were right about that too, I *was* in love with her. Which was fucking shitty.

I rolled out of her bed at 5am when I realized I was a possessive fucker that was wildly attracted to his best friend he was in love with, and I lashed out at her. I was jealous. I didn't like how that felt. It wasn't fair to Tama. I didn't know where to go from that point. Admitting to her how I felt put us further into limbo.

I met her five years too early.

I couldn't tell her how I felt and then tell her I had no plans to do anything about it. If I delved any further with her, I would hurt her. I would make promises that I would break. I would ruin our friendship to get my dick wet, and I wasn't going to do that.

It was brisk and snowing when I made it to my truck. I drove slowly home and avoided my roommates the rest of the day. Tama didn't message me until dinner time when she asked if I was going to come over or not. I told her I had plans, and we left it at that. My plans included microwave popcorn and rotting in my bed.

Thankfully the baseball season started so I didn't have to wallow in my own doubts for long. It was the perfect distraction. It was also the perfect excuse to distance myself from her. We went from seeing and talking to each other daily to every few days. I didn't pause to allow my emotions to take over. I had a mission and playing well was the only avenue to accomplish it.

It helped that she went to every home game and cheered me on through messages during away games. She didn't make me feel an ounce of guilt about taking time for myself. She made sure I knew she was around if I needed her and the shitty thing was, I did need her.

After she surprised me for my birthday with a party, I stopped avoiding her and started spending more of my free time with her. It took another month before we were bed sharing again. It was something that we fell back into. She never questioned my lack of emotional availability and to my knowledge never went on another date.

My tired body drudged through campus on a warm April day. I hadn't seen Tama in three days and I was missing her. So, when my last class of the day was canceled, I headed towards where she was supposed to be. She was walking and laughing with Ava. Her blonde hair was buffeting in the wind as she threw her head back in a laugh.

I liked that she was so close to her roommate. Even though Ava was terrifying and threatened to castrate me with her paring knife if I ever hurt her friend, she was the exact type of person that needed to be in my best friend's corner. She was small but fierce and I was grateful. I had no idea what she saw in Henry, but at least it took away the unease I felt towards him. Now the hatred only flowed one way. Him to me, and I could handle that.

Tama was wearing my favorite blue dress. Ava twirled next to her and then erupted in another fit of giggles. Seeing Tama laughing so freely made me smile. They were at the end of the quad heading towards the parking lot. They were both tiny, so I knew if I picked up my stride, I'd reach them in a few minutes.

They were waiting at the small crosswalk that separated the parking lot from campus when a white cargo van stopped and blocked their path. I watched in slow motion horror as three people in masks got out, surrounded Ava, placed a burlap sack over her head and plucked her up from the middle of the crosswalk. Tama dove into the sliding door as it slid shut.

I sprinted as fast as I could. I didn't know what was going on, but they had Tama. I caught up to the van that was stuck at a red light. I smacked on the doors and went to unlatch the slider when the driver unrolled the window.

"Can I help you with something?" she asked with a cool indifference.

I gaped at her, my chest heaving. "Let my fucking friends go," I yelled. Then I heard it; my girl was laughing. Ava was giggling and the driver rolled her lips in. "I take it, you know my unexpected passenger?"

"Give me the girls, and I won't call the police."

Tama would, I'd make sure.

The slider opened and Tama popped out, giggling. She turned back to Ava who still had a sack on her head. "Are you sure you're okay?" She laughed. Ava's sack nodded as she giggled. "Yeah, it's an initiation thing."

My arms were around Tama, lifting her up and carrying her away from the van that was still idling at the light. She was struggling in a fit of giggles as I made my way out of the street. I set her down and dropped my head to her level, checking her out for any marks indicating they hurt her. She had tear stains down her cheeks from laughing.

"I should probably explain," she choked out.

I looked into her caramel eyes before pulling her back into my chest. My heart was pounding through the adrenaline rush as I swayed her back and forth. I held her back out and let my hands roam all over her body. I checked her arms, swept my hands down her legs, then cupped her face as another giggle erupted.

"Are you okay?"

"Yes, Ava is being inducted in some secret society. We knew it was going to happen sometime today, but I acted on instinct. And we couldn't stop laughing. Once I joked that if Ava ever got abducted, I would jump in the trunk in solidarity. It turns out, I would," she finished with another laugh.

I tipped my head back, still working through all the emotions.

"Do we need to tell Henry someone took Ava?"

"He's tracking her phone. She got an anonymous note saying that her initiation started today. Henry's been on alert all day. But it's a good callout. Let me send him a quick message."

"Do you have any idea how fucking terrified I was?" I finally dropped my hands and then buried my face into her neck.

She smelled so fucking good. I inhaled deeply letting her scent calm me down. My nose skimmed the juncture of her neck and shoulder. I tamped down the urge to kiss her.

She giggled again. "I'm sorry. We didn't know how the initiation was going to go, and I didn't think I just acted. Wait, what are you doing? You have class right now."

I shook my head and dragged my nose up to her ear. "It was canceled," I murmured. My arms looped around her back and picked her up, so I wasn't slumped down. My fingers dove into her hair, cradling her head and the other hand was gripping her lower back.

"I'm okay, Rhys. Nothing happened. I'm really sorry you were worried."

I didn't put her down. I kept walking towards my house. She started to wiggle against me. "You can put me down. No one is going to take me," she said gently.

I shook my head.

"You're acting like a caveman. I can walk."

I grunted in response.

She laughed. "Me strong, you weak, you come with me," she said in a deep voice.

I set her down and looked at her. "You scared the fucking shit out of me. I don't want to let you out of my sight right now."

Her eyes widened as a small smile spread across her face. "If you are going to carry me, can it at least be a piggyback ride? I like being able to see from your height."

I snorted and adjusted my backpack to my front and squatted. She braced her arms around my neck as I looped mine under her thighs.

She squealed as I stood. I marched us to my house with her laughing in my ear. Her thighs felt good in my palms, but I shoved that thought away. By the time I made it to my house I could see the humor in the situation. She had calmed me by talking about her day and asking me about mine.

Setting her down in my foyer, I shrugged my backpack off my front. My body was tired before, now I was sweaty and exhausted from the adrenaline dump. She gave me a bright smile that was hard for me to not reciprocate. I let out a small chuckle at the whole scenario causing her to have another giggle fit.

After we calmed, I pushed her up my stairs.

"I need to take a shower and then I want to nap with you. Are you good with that?"

She grinned. "Yes, I was up late last night studying for my exam today." I stripped my shirt off and kicked my shoes off.

As the shower heated, I peeled my socks off before unbuttoning my jeans. Tama was standing in the center of my room, lips rolled in, all humor was gone from her eyes.

"Are you packed for spring break?" I pushed my jeans down my thighs.

She nodded. She was going to some resort in Puerto Rico with her roommates, but I didn't know the details. I had a huge baseball tournament all my spring break. I nudged my chin towards the shower, letting her know that I was heading in. I left my door open. Maybe it was an invitation, maybe not. I didn't know what I was doing when it came to Tama anymore.

Kicking my boxers off, my back was to her as I walked into my shower. "Tell me about this resort." I glanced behind me, Tama was standing tentatively in the doorway.

My eyes rolled to my soap, satisfied she was watching me. I washed my body, talking to her the entire time before I turned the water off and turned around. Her eyes widened and slid down to my dick which wasn't totally flaccid before gliding back to my face. She passed me my towel.

"Will is already complaining about Henry and Ava sharing a room. It's too bad you're busy for spring break. Nicole and I are bunking together because Matt will be with you. She's bummed that he won't be around, but at least I'll have someone not sucking face the entire time."

I wrapped the towel around my waist and rubbed the excess water from my hair. "I'd fucking love to go to the beach with you. We should plan something during my offseason."

She watched a water droplet slip down my chest and pool in my belly button. She sucked in a breath and turned around.

I fought the fist pump at the small win and ignored the complication it brought that our attraction seemed mutual. There were a million things I could have done at that moment, but none of them felt like the right thing to do. I dropped my towel and snatched a pair of boxers.

Tama had already made herself comfortable. Her shoes were off, tucked under the bed. The covers were nestled to her chin. She was looking at the ceiling with a soft smile on her face.

I got in bed after her and settled her against me. A sigh of relief that I had her, she was safe, and for now, she was mine, slipped out.

One Month Later

*Mama: Happy Birthday, honey.
Beckett and are going to
video chat you tonight. Yolanda,
Gerty, and Thelma may be on the
call too.*

*Me: Looking forward to it. Are
you taking the call outside the
house? Putting T and Y that
close together never works out.*

*Mama: We are going to call from
the activity room. At least Reggie
will be in there in case of a fight.*

Reggie was the security guard that was around to keep rowdy residents under control. You'd think he'd have a low-stress job, but Yolanda and Thelma gave him a run for his money. A few times he's had to break up very slow-moving fights between a few of the single men that were vying for Gerty's attention.

Ava knocked and walked into my room. She was balancing a plate of cornettos and smiling broadly at me. The pastries had different fillings based on the color oozing from the tips. Henry was following behind, watching the plate, no doubt hoping I didn't grab the lemon.

I chose the vanilla cream and settled against my pillows. Ava was a great baker, too. She learned from her nonna who had her own patisserie in Sorrento. When she came back from her winter break in Italy, she had a few more recipes up her sleeve and her cornettos were a favorite of mine.

Henry snatched the lemon one with a huge grin and sat on my desk. He didn't take his eyes off his pastry as he took his bite. His love of food is one of the things that bonded us together. It furthered my belief that Ava and Henry were a match made in heaven.

"So good." Henry moaned as he went for another bite. Ava giggled and sat down next to me. "Happy Birthday. Eat and get dressed. Lily and Nicole have a full day planned for us."

My eyes widened as I took another bite. Matt and Rhys were away for a game, but their flight was getting in this afternoon. We were all having dinner together, on my request. I wanted something low key and easy. Will was stressed about ending his first year at law school with a bang. Lily was preparing to graduate, but she had already been accepted to the business school at Pineview for her Masters. Nicole, Ava, and Henry were all in the stressful part of the semester where finals were on the horizon and chances for extra credit were dwindling. I wanted something low stress for all my friends.

My studies were also reaching a fever pitch, but I was still acing all my classes. I had signed up for a few summer courses to take online. My biggest stressor was the fact that the end of the semester brought me closer to the draft. Rhys had prepared me time and time again. When he drafted, he'd be given a little time to get to where he needed to be and then all bets were off.

I told him that I was going to help him with the move, in whatever form that took. Whether that meant finding him a place and packing him up or physically driving the moving truck with him, I was down for whatever capacity he needed.

"Am I allowed to know what the plans for today are or am I going with the flow?"

Ava's head tilted in thought. "I mean, I know what all we are doing, so I guess it's your choice."

I finished my pastry. "Give me a hint," I said.

"Spa day." She wagged her eyebrows.

I grinned. "Sounds perfect."

Lily paid for all of us to get hour-long massages, facials, manicures, and pedicures after time in the steam room. We relaxed together before separating for our own massage rooms. Ava and Henry, and Lily and Will were doing couple's massages and facials. Then we were all in the same room for the manicure and pedicures. It was funny watching Will jump every time he was tickled.

Henry hardly moved which made me certain he had a few pedicures in his life.

By the time we were done, all of us were feeling more relaxed. Lily, Will, and I were in one car when we left. Ava, Henry, and Nicole were in the other. Lily needed to run by the store to pick up some laundry detergent. We walked around together and ate the offered samples from the deli counter. I was getting hungry but didn't want to mention anything in case a meal was planned soon.

My phone buzzed in my pocket.

*Rhys: Happy Birthday! I'm home and
Whinny and Nathan want to wish you
HBD, come over!*

I glanced up to Lily who was smiling sweetly at Will as he tried to juggle the bouncing balls from the display. I cleared my throat.

"Just out of curiosity. What are the rest of today's plans?"

Lily smirked at me. "Dinner in a few hours, why?"

I held up my phone for her to read the message from Rhys.

"We'll drop you off."

I grinned and responded back to Rhys that I'd be over in ten minutes.

Lily and Will made their lazy way up to checkout before we finally made it to her SUV. I was getting anxious to see Rhys. Our friendship was still weird, but I liked it. We saw each other naked, regularly. Open door showers where we spoke about our day was the norm. I was upset at first that I wasn't tempting him, but then after I told Ava she told me it was a game of chicken. And I enjoyed playing chicken with Rhys. We hadn't done anything sexual, well except for the time he forgot about. But the tension was building between us.

Rhys was waiting for me on his stoop. He stood up and walked over to me with a wide grin on his face.

"Thanks for the ride." My words were muffled as I got out of Lily's car.

Rhys hugged me and swung me around before setting me down. His face was buried against my neck. "Fuck, I missed you."

He pulled his face away from mine and tugged me towards his truck. "Let's get some ice cream, my treat. It's not every day my girl turns twenty-two. It's your magic birthday you're twenty-two on the twenty-second. It calls for ice cream."

I chuckled at his enthusiasm and let him lead me over to his truck.

He ordered his favorite, birthday cake. I ordered mine, praline pecan. We sat on the bench where he told me about the scout that was at his game. An agent had been in touch with him. He was feeling giddy about the idea that he was going to make it.

We ate our ice cream before he turned back to me. He pushed a tendril of hair that had fallen out of my braid and tucked it behind my ear.

"You look beautiful." He let out a choppy breath and leaned into me. His eyes were on my lips as he licked his.

This is it.

"Hey Rhys!"

I tucked my chin down as he turned his head. Lydia strolled towards us. She bent down to hug him, shoving her boobs in his face.

"How have you been?" She went to sit on his lap. He slid over to avoid it, but it caused there to be space between the two of us. She sat down and turned her body away from me, giving me her back. She was always a little rude to me, so it was no surprise that she didn't acknowledge me.

I breathed out a sigh and finished my ice cream.

"You're interrupting something," Rhys said.

She glanced over her shoulder at me, lip curling. "It's just Tara. She didn't have a problem with this last year when we were fucking regularly."

I rolled my lips in and stood up to throw my trash away.

"Her name is Tama, and I don't give a shit about last year. You're being rude to my friend."

Lydia stood up and flicked her long red hair into my face. She leaned forward to kiss Rhys. He gave her his cheek. "Call me." She turned on her heel and walked away after giving me a reproachful look.

I walked the two steps over to the trashcan. With my hands empty, my palm rubbed my bicep a few times before he stood up and came to me. "Sorry about that."

My smile was a little too bright. "I'm used to it." I pointed back to the creamery. "I'm going to go wash my hands. Give me a minute."

He was running his hands through his hair when I came back. "That was shitty and I'm sorry she treated you like that. And that I allowed her to treat you like that last year." He stood up and walked over to me.

I chewed on the inside of my cheek. "It's fine. She did the same thing when she was with Henry, too."

He grunted. "I'm surprised Henry put up with it."

I let out a humorless laugh. "He didn't, that's why they didn't work out. But it didn't stop her from treating me poorly."

He sighed heavily. "Let's go home, Bully."

He grabbed my hand, lacing our fingers together and tugged me to his truck. I didn't know how I was feeling. Numb mostly to the disappointment that I was positive he was about to kiss me, and it was interrupted by Lydia, of all people.

"We are not going to let Lydia fuck up your day. She's a bitch and you're the best. Let's hang out until dinner, okay?" His pleading eyes were on mine as he turned his truck on.

My lips twisted to the side. I wanted him to take me home so I could process my disappointment, but he seemed adamant about hanging out. And I wanted to, mostly. I'd missed him. The past month had been crazy with traveling, games, and studying. He was burning the candle at both ends to graduate on time and be at the top of his game. If I told him I wanted to be alone it would make him stressed and that was the last thing I wanted.

His house was quiet when we made it inside. I stepped into the living room that led to the stairs when the lights flipped on.

"Surprise," voices boomed.

My hand flew to my chest as I looked back to Rhys who was beaming at me. "I told you I'd pay you back for my party." His breath tickled my face before he kissed my cheek.

Half the baseball team and all my roommates were standing in the living room. Nathan and Whinny were first to give me a hug. The baseball players that I knew waited in a line to greet me, and then the party started. Ava and Nicole had laid out a huge spread of food. Will and Matt were posted by the meatballs and were growling at anyone trying to add them to their plate.

Ava had made a large birthday cake that sat in the center of the table that was surrounded by other treats like lemon bars, cookies, and brownies. Henry was double fisting the lemon bars as Ava kept smacking his hand away as he tried to grab more.

Rhys made me a plate of BBQ sliders, corn salad, and fresh fruit before he loaded his own plate up. He guided me outside to his deck where a few of his teammates were sitting around the outdoor dining table. A few girls I didn't recognize were hanging around the keg that was primed and ready.

As the evening rolled on more people I didn't know showed up, no doubt hearing there was a party going on. I went back outside to get a beer for myself when my mom signaled that she was going to call in five minutes. Looping back in the kitchen, I grabbed a water instead. I looked around for Rhys so I could ask to use his bedroom.

He was talking to Nathan, rolling his eyes but grinning. I was a few feet from him when a blur of blonde pushed me aside and went straight for Rhys. She squealed and hugged him around his neck. He smiled down at her as he nodded at whatever she said.

I chewed on my lip and turned around looking for another resident of the house. I didn't want to interrupt Rhys's conversation. He seemed pleased to be having it. Whinny was eating cake with his hands.

"Can I borrow your bedroom?"

He gave me a lazy smile. "No hanky-panky, Bully."

I snorted. "My mom is going to call me. I need a quiet place."

He tipped his chin to the stairs. "You know the way."

I glanced back at Rhys. The blonde was still inches from his face. Her hand wrapped possessively around his arm. His eyes flitted in my direction before I turned around and headed upstairs to Whinny's room.

It was gross. His room smelled like gym socks, which made sense since there was a pile of dirty laundry that took up the corner. I cringed and flicked the light on before going to lock the bedroom door. The last thing I wanted was someone to come in expecting an empty room as a place to hook up while on the phone with my mom.

His sheets were crumpled, his comforter in a knot at the foot of the bed. I flicked his boxers off his chair with a pen I found on his desk. My phone lit up with a call. I took a breath to ignore the disappointment swirling in my gut at seeing Rhys with another woman. It had been weeks since we had been to a party, and even before he'd mostly stay next to me. It wasn't like last year where he'd disappear for thirty minutes and reappear, hair mussed, lips red, and eyes glazed.

"Happy Birthday," five voices crowed.

Gerty was sitting next to mom with Beckett standing overhead. The phone exchanged hands as I watched an elbow match between Yolanda and Thelma before Beckett stepped in and separated them.

There was a small knock on the door. I called out, "Someone is in here," and smiled back to my phone. That prompted the conversation about where I was and why I was in a stranger's bedroom.

The lock clicked as the door swung open. I whirled around with wide eyes.

"It's disgusting in here." Rhys walked right up to me.

"Who's that?" Gerty asked.

I cringed as Rhys grinned at me and pulled my phone from my hand. I cupped my face, feeling the flush burn my palms.

"You're a fox," Gerty cooed.

Rhys chuckled and made his introductions. He grabbed my hands and pulled me out of Whinny's room.

"Hold on guys. We are relocating to my room because my roommate is part pig." Rhys shut his door and locked it before smiling back at the screen. Gerty, Thelma, and Yolanda asked rapid fire questions. Rhys's head was tilted towards mine so we could share the screen while snuggled on his bed.

Beckett was scowling every time he was passed the phone. My mom kept giving Rhys a skeptical once over before the phone would yank back to Gerty. She was a relentless flirt. A few times Rhys blushed at the things she was saying. My mom snatched her phone back when Gerty asked Rhys's size and then asked him to tell her when to stop as she slowly spread her palms apart.

"Gertrude now is not the time for that," my mom said.

"But if not now, when? I'm an old woman. I live in the moment and don't buy green bananas. Those are my rules. Don't spoil my fun when there is a virile man in my face."

"You're such a slut," Yolanda grumbled.

"At least my vagina hasn't closed up from disuse, Landy," Gerty quipped.

"Hard to close a gaping hallway. Vince Degato said you're wide enough for him to set his testes in."

"And that's all for today. Tama, honey, I'll call you tomorrow. I love you," my mom said.

My face had curled into a cringe. Before I left for college my neighbors never discussed their sex life. Gerty confessed to me while she was drunk last summer that my mom had threatened all our neighbors to never mention sex to me or she'd have Bingo night canceled indefinitely. Now after I experienced the world outside of geriatrics and an overprotective mother, all bets had been off.

"See you online for our poker match," Gerty called as the phone went dark.

Rhys's chest was shaking in laughter. "You weren't exaggerating at all."

A grin spread across my face. "Grannies gone wild, remember?"

He chuckled and reached for me. "Why were you in Whinny's disgusting room?"

His hands rubbed up my arms as he tugged me to straddle on his lap. We had never been in that position before. I sat back closer to his knees and sighed.

"I didn't want to interrupt you to ask if I could use your room. And I didn't want to be using your room if you needed it."

He huffed a breath and tipped his head back. "I'm too drunk for this conversation," he murmured. I frowned at him. His hands rested on my hips as he stared up at me. "I want to kiss you."

I licked my lips.

"We are still friends if we kiss, right?"

My head bobbed rapidly as I leaned into him. One hand slid from my hip to the back of my head as he guided my face to his. His lips were warm. He groaned and tilted my head, his tongue seeking entry. I opened slowly. His hand on my hip tugged me closer to his body. I gasped at the size of his erection. He guided me up and down his hardened length as his urgent lips continued to kiss me. My dress had risen. My naked core was chaffing against his denim with delicious friction.

I gasped when he flipped us, so I was on my back.

He pulled his face away from mine. His eyes were wild as he glanced down at me. "Fuck, no panties."

He rested on his knees. His chest was heaving as he looked between my naked lower half and my face. His tongue traced his lower lip over and over again.

"You can touch me if you want to."

Please touch me.

He let out a choppy breath. "I can't give you what you deserve."

I rolled my lower lip into my mouth before nodding. "I know, but I still want it. It's my birthday, after all."

His eyes flicked up to mine. "I don't want to ruin our friendship." He looked in pain when he said it.

I shook my head. "You can't. What we have can't be ruined by having a little fun."

A relieved smirk crossed his face before he breathed deeply, looking at the ceiling. "We need rules."

I was going to agree to anything he said.

"No fingers, no tongues, no fucking."

I scowled, unsure what else was left to do. He chuckled. "We can jerk off to each other or dry hump." He looked down to my exposed lower half. "Or a version of it."

I nodded vigorously. "Okay, but your jeans are a little rough."

"I don't want to hurt you." He stood up and shucked his jeans off. His erection had pushed a huge tent out from his boxers. My eyes widened. It had been a while since I had seen it hard.

"Do you think my boxers will chafe you?"

I swallowed hard and whimpered. "I do," I breathed.

He yanked his shirt off before crooking his thumbs into the waistband of his boxers. His cock snapped against his stomach. He knee-walked back over to me. Kneeling in front of me like a Greek God. My body tensed.

Happy Birthday to me.

His palms slid up my thighs to the hem of my dress as he started to tug it up. I leaned forward and helped him, leaving me in only my lacey bra. He cursed under his breath as I shimmied out of that too. I gave him an innocent expression. "It's not like you haven't seen me naked before."

Leaning over me, his kiss was more tentative than before. He kept his hands bracketing my head as he settled his hips against mine. I gasped at how hot he felt. I spread my legs further, opening so the ridge of his head rubbed on my clit. My eyes rolled back as he found a rhythm with both his tongue and his hips.

He swallowed my moans as he rutted faster. My back arched as my calves looped around his naked butt, holding him to me as he grinded harder against me. His breaths were coming out in fast pants as my lips parted open in a cry that was muffled by his tongue spearing into my mouth.

Chest up, he squeezed my breast, rolling my nipples between his fingers, which made my orgasm extend, bowing my back, pushing further into him. He cursed and rutted harder before bracing himself on his palms. He slammed against me before his muscles tensed under my legs. Hot liquid coated my stomach as Rhys tipped his head back in a grunt. He rolled to the side.

"Fuck, I haven't come that hard in a while," he said. Then he started to laugh.

I turned to face him, smiling. "What's so funny?" I asked after another moment.

"I've wanted to do that for a very long time."

My brows furrowed. "You have?"

He rolled over to his back. His slowly softening penis was still resting against his stomach. "Fuck, yeah. I didn't want to mess anything up between us. I haven't been your friend in hopes something would happen. I genuinely like you as a person."

I bit into my lip. "Nothing's ruined," I promised.

He perked a brow at me. "Because we have rules. Our friendship comes first, right?"

I nodded. He rolled off the bed and came back a moment later with a wet sock. "Sorry, I don't own washcloths. This will have to do."

I giggled as he tossed the soiled sock in his laundry basket. "You're going to have to remember that you unpaired a sock or you'll think your dryer ate it."

He smirked at me. "I'll save the other one if we do this again."

I swallowed at the word *if* and nodded as I blew out a breath. Someone pounded on his door. I cringed.

His eyes widened. "I forgot we're hosting a party."

I licked my lips. "We should probably get dressed."

He groaned and leaned forward to kiss me. "Probably."

"I'm on the phone. Give me a minute," Rhys called, his lips still on mine.

I bit back a smile watching his naked behind walk to his pile of clothes. His brow perked when I hadn't moved. "We're good, right?"

I laughed. "Will you stop worrying? You're making me paranoid."

I leaned over the edge of the bed and snagged my bra. "We're good. I promise you, we're good." My dress got caught in my hair, so it took a moment to untangle myself. "I swear, one of these days I'm going to chop it all off."

He hummed. "You'll look beautiful no matter what."

My flush burned my cheeks as I stepped back into my shoes.

"Ready?" Rhys asked me before he opened his bedroom door and walked down to the party below.

Chapter 8

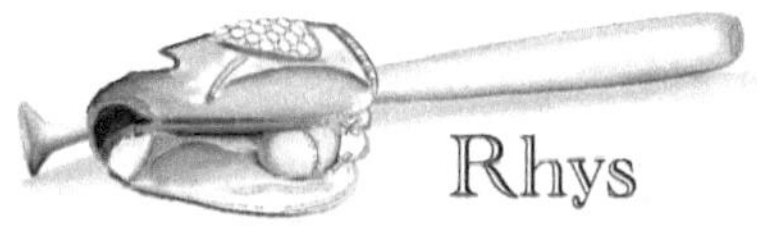

Rhys

Three Weeks Later

My gorgeous best friend was sound asleep in my bed as I packed my bag for the NCAA Super Regionals. It was where we stalled out before, but I was determined to make it past. I wanted a World Series win under my hat. We were good enough last year before Matt was taken out with a broken arm, and he had spent so much time with the pitchers this season that they were as good as he had been.

A few days after Tama's birthday my team had the Big 12 Championship which we won. It was an incredible feeling made even more special by the fact that Tama had flown to Arlington with her roommates to support the team. She was the first person I wanted to see when the final game finished, and we had cinched the win. I swung her around and damn near kissed her in front of my whole team. I held off. I wasn't sure how she felt about that, and I didn't want to make her uncomfortable.

At that point we hadn't hooked up again after her birthday even though we spent every night together. Seeing her splayed in front of me, tits bouncing as I let my ridge slide against her clit had been spank bank material for days. It wasn't until we had gotten home from Arlington that she initiated anything with me again.

We had been studying for finals together when she shoved her books to the side and straddled my hips. I grinned up to her as she cupped my face. She played by my rules and rode my dick to an orgasm. It opened a door for us. Now we were mutual masturbation and hump buddies.

Did I want more physically? Absolutely, but I was taking the gift of watching her cum every night as a decent alternative.

A few nights ago, I opened her nightstand and played with her little toys. I watched in fascination as the clit sucker made her legs shake. I wanted to replace my mouth with it but resisted. I jerked off on her tits and she winked at me as she rubbed it in and then licked her finger. It made my whole-body shiver just thinking about it.

Tama was finished with school, so she had been very generous with her time when I had been available. To say I was going into this tournament feeling relaxed and happy is an understatement. It helped that she and Nicole were going to fly and watch, but her flight was leaving a day after mine.

She slept while I leaned forward and kissed her lips. I hummed when she mumbled something in her sleep. Leaving a quick note and a copy of my key for her to lock up when she woke, I quietly closed my bedroom door.

Nathan and Whinny gave me knowing smiles when I strode through the kitchen.

"Tama's sleeping?" Nathan asked. He'd backed off since our last big confrontation. He no longer reminded me that I was in love with my best friend. Not that I needed a reminder, I knew with every single fiber of my being how I felt about Tama.

"Yeah, finals wore her out."

Whinny snorted. "Sure, *finals* are what we'll call it."

Grabbing the protein shake that Tama had made for me, I ignored the comment. We trooped out to my truck, tossing our luggage in the bed before making our way to campus. With school officially out the parking lot allowed first come first serve parking.

Matt Foust and Coach Daniels were talking next to the charter buses, strategizing no doubt. Foust had a brain for strategy, numbers, and finding players' weaknesses and strengths. He helped me with some batting when he noticed I was inconsistent with a slider pitch. Upped my batting average enough for scouts to notice.

Whinny settled next to me on the bus as we made our way to Denver International Airport. Most of my teammates fell asleep during the hour drive, but I was too amped to sleep. Whenever I closed my eyes all I could see was Tama cumming. Popping a boner while in a bus full of baseball players would open me up to a bit of hazing.

The flight was a little rowdy as most of the passengers were baseball players or family of the team. I kept to myself and tried to read the book I had seen Tama reading. The eBook was more discreet without the shirtless muscled guy on the cover. I had been reading through it whenever I was traveling. I had to set it down when the dude fucked the girl's ass as a punishment for mouthing off in front of his friends.

With my semi adjusted, I changed to *Ball Four* which had been highly recommended to me by my dad.

Halfway into the flight Whinny turned his body towards me. I stowed my phone and perked my brow, my silent question of 'what's up?'

Rolling his lips in before popping them out was his tic when he was gearing up to say something uncomfortable. "What's going on with you and Bully? And don't tell me you two are only friends. We share a wall. I'm not a creep, but she isn't always quiet."

My molars chewed into my cheek. I didn't know what to say that wouldn't betray her trust. "She *is* my friend."

"That you trade orgasms with?" His voice was low, but I still looked around the plane. This was not a conversation I wanted overheard. I gave him a quick nod.

"You convinced her to be your friend with benefits?"

I blew out a breath and shook my head. "It's different from what I had with Lydia. For one, I didn't give a fuck if Lydia messed around with other guys and vice versa. Second, I don't know what to call it because Tama and I haven't discussed it. We have rules in place, but we haven't defined anything. I'm going at her pace."

"But you're monogamous." He didn't question it. I was his party buddy and wingman who hadn't indulged in a random hookup in a while.

"Unintentionally, yeah."

His eyes cut in my direction. "Do you think Tama would be okay if it wasn't monogamous?"

My jaw clenched at the idea of our situation changing, but I still answered honestly. "I don't know. She was cool about it last year, but there have been a few times while we were out together where women flirted with me, and she didn't like it. It could have been because we were on a date and the girl flirting with me was rude to her, but I don't know. Maybe if the girl was nice to Tama she'd be okay with it."

Whinny's brow furrowed as he shook his head. "Would you be okay with it if it was reversed?"

"Fuck no," I said a little too quickly.

Whinny tilted his head. "Okay, so you are in a friend with benefits situation where you are monogamous?"

"It's more nuanced than that, but yeah." I could have told him about our rules in place, but I doubted it would make him understand. Also, I wanted to break every single fucking rule. Every time I saw her naked it made it more difficult to convince myself I was smart in implementing guidelines in the first place.

My thought had been: if I kept my hands and mouth to myself then it would be more emotionally detached. Like I was watching a live sex show. I could get off and not have a connection and vice versa. Now rubbing my bare dick up and down her bare pussy was a gray area, but I liked that too much to stop.

But after the first time I watched Tama get herself off I realized I was fucking wrong in my assumption. Watching her like that when she was so vulnerable was like sharing a secret. It was intimate as fuck, and it made me want more of it.

I already knew almost everything about her, and now I knew that the right side of her clit was more sensitive than the left. She got a full Brazilian every few weeks with Lily, but even during her growth phase it wasn't off putting. She liked when I played with her nipples, especially when I lightly bit them. I couldn't tell you a fucking thing about what Lydia liked or if she was even a natural redhead. I never cared enough to pay attention to what made her moan, and we only saw each other when she was completely groomed and dolled up.

"And she's okay with that?" Whinny asked.

The inconvenient truth was we never discussed it after we started hooking up regularly. "I've gotten zero complaints. Besides, she knows where my head is at. I can't give her a relationship. My whole life is going to change in a few weeks. She knows. She's okay with it. Even when we take the benefits away because I'm going to be gone, we will still have our friendship."

He nodded slowly. "And you'd be okay with Tama dating someone else next year?"

My stomach lurched. The thought made me want to puke, but I didn't want to deal with the consequences of what that meant. I played it off as a nonissue.

"I'm not worried about next year. Besides I'll probably be fucking a new bunny in every city. What sort of hypocrite would I be if I told her to wait for me? It's exactly why I don't want a relationship."

"Right, okay." He didn't sound convinced but changed the subject to what he was going to do after graduation. He wasn't going to draft. He had no desire to grind through the farm system and already had a job lined up at a marketing firm in downtown Denver. He was from Colorado, so I wasn't surprised he wanted to stay local.

When we were waiting for our baggage my teammate Remi Casey walked up to me and nudged my shoulder with his. He wasn't trying to bow up, he was just too big for his body. "I heard the Rays scout is going to be at the tournament."

I grinned. "Yeah, my agent or at least the guy I am thinking about signing with mentioned something about it. The Braves and the Mariners are also going to be there."

He whistled. "Your girlfriend is in my psychology lecture. She's hot as fuck, sweet too."

My jaw clicked.

He saw my expression and held his hands up. "No disrespect. Just making small talk."

My tongue swiped the front of my teeth. I wanted to correct him about the girlfriend comment, and maybe I would have if he hadn't complimented her. It didn't help that he was going to be in school for another year with her, and if I told him that we were only friends he might make a move.

"She have any single friends?"

Justified in not explaining my relationship status.

"Nope, her two roommates from last year are both with Reiser and Fousty, respectfully. Her other roommate is with Fousty's cousin." I turned to him. "I thought you were with Veronica Miller."

He grimaced as he shook his head. "No, she got back together with her ex. Turns out she was using me to make him jealous."

My upper lip rose. "That sucks."

He raised his hands. "Whatever, she gave terrible head and only talked about the dude."

Been there.

Countless hookups had used me to make their ex jealous. "Well, I know you want to draft, so focus on baseball. A relationship can fuck with your focus, and no piece of ass is worth your career."

His chin canted up. "Tama seems to have sharpened your focus. You've never played better, bro and that's saying something."

I fought back a smile at the compliment but swallowed it down that once again he thought that Tama and I were like that.

"She is the best friend I have ever had."

"Get your bags and go, we have a schedule to keep," Foust called out.

This is it. One more inning and we were going to the World Series. We needed to hold on for one more inning. I glanced over to the stands from first base. Tama was sitting next to Nicole, Lily, and Will. She had her hands clasped together, sunglasses covering her eyes. She was rocking back and forth, clearly nervous. I rolled my eyes back to the batter who had taken the batter's box.

Scott Drake had been on fucking fire on the pitcher's mound. He'd only let one hit so far. It was a pop fly caught by Remi.

I reacted the same moment the crack of the bat ripped through the air. The ball was heading right for me. I jumped to snag it, and fist pumped as the crowd roared. Drake caught the ball I tossed back to him, and I winked over to Tama who was still standing and cheering at my play.

Two more outs. If we shut this out, then we'd win even though we only had one run. It was my homerun, my second at bat.

The next batter struck out. Nerves pitched in my stomach.
One more out.

The bat cracked a screamer right for Drake's head. He hit the mound stomach first as the ball smacked into second base, popping up into Whinny's hand as he threw it over to first base. All pressure was on me. I snatched the ball from the air. The runner's foot was hovering over the bag as my hand slapped his hip.

A confused cheer rippled through the crowd and the umpires conferred together. Moments passed as they watched the replay before the umpire came out. "Out."

I threw my head back in a yell. My tendons strained in my neck as my throat went hoarse.

We were going to the World Series.

Rushing the mound, I scooped Drake up by the ass and shook him as the rest of my teammates met me in celebration. We were ushered to our dugout to keep our celebration classy. As soon as our opponents cleared off to their locker rooms we piled back onto the field where our friends, family, and fans swarmed us. My head was on a swivel as I looked for Tama. She was tiny compared to everyone else. I spotted Nicole who was at least 5'8" pushing through the crowd followed closely behind by Reiser. I could barely make out the top of Tama's dirty blonde hair. I rushed in her direction.

I yanked her up by the hips and kissed her like my life depended on it. She looped her arms around my neck. A few wolf whistles pierced the air around us before I realized what I was doing. I slowed my tongue and ended our kiss with a series of pecks. When I set her down, she looped her arm around my back as I held her under my arm.

"I'm so proud of you," she yelled over the celebration. Her eyes were bright with a few tears gathered in the corners.

I leaned down and kissed her temple before letting her go.

My parents were pushing their way through the crowd. I met them halfway, expecting Tama to follow me, but when I turned around, she was hugging Nathan and Whinny. My dad picked me up in a hug before setting me down for my mom to hug me next.

The night was a blur of celebration. Half the evening was spent with my parents and then the other half with my teammates as we went out to a pub to celebrate. I got there late and was informed by Whinny that I had missed Tama. My phone was completely dead so I couldn't ask her where she was. But I knew she'd want me to celebrate with my team, so I ignored the niggle of guilt about not celebrating with her.

She'd understand.

At one point a redhead sat in my lap and attempted to kiss me. I vaguely remember saying, "No thank you, ma'am, I have a girlfriend."

Offended by being called ma'am, she huffed and walked away. It wasn't until I was stumbling into my empty hotel room did I realize what I had drunkenly said.

Five Weeks Later

School had been out for almost two months, but I was still in Boulder, much to the dismay of the residents of Friendly Village. My excuse was that my summer classes were hard, and I needed to concentrate. I may have implied they were in person, but they didn't question it. Besides I was going to have a three-week break between summer classes and the start of fall semester where I was going to go home.

In reality, my classes weren't that difficult and only online. The reason for my dishonesty, I was savoring the last few weeks of Rhys.

I was completely shocked when he kissed me in front of his entire team. It was so claiming, and I wanted it to foreshadow more to come. Then within a few minutes he had run in the other direction. I knew it was to go to his parents, but he didn't imply he wanted to introduce me, so I slipped away to make it less awkward for him.

Then we missed each other during the post-win celebration. Whinny and Nathan bracketed my sides as they drank and got rowdy. I gave up at midnight that Rhys was going to show up where I was. Half the team was at a nightclub. Remi Casey had asked Whinny if he was going, clueing me in on Rhys's possible plans.

I swallowed down my disappointment when I made it back to my hotel room alone. It was silly and stupid for thinking one little kiss when my best friend was high on endorphins meant anything. He probably hooked up with a gorgeous stranger in the club.

It didn't stop me from going to the World Series. No matter how sad I was about not knowing where he was after his win, I wanted to support him in the biggest series of games he had ever played in his life. Lily, being rich as sin, was able to get us tickets to every game and hotel stays. She also used her dad's private jet to get us to and from.

It was an intense few games and unfortunately, they didn't win. It was so close, the other team simply played a little better. The celebration was obviously more muted than the weeks' prior. Rhys had signed with an agent and was happy in his own right, but he kept his professional win to himself while the rest of his teammates dealt with the loss.

Ava and Henry were in New York and Europe for the summer so I had our apartment to myself. Rhys's lease wasn't up until July 31, but Nathan and Whinny had already moved out.

Rhys and I spent the few weeks leading into the draft hanging out together. We still followed his rules, but I liked what we had. He'd entertain himself while I completed my week's work and then we'd eat, read together, and dry hump each other whenever the temptation presented itself.

It was a bittersweet routine that I was going to be sad to change when he moved. I wanted to broach the subject of making whatever we were official, but he had been clear. And the warnings from Griffin still rang in my head. Any relationship would suffer because of distance, but a new relationship would be doomed.

Speaking of Griffin, his new single was topping the charts. We spoke once a week through our chat as he detailed how things were changing for him. I never mentioned Griffin to Rhys. I didn't want to rock the boat. What Griffin and I had was friendly, and I didn't want him to think otherwise.

Warm hands cupped my shoulders and began to knead as Rhys's lips pressed into the top of my head. I set my textbook down and grinned up at him. He leaned forward and kissed my lips before hopping over the couch and sitting next to me.

"Are you nervous?"

It was the day of the draft. He had been clutching his phone and checking it constantly. His agent had told him to keep it nearby and be ready to answer.

He blew out a breath. "I feel restless."

I hummed and turned my body to straddle his hips. One brow perked as I leaned forward to kiss his neck.

The world paused when his phone rang loudly next to us. His wide eyes looked up to me. The television was on the draft as he saw his name splash across the screen.

"Holy shit," he whispered.

"Answer your phone."

He swallowed hard.

I listened with tears gathering in my eyes as he said, "It would be an honor."

I clapped my hands over my mouth as he hung up the phone. The television ticker was saying Rhys was picked by the Tampa Bay Rays during the first round. I leaned forward and kissed him. His hands cupped my cheeks. I could feel his smiling lips against mine, and then his cell went crazy.

He was on the phone for four hours between his agent, family, and friends. I made him dinner while he paced my living room. He kept nodding and then finally he tossed his phone on the couch and tipped his face to the ceiling.

"I fucking did it," he whispered.

"You did it."

His chest heaved as his emotions caught up with him. A few happy tears leaked down his cheeks as he recanted the negotiations his agent was doing, his signing bonus, and his family that had all reached out. Even estranged family members were congratulating him. I was so happy for him.

When we finished eating, he pushed his plate away. A worried furrow pinched his brow.

"What's wrong?"

His mouth opened and closed a few times. "If I sign with them, I'm going to be on their AA team, which is a big deal for someone straight out of the draft. They need a first baseman because theirs is on the DL. They want me in Montgomery in ten days. I'd only have about a month of the season to play." He chewed his cheek as his fingers rubbed together.

I didn't want to show him how sad I was at the prospect of him leaving. He had been working his entire life for this, and I was so proud of him. Showing him my trepidation of him leaving wouldn't make things easy for him.

I swallowed thickly. "We knew it was a possibility. What do you need me to do? I can look up apartments."

He shook his head. "No, the signing bonus is providing for my housing for the first six months."

I nodded. "That's great. What do you need from me?"

His brows puckered as he licked his lips. He swallowed hard before blowing a slow breath out.

"Will you go with me?" His blue eyes held me captive until I realized what he had asked me.

I blanched. I wasn't going to delay my education. I was ahead of schedule going to graduate almost a year early, but then I had my master's before my PhD.

He blinked at me and looked down at the table. His hand clenched in a fist before he dropped it down to his lap. His eyes darted away from mine to the ceiling.

"Like help me move," he clarified when I was quiet for too long.

I blew out a breath as a smile took over my face. "Of course. Are we going to drive or fly?"

"Drive, probably. We could make it a road trip to rival yours last year. Hit up national parks east of the Rockies."

I sat back in my chair. "I'd love that."

A slow smile overtook his face. "Then we should probably make some plans. I need to call my agent, deal with signing and then we can head to Alabama."

I giggled. "Not a sentence I thought I'd ever hear you say."

He chuckled. "Well, I'm a Montgomery Biscuit now, Bully."

Chapter 9

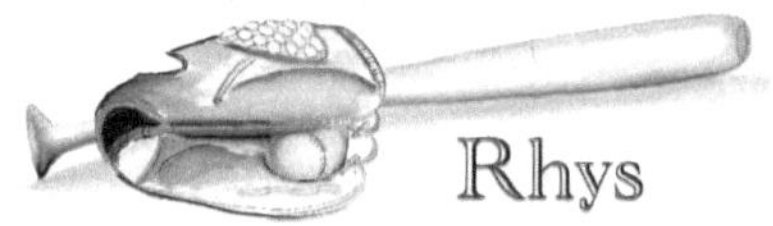

Rhys

So it turns out there aren't the same type of national parks between Boulder and Montgomery as there are between Boulder and LA. Tama still planned out a journey that was going to take a few days to get there. I signed the day after I was drafted. Tama mapped out our journey as I packed up my belongings.

I was going to share an apartment with another player for the first six months. I had looked online at the reviews of the neighborhood, so I knew what to expect. It came partially furnished; all I would need to bring was a bed and dresser. Which was all my truck could haul when loaded down with all my other belongings.

The custom truck bed topper my dad and I made locked up everything after I had packed it. I was leaving my mattress, so everything fit. Tama kept her bag behind her seat in the truck.

I clasped her hand as we pulled away from the house I had been living in for the better part of three years. My stomach twisted as she squeezed my fingers with hers.

"Okay, our first leg is the longest. It should take us about eight hours to get to Wichita. We can rotate drivers every four hours if you want."

I nodded at her as we pulled onto the highway. She was my navigator for the drive. She had also determined that we were going to listen to an audio book together. I'd been warned that there were some racy scenes. After the last book she read, I was already looking forward to it.

"Are you still good to stay in Wichita tomorrow? I was hoping to visit The Keeper of the Plains and there is a Frank Lloyd Wright house that we can tour."

I grinned at her. Each destination city we were slated to stay a day and relax. "Of course, let's see all that Wichita has to offer."

Wichita

Listening to that audiobook while driving was a bit torturous. Tama giggled when I had to adjust my raging erection. Then when it was her turn to drive, I spent half the time squeezing my dick, so I didn't cum in my pants. Fortunately, the main guy was an idiot and let the girl get away with two hours left of the book, so the graphic sex scenes took a small break.

We had an hour left of the book by the time we made it to our hotel. Road wary and tired, we checked in and took separate showers before heading out to eat dinner. Tama talked about our planned schedule while I watched her lips move.

"Are you even listening to me?"

I sucked in a breath, pulling myself from my stupor where I was imagining her lips wrapped around my cock. I shook my head. "Sorry, I was daydreaming."

She smirked. "I know. It was obvious when I told you that dinosaurs were going to eat my toes and you nodded at me."

I snorted out. "Sorry. You have my full attention. The nature walk sounds great. I want to stretch my legs."

Satisfied with my answer she went back to looking through the menu.

Hot Springs National Park

The drive from Wichita was an easy seven hours with stops to eat. We listened to another book, but this one was more of a fantasy, so it was longer. She warned me that we'd probably listen to this book on our way to New Orleans which was our next major city.

The little town outside of Little Rock that housed the hot springs was picturesque. Tama had made reservations for us to sit in the springs, something I was looking forward to. Being in the car for as long as we had hurt my back. I was used to walking around and being physical, so the nature made jacuzzi was a welcome plan.

Fiddling with the radio knobs, I confessed a little lie. "I had to tell the bed and breakfast host that we were married for them to let us stay."

Tama's nose wrinkled.

"Hey." I clutched my chest. "Don't make that face. I'm a fucking catch. I'm going to make millions. I have a good-looking face, and I'm decent to talk to."

She giggled and elbowed me. "I wasn't making a face because of the thought of marrying you. I was making a face because that's antiquated and old fashioned." She rolled her eyes up to the sky. "What are we going to do about rings?"

I clicked my tongue in thought. "Good point." We were driving slowly through the quaint downtown. I pulled into the parking spot of a little antique dealer/ pawn shop. "Come on, Bully, let's get our wedding rings."

She stumbled behind me as I tugged her into the little shop. There weren't a lot of options. Which was fine. We only needed the rings for the night. There was a his and hers rose gold set which fit my finger but was too big for her. They reminded me of a ring my grandmother wore and gave to my mom.

"I sell sizers you can pop in there, so the ring doesn't go flying," the shop keeper said in a twangy accent that took me a moment to understand.

"We'll take them."

Tama whimpered and tried to argue with me.

I grinned at her. "Come on, wife, you always told me you wanted rose gold jewelry to match the heirloom piece my mom has. I know you are upset that the racoon stole our wedding rings from the windowsill, but I think these are perfect."

The shop keeper smiled at us, probably thinking we were full of absolute shit. But it was a small town. It was possible the pawn shop owner knew the B&B owner. I didn't want to be kicked out of our room for some antiquated rule.

"It wasn't a raccoon. It was Tim Biggins' crows. I told you that he trained them to steal shiny things."

I grinned at her. "Is that why his house has all the bird feeders?"

Tama gave me a wide-eyed stare. "Yes, I heard that he also races his pigeons and that's how he paid his mortgage last year."

I bit back a laugh and turned to the shop keep. He was holding the two jewelry boxes out. I passed him my credit card. It was the best $150 I have ever spent. I slipped the ring on Tama's hand and then twirled the ring against my finger.

She gaped down at it before letting me guide her from the shop. I chuckled when she shot me an incredulous look. She went to take the ring off, but I stopped her.

"Not yet."

She gave me a shaky nod and directed us to our accommodations.

Our reservations for the hot spring were before dinner, so we quickly packed our backpacks with our swimsuits and borrowed towels.

We were going on a regular tour on our second day, but the first night was the only time we were able to get a reservation for one of the bath houses.

My jaw clenched when I saw Tama step out of the changing room. She was in a navy string bikini, and while I had seen her naked, she had never looked sexier. I wanted to pull the strings but shoved my hands in my trunk pockets instead.

We were directed to a public shower to rinse off before we got in. It wasn't overly busy, but it wasn't empty either. Most of the bath house attendees were paired off having quiet conversations. I watched Tama rinse off with rapt attention as her nipples pebbled under the cold shower water. We walked hand in hand into the hot water that bubbled from the pebble floor of the pool.

I sank to my knees, so my shoulders were submerged. Tama stood flat footed. I grinned that we were almost the same height. She smiled back before looking up. The sun was starting to set, painting the sky in a crazy red. I pulled her to loop her legs around my waist as we watched the sunset.

Crickets started to chirp as she turned to me. She glanced down at my mouth before I pulled her against my lips. We kissed like that until an announcement rang out that the bath house was closing and all guests were asked to vacate the pool.

Tama got out first. A coy smile tipped her lips before passing me my towel, knowing full and well I was sporting a prominent erection. I took a cold shower in the changing room, trying to calm down.

Tama had changed into a summer dress. Her hair was piled on the top of her head. *Fucking beautiful.*

I held her hand as we walked through downtown looking for a place to have dinner. We stopped by a little barbeque place that had a small dance floor outside. We ate and laughed at the ridiculous story we had made up about why we needed wedding bands.

A few people left their tables to head to the dance floor. I wasn't a great dancer, but I wasn't going to pass up the opportunity to hold Tama.

"Since it's our wedding night, you should dance with me."

She rolled her eyes and took my hand. We danced slowly, our feet barely shuffling from side to side. She was pressed against me, leaning her head against my chest. I kissed her neck and sighed at the contentment of the day.

The host of the bed and breakfast had milk and cookies waiting for us when we got in. Tama grinned at me when the host asked how long we had been married.

"A year. We couldn't afford a honeymoon until now. Tama loves hot springs so here we are."

She smirked at me and then made a polite chitchat about the cookie recipe. Watching her put a smile on my face. I was going to fucking miss her.

The stairs to our little room creaked as Tama's ass swayed. I gripped her hip when she shut the door and bent down to kiss her again. She whimpered against my lips and pulled away.

"Since it's our wedding night, I think it's about time we consummated our relationship, don't you think?"

I licked my bottom lip and swallowed hard. My temple bounced as I considered everything that could go wrong if I followed through with her request.

She chewed on her cheek for a second as a blush spread up from her chest to her face. A furrow pinched her brow before she ducked her head down and she turned her face away, cheeks red.

I shook my head. "I want to, Bully, you have no idea how much I want to."

Her head remained bowed as she nodded. I shook my head and hunched down to get into her eyeline. "If we do that, we can't guarantee nothing will change between us."

She rolled her eyes and sighed. Her swallow was audible. "Right."

"You mean so much to me. I feel like if we cross that last barrier off our rules then we are setting ourselves up for failure."

Still not looking at me, she took a step away and gave me her back. My heart dropped further and further and my throat became knotted with every step she took.

"If I could look into the future and know that we could continue on like normal, I wouldn't even question it." I needed her to understand. I needed her to look at me and accept what I had weeks ago. We couldn't take our physical relationship further without compromising everything.

She looked over her shoulder. "For my benefit or yours?"

My brows furrowed. "Both of ours, but it's a moot point."

A set in her jaw made the little muscle in her temple twitch. "I know for a fact that I can handle it."

I shook my head. "What we have been doing isn't the same thing—"

"We hooked up after the Grant date. You came over, kissed me, showered with me. You fingered me and went down on me. I blew you. You were too drunk to remember, but it happened. And guess what? I didn't turn into some moon-eyed girl with hopes you'd change your plans for me. I know you don't want to have a relationship. I'm not dumb. You're worried that *I'll* get clingy. But you're right it's moot. You don't even remember it."

I gaped at her as a lot of things connected for me. "Is that why you were upset the next day?"

She rolled her eyes, nostrils flared. "I told you that it was mortifying to be forgotten about."

I shook my head before I tipped it back to the ceiling. *Fuck, I'm an asshole.*

"I thought it was a dream," I admitted. "I thought you were in no way attracted to me like that. My blurry memories… I thought were some wet dream fantasy I had because I was sleeping next to you after I was jealous as fuck that you were going to hook up with Grant."

"Rhys, I've been attracted to you since the first moment I saw you sitting at that lab table while that rude girl practically humped your leg."

I snorted and then bit my lip. "You took my breath away."

She rolled her eyes. "You don't have to do that."

"Do what?" My brow pinched in confusion.

"Compliment me after I complimented you. My ego isn't that fragile, and neither is our friendship for that matter. You're worried your dick is going to ruin us? How powerful do you think that thing is? I watched you hook up with girl after girl for two years now and it didn't make me like you less as a friend. I know when you get on your team and you're traveling; you are going to be swimming in bunnies. I know what your real reservation about being in a relationship is. You don't want to cheat. And I get it. But once again, how powerful is your dick that you think one roll in the hay is going to make me forget the years of being indoctrinated into how your brain works?"

She crossed her arms over her chest and perked one brow high. "It doesn't matter anyway. I don't want to anymore. You don't do it for me."

I stalked over to her and lifted her up by the hips. Her back was against the wall when I took her mouth. She was lying to me about not wanting me anymore. I knew the second I swallowed her moan and her hands dove into my hair.

I hiked her dress up, so my hands held her bare ass and squeezed. She gasped in my mouth as my fingers curled around and started to finger her.

"Liar," I teased. I spread her wetness around. It was quiet enough in the room for us to hear my finger sliding in and out of her. She was impossibly tight. I groaned as my hips involuntarily bucked.

Her arm snaked between us, and she gripped me through my jeans. My stomach hollowed out as she stuck her hand down the waist band, fingertips grazing my head before she flicked the button open and eased my zipper down.

I carried her over to the four-poster bed and tossed her down. She leaned back against her elbows, and I dove forward, yanking her hips to my face and tasting the sweetest pussy my tongue had ever licked. She moaned into her palm that was clasping her mouth.

"You're fucking delicious." I nipped her thigh.

"I know, you told me."

I growled and dove back in, I wanted to drown in her scent. She yanked her dress off overhead and spread her knees wide apart. My hands worked up between us as I rolled her nipple in my fingers. My other hand went back to her impossibly tight entrance. I scissored my fingers to open her up and smoothed my thrusts to her g-spot. Her back bowed off the bed. I abandoned her nipple and pressed her lower stomach down, sucking her clit into my mouth.

She made muffled moans through her palm that she was biting into. Her eyes rolled to the back of her head, and I continued to rub her g-spot. Her breaths were coming out in short pants before her stomach hollowed out and her hips bucked up. Her hot liquid pooled against the collar of my shirt. I smiled against her clit, kissing her gently, until her body's latent tremors calmed down.

I kneeled back, wiped my chin on my shoulder, and tore my shirt off. I was never washing it again. I'd box it up so I could smell her delicious cum to get me through the times on the road.

Tama's head was still tilted back, chest still heaving. I leaned forward and bit her nipple before settling my hips into the cradle of hers. My jeans had slipped down, and my head was poking out of the top of my boxers. I used one hand to wiggle them down. I was going to take this as far as she wanted. Her heel helped me push my pants down as I kicked them off with my boxers.

I settled back against her. It was a familiar position that we had been in too many times to count. But this time was going to be different. I kissed her lips and hooked her leg around my hip so I could rub my dick against her clit. She was so fucking wet from her orgasm. I groaned at the heat. She always felt so good.

Her hips rolled into mine, we went out of sync, I plowed forward, and she sunk down. I was three inches deep, bare and gasping at how tight she was.

"Fuck, fuck, fuck." I paused and looked into her caramel eyes. "What do you want, Bully?"

She whimpered. "Keep going."

"I don't have a condom."

She blinked at me and bit her lips. "Keep. Going."

I groaned as I pushed the rest of the way in her. "You're choking the fuck out of me, baby," I hissed.

In all the times I had sex I had never felt anything this tight before. Either condoms deadened that much sensation, or she was impossibly tiny everywhere. My eyes rolled back as she gripped me. "Holy fuck. This feels so fucking good."

She cupped my cheeks to kiss me. The longer I stayed still the more she started to squirm.

"Please," she whispered against my lips.

My lungs let me sip in the air. "I'm clean and you're on birth control. How do you want me to finish?"

She let out a needy whine. "Inside me, please. I want to feel all of you."

I grunted as I pulled out and slammed back into her. She yelped and held her hand against the headboard to keep from banging her head against it.

I bent down and bit her nipple again as my hips pounded into her. Her tits bounced as I moved faster. She arched, feeding me more of her perfect body. I popped off her and went to the other nipple. My hips slowed down as I looked up to her from my lashes. Her mouth was parted as she murmured nonsense and moaned. I grinned as I went back to her lips.

She held me against her. Legs looped tightly around the small of my back, her hands holding my face. I lavished my tongue against hers. It was messy, lazy, and sensual as I started to feel the tingling sensation of my pending orgasm. I braced one arm against the headboard to keep it from banging into the wall as I continued to pound into her.

More nonsense mumbling and begging came from Tama. She threw her head back in a gasp as her pussy fluttered around me. She squeezed me so tightly it milked my own orgasm. I couldn't pull out all the way. Her legs tightened around my waist as I rutted forward again. I could feel every twitch of my release filling her up.

Collapsing onto her chest, I kissed her jaw and neck before I pulled out of her and slumped over. My lungs heaved. Tama's eyes were shut as if she were still in the middle of her orgasm. I leaned forward and kissed her eyelids before rolling off the bed.

I came back with a warm washcloth. "This place is fancy enough to have one of these." She giggled and shuddered as I cupped her pussy with the cloth.

Torn, wanting to play more with her but deciding that we had a few more days before I had to report and I was going to take advantage of every single one of them.

New Orleans

"Oh, do you mind boxing up an order of beignets for my wife," Rhys said to our waiter.

I rolled my eyes as my thumb played with the underside of the too big rose gold band. It was thin with an inscription on the inside that said *I know*. Rhys's inscription said *I knew*. I wish we had the history about the rings and how they ended up in the pawn shop in the middle of Arkansas.

He was *really* taking advantage of calling me his wife. It was surprising that someone as afraid of commitment as he was to be flinging the term around so willy nilly, but I wasn't going to stop him.

"Of course." The server bowed away. We were sitting on a patio in the French Quarter. A jazz saxophone player was crooning at the corner as the sun shone bright overhead. We got into New Orleans around midnight and walked around Bourbon Street. It was late and there were a few sketchy people around, but the vibe of the historic city was too cool to ignore.

Rhys and I got our palms read. My fortune was to be successful in work and adventurous in love. Rhys's was to be more successful than he dreamed but it was going to cost him in his personal life. They were generic enough answers that we thanked her and strolled through the rest of the street before heading into our hotel room.

Since our first night in Hot Springs, Rhys had been nearly insatiable. Every opportunity that allowed us a quickie, he was pouncing on me. Alone in our hotel room for ten minutes: he was on his knees pleasuring me. Got stuck in an elevator: his hand was up my dress. A crowded bar bathroom at midnight: I was swallowing him down my throat as he rutted into me making me gag. It was a good thing he liked gagging me because my reflex was sensitive.

Rhys wagged his brows at me as he sipped his iced tea. The server set down our to-go box and scooped up the cash Rhys had left out. "We are going to eat those later tonight when we need a snack after I fuck your brains out."

I choked on my spit. He grinned at me, grabbing my hand and pulling me away from the restaurant. We stopped in our cold room and groaned at how hot it was outside. I collapsed on the bed belly first. I was not one for working out and our days had been filled with either driving or walking around. Touring the hot springs was amazing. Walking around the French Quarter was beautiful. Knowing where every muscle in my legs was, not so much fun.

Rhys groaned behind me as he lifted the skirt of my dress up and held it against my shoulders. His zipper dragged down, and I shivered in anticipation.

I fully understood what Ava had meant when she told me that sex hurt until it didn't. Every time he pushed into me there was a pinch of pain. He was so big, and then a warm rippling euphoria as we built our rhythm together.

He jerked my hips up, pulling me to my hands and knees. He stood behind me and worked his way inside me. It was a new angle, but goodness gracious it was hitting something in me that had me collapsing at the elbows.

"Yeah, I know, baby," he said through gritted teeth. His hips slapped against me and his pace picked up. I was whimpering before I let out a keening cry when he started to circle my clit with his finger. "Yes, baby, squeeze my cock."

I was not expecting the dirty talk, but I was here for it. I moaned and bit my lip as the burning pleasure of my orgasm slid down my stomach. He pulled my body up, my back to his chest as he continued his punishing rhythm. He pushed my dress off my arms and squeezed me against his palm. "I fucking love your tits," he ground out.

I rolled my head to his chest as he looked down on me. He kissed me deeply, moaning into my mouth. His cum rushed into me and ran down my thigh. My tongue made languid circles around his before he pulled away.

He kissed my shoulder while pulling out. I shivered when he scooped up his cum with his hand before walking into the bathroom and returning with something that would clean me up.

Righting my dress, I let out a deep breath. He chuckled and kissed me quickly. "I can't believe we've been depriving ourselves of this for years."

A giggle slipped out. I had nothing to compare to, but I was positive sex with Rhys was my peak.

He smacked my butt as I bent over to put my shoes back on.

"Let's go, Bully. We have the catacomb tour to get to."

I whimpered but capitulated, following him back down to the elevator.

The tour was fascinating if not a little creepy. Rhys ground his erection into my back when we were in the dimly lit antechamber, the rest of our tour group in front of us. I could hear him hum in my ear as he nudged against my back.

I rolled my eyes and smirked over my shoulder. "You're insatiable."

He wagged his brows. "You're sexy as fuck. Come on, I'll be quick."

I scoffed and scooted my body away. "Absolutely not. Ghosts will follow us home and there will be a curse placed on both of our houses if we desecrate this temple."

He chuckled in my ear as he nipped my neck. "Fair enough. But I want you two more times before bed."

I shivered against him which was ridiculous. It was stifling hot and muggy.

We stopped in a souvenir shop. He looped Mardi Gras beads around my neck even though it was nowhere near the time of year. "Okay, now show me your tits," he joked.

I elbowed him in the stomach.

He bought a taxidermy alligator head that was small enough to fit in his palm. I squinted at it.

"What? It's cool and I want a keepsake to remember this trip."

He looped his arm around my shoulder and guided me out of the shop.

Gulf Shores

Rhys dove into the waves of the white sandy beach. It was empty for it being late July and hot outside. Our hotel was right on the water and within walking distance to several restaurants. It was our last full day of our trip before we had a small three-hour drive to Montgomery, and my flight was taking off late at night.

My gut hurt every time I thought about leaving. On one hand, I knew the bubble we were living in was unsustainable. He'd be traveling nonstop for the next month and then by the time his season was over I'd be in school again.

I *could* have agreed to travel with him, but it would have prolonged the inevitable. And I wanted him to bond with his new team. He wouldn't have that opportunity if I were hanging around.

It made my stomach twist as a nauseous wave rioted at the thought of him out at a bar with his teammates. A bat bunny would see him and pounce. He was the most handsome man I knew. Women couldn't resist his charms. I swallowed hard and buried the thoughts.

Rhys made his way up to me. I was sitting under an umbrella resting on the lounge chair provided by the hotel.

"The water is perfect. Join me." He braided our hands together as he tugged me into the waves. When we were out far enough to where I couldn't reach. He looped my legs around his waist and smiled at me. Water droplets slid down from his hair and dropped off his lips before he bent his face to mine.

His kiss was slow, tentative, full of longing on my part. He rested his forehead against mine, staring into my eyes before kissing me again. It would have been the perfect moment to admit to him my true feelings. That I loved him more than a friend. That I loved him calling me his wife. Even though it was scary and it would be hard, I wanted to try to have a long-distance relationship.

I swallowed thickly to keep all my thoughts to myself.

"Promise me our friendship can survive this," he whispered.

"I promise. Our friendship will survive the farm system just like you will. And before you know it, you'll be called up." My voice quivered and cracked.

He grinned at me and kissed me again. "And when I make it to the MLB what happens?"

"All your dreams come true."

"What if my dreams have evolved?"

I twisted my lips to the side. "Then you'll go after the new dream with the dedication you put into becoming an MLB player."

"What if you're my dream?"

My face crumpled as I squeezed my eyes tightly shut. It would have been so easy to admit everything to him. But I couldn't do that. I couldn't be that vulnerable knowing he couldn't give me what I deserved without hindering his goals. I'd never want to be the one to slow him down, and I had years left of school. I wouldn't be able to travel with him. I wouldn't be able to support him like he needed and vice versa.

"You're mine too, so I'm so glad we got to live in our dreams this week."

He blew out a breath and squeezed his eyes shut. I cupped his face and kissed him again. "I'm still your best friend. I'll still support you in every way I know how."

His Adam's apple bobbed. "I know."

I gave him a soft smile. "Are you excited to meet your roommate tomorrow?"

He shrugged. "I'm nervous to play my first game."

I hummed and squeezed his face in my hands, giggling at his pushed in cheeks, dramatically puckering his lips. "Don't be nervous. That's silly like this face you're making. You're going to do so great, and you know why?"

"Why?" he mumbled, his cheeks still smushed.

"Because you're a first-round draft pick from a D1 school. Your team made it to the World Series. The stakes to those games were so high and you scored a homerun in game one of the series. Your first game as a Biscuit is going to be child's play compared to that. Go out there and have fun."

The sex between us that night was different than all the rest. It was slow, sensual, and intimate. He kept his eyes locked with mine unless he was kissing me. Even when we finished, he kissed me for hours until we fell asleep.

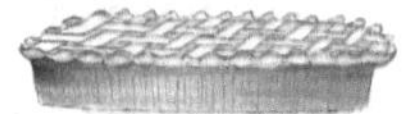

Montgomery

"Shane seems great."

His roommate was older than what I was expecting. He was a veteran on the team and tasked with breaking in all the rookies. He seemed a little gruff, but like an overprotective brother.

Rhys stroked his thumb against my cheek bone, staring at my lips. "I don't want you to go."

My nose tingled as I forced a smile to my face. The overhead speaker announced flights that were boarding and passengers that were needed at certain gates.

"I know. I don't want to go either, but you'll see me in a month, right?"

He nodded.

"And you can stay at my apartment for as long as you want."

He swallowed and nodded again.

"You can make it one month without seeing me. You're going to be so busy making new friends, traveling, and falling into the groove of your new team. One month is going to fly by."

"Kiss me one more time," he whispered.

I let silent tears splash down my face on the flight home. I had promised him it would only be a month, but I knew better than to get my hopes up. I knew we'd see each other, but he was

184

going to be more in demand than he thought he would be. I was going to support him the best I could; by being the friend he needed.

I twirled the rose gold ring with my thumb and hoped that everything would work out. I would make emotional sacrifices for him. I'd never let him know how much pain he left me in. I knew that I was flying away from a moment in our history that we'd never get to repeat again.

I'd never be his wife. He'd marry some gorgeous woman who would enthusiastically travel with him, and brow beat the bunnies away. He'd have the world cradled in his capable hands and I was so happy for him. My role in his life was always meant to be supportive until he had the right partner to take over.

Chapter 10

Tama

August

Me: Good luck today! Don't be nervous, you're going to kill it

Me: OMG! A HR first a bat? Congrats!

Rhys: I can't believe you know about that. My game wasn't televised!

Me: LOL! Not on TV but the game streamed online.

Rhys: You're literally the best.
I miss you so fucking much.

October

Rhys: Sorry I missed your call.
It's been crazy busy. Maybe
we can schedule time tomorrow?
I should have time after I promised
my dad an afternoon in his garage.

Me: Of course, whenever you
are available. No worries about
earlier, I'm sure your parents are
happily keeping you busy. I just
wanted to say I found the shirt
you were looking for last week.

February

Me: Happy Birthday!

Rhys: I still can't believe you
came out last weekend to
celebrate early. I'm about
to hit the gym, I'll call you

in an hour!

May

*Rhys: Happy Birthday! Check your
mail! Also, I'll try to be there for your
graduation. If not, I'll fly you to me
the following weekend. I need my
Bully fill.*

December

Me: Merry Christmas!

*Rhys: It would be merry if you
were here, but I understand your
mom and Beckett made plans.
I might be in LA next month for an
agent meeting. Want to meet up?*

*Me: My dear best friend, you may
be finished with school, but I am
not. I'll be back in Boulder next
month.*

*Rhys: Fuck, you're right. Maybe I
can stay with you next month
Before spring training. That okay?*

*Me: Of course! You know you're
always welcome!*

February
1.5 years after the draft

Me: Happy Birthday!

Rhys: I fucking miss you!

Me: Turn around.

May

*Rhys: I'm so fucking sorry I missed
your birthday and your call. I lost
track of time. Answer your phone!*

October

*Rhys: I'm going to be in LA for
Christmas. Please tell me we can
hang out.*

Me: Yes, times a million!

December

*Rhys: I'm so sorry that my meetings
lasted so long. I was intending on
spending the whole weekend with
you. I wanted more than a few
hours. Any chance you can go to
spring training?*

*Me: No worries and I will
have to check my workload.
I'll let you know, but count me
in wherever you are during my
spring break!*

February

*Me: Happy Birthday! I know you
are going to get called up soon!*

*Rhys: You know what it means if
I get called up, right?*

Me: All your dreams come true?

Rhys: Almost all

May
2 years, 9 months after the draft

Rhys: Happy early Birthday!
I'm traveling all day tomorrow
so I didn't want to miss it like
last year. I miss your face!
Being on the 40 roster means
I have to be flexible.

December

Me: Merry Christmas!

Rhys: Are you ready to start
your doctorate? I can't believe
I missed your graduation! Why
didn't you tell me you are walking
a full semester early? I should
have known, you got your first
degree early too.

Me: I am ready and don't worry
about the graduation. I sent you
an invite, but the card came back.

Rhys: Fuck, I moved and I forgot to
tell you! Sorry, speaking of moves-
You nervous to head to Seattle? I'm
so excited you're getting your PhD from
University of Washington. When I visit
my parents I can see you so easily!

February
3.5 years after the draft

*Me: You made the 25-man roster
on your freaking birthday! I am so
proud of you! You did it! Also
Happy Birthday!*

*Rhys: I'm still in shock! You were the
first person I wanted to tell, but you
beat me to it. Can I send you opening
day tickets?*

*Me: Like you have to ask! I'll be
there.*

March

*Rhys: Where did you go? One
moment you were beside me
celebrating the next you're gone.*

*Me: Sorry, I'm so happy for you
and proud and you deserve all
the accolades. I didn't want to
spoil your celebration of your first
MLB game, but I wasn't feeling*

well. Enjoy your night, don't worry
about me.

Rhys: Is this because of the blonde?
I told you to ignore her.

Me: No, I have a migraine. I've
been staying up late to get ahead
in school so I could take this trip.
It just caught up with me.

December

Rhys: Merry Christmas, Bully!
Do you think we can meet up
next month? I know you've been
busy with school, but I need to talk
to you.

January

Me: Krista seems really great!
You didn't need to fly to Seattle
to tell me about her though!
But it was nice seeing you.

Rhys: I did though because you
are my best friend! I wasn't
expecting her to surprise us.

June

Dear Tama,

I know you received the wedding invite and were probably thinking why didn't it have an RSVP card. It was intentional. The thing is, Rhys invited you out of pity. He knows that you don't have a lot of friends and he didn't want you to find out about our wedding from social media.

The reality is I am marrying him and you being there will be weird and awkward for me. Please allow me to have the day that I deserve and don't come. Please consider this your official un-invite

Krista

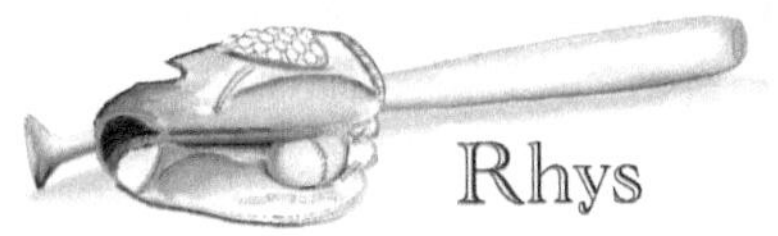

Rhys

July
Five Years After the Draft

A harsh breath rattled past my lips. My nerves were making my stomach lurch. *I'm making a mistake.* I loved Krista, I did. She told me I did, but it didn't feel right. It felt rushed and not as easy as I thought a committed relationship should feel like.

I had zero say in the wedding except for my two groomsmen. I had to negotiate hard about the date. She wanted me to take two weeks off work in June. Which wasn't going to happen, so we compromised to get married during the All-Star Break.

I didn't have final say on who was invited and we had been fighting nonstop for the past two months.

It's just cold feet.

What I needed was Tama. She'd calm me down and tell me I was doing the right thing. She'd cheer me on like she had my entire life. I twirled my rose gold ring around my right finger. I had switched hands when I started my first spring training. Too many of my teammates asked me about my wife, and it messed with my head to see it and know it wasn't true.

Our friendship had been strained since Krista was introduced. I had only seen her twice in sixteen months, which wasn't the norm. We had made a point to see each other every two months since I drafted. My MLB schedule was less forgiving, and her PhD program was ramping up, but our connection was still strong. I knew she was my soulmate, and I needed her.

Nathan tilted his head at me. "You don't look very good, bro. Are you hungover?"

I shook my head. "Krista made us have a dry bachelor/bachelorette combo party two weeks ago. I was sober as a bird last night."

Whinny's upper lip curled into a grimace. "Sorry I missed it."

The sarcasm in his voice was unmistakable. It wasn't what I thought my bachelor party would be like either, but what did I know? I had never been married. I had hardly had time to consider being in a real relationship before she gave me a proposal deadline. We had only been dating a few months at that point.

I'm going to be sick. This is a mistake.

"Honey, I found the garter belt Krista was freaking out about last night. I checked her room, but she didn't answer. Do you think you can give it to her?" My mom walked into the room looking harried and holding the garter belt like it had burned her.

I let out a shaky breath and nodded. *Maybe seeing Krista would calm me down. She'd tell me how perfect we were for each other. She told me I loved her all the time.* Wait…did I love her?

I wrapped the light blue garter around my wrist and took off to the bridal suite. No one answered when I knocked, but it didn't stop me from strolling in. I looked around the room and went straight for the closed bathroom.

"Oh god damn it," Krista hissed.

I frowned. I pushed the door open, worried she was sick or hurt. Nope. My bride-to-be was sitting on the counter, dress hiked up to her chest. Her stepbrother eating her pussy like it was his job. Her head was pushed against the mirror as her breath gasped from her lungs.

I backed away from the door and made myself comfortable on the couch. A numb relief pulsed through my body, like icing an injury. I knew it was a mistake to marry her, catching her made my decision guiltless.

She stumbled out of the bathroom with a grin on her face which quickly dropped when she saw me.

"Have fun in there?" My tone lacked all anger. If anything, I sounded like I was in on a huge joke. I guess in a way, I was.

"It's not what it looks like."

I chuckled and walked over to her. I delicately gripped her hand and slipped the 3-carat diamond engagement ring from Krista's finger.

I initially proposed with a single carat, but Krista complained it was too small. I should have known then.

"Thanks," I said and strolled out of the door.

Most of the guests were already seated. Nathan and Whinny gave me worried looks as I motioned for them to follow me. I strode straight to the front of the garish church. I wasn't remotely religious.

The gathered guests quieted down. I grabbed the mic and tapped it to make sure it was hot. Feedback ripped through the air and echoed against the domed ceiling. The last few whispers stop.

"Hey everyone, I don't know most of you because Krista is a bit of a control freak." A few chuckles trickled from the crowd. "Anyway, there isn't going to be a wedding today. If you want to know why, ask the bride and her stepbrother, but I would ask him if he washed his hands before you shake it because it was palm deep in her pussy."

A few shocked gasps followed my announcement. "Anyway, head to the reception now. It's a party where I didn't get married to a gold-digging cheater. Eat, drink, and celebrate." Feedback from the dropped mic overwhelmed the initial gasps from the guests.

Nathan and Whinny followed behind me out of the chapel at a fast clip. I stopped outside the double doors that closed the guests off from me.

"Where's Tama?"

Whinny palmed the back of his neck. I looked back to the nave; positive she would be running out any second. My parents were busy talking to the wedding planner. My dad caught my eye and tipped his chin to the exit, motioning for me to leave.

Nathan blew out a breath. "I didn't see her, man."

Whinny pushed me farther down to the atrium when we heard Krista's shrill voice.

I shook my head. "I told her when Krista sent the invitation to keep an eye out for it. She said she wouldn't miss it. I know her mom's vow renewal was yesterday, but she said she'd fly from Palm Springs to here. She wouldn't miss it."

Whinny gripped my elbow and pulled me to the parking lot. Nathan was hot on our heels. He shoved me in the back of the car and looped into the driver's side.

Nathan leaned in through the window. "I'll look for her. Get him out of here."

Whinny sped off like a bat out of hell. I grabbed my phone and called Tama. My call wouldn't connect. I tried again and the service dropped. I rolled my head against the headrest and closed my eyes.

"Where are we going?"

I blew out a breath. "Take me home. I need to change the locks."

Whinny made an abrupt right. I called my agent and told him what was going on. A locksmith and a moving service were waiting at my front door. I directed the locksmith to switch out the locks and the moving crew to pack up all of Krista's things. Everything was done within an hour. Krista's shit was loaded into a storage unit, and the man at the front of my gated community was given information to bar her from the neighborhood and direct her to the storage unit where her stuff was.

Relief swept through me like a load was lifted from my shoulders. I wanted to see and kiss Tama like it was before Krista. I hadn't kissed her since my first MLB game, and it was nearly torturous thinking about why I had deprived myself. Then I was going to beg her to move to Tampa. Not seeing her since January was torture.

My skin itched as the feelings I'd been ignoring since draft day arose. I still loved her. It's probably why I wasn't freaking out over Krista's infidelity. I was never in love with Krista, not when Tama still held that spot.

"Are you about to have a mental breakdown?" Whinny passed me a beer.

I shook my head. "Nope, you saw me. I was thinking about calling it off. Catching her cheat made my decision easier, and now I don't have to worry about the prenup, alimony, or any other bullshit."

"Well, alright then."

My phone buzzed with a message from the front gate that Nathan had arrived. I walked over to the front door and swung it open getting ready to scoop Tama into my arms. I scowled when Nathan got out of his car alone and winced when he saw me.

"She didn't come."

I shook my head. "What do you mean, she didn't come? Is she in the hospital?"

He blew out a breath and took the three steps up to the door. He passed me his phone. A picture recently posted of Tama was cued up. It was on Ava Reiser's Insta account, she had become a bit of a ballet phenom in the past year, so I wasn't surprised to see that Nathan followed her.

Henry's arm was slung around Tama's neck, and she was smiling softly at him. The image of palm trees with mountains in the background was beautiful and very clearly not in Tampa.

My heart pinched as I grabbed my chest and collapsed on the steps. I couldn't catch my breath. *She didn't come to my wedding. The most important person in my life. The most important day of my life and she didn't come.*

I don't know how long I sat on my steps staring at the brick walkway. I know I sat through my parents checking in on me, a rainstorm, and a food delivery before I stood up and walked to my empty bedroom.

She didn't come.

Tama

Me: Happy Birthday! I know we haven't talked in a long time, but I didn't want to put Krista in an awkward position. I don't want to put you in a bad spot. I know

(Message Not Delivered)

Me: You just hit a Grand Slam!
(Message Not Delivered)

Me: I'm graduating with my PhD
today.
(Message Not Delivered)

Me: Merry Christmas!
(Message Not Delivered)

Me: Happy Birthday!
(Message Not Delivered)

Me: It's moving day! I bought a
house and renovated it. It was
daunting, but I'm so excited!
(Message Not Delivered)

Me: Congrats on making the All-
Star team! You're having an
incredible season!
(Message Not Delivered)

Me: You did it! A World Series
win after your grand slam!
(Message Not Delivered)

Me: Merry Christmas!
(Message Not Delivered)

Me: I wrote a book!
(Message Not Delivered)

Me: Happy Birthday!
(Message Not Delivered)

Me: My book just hit the NY
Times Best Seller List!
(Message Not Delivered)

Chapter 11

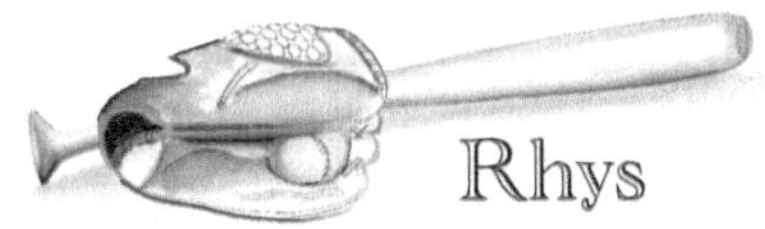

Rhys

Eight Years After the Draft

I clenched my fists in a silent victory as I hung up the phone. My agent had secured one of the highest trade deals in MLB history, and I couldn't be more thrilled. It's not that I didn't love being a Ray. Tampa Bay gave me my career. They trained me and gave me the skillsets needed to win the World Series.

Around the same time as my contract was coming up, my dad was diagnosed with macular degeneration. My mom didn't like to drive, so I asked my agent if Seattle would be interested in having me on their team. It turns out they were and while I was sad to leave the Rays, I was happy to be closer to my aging parents.

They had a small support system. About a year ago they got a new neighbor named Trudy that had made an impact on their life. Trudy had taken a liking to my parents and vice versa. First, I thought Trudy was a young girl, but later I became positive Trudy was closer to my parents' age. She lived with her mom who was a spry eighty-year-old that taught my mom how to knit. Regardless Trudy and her mom took my mom grocery shopping and hung out with my dad in his garage.

I heard so much about Trudy that I felt like I already knew her. My dad described Trudy as big, gray hair, blue eyes. It confirmed my theory that my parents' new neighbors had a Golden Girls/ Grey Gardens situation next door.

While Trudy's support had been great and I was appreciative, it was nothing compared to what I would be able to do. I had the means, though my family rejected anything that was extravagant.

It was like pulling teeth to get them to agree to go with me to whichever Caribbean island I wanted to celebrate the holidays at. After I paid off most of their mortgage, they wouldn't allow me to buy anything more than a vacation once a year. So, paying for an assisted living company to check on my parents was out of the question.

They'd scoff at the idea of needing one and then would refuse service when my mom researched the price of it. When Seattle confirmed that not only they wanted me, but they were also willing to pay big bucks to have me, I jumped at the chance.

It was the middle of the season so there was no way I'd be able to sell my house in Tampa while looking for a new home in Seattle. That would all have to wait until November. In the meantime, I was going to surprise my family. They'd be more than happy for me to stay in my old bedroom while I finished out my season.

My cool weather wardrobe needed a refresh. I was going to need to pack and hire a moving company, but I wouldn't have to hassle with the minutiae of every decision.

It was leading into the All-Star Break. In a few days I'd fly to Seattle. I'd land around the time the announcement of my trade will become public. My parents were going to be thrilled.

Once the season was over and I was settled in my new home, I'd find her. I had no idea where Tama was. She'd moved after the wedding invitation went out, so my address for her was useless. A fact I discovered when my assistant attempted to return the wedding present, and it was sent back. She was a ghost on social media, and I didn't have control of my account to send her a message. I only looked for her in the offseason. I didn't want to chance seeing her happy without me in her life while I was in the middle of the season. It would fuck with my head, and I couldn't afford that.

I needed to confront her in person. A text would never convey the damage she did. I needed to see the realization in her eyes when I told her how much she hurt me. I needed to remind her that she broke her promises. I needed closure in that relationship. When she ghosted me on my wedding day and then went radio silent, I focused heavily on my game.

I put on twenty pounds of muscle and blew my batting average out of the water. Krista remained a thorn in my side for the better part of a year. She tried to sue me for public humiliation, but my lawyer was a fucking shark and got the case thrown out. My agent had tracked down every single guest and had them sign an NDA.

Most of the guests were at the wedding reception when he helicoptered in with a notary. There were a few holdouts that he paid off, but it was still cheaper than the lawsuit Krista tried to file.

I pulled my suitcase down and started packing. The little gator head that sat on my dresser and my rose gold ring that was sitting in its teeth were shoved in a sock for safe keeping. I grabbed my raincoat.

My virtual assistant sent me a few flight options to Seattle. I grinned and sent my confirmation. I was going to have a busy few days, but going home was going to be worth it.

Tama

"Don't look at me like that," I said to my one -hundred-eighty-pound Cane Corso Napoleon Mastiff mix.

He was first a medical dog rejected for being too big then a police dog dropout for being too friendly. His blue eyes were intense missiles to strike fear, but he gave guilt-inducing puppy eyes with those babies. Beckett drove him up to Seattle when I had moved into my own place after graduation. He didn't like that I was alone and wanted me to have some sort of protection.

Gertrude, named accordingly from my lost bet, was stubborn as a mule and smart as a fox. I had taught him how to use talking buttons when I first adopted him. He was the most needy and handsome boy in my life, and I was too exhausted to get out of bed.

I had completed my PhD in psychology and immediately went into a study of emotions and brain functions. Henry and Lily paid for my private study when grants fell through. We paid one hundred participants for three days of their time while I

206

performed several brain scans while they recalled memories tied to strong emotions.

Every participant had to sign an NDA and allow me to use their stories as well as their brain scans in any published works. I studied the effect of grief, heartbreak, and loss; love and happiness; sex and kinks; and trauma and pain on the brain and body. I checked blood flow to the brain as well as hormone levels in the blood while recounting their memories or having sex. All audio was proprietary that I used to narrate what was happening to their brain as they spoke.

Lily and Henry funded one year of research, so I had to make it count. I worked fifteen-hour days, six days a week. And then I spent a few months writing a book called 'The Science of Heartbreak'. And because Henry is an algorithm genius, he knew what to do to make my book go viral. It had been on the NY Times best-selling list for four months straight.

Several podcasters interviewed me, and I did a small book tour. I only went to a few cities. I didn't want to leave Trudy for too long. Henry wanted me to go on television to promote my book, but I wasn't ready to do that. I didn't want my image splashed everywhere. My anonymity was precious. Which was a very different approach than he had with Ava.

Henry also made Ava go viral for her ballet skills and now she was a worldwide phenom that was sought out to dance in ballets. I was so proud of her.

"Lazy," the deep voice of Trudy's dog button said from his room. Henry thought it was hilarious to use James Earl Jones' voice when Trudy 'spoke'.

I groaned. "I'm not lazy, I'm tired. I had to wake up at 3am to do that London podcast," I called out.

"Gertrude outside."

I whimpered and pulled my phone out. I had set my locks to be controlled virtually. All the doorknobs were lever handles so he could open every door with his paws or snout. I clicked through and unlocked the patio door.

"It's open," I called.

The beep of my patio door signaled he was outside. I snuggled back into my pillows. No doubt he was eating apples from the tree in our backyard to stave off his hunger. He was a big boy and had a huge appetite. He was also spoiled. I made all his food, but he was like a child to me, so I was happy to spoil him rotten.

My phone buzzed in my hand.

Griffin: I heard you in London today.
I still can't believe my fiancée wrote a
fucking book. I thought you wanted to
fuck while your brain was being scanned
for a kink, not writing material.

I snorted at his message. Griffin and I were *not* engaged. The last time I saw him he was worried about his grandma seeing him get married while she was alive. He asked me to marry him if we were both still single at forty, giving him enough time to fuck every groupie and still give his grandma a few years of cushion to live.

He and I had a weird long-distance friendship. We saw each other occasionally, more in the last two years. He bought a house in Vancouver when he wasn't touring. When he was home, he'd visit me often.

As one of the subjects in my study, he volunteered to help me with the sex portion of the experiment. Wanting to be able to assure my participants that it was easy and not distracting, I went through the entire process first.

By the end of the study, I had noticed one thing that solidified my relationship with Griffin as friends with occasional benefits. The couples that had sex and were in love with each other had very different brain activity than those who weren't in love. It was fascinating, and I was looking forward to writing my book about sex and kink on the brain. My brain scan with Griffin confirmed what I knew. We weren't in love with each other.

> *Me: I wanted to do both. How's London?*

Griffin: Rainy as fuck. The tour is almost over. I am looking forward to a nice break. It's too bad you couldn't join me this tour! I missed you. Please tell me you will be around in September?

> *Me: Probably so, but Henry has set me up with a part time job as a high school counselor. His aunt is the superintendent and they needed someone part time to help teens deal with their emotions.*

Griffin: I didn't know you were that kind of doctor. I have so many fantasies involving being on a shrink sofa and then seducing her.

I snorted.

*Me: That's actually not that
uncommon. And I'm not really
that type of doctor. I specialize
in research, but I am qualified
and it'll keep me social while
writing my next book.*

*Griffin: I'm going to read your current
one. Your interview sounded so cool.
I'm so fucking proud of you. I told the
girl blowing me this morning that you
and I were getting married. She wasn't
as impressed as I thought she would
be.*

I rolled my eyes. My doorbell rang. I wrote to Griffin telling him I had to go and pulled my robe on while running my fingers through my chin length hair. Cutting it was a huge decision that I didn't regret. It had been three years since I chopped all my hair off. Ava was concerned because the timing lined up with Rhys's wedding.

Don't think about Rhys.

My heart still hurts at the death of our friendship. I knew it would happen eventually, but I didn't think it would be so abrupt. We spent years seeing each other whenever we could. He'd spend time with me during his offseason, holidays, and birthdays.

Then he met Krista, and I didn't see him again after he told me about his relationship. I was shocked when he told me about

210

her. Even more so when I met her…again. She was the mean as nails bat bunny blonde who talked about me in the bathroom after Rhys's first MLB game.

It felt like a sucker punch right to the gut when I saw her fake smile again. I had the hapless hope that the reason why he wanted to talk to me was that he was ready to have a real relationship. He had made it to the MLB.

I wouldn't say I had been waiting, but I had been hoping. I had dated a few guys off and on, nothing close to how I felt about Rhys. We had a non-comparable connection that I hadn't had with anyone else, and I hoped he felt the same way.

Turns out he *was* ready for a relationship, just not with me. I was the stupid girl that crossed her fingers for five years that he'd tell me that I was his and he was mine. We came close on our road trip to Montgomery, but it was a flash in the pan. The pinnacle of our friendship. It wasn't the start of something; it was the beginning of the end. And then with Krista in the picture, our friendship was pushed off a cliff and exploded in a fiery death.

I pulled my door open and grimaced. Trudy was standing next to my neighbor, wagging his tail. "Hey Tom, he jumped the fence again?"

He chuckled and stroked Trudy's massive boney head. "You know it. He dug up some of Rita's carrots before I stopped him."

I squeezed my eyes shut. "I'm so sorry."

Tom chuckled. "No worries, this big boy took some carrots off our hands. The bounty this year has given us far more than we can consume. I didn't want you to check your backyard and not see him back there."

I held the door wide open. "Inside."

Trudy bounced passed me and went right for his buttons. "Gertrude, hungry."

Tom chuckled again. "Rita wanted to know if you want to come over to dinner tonight."

Tom and Rita had welcomed me to the neighborhood with open arms a year and a half ago when I finally moved into the house I had renovated.

I had first given all my neighbors a basket of muffins. That turned into me inviting Rita and Tom over for dinner when they returned my basket and Trudy after only two days of being in my new home. He jumped our fence and rifled through their garden. Fortunately, they loved my dog and watched him whenever I had to go out of town.

Four hosted dinners passed before Tom and Rita invited me over to their house for a meal. I didn't hesitate to accept. I loved them. They were like a long-lost aunt and uncle that I adored getting to know. The dinner started out fine, normal, and then they turned the baseball game on. Despite my friendship with Rhys being done and over I still watched his games. It was then that I made the discovery that my new neighbors were Rhys's parents.

It was so obvious in hindsight. Rhys had Rita's eyes and Tom's build. Their house was covered in childhood pictures of him, but he was so little I thought I was imagining things. It wasn't until they pointed Rhys out on the television and said, "That's our boy," that the dots connected.

I didn't want Rhys to think I was some crazy stalker getting close to his parents in his absence. It's not like *I* found this house. I had Nathan to thank for that. He hooked me up with a real estate broker.

The house needed so much work, but Nathan convinced me that it was worth it. It was in a coveted neighborhood. It was close to nature trails and in an established area with big lots not far from downtown and the water. After that dinner I confronted Nathan who acted coy, but I knew the truth. He intended for me to live next to Rhys's family.

I had a serious conversation with Tom and Rita about how it was going to work for us to be neighbors and friends. They confirmed that Rhys used to talk about me all the time. We all agreed to not tell Rhys about me and in exchange they wouldn't talk about him to me. I didn't want to hear about how blissfully wedded he was.

The only thing they had ever said about Krista was that they didn't like her, but I stopped the conversation in its tracks, inducting our number one rule: we don't talk about his personal life. They promised to give me a heads up when he was going to visit. It ended up being a moot promise. He hadn't been home in three years.

"Dinner sounds great. What do you want me to bring?"

Tom rubbed the back of his neck. "Bring Trudy over and maybe those apple turnovers."

I chuckled. "No problem. I'm heading to the grocery store later. Do you need anything?"

"You're so sweet. Rita may take you up on a ride." Recently Tom had been diagnosed with night blindness and the beginning of macular degeneration and Rita wasn't big on driving, so I drove them to most places after the sun went down.

"Gertrude, hungry."

I glanced over my shoulder. "Let me feed the beast. I'll message Rita in a little bit."

Trudy was standing next to his bowl. His paws and snout were streaked in dirt from his gardening adventures.

"You can't steal food." I pulled out the container of ground turkey, apples, carrots, avocado, chicken hearts, and squash. His breakfast was different from his dinner, and I rotated between seven different meals over the course of the week.

He grumbled in his deep groan. It sounded like he was saying, "I know."

I rubbed his boney head as I set his bowl down. His velvety ear had dried mud on it. I scowled at him. "You're going to need a bath now," I warned.

He scooted his bowl away and turned his back, ignoring me. I chuckled at him and walked back into my office.

Another ten podcasts to interview me were scheduled as well as orientation dates for the school district. I had a few weeks before the beginning of school. I didn't need the money. The book's success on its own kept me afloat. I had also inherited a large sum when Yolanda passed away. I was sad about it for the longest time. Nothing compared to the grief that Thelma was experiencing though.

Every time I visited my mom and Beckett, Thelma would talk about how much she missed her best friend. It was a real surprise to hear her speak so lovingly about a woman she had literally told to suck on a poison dart frog for crocheting a tea cozy for Johnny Kilmer which Yolanda had relations with once two years prior.

Between the book and the inheritance, I was set for life as long as I lived fairly simply. The counselling gig was more about Henry making sure I didn't let my world get too small. He knew that when I was focused, I closed myself off and didn't socialize. He was still the best friend I had ever had. Like a brother shelling out his platonic love and advice. His wedding to Ava was coming up, an event I was looking forward to.

They were getting married in Paris between Christmas and New Years. They had been engaged for a few years, not in a huge hurry as Ava's career took precedence. He had rented out Disneyland Paris for the evening. All the guests were going to be given free rein to ride as many rides as they wanted until midnight. I had never been to Paris, so I was ecstatic to go.

Trudy nosed his way into my office and stretched across my feet. He was needy with separation anxiety if he didn't know where I was. I had to videocall him the few times I had left him to visit Lily, Nicole, or Ava. Tom and Rita let him sleep in their bedroom, otherwise he'd pace their house and try to escape to come home.

I had let him stay by my side since I adopted him. He was the best lab assistant anyone could have asked for as I performed my brain scans. He kept me company and didn't argue with me. He didn't have his buttons in the lab.

He licked my bare toes before yawning and walking into the bathroom. A few minutes passed and he trotted out of the office. "Gertrude, poop."

"I know, I can smell it," I called out. The unexpected benefit of having a dog the size of Trudy was that he could sit his butt on the toilet and do his business. He hadn't quite figured out flushing. His big paws weren't nimble enough. The downside was I had to keep the toilet seat lifted so we deemed the office toilet as his. I was grateful that I didn't have to pick up his turds that were bigger than my hand every day. I flushed the toilet. He got a treat from the box on my desk for being my good boy.

I went through the pre-interview questions for the upcoming podcasts and made myself some breakfast. Trudy drooled as I scrambled up some eggs. "You already ate."

He grumbled and dramatically collapsed at my feet. "We are going for a walk after this and then you're getting your bath." His tail thumped against the hardwood floors once in agreement.

It was a cooler day in the Pacific Northwest. It took me a while to get used to the weather. I grew up in the desert, so rain was a new concept. Even in Boulder we only got rain sporadically and snow during the winter, but it was still a sunny place to live. The constant drizzle took less time to get used to than I thought it would.

Trudy walked at my pace. There were a few trails near my house. One of the things I loved about my neighborhood was that it was established. Most of my neighbors were a little older with children my age. My neighborhood was quiet and well maintained. I also felt more comfortable around an aging community.

Beckett ran the crime statistics for my area and helped me negotiate when I bought the house. It was run down as the previous owner was a hoarder, leaving some structural damage from the weight and moisture of the hoard. Mom flew up and helped me paint and pick out furniture after months of renovations. It was the first time in my life that I was living in something that was completely catered to me. All my college life I lived in housing made for students. Even in my PhD program I opted for a furnished student apartment.

Trudy peed on several trees as he sniffed beyond the trail. Dogs and their owners stopped in their tracks when they saw us together. I had to reassure more than one walker that Trudy was harmless.

A small terrier barked irritably at Trudy. He sniffed in her direction and kept going, uninterested in her drama.

"Are you sure you can handle that thing?" the uncontrollable terrier's mom asked.

I gave her a forced smile. "I'd say so. Between yours and mine, mine is calmer and nonreactive."

She sneered her lip at me and yanked her dog off the trail. Her terrier had been pulling so hard on the leash to get to Trudy, she had choked herself out. Her barks were interrupted as she coughed. The terrier owner stormed off.

An older woman walking her lab laughed. "Isn't it so ironic that the unbalanced dogs get a pass because they are small and bigger dogs can't step out of line for one moment?"

I grinned up at her. "It's the owner, not the dog. With a different dog mom that terrier would have been fine."

The older woman laughed. "I'm Libby, this is Hendricks."

I made our introductions. Trudy sniffed Hendricks's butt and then wagged his tail. He turned his head to look at me. His big blue eyes dipped down showing the whites underneath. I knew the look. He wanted to play. "We'll play when we get home." He grumbled his bassy backtalk.

Libby laughed again. "There's a dog park around the corner. We were heading to it if you want to join us."

"Sounds great."

The small talk was nice for both of us. Older people had the tendency to be lonely and would engage in conversations with strangers to feel human connections. Libby and I talked for thirty minutes while our dogs frolicked in the busy dog park. When Trudy was finished, he rested his big head on my lap and gave me his wide puppy eyes.

"Well, it looks like he's ready to go."

We made our goodbyes and headed back home where he got his weekly bath. It was an entire process. He had so many wrinkles around his face and neck that I had to make sure all were cleaned out. Then we had to go through the process of drying him. I had bought him special headphones to help tamp down the noise of the hair dryer after he kept running off to tell me "ear pain" repeatedly. I gathered it was too loud for his sensitive ears.

His silky gray fur was brushed until it was dry and shiny. "You're such a handsome boy," I cooed to him.

I sent Rita a message that I was heading to the grocery store and dropped Trudy off to hang out with Tom who was busy in his garage. Trudy and Tom worked well together. He had taught my dog what certain tools were called and laid them out for Trudy to grab. It was funny to watch Tom mutter, "Get me the wrench" and my dog pulled it into his big jaws and walked it over to him, thumping his tail into everything along the way.

"Have you heard from him?" Rita asked tentatively as we pulled into the parking lot. I didn't have to ask her to specify. I shook my head.

I hadn't heard from Rhys in a long time. It didn't stop me from sending him holiday and birthday well wishes, but every single message went undeliverable. It was clear that he had blocked me. I still messaged him when big things had happened to test the waters to see if I was finally out of the doghouse and unblocked. My last undeliverable message was sent four months ago.

"I still can't believe you were my almost daughter-in-law," she murmured.

The comment sliced my heart. I swallowed hard and gave her a sad smile. "I hear the nectarines are perfect right now."

She took my change of subject with grace. "You should make a pie with them."

I grinned over to her. "I'll think about it. Sorry I missed our knitting circle yesterday. My agent had scheduled a few interviews that overlapped our time together."

Rita waved her hand in the air. "Honey, I'm retired, I can have a knitting circle whenever you're available."

I taught Rita how to knit a few months ago. She was getting better but still needed practice. She was a retired teacher that would substitute occasionally. We were technically going to be coworkers because of my new part time job. She had already given me all the gossip about the teachers and administration.

We made our way through the grocery store gathering our goods that we needed for the next week. I helped her carry her groceries in as Trudy bounded towards me. Tom had a grease stain on his cheek, black crescents under his nails, and a smile that stretched wide making his eyes sparkle.

He had taken a break from his hobby when getting up and down to get the right tools was too hard on his knees and back, but with my dog as his sidekick he was tinkering on projects again.

The current project was a 1976 Chevelle that had taken the better part of three years. The unspoken elephant in the room was that Rhys's absence is what had prolonged the project.

My goodbyes were short as I headed back home to make dessert. With a few apples plucked from my tree, I began making the requested apple turnovers. I tossed a few slices to Trudy as I diligently made the dough and filling.

Trudy led the way back over to Tom and Rita's house.

"I was thinking about making a gate between our yards. That way it's easier to get Trudy to and from. Also, we could expand our game of fetch," Tom said hopefully.

I shrugged. "I have no problem with that. As long as you're okay with Trudy using your garden as a buffet."

Rita laughed and ran her fingers into Trudy's silky fur. "I'm thinking about having a greenhouse built, so that should be fine."

"Dinner is ready," Rita said once we made our way into the kitchen. Tom had washed up and was filling his plate. I dropped off the apple turnovers and followed Tom.

We were sitting down to eat when the front door opened.

"Mom, Dad?" Rhys called out. His voice was like an arrow to the heart. Exactly how I remembered it. Pain and shock froze me to the chair.

I gave my hosts a wide-eyed stare and slunk down to the ground. Deep breaths filled my lungs while I gathered my bearings under the table. Trudy licked my face before I scrambled to my feet.

Rita shook her head like she had no idea he was coming.

"Thought I'd surprise you. Where are you?" he called out.

I pointed to the patio door. Tom gave me a silent nod as Rita rushed out of the dining room to greet her son. I launched myself out of the Goodman's backyard. Trudy was fresh on my heels. My hands were shaking with adrenaline as I yanked my door open.

With my head against the wall, I let my weight carry me down to the ground, sliding to my butt.

What the heck is he doing here?

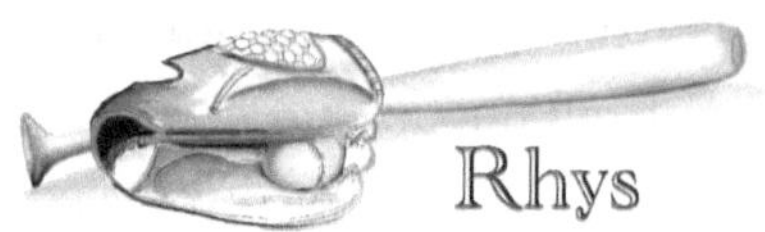

"Mom, dad?" I called out as I unlocked their front door. Their house smelled like pot roast. I took a deep breath and hummed at the familiar scent of my childhood. When they didn't answer back, I walked into the living room. I knew they liked to watch tv while they ate. "Thought I'd surprise you. Where are you?"

My mom rushed into the living room. Her cheeks were pink as she gave me a watery smile.

"Honey, what are you doing here?"
Ouch.

She pulled me down for a hug as my dad walked in after her. There was a nervous energy in the air.

Oh god, did I interrupt them having sex?

My dad hugged me when my mom let me go. "Good to see you, son. We were sitting down to eat. Have you eaten?" He looked beyond my shoulder to the front window with wide eyes. I tried to glance behind me to see what my dad was looking at, but my mom yanked me towards the dining room.

"Come on, let's eat."

I scowled at the three plates. "Expecting company?" I pointed at the untouched food neatly separated in equal mounds on my mom's favorite china.

My mom waved her hand. "Trudy was coming over but had to cancel at the last minute. There was an emergency with their mom."

"Is her mom okay?"

My dad coughed. "Fit as a fiddle, it was, uh—"

"An issue with the sprinklers kind of emergency," my mom interrupted.

I frowned. "Sorry about that. I want to meet Trudy."

My dad was gulping back his water. He choked and sputtered. "Trudy's great," he wheezed.

My mom patted my dad's back as she pointed to my plate. "Dig in honey."

My stomach grumbled. While I had a personal chef meal prep for me, nothing compared to my mom's home cooking. Well almost nothing.

I pushed my empty plate away as my mom came in with another dish with desserts on top.

"Trudy's mom made us apple turnovers."

Helping myself to two, I moaned into the bite. I hadn't had an apple turnover in ages, and these reminded me of college. I chewed through my dessert as the happy memory was doused by a bitter edge of Tama's disappearance in my life.

I chewed slowly and tried to push the emotions away. It was uncanny how similar the turnovers tasted to my former best friend's recipe.

"Aren't they amazing?" My dad dusted the crumbs off his shirt.

I nodded.

"Yes, Trudy's mom is quite the accomplished baker." My mom gave my dad a pointed look.

"Does Trudy's mom have a name?"

My parents both gave me a wide-eyed stare. My mom's cheeks flushed again before my dad cleared his throat. "Isla."

My mom nodded vigorously. They were acting weird.

I licked the front of my teeth. "Do you think I'll be able to meet Trudy and Isla?"

My mom turned to my dad and grabbed his plate. "Are you done, honey?"

"Yeah." I pushed my plate in my mom's direction. I looked over to my dad, waiting for him to answer my question. My mom busied herself out of the dining room.

"I don't know. Trudy is special," my dad said slowly.

Definitely a Grey Gardens situation then.

"So, what brings you to our neck of the woods? It's midseason, we weren't expecting you in Washington until August 8."

I couldn't hold my smile back. "Well, breaking news, Dad, I'm being traded to Seattle."

My mom's head popped into the dining room. "Don't mess with me," she said. Her eyes misted.

I held my hands up. "I'd never mess with you about this, Mom. I know how much you've wanted me to be a Mariner since I was a kid. An opportunity came up, and I took it."

My mom's arms wrapped around me as she sobbed into my shirt. I knew living on the other side of the country had been hard on my parents, but I wasn't expecting this reaction. I patted her back as my dad hugged us both.

"This changes everything," my mom wailed. "You can have it all. We can have it all."

I wiped a gathered tear with my thumb. "I hope you don't mind, but since it's midseason I won't have time to find my own place."

"You don't even have to ask." My mom squeezed me harder.

When the hugs stopped, I leaned into the doorframe while my mom and dad washed the dishes. "I'd like to meet Trudy and thank her for helping you guys out."

My dad gave me an awkward smile. "Well, Trudy will let you know when they are ready to be met."

My brows puckered. "Is Trudy nonbinary? You keep saying they."

My mom's head tilted to the side as her eyes darted back to my dad.

He cleared his throat. "Trudy is very special. Want to see where I am at with the Chevelle? Trudy's been helping, but it's not the same as you helping me."

I grinned at him. "Lead the way."

Chapter 12

*Rita: He's home for the break. I'll
let you know more when I find out.*

Rita: He's being traded to Seattle.

*Rita: And he's staying here until
the end of the season.*

I whimpered at her last message. I couldn't handle being his
neighbor. I couldn't handle being around him again. For one, he
hated me. And second, even if he didn't, I couldn't allow myself
to fall back in love with him. The first time around nearly killed
me. I couldn't handle seeing his happy marriage rubbed in my
face.

Me: What about Krista? I thought

*Rita: Honey, if you ever let us
talk about it, you'd have known.
He never married her. She
cheated on him on his wedding
day. He called the whole thing off.
Now don't repeat that. I had to sign
an NDA.*

My chest heaved at the information. His biggest fear was being cheated on or cheating and it happened to him on his wedding day, and I wasn't there. I should have told Krista to take her un-invite and shove it, but I thought they were happy. She pawed all over him and treated him like he hung the moon. It was devastating to see him reciprocating her affections, but I was still going to go to his wedding until that letter came.

Henry told me it was kismet and to be glad I didn't go. He stayed close to me the entire time we were in Palm Springs for my mom and Beckett's vow renewal. It was closer to a real wedding since the first one had been pretty fast in the courthouse.

My mom insisted I invite my college friends and I was lucky enough that not only Henry and Ava went, but also Matt and Nicole Foust as well as Lily and Will Reiser.

Lily and Will…. I needed help. I needed an escape. I'd have gone to Henry, but he and Ava were in Australia. And Nicole and Matt were visiting her sister in San Francisco.

*Me: SOS! I need a place to go for a
few days.*

*Lily: Is this a murder situation? I'll
provide an alibi, but you need to ditch
the phone.*

I giggled.

*Me: I may die, but no one has been
murdered. As you know my neighbors
are Rhys's parents.*

*Lily: A fact that has concerned me for a
year. Wait. OMG, I just saw the news.
He's being traded to Seattle?!*

*Me: And staying at his parents' house
until he can buy a new place.*

Lily: What do you need from me?

*Me: An escape. He's home for the
break. I need a few days to get my
head on straight.*

Lily: Want me to send the jet?

*Me: That'll take too long. I'll book a
flight for tonight. See you in a few
hours.*

I switched my conversation over.

Me: I'm heading to LA for a few days.

Rita: Of course. Whatever you need.
I'll let Tom know and we can come
get him.

I scampered to my room and yanked my luggage down. Trudy whimpered before he left my bedroom.

"Gertrude pain."

I grimaced. He was telling me he was sad. I didn't have a sad button. He had a 'hungry' and 'pain' button. So, when he didn't like something, he would tell me it pained him.

"I'm sorry. Tom and Rita are going to take good care of you. It's only for a few days," I promised.

He grumbled and walked back into my bedroom and laid across my bag. I harrumphed as I tugged my clothes out from under him. "I know, but I have to do this." He sighed and turned his head away from me.

With my bag packed, I messaged Tom to let him know that I was heading out. He met me at my garage, hand outstretched. I passed Tom the cooler bag of premade food. Trudy whined but trotted after Tom who promised him treats.

My flight to LA was fast. Lily had a driver waiting for me when I landed. She left the light on for the pool house in their backyard. I breathed in the familiar dry hot air. My heart hadn't calmed down until I slipped into the cool sheets.

Lily's daughter Elise woke me up early, squealing as she climbed onto my bed. She was an adorable blonde-haired, blue-eyed toddler with energy and sass. She snuggled into me as Lily sat on the bed.

"Tell me everything," Lily said and passed me a coffee.

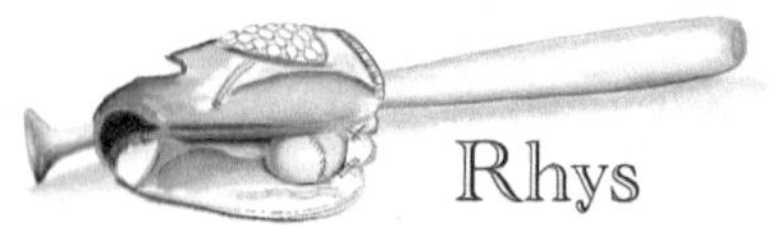

Rhys

I stretched my arms over head. My childhood bed was only a full-size mattress, so my feet hung off the end when I stretched my body out. The house was quiet early in the morning. I had gone to bed early. I wasn't used to west coast time, and my body was on my baseball sleep schedule.

My parents' bedroom door was propped open at the end of the hallway. I walked across to the bathroom that was used by guests, but it was primarily mine. I paused at the doorway and blinked, rubbing my eyes. The biggest dog I had ever seen in real life was backed up to the toilet. He grumbled as he looked over to me before turning his big head away. The distinct plop of his dog shit hitting the water made me gag. He took a few steps away, nosed passed me, and went straight into my parent's bedroom.

The dump he left behind was a monster. I flushed after him and took my morning piss, still not convinced I was awake. The kitchen was empty when I made some coffee. The slow clicking of dog claws on the hardwood floor made me perk my head up as the horse-dog made his way towards me. He sat at my feet and gave me the most pathetic puppy eyes. He was a gorgeous dog for being a beast. "Are you hungry?"

He walked over to the patio door and pushed his nose against the knob trying to open it. I let him out and watched in fascination as the dog pissed in every corner of the yard. He trotted back inside and sat at my feet. I squinted at him and moved to read his tag. *Trudy*

228

I snorted and shook my head. *What the fuck?* Trudy isn't some older masculine female boomer with a penchant to knit and fix up cars. Trudy was a fucking dog. And a boy dog if his under carriage was any indication.

My dad walked into the kitchen, scratching his ass and yawning. He paused when he saw me and flicked his eyes to the gray beast who was thumping his tail against the floor. "I take it you met Trudy."

I nodded slowly. "Is there a reason why you didn't tell me that Trudy was a dog?"

My dad rubbed the back of his neck. "We didn't tell you he was a human either. I know I told you once that his bark was loud."

I scoffed. "I thought you were using a euphemism like Trudy's bark is bigger than her bite, that she's a loudmouth."

My dad chuckled. "He is mouthy, but he doesn't have his buttons here." He turned to the dog. "Breakfast?"

A booming bark that would scare off any intruders rang through the house. "Trudy's mom had an emergency and had to fly to LA last night. We are watching him for a few days. We keep the toilet seat up in your bathroom. He's potty trained. He follows a variety of commands, and he's going to need a walk in a few hours."

"Her sprinklers required a trip to LA?"

My dad's cheeks flushed. "Separate emergency."

"Huh, okay." I wasn't going to push for the reason behind his ruddy cheeks or fidgeting fingers. But I had no doubt the subject of Isla and Trudy made my dad anxious.

I waved my hand to the horse-dog. "You watch Trudy a lot?" I leaned my hip against the counter as my dad picked up the dog bowl and rummaged in the fridge. I turned around to fill up my mug when the coffee maker beeped.

"Trudy hops the fence, so I see him often."

"I take it Isla isn't an eighty-year-old woman living with her aging daughter."

My dad laughed and shook his head. "No, Isla is closer to your age."

Interesting. "Is she hot?"

My dad scowled at me. "She is a wonderful young woman. She helps us out a lot. I view her as a daughter, so I won't answer that question."

An uggo then.

"Well, I'd still like to meet her and thank her for taking care of you guys."

My dad chewed his lip. "She's private, Rhys. She may not want to meet you."

My brows rose. "I want to at least pay her for gas and her time."

My dad sighed. "She won't take money, I tried. She's independently wealthy after inheriting a small fortune, and she's a best-selling author. She helps us out because she likes to."

I sighed. "Okay. What book did she write, maybe I've heard of it."

My dad grimaced. "It's like a self-help book. I doubt you have."

My mom walked into the kitchen and scratched Trudy's head before smiling at me. "How'd you sleep?"

"Fine." I squinted at my dad as his nostrils flared, and he tipped his head towards the bookcase. My mom rolled her eyes.

My parents were being weird as fuck. They were cagey as hell whenever I mentioned Isla. When she Face Timed her dog, my parents rushed to the back yard to take the call. I watched from the window as Trudy did a happy dance and twirl around while barking.

I volunteered to take the beast on a walk. I was stopped by an older woman who clearly knew Trudy because she spoke directly to him. "Are you Trudy's dad?"

I smirked and shook my head. Pet parents were so weird about the ownership of their dogs. "No, I'm just walking him."

She grinned. "You seem like you can handle him. I was worried when I met his mom. She's a tiny thing, but Trudy's a good boy."

The 'good boy's' tail whipped my thigh as the black lab sniffed and licked his face.

I held back a grimace. "I haven't met his mom."

"Oh, she's a doll. She's the sweetest and so beautiful both inside and out. You should really get to know her."

I grinned and waved goodbye after her advice. I already had plans to meet my parents' neighbor, but knowing she was pretty, according to a stranger, made me more intrigued to meet her.

I didn't get a chance before the end of the break. She had come home late the night before I had to report. Then I had two back-to-back series at home against Houston and Milwaukee. She was apparently busy. She never answered the door when I tried. It seemed she only answered the door in the morning when Trudy was being returned from hopping the fence.

Then I left for a series in LA against the Angels. I was stoked to see Will Reiser and Matt Foust. Will was the team lawyer, and Matt was the team scout. It was incredible to see them. I resisted the urge to ask them about Tama. I knew they'd know. But I didn't want her to be given any sort of heads up. I wanted my confrontation to be as abrupt as her abandonment of me had been.

After LA was a series in Oakland. I was on game two of a four game series against Texas, but at least it was at home. I was going to be in Seattle for another ten days playing against Texas, Cleveland, and then the much-anticipated game against the Rays.

I'd finally have an off day on Aug 11, but the team PR person had set up a meet and greet with my old high school. I was happy to do it if it meant I could inspire the next generation of ball players.

In the limited time I had spent at my parents' house I learned a lot about Trudy. My dad was correct in saying he was special. I watched in fascination as he grabbed wrenches, screw drivers, and rags for my dad as he was under the Chevelle. I also accidentally ate Trudy's food for lunch.

I wondered why the dog wouldn't stop whining and drooling as I went ham on a ground beef and pumpkin casserole. It was savory and sweet. It needed a little salt, but I wasn't going to complain about a ready-made meal that met my macros. My dad laughed his head off when he saw me. But seriously who the hell makes their own dog food?

I also learned that Isla was a very private person. She hadn't come over once when I was in town. Trudy would jump the fence most mornings, and my dad would bring him back to his house after showering him with attention and carrots.

It was too early. I should have slept in, but I was still on East coast time. My parents had stayed up late with Isla watching my game, so they were still sound asleep by the time I made it to the kitchen to make some coffee.

Trudy was sitting on my parents' deck, chowing down on a few carrots he had plucked up. I opened the door and let him in. He nudged my hand in a thank you as I scratched his velvety ears.

I made some eggs for me and for the dog that was so important to my parents. He drooled on my knee as I set his plate down and ate my own food. When I was done eating, I zipped my hoodie over my bare chest and decided to take Trudy back home.

He looped out in front of me and nosed the doorbell with his snout.

I stood next to him on the stoop and ran my fingers through my hair to make sure my bed head was under control. The door swung open as my heart went into a freefall.

Tama *Isla* Bulris stood in front of me. Her wide caramel eyes exactly as I remembered. She squeaked and slammed the door in my face. Trudy barked in indignation. I was rooted to the spot.

What the fuck was going on?

I pushed the front door open. Trudy trotted in front of me.

"Gertrude, hungry," a deep voice called out.

My mouth gaped.

"A little warning you were bringing Rhys over, Trudy. We talked about this," Tama hissed.

"Gertrude, hungry."

"I know you're hungry. I'm having an existential crisis," she hissed back.

I rocked back on my heels before turning around and leaving the same way I came. My dad greeted me at her gate. His eyes were apologetic as he waved for me to follow him home.

"What the fuck is going on?" I asked my dad as soon as he shut the garage door.

He scowled at me. "Language, son. I know you're mad but that's not an excuse."

I held my hands up. "Are you aware who your neighbor is?"

My dad gave me a guilty grimace.

The air left my lungs. "And you didn't think you'd tell me that my former best friend was your next-door neighbor? Wait, is this why you only called her Trudy's mom?"

"Yes. We didn't know we were all connected to you until we had known her a month. She moved in and brought us muffins. Have you ever had her pumpkin muffins?"

I scowled at him. *Those were my fucking favorite.*

My dad held his hands up again. "She invited us over for dinner after Trudy hopped the fence. Your mom loved her immediately. We invited her to dinner, and we figured it out. Then she asked us to separate our relationship with you from our relationship with her. She explained everything, and I don't blame her for not wanting you to know she was our neighbor."

Rearing my head back like he had slapped me, I said, "What's that supposed to mean?"

An unamused glare briefly crossed his features. "I'm paraphrasing and drawing my own conclusions based on what she said, and her friend Henry shared, but you strung her along for five years only to plan to marry another woman."

I blanched. "That's not what happened, and Henry hates me. There is no way he gave you an unbiased opinion."

Crossing his arms, my dad raised one shoulder higher. "I told you I drew my own conclusions. You spoke about that girl for years and then you decided on a whim to marry that Krista woman. I thought you took a fast pitch to the head, but I kept my mouth shut."

Blinking rapidly at him, I absorbed what he was saying. "You lied to me because my ex-best friend asked you to?"

One shoulder hitched higher. "If that's how you see it, sure. I'd like to say I protected a vulnerable person."

I flung my hand out towards Tama's house. "She clearly stalked me to get to you. She's not a vulnerable victim. She abandoned me on my wedding day and iced me out for years, Dad."

An annoyed huff pushed from my dad's mouth. "Inaccurate and unnecessarily cruel. Talk to me when you're ready to handle the truth." My dad walked back into the house with heavy footfalls and shook his head.

I made myself scarce before my game. I was in too much shock, too pissed, too relieved, too frustrated to process anything. And in the middle of a series wasn't the time to start. I pushed all my thoughts about Tama in a box and swallowed it away like I had been doing for three years.

*Whinny: How's it been playing for
your childhood team?*

I read the message with a grin. It had been about eight months since I had seen Whinny. He was still in Denver, still single, and still my wingman whenever we went out.

After the Krista drama I went a little crazy fucking bunnies. After about six months of the bullshit, he and Nathan sat me down. It was a necessary talk. I was being reckless.

Players were being embroiled in paternity scandals, and I had spread my seed in enough cities to worry about having unknown children around. I was always careful and used a condom I provided. I always put it on myself, and I took it with me when I was done. All the women signed NDAs and team security escorted them away when I was done with them.

After the intervention I was more selective. The past year my dating life was nonexistent. I didn't mind. I was thirty, single, never married (dodge a bullet there), and no prospects. I wanted a relationship with companionship and the securities that came along with one. Finding someone on the road was impossible. I was holding out to the end of the season before I attempted to date someone real. Not someone I met at a bar who knew my stats better than I did.

> Me: Almost a dream come true.
> I found Tama.

Whinny:  How'd that go?

> Me: Not well. She stalked my parents and moved in next door.

Whinny: That doesn't sound like Bully.

> Me: Whose side are you on?

Whinny: I'm Switzerland. But you need to talk to Nathan.

⚾ ⚾ ⚾

> Me: Why the fuck do I need to talk to you about Tama?

He better not be fucking dating her.
I'd fucking murder him with my bare hands.

Nathan: I'm great. You're killing it in Seattle

> Me: Just put me out of my misery.

236

*Nathan: My cousin may have been her real
estate agent.*

Me: So, you knew she was stalking me?

*Nathan: Whoa, whoa, whoa. She didn't know
who her neighbors were, but I take it she does
now.*

Me: What the fuck is going on?

*Nathan: I may have suggested the vacant
house for my cousin to show her. I may have
known that your parents lived there. And I may
be in the frame of mind that you're both too
fucking stubborn and needed to talk.*

Me: She abandoned me.

*Nathan: You know the difference between me
and you? I asked her what happened.*

Me: What the fuck happened?

*Nathan: A conversation you need to nut up and
have on your own.*

*Me: She doesn't want to talk to me.
She's never reached out. And she
slammed the door in my face.*

Nathan: I don't know about the door, but I do know you blocked her number.

Me: I didn't block shit.

A sinking dread filled my gut. After Krista, I passed my phone off to my agent. He cloned it and only forwarded messages to me from my approved list of people. He had the service block every woman on my phone except my mom. I beat my head against the lockers as my teammates filed out.

"You played well tonight, Goodman," Coach Jimmy called out. I nodded in his direction and plucked my phone back up.

Me: I need you to unblock Tama Bulris.

David (agent): Give it an hour. You killed it tonight.

There wasn't a way for me to get undelivered messages, but at least if she ever wanted to text me, I would get them.

What am I thinking? I live next to her!

I took a car service to my parents' home. My cars were being shipped to Seattle and stowed in a garage until I bought my next place. The lights were off in both houses, but it didn't stop me from marching up the steps to Tama's and pounding on the door. The deep intimidating bark of Trudy rang through the night. There was no way she didn't hear me.

I stood on the steps for an hour, knocking and waiting until I stomped over to my parents' house. She was trying to hide, but I wasn't going to let her. I had spent three years wondering, worrying, being pissed off and it ended soon.

Chapter 13

"**D**arren has a small dick, but he's nice. And I think because it's so small it probably wouldn't hurt for my first time, you know?"

I blinked at the teen sitting in front of my desk. Laura, I think her name is. I looked down at her student file. Yes, Laura. She had been recommended to me by her homeroom teacher. Laura was crying in the bathroom her first day of school.

I cleared my throat. "Why don't we talk about why you were so upset on Thursday."

Laura blew out a breath. "It was nothing. My period has started which meant I couldn't wear my new white jeans to school. I was crying because I saw Rebecca Baker wearing the exact same pair and now I have to wait to wear them, or she'll call me a copycat."

Yeah, that's nothing alright.

"Do you often cry like that when you are disappointed?"

She shrugged. "I mean, like I said my period had started. Anyway, yay or nay for choosing a small dick for my first time."

The ticking of the clock pulled my attention away. We had a school assembly in five minutes where I was supposed to be introduced and then they were having some welcome-to-school rally.

"I feel like the size of his penis shouldn't be a factor in choosing your partner. You should be more focused on how he makes you feel as a person."

Laura gave me finger guns. "Got it. You got any condoms?" She looked around my desk, moved my box of tissues to the side, and frowned when she didn't discover a bowl of prophylactics at her disposal.

I cleared my throat. "I believe there are some in the nurse's office."

Laura shrugged. "I'll pull and pray after my next period."

My eyes widened. "Don't do that. The pullout method isn't reliable unless you are diligent about tracking your cycle. Also, your first time will be possibly bloody. A condom will keep it sanitary. And they protect more than just from pregnancy."

Laura blew out a breath. "But the nurse is a hundred years old."

A smile cracked my lips. "Doesn't mean she's a prude. Ask for a condom. If you are old enough to have sex, then you are old enough to ask for a condom. If that's too embarrassing for you, then you need to think about if you are mature enough to make this decision."

"You're so wise. Okay, I'll ask Nurse Ratchet for a condom and tell Darren the good news."

I blew out a breath as she breezed out the door.

"Ready?" Genevieve popped her head in my office. She was Henry's beautiful aunt. Her auburn hair was a little lighter than

Henry's and her accent wasn't quite as pronounced as his mother's, but I could see the resemblance.

"We are going to go over the beginning of school rules, introduce a few teachers and you, and then we have a special guest as a motivational speaker."

"Sounds good." Following in her wake towards the gym, the loud rumble of a thousand students bled out into the hallway. Lily had trained me well in wearing high heels. I hated them but at least I was close to the same height as some of the students.

Henry's cousin, Weston, who was a science teacher at the school, tipped his chin and scooted over so I could stand next to him. He was the same tall and broody handsome that Henry was, but he was more reserved. His hobbies were geared more towards science fiction and Scrabble than bondage like his cousin.

He was sweet and had been a decent friend to me since moving to Seattle. His shoulder bumped mine as Principal Howard talked about her expectations for the year.

I leaned into him. "How long do these things last?"

"An hour," he whispered back.

I followed the rest of the faculty taking seats on the side of the stage. There was no leaving early without all the students seeing. I checked my watch and held back a groan. Trudy was going to get antsy without me home. I was three hours into a four-hour workday and already jonesing to see my boy.

He was with Rita and Tom, he was fine, but it turns out I was as needy as he was. I hadn't let him out of my sight since Rhys stormed back into my life. I had avoided answering the door. His parents would invite me over during his games, so we were all able to still see each other, but I was firmly in the avoidance category of how to handle Rhys Goodman.

"We are also pleased to welcome to the faculty this year, Dr. Tama Bulris. Some of you may have heard of her. She wrote the best-selling novel 'The Science of Heartbreak' and has been making waves with her funny and sincere interviews. She has agreed to work with you all this year Monday, Wednesday, and Friday from 8am to noon. You can sign up for half hour slots as her calendar dictates." A mumble of excitement rippled through the crowd.

"Stand up," West whispered to me. I was in the front row, corner closest to the principal. I gave the students a quick wave before smoothing my pencil skirt down to take my seat.

"And now what you have all been waiting for. I am pleased to introduce our next guest. He attended here not too long ago. I was his English teacher, so I know him well. He has proven himself as an elite amongst his peers. Please help me welcome your new Mariners first baseman, Rhys Goodman."

Gasps, hoots, screams, and clapping rang out as my shoulders shrank inward. He looked good, more muscular when I saw him last. I couldn't count slamming the door in his face. It was only for a second and then slam. He approached the stage like a panther.

His face was smiling towards the crowd. One muscular arm was waving as his thick thighs took the stage steps. He was wearing a pair of chinos that had been tailored to him, no doubt. His button up shirt was rolled to his elbows and straining against his biceps. His dark hair was a little longer, messier on top, and he had stubble across his square jaw. His gaze scanned the auditorium briefly before he grabbed the mic.

"First, let's give a hand to your teachers. My mom taught here for thirty years, and she still subs occasionally. I know they don't get enough praise, so give it up for them." He swung his body to face the rows of faculty. Our eyes locked. I sucked in a breath. The easy grin on his face dropped as his brows puckered. He let out a huff that vibrated the mic and turned back to the crowd, shaking his head as if he had seen a ghost.

Throughout his motivational speech he kept glancing back at me as if to make sure I was still there. My eyes were on the exit. I was tapping my foot, trying to calm my nerves. Finally, he passed the mic back to the principal, but he marched right over to me to stand. He was close enough that the heat from his thigh warmed my arm.

Principal Howard gave instructions on how to get Rhys's autograph. He was going to be making himself available in the cafeteria for students to come up during their lunch. As soon as the assembly was released, I shot up from my seat and made my way to the exit as Rhys gripped my bicep. "Where do you think you're going, Bully?"

I shivered as his warm breath tickled against my neck. "I have to go. Trudy needs me."

His fingers twitched against my skin. "We need to talk," his tone was harsh considering he was whispering. I swallowed thickly.

A few teachers came up to Rhys to introduce themselves. West stared at where Rhys was holding me captive with a perked brow. I shook my arm out, and he finally let me go. I slipped into the clamoring crowd of high schoolers ducking so they were all taller than me and into my office. I grabbed my purse, keys, and locked up. He may have wanted to talk, but he had to be here for another two hours, and I had to go.

Trudy did his happy toes dance when I picked him up from the Goodmans. Even though he'd already been walked by Tom, I took him on another walk. I needed to clear my head. Avoiding Rhys wasn't going to work forever and now he knew my work schedule. Who's to say he wasn't going to bombard me at school again because I refused to answer my door? I couldn't have that.

It looked like it was time to stop avoiding the man that had been haunting me.

Rhys was sitting on my stoop by the time we got back. My heart started to pound as he stood up and wiped his hands on his pants.

"I thought you were icing me out again, but I didn't hear Trudy bark."

I unlocked the door. "Mom, pain."

Darn this dog and his nose.

He could smell the adrenaline hitting my blood stream. When my blood sugar got too low, he'd say, 'mom hungry'. He appeared in the doorway, tilting his big head making his ears flop.

"I'm okay, Trudy."

"Are you sick?"

I shook my head.

"How does he know to warn you that you are in pain?"

I blew out a slow, steady breath, forcing my shoulders to inch down. "He can smell my adrenaline."

Rhys's face softened. The pucker in his brow smoothed and the tension bracketing his mouth relaxed. He kneeled to pet Trudy. "I'm not going to hurt your mom."

Again.

"I like your hair," Rhys said after a long moment of silence.

I swallowed. I wanted to fidget and run my fingers through it, but I shoved my hands behind my back and balled my fists.

"My dad told me about the pact the three of you made."

I winced. "It wasn't to keep a secret from you. It was…" I was at a loss for words. I could have told him it was for my mental health but that would open a can of worms.

"Just a byproduct then. I don't want to talk about how you've befriended my parents after you abandoned me."

"I didn't abandon you." My hackles rose.

"You didn't come to my wedding," he yelled.

I took a step back as Trudy growled at him. He nudged his head between us and pushed his butt against my hips, pushing me back further. Rhys put his hands up and took a few calming breaths.

"You didn't come to my wedding. Do you know how much it fucked me up that my best fucking friend didn't show up to my wedding when you told me you'd be there?"

Patting Trudy's hind quarters, I nudged him to stand down. "You didn't want me there. I was a pity invite. I was a hanger-on from college. You didn't want me to see you had gotten married when it hit social media."

"That's not fucking true."

I rolled my eyes. "Then why did I only see you once after you and Krista started to date. And don't tell me I don't know what I'm talking about. Krista introduced herself to you the night of your debut game."

"How the hell do you remember that?"

"She joked to her friends about how ugly I am, and how you only kept me around to stroke your ego. She saw me and said, 'you have to know he's out of your league.' And then after I officially met her after Christmas, she pulled me aside and told me that I was the friend you pitied because you knew I had a crush on you."

A devastated expression crossed his face. "That didn't happen. Why didn't you tell me that happened?"

"Oh buddy, it sure did. I didn't believe her at first and then the wedding invite came without an RSVP and an accompanying letter telling me I wasn't invited. I thought about it. You *had* pulled away. You met her, and I didn't see you again until ten months later when you told me you two were together. I didn't even know you were looking for a committed relationship! Even if I didn't believe her bullying me and trying to push me from your life, you wanted *her*. You chose *her* to be your wife. That takes precedence over friendship!"

Trudy whined. "Ear pain."

I huffed a breath, realizing I had been yelling. "Sorry, Trudy. I'll keep it down."

"I didn't mean to pull away. I was trying to dedicate time to my relationship."

Yeah, the one not with me.

"It's in the past. You made your choice. You seemed happy with Krista, and I wasn't going to stand in the way of your happiness."

His brows puckered again. "Why couldn't my parents tell me about you?"

I chewed my cheek. "I didn't want to see you. I knew that if you cared, you'd want to confront me about not going to your wedding because that's the type of man you are. The last thing I wanted was for you to show up at my house with Krista and tell me what a terrible friend I was while I kept my mouth shut about Krista's letter."

"I never married Krista."

I looked down at my worn sneakers. "Yeah, Rita told me that the other day."

He huffed. "You wanted nothing to do with me so badly that you didn't let my parents tell you that I left her at the altar after catching her cheating on me with her stepbrother?"

I blanched. "Her stepbrother? Jeez. It's a weird kink. Henry's ex had a thing for her stepbrother, but they met when she was seventeen. I'm not trying to yuck somebody's yum. But there is something that feels wrong about it. I mean maybe if they became stepsiblings while older like Raven, but if you were raised with that person." I made a face.

Rhys gave me a deadpan stare.

"Not the point of your story. I'm sorry she did that to you. And I'm sorry I wasn't there to help you through it."

He let out a deep breath. Silence blanketed the room. He seemed calmer, like all he wanted from me was an apology and a reason. Now he had it, he was fine. His anger had always been like that. A lit match that flamed out quickly, hardly burning your fingertips. "So where does that leave us?"

I rolled my eyes. "You living your life, me living mine. At least now your parents won't have to tiptoe about us to each other."

"No interest in picking up where we left off?"

I reared back as pain lanced through me. Where we left off was him committing to someone else after implying for *years* that I was going to be his and he was going to be mine. I was never going to be enough for him, and I would be damned if I let him back in like that again.

"Oh fuck, are you with someone?" he whispered. I didn't have a chance to answer. My laptop started to ring. I looked at my watch. "I need to get that." Turning on my heel, I rushed into the office to answer the scheduled podcast interview.

The questions asked were pretty boilerplate. It was the same series of questions repeatedly: Why do I think the book resonates with people? Everyone has experienced heartbreak, and everyone is a little voyeuristic into others' pain. Do I have a sequel in the works? Yes, one for sex and kink, one for happiness and love. What is advice I would give to someone dealing with heartbreak? You aren't alone, what's happening to you is normal and talking through it helps.

"You have been linked to some notable people in the past few years, Lily Young who is taking over ML Properties with her sister in the coming years, Ava Reiser the ballet phenom, Griffin DeMarco from the Dumb Youths, Henry Foust who has made a name for himself as the stock market guru. We even dug a little deeper and know that you were once very close to Rhys Goodman. All very influential people in their own fields. Tell the listeners, are some of the anonymous stories from them?"

I let out a nervous laugh as Rhys leaned his shoulder against the doorway. I could have sworn he had left. My mouth gaped before I focused on my answer. "I was very fortunate while I was at Pineview to meet all those people. Lily, Ava, Henry were all my roommates at one point."

"What about Rhys Goodman and Griffin Demarco?"

I swallowed. This was not a part of the prescreened questions. "All my friends from school. Like I said, I was very fortunate to meet some amazing and talented people while I was in college."

I evaded the question as much as I could and then thankfully the podcast ended. Rhys was walking around my office, looking at the pictures on the walls. There were photos from Friendly Village and Pineview. He was in a few. I had more pictures I hadn't had framed yet. I was thankful that I'd been too busy otherwise the pictures from our road trip would also be on the wall. One look at those and he'd know I was madly in love with him then.

He chuckled as he pointed to the picture of Whinny, Nathan, and him celebrating their Super Regional win. "We look so young," he said quietly.

I strummed my lip with my teeth. "It was a long time ago." I sighed when he sat down in my reading chair.

He wiggled his shoulders and removed the pillow from the small of his back, placing it on the table next to him.

"Make yourself at home."

He grinned at me. "If I'm choosing between your house and my parents—"

"That's not happening."

God forbid we were actual roommates. I had a fighting chance of avoiding him if he were next door. If he were living with me, he'd wind up in my bed to cuddle and I'd be back to being his backup plan.

Never again.

His brow furrowed before he clasped his hands in front of him.

"What else do you want to talk about Rhys?"

His gaze flicked to mine. "Are you with someone? You seemed close to that guy at school."

I chewed on my cheek. It would be too easy to say yes. Weston would play along, no questions asked. He knew Rhys from high school, though they weren't friends. Henry had complained to him a few times, so he'd pretend out of solidarity to his cousin.

"Which guy are you talking about?"

"The tall, brown-haired guy that was sitting next to you."

I rolled my lip in. "Does it matter if I'm with someone?"

Evade, evade, evade.

He blew out a breath. "No, I'm just curious."

I blinked at him. His phone vibrated as Rhys reached into his pocket. He read his message and tucked it back without answering. "My mom wanted to know if I'd invite you to dinner. She's making roasted chicken."

I sighed heavily. I loved Rita's roasted chicken. I highly suspected the invite was intentional knowing Rhys didn't have a game. "Yes, I can attend dinner."

He grinned at me. "Your boyfriend won't be jealous if you're having dinner with me?"

I shrugged. "I'm not allowed to have dinner with a guy I used to know from college?"

He squinted at me. "We were more than that."

I lifted one shoulder. "We were, but not by much. We were friends until we weren't."

A determined set flared in his jaw. "Well, I want to be your friend again."

Of course he did. He had nothing but benefits from our friendship. It never hurt him. It certainly didn't render him practically catatonic. I needed to be scooped out of bed by Griffin, who flew from Scotland because he was worried about me after I discovered Rhys blocked my number.

I gave him a patronizing smile. "We can be friends again, but it'll never be like it was."

It can't be.

He hummed and looked down to his knees again. "Can I meet that guy? What's his name?"

I looked over to Trudy who had sauntered into the bathroom. Rhys's lip rose high on one side as the loud plops of Trudy's poop hit the water. He bounced out and announced his bowel movement.

"Are you talking about Weston?"

Standing up from my desk, I passed by Rhys who was still sitting in the chair. I flushed after Trudy, washed my hands, and rattled the treats making Trudy bound towards me. A glob of drool leaked from his jowl as he sat.

He didn't leave my side after that, laying at my feet as I took my seat back at my desk.

"If *Weston* is the guy sitting next to you today, then yes." A pink flush colored high on his cheekbones and ear tips, his nostrils flared. He pumped his clenched fist before smoothing it down his thigh.

"Weston is Henry's cousin. I'm surprised you didn't recognize him. You two went to high school together."

Rhys rolled his head back. "Of fucking course you're dating Henry's cousin. Are you sure he'd be okay with you having dinner with me?"

I shrugged. "He doesn't control what I do. Anyone that tells you not to talk to someone isn't being respectful of your autonomy, and it shows massive trust issues. I've never given anyone a reason to doubt my loyalty in a relationship."

He squinted at me. "You weren't loyal to me on my wedding day."

"We already covered this, and we weren't in a relationship. We were *never* in a relationship. We were friends and your fiancée told me that I needed to leave you alone. I wasn't going to rock the boat in your *actual* relationship. You made a commitment to *her*, and I respected that. If you have a problem with how things worked out, you should take that up with Krista."

He growled at me.

Trudy growled back. I chuckled and stroked his soft ear.

"Can I ask you something?" I tilted my head. "If I were single, what would you do?"

He rolled his eyes to the ceiling, a smirk playing across his lips. "I'd kiss the fuck out of you."

I scoffed. "That's not very friendly. I only kiss friends I give benefits to, and you are no longer in that category. Besides, haven't you spent three years thinking I abandoned you?"

"I'm still salty about it, but I'm starting to understand what happened."

I licked my teeth as my phone buzzed.

*Rita: Rhys said you are good to come
to dinner. I'm so pleased you two are
getting along again. Tom wanted to know
if you can bring over some ice cream.*

My lips twisted to the side at the message. Rhys and Trudy followed me into the kitchen as I pulled out my ice cream maker and ingredients.

"What are you making?"

"Your dad has requested ice cream. Since your mom is making my favorite, I'm willing to make his."

Rhys hummed. "My mom's roasted chicken is your favorite?"

My gaze flicked over to him as I measured the heavy cream into the pot. "If you want to be my friend we need to have rules."

He wagged his brows. "I loved our rules."

I gave him an unamused glare. "You can't come over whenever you want. You need to let me know you are coming."

"What if I'm bringing Trudy home?"

"Your dad is putting a gate in between our yards. He'll be able to get inside through the patio door. He knows how to let himself in once that gate is finished."

"Fine, what else?"

"I'm not interested in a physical relationship with you." It was a bold face lie but it was for my protection and maybe if I said it out loud, I'd believe it.

"Obviously, you have a boyfriend."

"Even if I didn't," I started.

He held his hands up. "I get it. What else?"

"This is probably completely moot, but if we are together in public and anyone is rude to me, I'm leaving. I'm not going to put up with women vying for your attention, treating me like I don't exist, and you turning a blind eye."

"I can't control people coming up to me."

"You can't control the approach, but you can put a stop to the rude behavior. And before you get your panties in a twist and call me a jealous child. It's not about jealousy; it's about being blatantly disrespected and dismissed. My self-worth suffered greatly as your friend. I'm not putting myself through that again."

He squeezed his eyes shut. "I'm sorry, I had no idea."

"Yes, you did. You chose to ignore it. I let you get away with it, so I was as complicit as you. But that is why I am warning you now. I'm worth more than that. You want to give people the time of day that treats me like crap, this," I waved my hand between us, "isn't going to work."

"That's fair. I have one rule of my own."

I continued to stir the cream and milk mixture until the sugar was dissolved. "I'm listening."

"I want to meet Weston."

I groaned and tipped my head back. "Why? You went to high school with him."

"I was an asshole in high school and don't remember him. If he's important to you, then he's important to me. Can I meet your boyfriend?"

"You realize you have zero negotiating power in this."

He smirked. "Come on Bully, let me meet your boyfriend."

I sighed. "I'm going to have to pass. Sorry our friendship is not going to work out."

Rhys grunted. "Are you afraid he's going to be intimidated by me?"

I snorted. "Nope."

"Is he a fan? Are you worried he's going to embarrass you by fan-girling?"

"Good God, you are so full of yourself. Rhys, no he's not a fan. He's not intimidated by you."

"Then what is it?"

"He's not my boyfriend."

I pulled my cabinet open and grabbed the stash of mini candy bars that Henry had left behind. I started to unwrap and chop them up for the mixture. Rhys was quiet behind me. I kept my eyes on the task, waiting for my mixture to cool. My back was to him as I waited for him to say something. The cream mixture poured smoothly in my ice cream maker. Still silence.

When the quiet was too much to handle I turned around. His smile was obnoxiously big. I rolled my eyes and turned back to the dessert.

"Make yourself useful and get the jar of caramel from the fridge," I called over my shoulder.

The refrigerator opened with bottles clanking together and closed a moment later. The jar appeared in front of me. It was the closest he had come to me. He smelled the same. I took in a slow breath and closed my eyes, memories assaulting me before I pulled them back.

I flicked the machine on and took a step away. "I'll see you at dinner."

Rhys was still grinning at me. "Yes, you will."

Rhys

"How'd it go?" my mom whispered.

She looked over her shoulder. My dad was snoozing on his recliner in the living room.

I shrugged. "She explained to me what happened and why she didn't come to my wedding."

"Well, that's more than your dad and I know. What happened?" she hissed.

"Why are you whispering?"

"Your father doesn't want me to meddle," she whispered back.

I chuckled and rubbed the stubble on my chin. "Krista happened. She was rude, lied to Tama, and sent her a letter telling her she wasn't invited."

My mom scoffed. "I never liked her. I could tell she was rotten. Now, Tama, she's the ideal daughter-in-law."

I rolled my eyes. "Calm down Mom, she barely agreed to be my friend, and I think it's more for your benefit than mine."

My mom shrugged. "Probably, but I'm not afraid to exploit it if it means I get you two back together again. You were so happy when you were friends. Which reminds me." She took the hand towel from the oven handle and whipped it in my direction.

"Hey, what was that for?" The welt on my arm from her assault burned.

"That was for having the perfect girl and tossing her aside to propose to that awful woman."

"That's not what happened."

"Tomato, potato. You never asked her to be more than a friend. For that I may never forgive you." She stuck out her tongue.

Her remark struck my solar plexus, and I rubbed at my chest. I couldn't tell my mom about our road trip and how I practically begged her to stay with me. When I told her she was my dream, and she told me that a dream was all we were ever going to be, it crushed me.

I sighed. "Do you need any help with dinner?"

She chuckled. "And have you burn it? No thanks. Your laundry needs to be rotated. Why don't you do that."

"You didn't need to do my laundry, Mom."

"I know, but I don't mind. You've been so busy with the last few series, and you are flying out tomorrow morning bright and early and won't be home for another ten days. I wanted you to be able to relax today."

I leaned forward and kissed her cheek and headed to the small laundry room. My parents had the same dryer as when they got married. It was mustard yellow and still worked like a charm. The washer was replaced two years into their marriage, so it was an off-white model with a turn dial that clicked and had to be pulled out in order to make the thing work. No fancy setting or chime when it was done, but it was reliable.

Anxiously cleaning my room, I contemplated removing my homage to early 2000s baseball from my walls. My parents hadn't changed a thing since the day I left for college. I still had the same navy sheets with a tear at the foot of the bed. My dresser from when I was a baby still had Superman stickers on the side from when I was four and into stickers and superheroes.

I don't know why I was cleaning and contemplating making the room look like a man lived in the space. Maybe I had hoped that Tama would want to see where I slept. Which was ridiculous. She had been clear about keeping our friendship platonic. *Then why did she imply she had a boyfriend?*

My only assumption was she wanted me to have a real reason to stay away. Her willpower wasn't going to hold up, and she had the willpower of steel.

We had both been attracted to each other for *years* before she invited anything from me. I still hated the fact that I didn't remember our first time hooking up. We more than made up for it during our road trip and the subsequent visits to see me.

I didn't keep a tally, but we had a running hook up of every few months until I met Krista. She *did* make me wear a condom after my first spring training and every time after that, but I didn't question it. I was happy with what she was willing to give me.

With my bed made, I looked at my room with fresh eyes. It wasn't my fancy master suite with a king bed and views of the ocean, that's for sure. It looked like a fucking kid lived here. My house in Seattle was going to be impressive. I wanted a view of the water and the mountains.

Trudy's deep rumbling bark echoed in my parents' living room. A shiver ran down my spine, and I checked my pits and breath. I reapplied deodorant and casually walked out of my room.

Tama was in the kitchen with my mom, Trudy, on her heels. She was wearing a yellow dress that hit above her knees and sandals. Her short hair had a subtle wave to it that I had never noticed before. She looked so pretty and casual. It was a change from her tight and sexy as fuck pencil skirt and four-inch heels that I saw her wearing at the high school and then the sweatpants and t-shirt from when she took Trudy for a walk.

Her legs and arms looked more defined than when I last knew her. She was once twiggy, now she looked like she had worked out, no doubt the beast panting at her feet was the reason.

My dad came into the kitchen and looped his arm around her shoulder in a side hug. She grinned up at him and passed him a container of ice cream. "I added more candy and caramel this time."

"You're the best." He scooped up the container with both hands and peeked inside.

"Put it in the freezer until we are ready to eat it," my mom called out from the oven. "How are you doing honey? How was school?"

Tama shrugged and glanced in my direction.

"I wasn't expecting to be the one helping a girl decide who to lose her virginity to, but you know, fine."

My brows rose as my mom laughed. "Teenagers are horny monsters. What did you tell her?"

Tama blew out a breath. "Boilerplate answer. Don't give it up to anyone, make sure they are good to you. She told me he was nice and then asked me for condoms."

My dad snorted. "I'd say advice hasn't changed, but I'm afraid in my day the counselor would tell us only about abstinence."

Tama grinned. "And then there was a birth rate explosion. It's no surprise now the birth rates are declining as sex education increases. She told me she was going to go with the pull and pray method, and I had to point out the flaws in that plan." I chuckled.

She glanced over to me like she had forgotten I was there.

"I heard you wrote a book," I said.

My mom looked down at her plate as Tama's cheeks blushed. I didn't mention I listened in fascination as she answered all the podcasters' questions.

"I did."

"It's wonderful. You should read it," my mom said.

Tama shook her head. "I doubt it's his style of reading. It's full of medical jargon."

258

My mom waved her hand. "Yes, but it's after you read the anecdotes from each of the participants. They are all beautiful and heartbreaking stories. I cried a few times while reading them. And then she does a brilliant job explaining what is happening in the brain as we deal with heartbreak. It's fascinating how someone that experienced a difficult breakup had similar brain scans as those grieving the death of a loved one."

Tama gave my mom a soft smile. "I'm glad you enjoyed it. I was worried the stories would be too depressing. I tried to give a little hope at the end by letting the reader know how they coped."

"Yes, it was a nice touch. I think it would have been a little too heavy otherwise." My mom turned back to me. "I have a copy. You should read it when you have the time."

I cleared my throat. "Sounds good."

"Dinner smells great, shall we eat?" My dad gave my mom a hard stare. She rolled her shoulders back like she didn't notice.

"Yes, I'm starving," Tama said.

"Guests first." My mom motioned for me to go.

My brow pinched. I wasn't sure if it was an insult to be called a guest in my childhood home or be delighted that they didn't consider Tama one.

"That podcaster today asked some tough questions." Delicately cutting through her chicken, my mom looked up to Tama, waiting for her response.

Puffing her cheeks out, Tama rolled her eyes. "They asked questions not included in the pre-interview."

My mom leaned forward. "But you can tell me was Griffin Demarco a part of the study?"

Blush rose high in Tama's cheeks. "In a manner of speaking." Her eyes flicked up to mine before turning towards my mom. "He was a sexual partner of one of the participants."

What the fuck did that look mean? And who the fuck is Griffin Demarco?

An almost squeal punctuated my mom's excitement for the gossip. "What about Ava? I've seen her videos; she's such a talent. I was so surprised that she's so tiny in person."

"Well, she does stand on her toes when she dances," my dad joked.

My mom swatted at him.

"I personally knew half of the participants. Of course this is confidential, but yes Ava was a participant. Henry and Lily also helped me out. I was very fortunate that all my friends lent their brains to support me."

Not me. Wasn't asked.

We finished eating dinner, and my mom directed us all to the deck so we could enjoy the evening. She held my dad back, asking him to help carry the bowls outside. Tama made her way to the patio. It was unnerving that she felt so comfortable in my parents' home, a place I hadn't been for years.

The sun was setting, casting Tama in a golden glow against the orange sky. "You look gorgeous."

I reached out to her and swiped my thumb against her cheekbone. Her skin was as silky smooth as I remembered. A tendril of hair waved in the light breeze, and I pushed it behind her ear.

She blew out a breath and took a step away from me. "Thank you for the compliment."

It was too formal, and I didn't like the space between us. But I didn't want to make her feel uncomfortable, so I changed the subject before I tried to kiss her. "It's incredible that you wrote a book." She nodded.

"What inspired you?"

She sucked in a breath through her teeth and turned to the patio door that was swinging open. My dad walked over to her and passed her the ice cream.

"You weren't joking about the extra caramel and candy." My dad sounded giddy about it.

She chuckled and shook her head. "I aim to please. Let me know if there is a candy combination you want me to make next time. I used the leftover candy from Henry's last visit."

How often is that fucker here?

"Tell him I said thanks for the tip on the stock. I made a mint, enough to buy my next project. I'm waiting to finish the Chevelle before I bring her here."

I swallowed my annoyance that my dad had a personal connection with Henry and seemed to like him. "What did you get?" I loved talking to my dad about cars. The past few years had been too busy for me to take notice or ask about my dad's hobby. I needed to make a point as soon as the season was over to help him with the Chevelle that he had purchased years ago.

"1977 Porsche 911 S 2.7 Targa."

I whistled. My mom and Tama nodded on without trying to be patronizing, but I knew if they understood they wouldn't just nod.

Trudy let out a loud whine. Tama scowled. "Dairy hurts your belly, and the last time you ate chocolate I had to air the house out for three days." I swear to god the big dog said, "I want it," in a whiny grumble.

"You can't have it," Tama replied back.

My dad chuckled and stroked Trudy's ear. "I told you Trudy was special."

Chapter 14

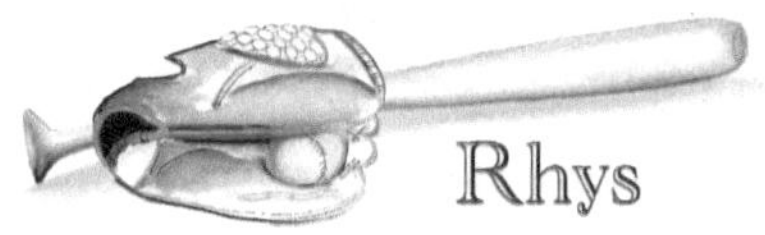

Rhys

altimore, New York, and Philly, all the towns blur together post mid-season. The biggest difference is that my final destination for my single day off is a rainy, cool-weather city versus spending the day at the beach with my teammates, hosting a party for bunnies to go topless at my pool. Because who lives next door, I'd never exchange a sunny beach for the chance I'd catch a glimpse of Tama walking Trudy in the rain.

A month ago, I was looking forward to confronting her, getting closure, and moving the fuck on. Now, after knowing what I do, there was no moving on from Tama. I had asked Nathan to confirm what Tama had said about my wedding. He told me that she sent him a picture of the letter that Krista had sent. She paraphrased it to make it seem less cruel.

When I read through the blurry image I was enraged. It made me want to confront Krista, but any communication with her would be bad. I was done with her. I never wanted to speak with her again.

Whinny was aware of the letter, too. Though, he hadn't read it. He also knew about Tama living next door to my parents and told me the reason for his intervention a few years ago. He knew that Tama was hurting. He was hoping I'd pull my head out of my ass and talk to her.

He also let slip that Nathan had visited Tama at her house, another secret I didn't like, but being mad seemed pointless when I had spent three years mad at some manipulated miscommunication.

The charter bus from the private airport parked in front of our practice facility where everyone had parked their car. It was late afternoon Wednesday, and I didn't have to work again for a full 48 hours. My primary car had been delivered while I was away, so I was glad I wasn't going to have to use the car service anymore.

My parents' house was empty when I arrived.

Me: I'm home. Where are you?

Mom: Eating dinner at Tama's.

I sighed. It wasn't an explicit invite, and I wasn't going to go over without that. She gave me boundaries, and I was going to do my best to respect them.

Mom: Tama said you can come.

Trudy let out a single bark to announce my arrival. Tama gave me a soft smile while my mom hugged me. My dad stayed seated, eating what looked like fried chicken. My mouth watered. From what I remembered, no one made fried chicken like Tama.

"Help yourself." Tama pointed towards the kitchen.

It took a moment to find the plates, silverware, and a glass for water. Then I piled my plate. I photographed my fried chicken, green beans, dinner rolls, and au gratin potatoes and sent it to my group chat with Nathan and Whinny.

Nathan: Son of a bitch. I'm chartering the first flight.

Whinny: Don't tell me I missed the apple turnovers.

Me: You did, but that was the first night I spent in Seattle before I knew she baked them.

Trudy's nail clicked against the hardwood in his slow walk to the kitchen. He was going to beg for food. I looked at my plate and didn't want to part with a single morsel.

"I know you already ate," I whispered to him.

The chair next to Tama was vacant so I took that spot happily, even though there were three seats to choose from.

"You're in for a treat, son," my dad said with his mouth full.

I chuckled. "I'm well aware. This was one of the many favorite meals she'd make for me while I was in school. Nathan and Whinny are jealous right now." A groan slipped past my lips as I ate my first bite. "Good lord, Bully, you've only gotten better with age."

"Bully?" my mom asked.

Tama cleared her throat. "From my last name."

"Oh, of course. I was thinking I missed a huge part of your friendship. But there is no way you were a bully ever in your life."

Tama gave my mom a half-smile. "No, definitely not a bully. How was work for you today?"

I wasn't aware my mom was subbing today. I listened to her answer, and my dad shared his day. They turned to me. My cheeks bulged at the amount of food I had shoved in my mouth.

"What?" I chewed through enough to swallow.

"Your dad asked how your trip was," my mom said.

I wiped my mouth. "Sorry, I was concentrating on how good everything is. I haven't had food like this in years, I guess my hearing stopped working."

Tama let out a nervous laugh. I reached over and squeezed her knee and described the bunny drama that happened between a few different rookies.

Tama was chewing on her cheek. She adjusted her leg making my hand fall away.

"I wasn't there to witness it, but Carlyle, the second baseman, gave me his firsthand account."

"Were you feeling sick? You told me you love the bar scene in New York," my dad said. *Thanks a lot for that, Dad.*

My mom cleared her throat. "That was years ago, Tom. Clearly, he's matured since then."

"It's been a year. You remember when we were in Jamaica last December, and he went on and on about that one bar near Brooklyn. They were hosting a wet t-shirt contest but some of his teammates participated, and he got roped into it."

What the hell, Dad?

The tendons in my mom's shoulder flexed. "Ouch," my dad muttered as my mom's hand reappeared at the table.

I cleared my throat. "That was good fun. I don't indulge in the bar scenes anymore. I want to concentrate on other things and getting drunk wasn't getting me to those goals."

My dad chuckled. "What other goals could you possibly have?"

I licked my lips and looked at Tama's profile. She was looking over at Trudy whose head was above the table, closer to her shoulder. A line of drool was slowly easing its way to the floor. "I'm thirty, I want a real relationship with someone that makes me happy. I'm not going to find that in a bar on the road. Spending too much time in that scene will distract me from what I want."

A light blush creeped up Tama's neck. Then her lip curled in disgust as Trudy moved his head and whipped his drool on Tama's foot.

"Well, I think that's wonderful," my mom said. "Tama and I were talking about something similar today. I guess her mom is wondering about grandkids. What did you tell Melody, Tama?"

She blew out a breath as she leaned forward and wiped her foot off.

"That Trudy is as good as she's going to get unless the man of my dreams lands in my lap. Which obviously isn't going to happen. I don't live in a fairytale and experience has taught me that men are adverse to commitment with me."

Ouch.

I didn't want to assume she was talking about me but my mom scowling pointedly at me made me reverse that thinking.

"I like that Griffin kid," my dad said. "He knows cars and helped me teach you how to change your oil. Where's he now-a-days?"

Why was my dad being the biggest cockblock in the history of the world?

Tama blushed harder. "Griff is in Europe right now. His tour is finishing soon. Maybe he'll swing by on his way to Vancouver. I'll tell him you said hi next time I talk to him."

"Oh Tom, Griffin is a handsome, charming, sweet boy, but he's a rock star. Do we want our Tama with someone who has groupies following him around wherever he goes?"

Our Tama?

My dad turned his head to look directly at me. "You're right. *Our* Tama deserves someone's undivided attention. She shouldn't have to compete with some woman hoping to screw a famous person."

My mom elbowed dad hard.

Tama cleared her throat. "Like I said, I attract men who are adverse to commitment. Who is ready for dessert? I made banana pudding with homemade lady fingers and whipped cream."

"I'm not going to say no to that." My dad pushed his empty plate away.

Tama's chair bobbled as she abruptly pushed it back. Trudy was hot on her heels. I gave both my parents a look that said, 'what the fuck'. My dad shrugged.

"Rhys, why don't you help Tama carry the pudding to the table," my mom suggested.

Tama was leaning on the counter, shoulders up to her ears as she took in a few deep breaths.

I had never seen her like that before. She looked rigid with stress, and I hated it.

"You okay?" I whispered.

She sucked in a breath. "I'm good, needed to take a moment. Your mom isn't subtle."

I smiled. "Yeah, I noticed. If she's making you feel uncomfortable…"

She shook her head. "Your mom is fine. Your dad too. Let's drop it." Her head disappeared into the fridge. She set a large dish of banana pudding on her island and grabbed bowls from the cabinet.

"Do you want to serve it up here or in the dining room?" I grabbed the spoons.

"Here is fine." She scooped healthy portions in each bowl and then went back into the fridge to dollop each dessert with whipped cream. She sprinkled graham cracker crumbs on top. I followed her back into the dining room. My parents were hissing back and forth to each other. My dad looked annoyed, my mom looked pleased with herself.

"This looks wonderful, Tama." My mom accepted hers with a toothy smile. We ate in contented silence.

"Why don't you help Tama clean up. I'm going to take your father home." My mom tugged on his elbow.

"That's not necessary," Tama said.

"Nonsense, honey. You cooked; he'll clean."

My parents left hastily and then the silence that followed was a little less contented. I pointed to the kitchen. "I'll get started."

"You don't need to. I'm sure you are tired from all the traveling. Go home and sleep."

I shook my head. "I'd rather be here. I missed you."

She rolled her eyes. "You saw me ten days ago."

"I meant the past three years. I missed you every single day."

"Don't do that," she said quietly.

I hated that she didn't want to think about how much I missed her during our time apart. I looked down at the empty table before pushing away from it. "I'll get started."

Tama made herself scarce. Her kitchen had been updated and had a dishwasher that worked, unlike my parents, so it was an easy clean up. I wiped down the granite counters and thought of the possibilities with my parents' house.

They refused to let me spend any money on it, but Tama's house was a testament in how nice we could make their home. The neighborhood was already coveted for its larger lot sizes and proximity to the city and nature trails. Most of the homes were owned by the original owners or their children.

I vaguely remembered who lived in the house before Tama. We referred to it as the Hoarder House or the Witch's House. You could see piles of stuff blocking the windows. My dad said when the house went for sale the contractor Tama hired had to air the house out for a week. It smelled like hot garbage and death.

Now it was a clean slate with mid-century tastes to reflect the house's age. It was cozy in the living room, with soft surfaces to lounge on. I had already seen the office which reflected the same taste as the rest of the house. It was chic without being stuffy. I loved it, and I was impressed by what she was able to do with it.

I walked around looking for her when I was finished. She was sitting in her office with Trudy resting at her feet. Her laptop was open in front of her. She was leaning forward, reading. Her eyes gazed up at me as she sat back.

"All done?"

"Yep." I took a seat in the reading chair I had sat in weeks ago after I confronted her and learned how misguided my anger had been. "All done. What are you working on?"

She licked her lips. "Reading emails from my publisher. They are telling me whether my book on sex and kink should come out before my book on love and happiness. I have been advocating for love and happiness after heartbreak. It feels like an easier transition. My publisher wants 'The Science of Kink' to come out next. He's arguing that kink can and should come before love and happiness."

I blew out a breath, surprised by the change in conversation. "What are you going to do?"

She shrugged. "Follow his professional advice. I have most of my research done. Of my one hundred subjects, fifty had true kinks, so it'll be interesting to show the differences on taboo sex on the brain versus standard traditional sex. Something really interesting though, the subjects that were in love with their partners had different brain activity and hormonal changes. Ava's brain scan was beautiful. I knew she loved Henry, but there is nothing like seeing the proof backed by science."

I didn't know what to say, but I had a million questions.

She giggled. "Go ahead and ask."

"Did you watch one hundred participants bone?"

She laughed out loud and shook her head. I fucking loved her laugh. "Firstly, the bedroom had no cameras inside. There is audio. I asked for narration so I could understand what was happening while it was happening. The participant was hooked up to the MRI, so there was some limitation on what could be used. We stayed away from metals, so there were a lot of leather substitutes. Some participants got into the idea that I was in the next room, some took longer to climax."

I wagged my brows. She rolled her eyes again and looked me right in the eye as if challenging me.

"Second of all, I was one of the participants so it would have been ninety-nine. I was the first to make sure the accommodations were comfortable, and the climax was possible."

I chewed into my cheek hating that someone fucked her and it wasn't me. I wanted to ask who the lucky guy was, but I resisted. It wasn't my business, and it would have made me too upset. Which was ridiculous, I had plenty of sex after our friendship dissolved. Plenty before it too.

She had never rubbed it in my face when she had other partners. She never mentioned a specific instance before everything happened, and it was throwing me off and making me insanely jealous.

Change the subject before you ask something stupid. Like who the fuck is he? Or were you in love with him?

"When did you start your study?" I asked after a moment of silence.

She looked thoughtfully at me before answering. "About a year and a half ago. It was a continuation of my senior thesis which was on grief and heartbreak. Which was personal to me at the time."

My gut twisted that she went through something painful without me. "Who died?"

"Yolanda."

I bit hard into my lip as my stomach swirled. A woman she adored died and I wasn't there for her because I was in my own head and pissed at the world.

"I'm so sorry."

"Death is the inescapable fact of life. Turns out she did write me into her will. I was the sole beneficiary. This is the house that Yolanda built." She waved her hands around. "She was a two-time widower. She told me once her first husband was an oil baron. I figured she was exaggerating, but nope."

I looked around the office, my gaze snagging on a picture of Tama playing poker with a bunch of old women. I'm positive I recognized Gerty in it. I looked at my watch and saw how late it was. But I didn't want to leave her. I wanted more one-on-one time before my next series started. "What are you doing tomorrow?"

She swallowed before looking away from me and licking her lips. "Taking Trudy for a walk and running some errands."

"Want some company?" I sounded like a hopeful fucker. There was a desperate lilt in my words.

She bit into her lip. "You should rest on your off day. I know you only get one day off every six. Exhaustion will affect your game, and your team is in playoff contention."

"I love that you know my game schedule."

She rolled her eyes. "Just because we stopped talking doesn't mean I stopped caring. I'll always cheer you on. You've worked so hard and deserve all your successes."

I sat back, blown away by her sincerity. I swallowed the lump in my throat. She was a better friend than I ever deserved. "I made a lot of sacrifices, though."

She shrugged. "I'm sure the millions in your bank are a reminder that all your sacrifices were worth it." *Not if it meant I lost her for good.*

She grinned at me and stood up from her desk. "I'm going to bed. You can let yourself out. I remotely lock my doors." She stretched her arms over her head, rising on her toes. Trudy did his own stretch and led the way out of the office.

I took a deep inhale. Her fragrance was more concentrated by her desk than in the rest of the house. I closed my eyes to the apple and jasmine smell that made me feel at home. As requested, I let myself out and headed to bed. She was right, my body was exhausted.

I rubbed the crust from my eyes. Sleep eluded me most of the night. The conversation with the Goodmans about relationships plagued my thoughts and dreams. As did Rhys's announcement he wanted a real relationship. Though he had one of those before, proposed and darn near got married, so it was less than pointless to think I'd be seriously considered. Exhibit A: he had me and chose beautiful Krista when he was ready to commit.

Trudy had requested food twice and I had already let him out. It was a matter of time before my neighbor brought him back. I also knew it would be Rhys despite the early hour. He seemed hesitant to leave after he finished with the dishes. A part of me wanted him to follow me to my bedroom, but I was glad he respected my boundaries. It was not something I was expecting from him.

Relief pulsed through me when he left. Hiding the real reason behind my thesis was difficult while he looked at me with heartbreak over Yolanda's passing. What I wasn't prepared to tell him was that *he* inspired my thesis. My mourning our friendship, my realization that I will never be enough, my grief that he chose someone else, that's what haunted me my final year during my PhD program. The fact I couldn't get over it. Yes, Yolanda did pass away around the same time, but her death was not the primary cause for my depression. She had lived a full life and passed peacefully in her sleep at 92. It was the death of hope that did me in.

The process of getting ready gave my mind something else to focus on. I washed my face and brushed my teeth to wake myself up. Trudy's walk was a long walk through the nature trails that ended near a cafe where I would get breakfast for myself. It was sprinkling lightly, nothing I hadn't gotten used to in the years since I moved from the desert.

My tight spandex pants that dried quickly when wet were essential to wear on a rainy hike. I ran a brush through my hair and popped a hat on. My waterproof trainers were near my front door.

I gathered my pack I brought while taking long walks with Trudy. It had my essentials: pepper spray, even though I doubted anyone would be crazy enough to attack me with Trudy by my side; a collapsible water bowl; water bottles; a small towel to wipe his paws; and a rain slicker in case it started pouring. Trudy had one too, so I didn't have to mop my entire house if he got wet and shook his massive body to dry off.

My doorbell rang, so I unlocked the front door remotely. My dog bounded into the house a moment later and went right for his buttons. "Gertrude, hungry."

A light chuckle from the entryway made my shoulders roll in. I recognized Rhys's deep rumble and sucked in a breath before sticking my head around the corner to see him looking around my living room.

"Thanks for bringing Trudy. I think your dad is planning on starting the gate this week."

Rhys turned around and grinned at me. He was dressed in workout clothes. He hadn't shaved, but I liked the darkened scruff around his jaw. His eyes raked up and down my body. "Morning, gorgeous."

My cheeks heated. My clothes were far tighter than I would have ever worn around him. You could see every curve of my leg and butt in the athletic pants. Something I noticed his eyes had zeroed in on.

"You look ready for that walk."

I set down Trudy's bowl. He was tapping his paws happily, thumping his tail into the cabinets. "I'm taking the east trail. The one that leads to the small shopping center with the cafe and farmer's market."

Rhys's brow furrowed. "That's like two miles one way."

I shrugged. "It takes a lot to wear Trudy out. We normally walk three miles a day, so an extra mile is nothing. Plus, it stormed yesterday morning, so your dad had to cut their walk short."

He smirked at me. "Do you remember when you'd refuse to walk to my house if you had your backpack on because it was too far away? I had to give you piggyback rides."

I snorted. "In my defense the altitude messed with me. Also, I didn't need to work out. My metabolism was able to handle anything. Like you, I'm thirty, things have changed in that regard. And lastly, Trudy acting like a psycho later because he's hyper is a punishment for feeling lazy and not taking him for his walks."

"Well, I'm feeling well rested and looking forward to a long walk. My offer stands to accompany you on your errands today."

I squinted at him. "Was it an offer or an imploration?"

He grinned. "I'd beg to spend more time with you if it would make a difference. I'll drop to my knees right now."

I rolled my eyes. "That's not necessary."

Trudy rubbed his head against my stomach before walking away. "Gertrude, walk."

"That's our cue if you want to join us."

Rhys grabbed my pack before I could and pulled it on his back. "You've got water?"

"For me and Trudy, but I'll share with you if I must."

He wagged his brows. "Let's go, Bully."

Trudy patiently waited while I strapped him into his chest harness. Rhys led the way to the empty trail. It was misting rain. We chatted about how he likes his new team, things he missed about his old team, and the hassle of getting his house ready to sell.

Some of his old teammates were still using his house as a party pad, as discovered by his real estate agent. He was going to be in Tampa Bay in a few weeks and was planning on changing the locks to the house and picking up a few things he didn't think he'd need but now wants.

"You should come with me to Tampa."

I rolled my eyes over to him. "And see your sex palace? Pass."

He laughed. "No, because there is a great view of the ocean at sunset, I want you to see. You remember our road trip, and we watched that crazy sunset while in the hot springs?"

I chewed on my lip. It was one of my favorite memories. That day meant more to me than I could ever admit to him, so I had mentally cataloged everything about it.

"The day I viewed the house, the sun was setting. That same crazy orangey red took up the whole sky. I bought it because it reminded me of you. I have watched countless orange sunsets on my back deck, thinking about that trip. I want you to see it. Will you at least think about going with me? It's not until Labor Day. You can fly into Tampa Sunday late afternoon. We'll time your flight to mine and then you can fly out Tuesday night, so you don't miss school on Wednesday."

My nose tingled at the memories he evoked. "That's in nine days."

"I know. I'll buy your tickets. My game isn't until late afternoon Monday and Tuesday, we can spend our mornings on the beach."

My brows pinched in confusion about what to do.

"It's a six-bedroom house, you can have your own room. I want you to see the sunset," he said quickly.

Going would put me in dangerous territory. I'd get caught in his seductive web for sure. "Can I think about it?"

"Of course. Yes, think about it. Anything I can do to sway you, I will. I'm selling the house and buying one here, so it's my last shot to show you something I've wanted you to see for four years now."

I sighed and turned to watch Trudy nose his way down the trail.

"My parents will watch Trudy. Fuck, I'll charter a private jet, and you can bring him."

I rolled my eyes over to him. He held his hands up. "I'm offering, you don't have to accept."

I blew out a breath. "I'll think about it, but it won't be necessary to go private. Trudy doesn't like flying. It hurts his ears."

He smirked at me. "That's fair."

He changed the subject to what I had been doing for the past three years. We skated around relationships and hookups. I didn't want to hear anything about his wild times while single in the MLB. I doubted he wanted to hear about my experiences with Griffin if I had to guess based on the way his jaw tightened when I told him that I was the first person to have sex while getting my brain scanned for my study.

"I can't believe you got a job offer in Florida and turned it down," Rhys said.

I shrugged. "Henry and Lily had already offered to pay for my study. Why work for someone else when I could work for myself."

"Because we would have only been thirty minutes away from each other," he said with wide eyes.

Which was exactly why I turned it down.

It had been a great opportunity working at a lab where they were researching sleep, depression, and mental illnesses. The study is still ongoing, which meant the results weren't what they were expecting. I was looking forward to reading the medical journal.

"Correct, but you had blocked my number by then. I had also just finished renovating the house, and it was a labor of love to pick everything out."

Rhys grunted. "I didn't mean to block your number. When everything happened with Krista, I had my agent control my phone. He blocked every woman except my mom and only forwards messages to me that are on the approved list."

The fact that I wasn't on the approved list spoke volumes.

"What's done is done. Besides, I love my house. I love my neighborhood and neighbors. I'm not moving if I can avoid it."

He rubbed the back of his neck. "What if you want to have kids and expand your house. Would you consider moving?"

I shook my head. "You've seen my lot size. I could easily expand. Besides a part of the renovation was a small addition to expand the main bedroom, bathroom, and closet. While we were drawing up the plans, I added a basement space that can easily be finished. The concrete patio off the dining room is rated as a foundation. It runs the length of the house. I had initially planned on expanding even further, but since it's only me and Trudy for the foreseeable future I held off on those plans."

He blinked at me. "Where is the entrance for the basement?"

"I converted the hall closet to a staircase."

His eyes widened. "No shit. I feel like I need a tour of your house. Your layout is or was the same as my parents. I love what I've seen so far, so I'd love to see more."

I giggled. "Why do I feel like you are wanting to see my bedroom?"

He smirked at me. "That's a bonus. Seriously, Bully, I want to see and hear about your big plans for the house."

I sighed. "Well, if I were married with two kids, I'd want to add two more bedrooms and bathrooms. The original plan was to add a bedroom and have the bathroom be a jack and jill to the existing bedroom that way the guest bedroom would still have their own bathroom. But since I have converted the second guest bedroom to my office and Trudy's bathroom, I'd need to add two bedrooms and probably two bathrooms. They couldn't be huge bedrooms, and the bathrooms would have to be efficient, but there is room."

He grinned at me. "You'd have a five-bedroom house with four bathrooms?"

I shrugged. "Possibly, but I would want children to fill those rooms and that's not going to happen."

He stopped and tugged on my arm. I looked over my shoulder at him expecting him to be pointing out something on the trail like a bird or fat squirrel.

His face was pinched in confusion and concern. "Why can't that happen? Were you sick? Did something happen to you where you can't have kids?"

I rolled my eyes. "This is the second time you've been worried about me being sick. Seriously, I'm healthier today than I was at twenty. Do I look sick?"

He vehemently shook his head. "No Bully, you look perfect. I worry that I missed serious shit while I was throwing a tantrum like a little bitch."

I snorted. "You were justified in your anger. I hurt you and it's okay to feel upset by that."

"Yeah, but if I would have tried to hear you out…"

I shrugged. "What's done is done."

He gripped my hand and tugged me towards him. His big arms surrounded me in a hug. The misty weather had started to make our clothes damp. I was momentarily shocked at the cold fabric against my cheek and arms before I realized we were embracing. It was the first true hug we had shared for over three long years. He buried his nose into my neck and took slow even breaths. I closed my eyes, his woodsy scent surrounded me, making my eyes prick as happy memories assaulted me.

"You're still more perfect than I could ever deserve," he murmured against my ear.

I let out a slow breath, controlling my emotions. His cool nose trailed from my neck to my jaw. He pulled back enough for his gaze to focus on my lips before staring into my eyes.

Trudy's boney head nuzzled against our stomachs, separating us enough to break eye contact. I blinked rapidly and silently thanked Trudy for the assist. "Do you need some water?"

He let out a loud bark. Rhys was still staring at me. I rolled my lips in and motioned to take the pack off his shoulder. He shook his head as if clearing his thoughts, pulled the bag to his front, and dug out the collapsible water bowl and water canteen. Trudy lapped noisily until the bowl was dry and he started to trot away.

The bag zipped behind me, and I glanced back to see Rhys packing the bowl and water back up. I was grateful for the silence while I collected my thoughts on the almost kiss. It was a slippery slope to let him in like that. He may have said he wanted a committed relationship, but he never said he wanted one with me. I wouldn't survive it again if I let him in and he found someone better.

The cafe was empty when we got there. Rhys took Trudy to the covered patio as I went to the counter to order some breakfast and coffee. He was muttering to Trudy, scratching behind his ears. "You're a bigger cockblock than my dad."

I giggled and passed him his coffee and sat down across from him. The rain was starting to pick up. It was going to be a muddy walk home, but it wasn't unfamiliar to me in the least. I liked walking in the rain.

Rhys smirked at me as he took a sip. He moaned. "You remembered my coffee order."

I tittered. "It's been like three years, not three decades. It's not a big deal."

He chewed his lip before looking off to the side. "Krista never remembered my coffee order."

I sucked in a slow breath through my teeth. I wanted to retort back that she was a self-absorbed jerk, but I had a feeling he knew that now. "Well, I guess you live and learn. If remembering your coffee order is important, you should put that on your dating profile as non-negotiable."

My joke didn't land as he scowled at me. He traced the mouth of his to-go cup with his finger. "I don't need a dating profile."

I giggled. "You're right. I forgot you're mega famous. You could crook your finger and get any woman you want."

"Not any." He perked his brow.

I mimicked his expression. "You're right again. You'd have a hard time with some married women. Save the heartbreak and go for singles only."

"I'm having a hard time with a five-foot-tall blonde doctor with a dog that's twice her size."

"They are a nuisance around these parts."

Evade, evade, evade. I wanted to believe him, but we've done this song and dance before. He may want me to be his, but he didn't want to be mine.

"Are you Rhys Goodman?"

I didn't hear her approach. The rain hitting the awning we were sitting under was loud enough to conceal her heels tapping against the pavement.

She was pretty. Red hair was pulled back in a long ponytail, curled into soft waves. Her bright green eyes were striking as was her smile. She reminded me of Lydia. Leaning closer to our table, she placed herself between me and Rhys. Her back was turned towards me.

"I am." He didn't seem annoyed to be interrupted. I'm sure this happened to him all the time.

"Oh my god! I thought that was you. I'm so excited that you are finally in Seattle. I've been following your career for years. I'm Hailey."

I couldn't see Rhys's whole face. Hailey was blocking my view. Only the edge of his cheek and jaw were visible to know he was smiling at her. She was tall, beautiful, outgoing… exactly his type.

"Thank you, I love meeting a fan."

"Oh, I'm more than a fan. What are your thoughts on your upcoming game in Tampa? I know we beat them a few weeks ago. Are you nervous about the crowd turning on you?"

"I think they'll be some upset fans, sure. But I am trying to have breakfast with a friend now."

Hailey glanced back at me and gave me a quick smile. "Perfect, she can take our picture." She shoved her phone into my hand.

Her arm looped around his shoulder and right before I took the picture she kissed his cheek. Rhys scowled at her but didn't say anything. She snatched the phone from my hand and turned back to Rhys. Her hip bumped my elbow, and her long hair swatted my face. I closed my eyes and took a deep breath.

This was why I couldn't be with him.

"I heard you are planning on buying a house on the water. I'm a real estate agent and have some properties that I think you'd love."

"I'm not looking during the season and like I said, I'm having breakfast."

"Right of course, let me grab an autograph, real quick." She turned around and pulled my unused napkin from the table, letting my silverware clatter onto the metal tabletop. She passed it to him with a pen. Rhys's jaw clenched and temple bounced, but he smiled at her and signed the napkin.

"I have something for you, too." She giggled and pulled out a business card.

"I'm available whenever for whatever."

Her hair swished against my cheek as she left. Trudy grumbled with a sigh as he readjusted himself at my feet.

"Sorry about that," Rhys whispered.

An amused smile ticked my cheek even though I was annoyed. "Comes with the territory."

The waiter appeared a moment later with our breakfast sandwiches. After Hailey my appetite was nonexistent.

I ate a few bites and set it down. Both Rhys and Trudy were eyeing my food. Rhys had finished his sandwich quickly. I pushed the plate away. "You can have the rest."

He shook his head. "Surely that's not all you're going to eat."

"Lost my appetite."

He closed his eyes and shook his head. "I'll ask for a to-go box." He got up and went to the order counter. Hailey approached him again. She squeezed his bicep and flirted. He gave her easy smiles and posed for another picture.

Rolling my eyes, I watched as my stomach soured. She probably saw that her eyes were closed in the picture I took of them, and her head was tipped back in an unflattering angle giving her a double chin.

Pulling out my rain slicker, I got Trudy into his. It always made me giggle seeing him dressed in a raincoat. He gave me unamused glares but never tried to shake it off.

Rhys packed up the sandwich and put it in the bag before grabbing Trudy's leash. "Ready?" He flipped his hood up from his athletic jacket and pointed towards the patio's exit.

Hailey waved and blew a kiss from her car. I rolled my eyes and took the lead towards the trail.

The sound of the rain hitting the hood of my slicker was loud in my ears. It drowned out a lot of thoughts and made small talk nearly impossible.

Twenty minutes into the walk back and the rain let up enough for me to hear the wet trail twist under foot.

"I'm sorry about earlier," Rhys said.

A shrug dropped my shoulders dramatically. "It is what it is."

He sighed heavily. "I feel like shit though."

I shrugged again. "The days where I put your emotional wellbeing above mine are gone, Rhys. You feel bad, make different decisions."

He groaned. "I don't know what I could have done differently though, but you're still pissed off."

A humorless laugh vibrated my throat. "If roles were reversed, would you be mad?"

He shook his head. "No, I'd understand what being friends with a celebrity would entail."

I snorted. "Bullshit. I'm not mad that you're a celebrity. I'm not mad she approached you. I'm not even mad that you posed for two pictures and let her kiss and grope you. That comes with the territory when you refuse to put up boundaries with fans. But if you are telling me you'd *understand* if a man came up to me, pushed you out of the way, smacked you in the face twice, and acted like you were only there to take their picture, you'd be fine with that. Bull. Shit."

Rhys blinked at me. "I've never heard you curse before."

Huffing an annoyed breath, I stormed forward.

"I didn't see her doing that. I'm sorry. I'll do better next time, I promise."

I didn't respond. There was no point. I doubted he would do better next time. I'd have to make a point that either 'next time' didn't happen or if it did, I was mentally ready.

"What other errands do you have to run?"

"I'm taking your mom grocery shopping. I have laundry. When I get home, I'll need to mop the floors. I know we'll track mud in, and Trudy will get water everywhere when he shakes off the little rain still coating him."

"What about dinner plans?"

My eyes rolled, but I didn't voice my response.

"Would you have dinner with me? I want to make a re-do from breakfast."

I shook my head. "That's a bad idea, Rhys."

He groaned. "Why? I promise what happened back there won't happen again. I want to take you to dinner to apologize."

Concentrating on the trail, I refused to look at him. "You've said the words. Food isn't going to make them any more sincere."

He huffed but didn't add anything else.

By the time we got home I was starving and mentally exhausted. Rhys stood at the front door as I pulled Trudy's slicker off and wiped his muddy paws with the towel. He shook his huge body while on the front stoop before he bounded into the office. I kept my eyes down as I dried my legs and slipped my shoes off before going into my home. Rhys didn't follow me in which I was grateful. I needed a minute to myself.

Chapter 15

Tama

"Thank you so much for going to his game with me. Tom gets too into it, and I wanted someone not crazy to sit with." Rita led the way to our prime seats for Rhys's game.

She had asked me while we were grocery shopping and practically begged. Her reasons ranged from: Tom's fanatic ways; Tom's difficulty driving at night and how the game would be over after sunset; her love of ballpark hotdogs; and my personal favorite 'it's drone night, you know I love those.' In all the time I had known Rita she had never once mentioned her love of drones. I was positive she didn't know what one was.

I hadn't been to a baseball game in years. The sun was peeking through the clouds, warming up a cooler day. Our seats were great, sitting right behind the dugout. We were close enough to hear the banter. Rhys beamed at me when he saw me sitting next to Rita. I was still feeling uneasy after the interaction with Hailey so his happiness to see me made me feel a little jaded.

Rita had taken her knitting out. She was a big baseball fan, but she got too anxious during important games, so she told me she brought something to distract her. I helped her when she got stuck and chatted about ballpark food. As soon as Rhys went at bat Tom went crazy. I had never seen him so verbose. If it wasn't so jarring, I'd have thought it was funny.

Rhys hit a double. It changed the momentum of the game. It was exciting and I loved seeing him in his element. He high fived his teammates and celebrated the win when it was over. Rita led us to a suite for the family to hang out after the game while we waited for Rhys to shower and have his post-game interviews.

"The wives separate themselves from the girlfriends. If you don't have a ring the wives won't waste time getting to know you," Rita whispered. "We've only been up here a handful of times, but we were welcomed nicely considering we are permanently in Rhys's life."

I snorted. "Makes sense to me."

She grinned and introduced me to a woman with two kids at her feet. "This is Julia Newman, she's married to Colin Newman, the catcher. Julia, this is Tama Bulris, she's been a friend of Rhys for years," Rita introduced me.

Julia's eyes widened. "Not Dr. Tama Bulris? As in the author of 'Science of Heartbreak'?"

My cheeks flushed. "Guilty."

Julia reached over and hugged me. "I love your book. It helped me with some personal struggles. It was nice to be able to relate to so many people and not feel so alone as I dealt with my own loss. I loved understanding what was happening in my body. It made so many things make sense and the guilt of not being able to pull myself up by the bootstraps lessened dramatically."

I gave her a soft smile. This was a common thing shared with me. It was part of the reason for my book's success. "I'm so happy you found something positive from my research. It was why I shared it with the world."

"How long have you been friends with Rhys?"

I blew out a breath. "The better part of ten years."

"That's incredible you've maintained a friendship with an athlete like him that long."

My genuine smile flattened at the comment. A heavy arm wrapped around my shoulder as Rhys kissed my temple. His fresh cologne smelled incredible.

"I'm so glad you came today," he whispered against my neck. His nose glided up as he kissed my face again.

"Hey Julia, you met my girl?"

Her head tilted as she looked between the two of us and squinted. "I did, she mentioned you two have been friends for about a decade."

He chuckled. "Met her in college. We hit it off in the biology lab as partners. Became instant best friends. The past few years we couldn't see each other, but living here now means I get my best friend back."

Julia's brow furrowed as if she were thinking. Then her shoulders dropped, and she looked at me with sympathy. I chewed onto my cheek, knowing that if she read my book then she just figured out my heartbreak story. She cleared her throat. "That's so wonderful."

Turning to me, she rubbed my arm. "I hope I see more of you."

I didn't mind sympathy, but I hated pity. Julia pitied me and my unrequited affections in college. I forced a smile.

"Let's get some dinner before it gets too late." Rita tugged on Tom's elbow. He was busy talking to Greg Tompkins, the shortstop.

"Who drove?"

I raised my hand. Rhys frowned. "I was hoping you'd ride with me but thank you for driving my parents."

Rita gave directions to the restaurant that they liked to go to post games. We got there about ten minutes before he did. The restaurant was busy, so we expected to wait, at least until Rhys came in and we were whisked towards a table. Heads turned in his direction as we walked through the dining room. A few women scrambled to their feet and followed us.

"Oh my God! Rhys Goodman, I loved your Calvin Klein ad," some brunette crooned as she stepped between Rita and Rhys.

He scowled at the woman and turned to his mom. "Are you okay?"

Rita nodded and stepped to the side as Rhys lightly gripped his mom's elbow and adjusted her in front of the woman. "I'm having dinner with my family. I appreciate the support, but time with my family is important to me. If you leave your information with the hostess, I'll make sure you get an autograph."

The pit in my stomach soured as I listened to him ask the server to keep fans away and to let the hostess know about her possibly collecting fan's information. He passed the kid a hundred-dollar bill. When Rhys excused himself to wash his hands, I smiled brightly at Rita and Tom.

"That's great how he handled the fan earlier."

Rita flapped her hand dismissively. "He's been doing that since he was drafted. I don't mind going out with him. I know he won't put up with anyone disrupting our time together."

So, he's always known.

My chin quivered as I turned to Rita and Tom. "I'm so sorry to do this, but I have a headache. Are you okay to ride with Rhys?"

Tom sighed and gave me a knowing nod. Of the two he knew the most about the details on how Rhys had treated me. He was easy to talk to, like his son. He had asked most of the questions in a delicate way that made me want to spill my guts.

Rita frowned. "I have some medicine. Maybe you're dehydrated." She started rifling through her purse.

I stood up. "It's fine. Trudy will be missing me anyway. I'll see you tomorrow."

My exit was hasty, desperate to leave before Rhys made his way back to the table. I saw out of the corner of my eye he had been stopped at the bar by a beautiful woman. I ducked my head to be out of view and headed to my car.

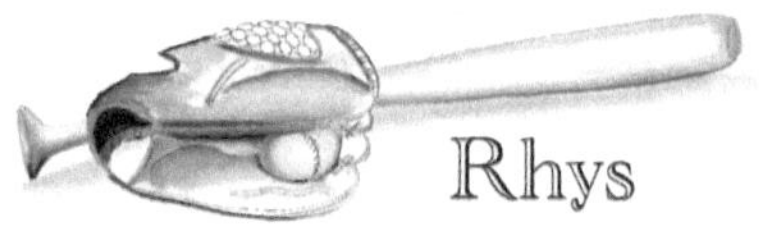

Rhys

I pocketed the phone number of the woman from the bar. I had no intention of calling her, but it was a dick move to toss the paper in front of her. My mom's brow was furrowed as my dad hissed at her. Tama wasn't at the table. My eyes darted around as I pulled my seat out.

"Sorry, that took longer than I had planned. I got stopped on my way back. Tama in the bathroom?"

My parents looked at each other as my dad cleared his throat. "She had a headache. She went home. You're okay to drive us after dinner, right? If not, I can call a cab."

My brow furrowed. "Of course I can take you home. What do you mean she had a headache and went home? She seemed fine when we got here."

My stomach twisted as my heart pounded. I couldn't put my finger on what I was feeling. It was like the echo of disappointment I had felt on my wedding day when she wasn't there. Obviously, the pain wasn't nearly as debilitating, but it was there. There was the same confusion I experienced after my first MLB game, and she left. I doubted she had a headache. That was her go-to excuse when she was feeling upset. I had no fucking clue what I had done.

I made a point to reject all fan interactions around her. I shut down the woman who was rude to my mom. I showed her that I had boundaries, and she still left.

"I think she was dehydrated," my mom said. She was worrying her lip. The waiter came and dropped off our drink order.

"Did I do something wrong?"

My mom shook her head. Dad winced and took a sip of his whiskey.

"What did I do?"

He blew out a breath as the server came back to tell us the specials. My mom spoke before I could, giving him her order which made my hope to leave as soon as possible moot. There was no way I was going to deprive my mom of her favorite restaurant.

Dad avoided my gaze as he fidgeted with his glass and napkin.

"What did I do?"

He winced as my tone lilted towards begging.

"You didn't do anything wrong. You handled those fans exactly how you always have around us, but I think that was the problem."

"How?"

My dad leaned forward. "You showed her that you've always known what to do, you chose not to around her."

His words hit like a sucker punch. He was right. I had no idea how he knew, but he was right.

"You've never seen me out with Tama before. How would you know?"

He nodded to the server who was setting down the basket of bread. He buttered a piece for my mom before snagging a slice for himself. "I've heard from more than one person how you've treated her in the past. It's why I don't think it's in her best interest for you to pursue anything with her."

I blanched. "What about what I want?"

"It's only *ever* been about what you want, son. I understand that maybe I was given skewed and biased points of view, but Henry and Griffin both shared similar examples, different instances. I would be thrilled to welcome Tama into the family officially, but not at the cost of her mental health."

Who the fuck is Griffin again?

My mom gripped my dad's forearm before turning towards me. "We can fix it. Tama is a woman that needs to see to believe. You showed her you are capable tonight, now you must prove to her that you can treat her right."

The endorphins from my win and seeing Tama cheer for me were long gone. I tried to enjoy dinner after my mom changed the subject, but everything felt off. My dad's words were haunting me. He had always been my biggest fan but, in this instance, he wasn't on my side.

It had been three days since the restaurant, and Tama had been scarce. All my games had been at home, so I had more opportunities to try to talk to her. She was shutting me out.

My dad had created a gate linking the backyards like he had promised, so there was no longer the excuse to take Trudy over. She didn't answer the door when I knocked, and Trudy didn't bark which meant they were on a walk every single time I tried to see her. It was frustrating. How was I supposed to apologize if she wouldn't talk to me?

I had three and a half more days before I headed to Cleveland and only five days to convince her to meet me in Tampa. I slumped my head against her front door as I waited for her to come home from her shift at the school.

She pulled into her driveway slowly. Before she got out of the car, she closed her eyes and took a few deep breaths. I hated that she had to brace herself for interactions with me. As I stood up to greet her, she gave me a bright smile.

"You played great last night. I thought your dad was going to blow his voice box out when you hit that homerun."

"Why are you avoiding me?"

She swallowed hard and unlocked her door. Trudy came bounding towards her, wiggling his butt as she scratched his head.

"I haven't been avoiding you. I think we keep missing each other."

I followed her into her kitchen and watched her make herself a sandwich. "Want one?" She pointed to the hoagie that had strips of her fried chicken, tomatoes and lettuce from my mom's garden, and her homemade aioli.

I scoffed. "Of course I do, that looks incredible."

She giggled and passed me the one she had made and made one for herself.

"See, I'm not avoiding you," she said with a soft smile.

I chewed through my bite and bit back a moan. Even her leftovers were good.

"You were, but that's okay. I'm not going to let you anymore. I'm taking you on a date tonight."

Her cheeks bulged at her bite. "No, you aren't. You have a game." Her words were muffled from the food as she tried to speak around it.

Fuck, I did.

I nodded vigorously and took another bite. "Fine not tonight, but I am." My words were just as muffled. I worked through the food and swallowed. "I'm taking you out on a proper date."

She shook her head.

I nodded back. "How can I prove to you that I'm boyfriend material if you won't let me date you?"

She blanched at me, dropping her sandwich to her plate. "What? Like a mock date where I critique you, right? A role reversal from college but this time it's you wanting a relationship."

I smirked at her. "No, like a real date. I want to be your boyfriend, but I need to prove to you that I can be."

She whimpered and looked at the ceiling. I set my plate down and walked over to her. I was close enough with her head tilted back that I loomed over her, looking down at her petite frame.

"I want you to be my girlfriend, but I need to prove to you I'm worth it. Let me take you on a proper date."

She blinked up at me, swallowing thickly. "When?" she croaked.

I leaned down and kissed the space between her lips and her cheek before trailing my lips across hers on the way to her ear. "Wednesday night after my game."

Goosebumps bloomed across her neck. I wanted to lick her, but I stepped back giving her some space.

She let out a shaky breath. "Okay."

My smile stretched across my face. "Okay." I grabbed my sandwich for another bite.

I was nervous as fuck when I showered after my afternoon game. I had less than two hours to shower, shave, drive across town, pick up Tama, and head to the restaurant for our reservations.

My mom had helped me plan the date. She reminded me to order flowers and picked up my suit from the dry cleaners. My dad was ignoring the fact I was going against his wishes and trying to date Tama.

Speaking of the devil, he was talking to Tama where the backyards merged. The gate he had created was large and motorized that slid against the existing fence. It made the opening around eight feet wide which was plenty large for Trudy to run and play. He was showing Tama the remote and how to activate the motor if she wanted to close the yards off. Trudy was running back and forth wagging his tail at the new large dog run.

Tama noticed me as I walked to her patio from the side gate. Her eyes widened on the flowers in my hand and the suit I was wearing. I opted to not wear a tie, if I wanted to be lightly choked all night, I'd ask Tama.

She looked beautiful in my favorite blue dress she used to wear during the warm spring and summer days while we lived in Boulder. Instead of Vans she was wearing strappy heels that made her calves look incredible.

My dad nodded as she walked over to me. I leaned forward and kissed her cheek before handing her the bouquet of tulips, peonies, gardenias, lilacs, and jasmines. It was an explosion of fragrances and color.

"There is a little card tucked in. It explains what each flower means." I followed her into her kitchen. She placed the bouquet in water. "You look beautiful. You always do in that dress."

Blush colored her cheeks before rolling her pink lips in and nodding towards the door. "Your dad is all set up for Trudy. I'm ready when you are."

My palm rested on the small of her back as I led her to my Rivian.

"This is quite different from the truck."

I grinned at her and helped her ease into her seat. "I still have it. It's being shipped here as we speak. I had to rent a garage to store my cars. I use this one because it's the most practical."

Tentatively sliding my hand to hold hers, I felt like a teenager busting moves and feeling nervous as shit that she was going to reject me. She laced our hands together and squeezed.

The drive to the restaurant was a fast thirty minutes as I made my way right to the water while fighting traffic. I paid for a valet and wove through the packed waiting area. The hostess' eyes lit up when she saw me, and I crossed my fingers she didn't flirt.

"We have the private dining room ready for you, Mr. Goodman." Her cheeks turned a ruddy color. She looked over to Tama. "If you'll follow me."

Excited whispers hummed as we walked through the dining room. A few people stood up, but I looked at the motion and shook my head. Most fans understood and respected the notion that I wasn't entertaining autographs. A few women attempted to approach, but we kept moving until we were closed in the private dining room.

Opening my wallet, I pulled out a few baseball cards that I had signed. I handed them to the hostess. "Can you give these to each of the fans that started to come towards us. Also, if anyone inquires if it was me, pass those out. I'd like to have an uninterrupted evening with my girlfriend."

The hostess' eyes went wide as she looked at Tama who was blushing wildly. She took the cards before closing the doors behind her.

Tama blew out a breath. "You know, just because I agreed to one date doesn't mean I'm your girlfriend."

I shrugged. "Yes, but I'm testing a theory that if I say you're my girlfriend the bunnies will back off a little."

She twisted her lips to the side. "As long as you know this," she waved her hand between us, "isn't some exclusive done deal. I'm still getting used to the idea of being your friend again."

"That's fair."

The noise from the restaurant heightened as the private dining room door swung open. Our waiter swaggered in. He had two waters in his hand. He gave us the opening spiel and described the chef's recommendations. I opted for us to have the tasting menu, knowing it would take a few hours. Anyone in the dining room when we arrived wouldn't be by the time we left. I'd be able to make a swift exit without being stopped.

I ordered a bottle of wine and watched the flush climb to her cheeks as she drank her glass.

"So inquiring minds want to know. Now that you have made it, is it everything you thought it would be?"

I chuckled and shrugged. "The money is. I was able to pay my parents' house off. Well, all but ten grand. My accountant said it would help them with tax write offs to still have a small mortgage. They were my reason for wanting to make it big. I wanted to pay them back, and I have."

She gave me a soft smile. "Anything that shocked you?"

"This is going to sound naïve, but it's hard work. It's not just showing up and playing. The workouts are grueling preseason. The season is so fucking long with very few off days. It's hard on my body. The celebrity aspect I expected, but people's team loyalty makes them forget that we are actual human beings. We didn't choose the team we were traded to, for the most part. We are working like anyone else collecting a paycheck. We go where we have been told to go. But fans turn their backs on you quickly."

She hummed with a nod.

"What's your favorite part?"

I grinned. "Getting paid to play a game. I'm lucky in the position I'm in. As long as I stay healthy, I have a long career in front of me. I signed a seven-year contract with five years of no trade option. I'll probably end my career here, which makes me happy. This is always where I planned on ending up."

She smiled brightly; her eyes crinkled in the corners. The waiter came back, poured Tama another glass and dropped off our first course of seven. "Okay, last question about your job. If you could talk to your younger self, what advice would you give?"

"Kiss you sooner."

She snorted and rolled her eyes. "I'm serious."

"So am I. If I kissed you sooner, I would have had more time to confront my feelings for you."

She looked down to her small plate. "Don't say that. Lamenting on the past will not change anything."

I sighed, chewing onto my cheek. "Okay. What about you? Same questions."

She tapped her chin. "Is being a doctor everything I thought it would be? No, I thought I'd have more patients and help people talk through their problems. The job at the high school gives me some insight on what I thought I'd be doing, but I loved the research study and writing my book.

"Anything that shocked me? Well, I pre-screened a lot of people to see who had the most relevant life experiences for my study, so I heard about a lot of kinks. I'm not judging, what gets you off, gets you off. Honestly most kinks come from some Freudian experience in early childhood. Doms or people into bondage had experiences where they felt powerless or used when they were younger. Same for some subs, but they are empowering themselves by choosing to be dominated, removing themselves as a victim. I think the most shocking thing would be scat play."

I choked on my sip of wine, tapping my chest as I tried to clear my throat. "Please don't tell me it's what it sounds like."

She grimaced. "It is and it's not sanitary."

My face twisted in disgust as she giggled.

"My favorite part is knowing my research and book have reached the targeted audience. There is a collective relief that comes from feeling recognized for something that made you feel isolated. Heartbreak and grief are common and how you react may seem weird or extreme, but it's not."

I gave her a soft smile. "I'm so sorry I wasn't able to support you through Yolanda's passing."

She swallowed hard. "And advice to my younger self?" She chewed on her bottom lip. "I'd encourage myself to create boundaries far sooner in life. For instance, my mom wouldn't let me leave our community until I was twenty. I let her make those decisions for me."

We sat and talked through all seven courses and a bottle of wine, which she drank the majority of since I drove. The soft lighting made her skin look silky in the candlelight.

I reached forward and stroked her cheek with my thumb. She closed her eyes at the contact.

"I want to kiss you," I admitted.

Her eyes were slow to open as her gaze bounced between my eyes to my lips.

The door to the private dining room opened again. Our server gave us a knowing smirk. "May I take your valet ticket to have your car ready?"

I handed it over as well as my credit card to settle our bill.

When everything was paid and ready I took Tama's hand and guided her through the still full restaurant. Patrons looked up from their seats, but we were moving too quickly for anyone to stop us. My SUV was cued up and waiting.

The drive home was full of, what I hoped, sexual tension. It had been a while for me since I had shared my bed with anyone. I didn't want to make assumptions, but I was hopeful. I parked on the street between her house and my parents. She waited for me to join her on the stoop.

My nerves ratcheted up as I took the last steps behind her. She glanced up to me with a nervous smile on her face and unlocked her front door.

"Trudy must be spending the night with your parents," she said when the horse-dog didn't greet us.

I remained on the stoop as she stood in her entryway, taking off her high heels and rolling her ankles around before she looked over her shoulder at me. "In or out Rhys."

I silently pumped my fist. "In."

"You want that tour?" Her shy smile was back.

God yes.

She opened the door to what would have been my parents' linen closet and turned the light on. I followed her down a set of stairs. The space was decent in size with a door that led out to the side of the house, under where her bedroom was. There were a few boxes, but it was mostly empty.

"This could be a home gym."

She snorted. "Rhys, the extent of my workouts consists of walking my dog. I have no use for a gym."

But I do.

I shrugged. "Maybe your future husband will want one."

She rolled her eyes and headed back up the stairs. I followed behind her, watching her sexy ass sway back and forth as she ascended to the main floor. The next door she entered was in the same spot as my parents' bedroom. I blew out a whistle. It was easily twice the size with a huge king bed, reading area, and spot to watch television.

She giggled. "I spent the most time on this wing of the house. There was structural damage from the moisture of the hoard. Since we had to replace major beams and the foundation, we expanded and added the basement. Here's the closet." She opened French doors into a dressing space the size of my childhood bedroom. Only half the hanging space was used.

"It looks like you're reserving that side for the right person."

She shrugged. "Maybe I still don't like shopping."

I followed her to the bathroom. "Now this is nice."

I wagged my brows at the two-person shower with a bench. The soaker tub was long and deep enough for me to rest after a hard game, and two vanities. Dark gray slate octagon tile covered the floor until the river stone shower floor. The shower wall looked classic with marble subway tile. There were built-in alcoves for her soaps with a tile mosaic along the back, a rain showerhead in the center of the ceiling and two massage bars on either side of the shower. The vanities had a midcentury vibe to them.

"I can't believe you did all this. Has my mom seen it? I've been trying to convince her to upgrade the house for ages. She always complains about how small her bathroom is."

Tama smirked at me. "She's seen it briefly. I love your mom, but we don't have spa days together and spend time in my bathroom gossiping like I used to do in college with my friends."

She rang her hands together before smoothing her palms down her dress. "So that's the addition." Her eyes met my gaze. Her plump bottom lip disappeared behind her teeth as she turned on her heel and walked back into her bedroom.

"I'm jealous," I admitted.

She chortled. "Of what?"

I grinned at her as she looked over to me from her shoulder. I approached her slowly and wrapped my arms around her waist. My nose trailed from her neck to her ear. She sucked in a slow, controlled breath, but goosebumps bloomed where I had touched.

"Of the two-person shower that looks like the perfect spot to fuck. Your gigantic bed that I would spend hours pounding you into the mattress. Take your pick."

A choppy breath stuttered from her lungs as she turned her face. She barely brushed her lips against mine, but it was enough of an invitation. I spun her around and kissed her mouth with all the pent-up desire I had been feeling since I laid eyes on her. My hands dropped from her waist to her ass as I pulled her to my height. She wrapped her legs around my hips as my fingers kneaded into her firm cheeks.

Gathering the skirt of her dress with my fingertips, I was rewarded with the warmth of her bare wet pussy. I groaned into her mouth before pulling away.

"I forgot you don't wear panties." I deepened the kiss as my fingers swirled around her clit. She gasped in my mouth, and that turned to a whimper when I adjusted my grip to tease her entrance.

"I want you so fucking bad." I pumped one finger into her impossibly tight channel. She nodded as her soft pants tickled my neck. I walked us over to her bed, kissing her neck and shoulder before setting her down.

Her eyes were lust drunk. I went back to kissing a trail from her neck to her chest, pulling her dress down her arms. I bit her nipple through the lace bra before working the straps of that down too. Her tits were as perfect as I remembered them to be. Full, natural, almost too big for her tiny frame, but perky all the same.

I pushed them together and buried my face between them. Her scent was concentrated and intoxicating.

"Are you motorboating me?" she giggled.

My head bobbed into her cleavage and bit the inside of her tit before looking back into her caramel eyes.

My hands worked down her torso and grabbed the hem of her dress. She raised her hands up and helped me rid the garment out of my way. With only her bra loosely wrapped around her waist she looked wanton and ready. I dipped my face down and licked a path from her belly button to her clit.

"I want to eat your needy little pussy. It's my favorite dessert, and then I'm going to fuck you until you're hoarse from screaming my name.

Her back arched as my lips surrounded her clit and sucked.

"Use your fingers too," she gasped.

Yes ma'am.

"You can do anything you want to my body if you think it'll bring me pleasure. As long as I get to do the same to you."

Fuck yes.

Pushing two fingers inside her, I crooked them forward, finding the rough skin of her g-spot. The keening whimper she let out made me know I was hitting it right. I lapped at her clit and pushed her belly down, creating the perfect angle and pressure.

"I'm so close." She let out a breathy mewl that made shivers run up my spine.

Perfect.

I stopped everything and kneeled in front of her. She propped herself on her elbows with a look of exasperation on her face.

I chuckled. "I need a towel."

She pointed to the bathroom. I rearranged my hard dick to relieve some of the pressure and tossed my suit jacket on the back of her reading chair. My button up shirt dropped from my shoulders as I checked the small linen cabinet next to the shower.

Tama had removed her bra but was still spread out on the bed.

"Lift your sexy ass up."

The towel was rolled in half to lift her hips. The other half was going to catch the mess I was going to make of her. I settled back on my bare stomach and flicked her clit with my tongue. My smile spread against her thigh as I watched her body shiver. I kissed her pussy sensually like it was her mouth before I worked my tongue back into a loud and messy lapping. My fingers resumed their tapping against her g-spot.

Her hands snaked into my hair as I pushed her lower stomach down. She was mumbling nonsense. I added my thumb to rub against her clit as I flicked it relentlessly with my tongue. Her back arched, and I sucked on her pussy.

Her loud moans were music to my ears as she squirted into my mouth and down my neck. Her thighs were bouncing against my shoulders as I licked her through the tremors. Her body slowly relaxed. I grinned up to her, thighs framing my view. Her head was still tipped back, tits rising and falling as she caught her breath.

I used some of the spare towel to wipe my face and chest. I tugged the wet fabric away and tossed it on the floor. Tama looked at me lazily before sitting up.

"Your turn."

A shiver ran up my spine at how she was looking at me. Her gaze roamed my chest and stomach. I was ripped in college, now I was fucking jacked.

She bit her lip. "Get naked and lie on the bed."

I scrambled to my feet like an overeager kid about to get his dick wet for the first time. I shoved my pants and boxer briefs down together. My dick slapped against my stomach. Tama moved off the bed and invited me to the spot she had occupied.

My breathing was choppy as I tried to calm down. I was on the fucking edge of cumming from hearing her cum. The fact that her taste still lingered on my lips was driving me crazy.

Tama came back into the bedroom holding a few things. "I want you to be open-minded."

I blinked at her as she held up a blindfold. I had played with sensory deprivation a few times. I didn't fuck with breath play, but I understood the appeal of not seeing during sex.

She crawled towards me, tits swaying as she straddled my hips. My cock twitched as she slid her wet pussy up my shaft while she placed the blindfold around my eyes. She adjusted my hands to over my head. My lips parted in shock as the cool metal of a handcuff clicked into place.

"Oh fuck." I swallowed hard trying to not think about who taught her this. Was this something she sought out on her own? I hated the idea of her with anyone else, but it would have been hypocritical in the highest degree for me to say a word. It's not like I spontaneously figured out the g-spot and how to make a girl squirt.

I should have expected the cuffs around my ankles, but I didn't. "You aren't going to leave me like this are you? This isn't some prank?"

She giggled. A cap opened. "No, I figured if you were tied up, you'd be less likely to tell me no."

"I'm telling you right now, if it involves you naked and me cumming, I vote yes."

She laughed again. "Good."

The bed shifted and then there was hot wet suction from her mouth on my cock.

"Fuck, yes," I hissed.

She licked me like I was an ice cream cone and poured warm liquid on my dick and slicked her hand up my shaft. My toes curled as lube dripped down my balls. Then her hands gently massaged them as her mouth surrounded my head.

This is heaven.

She gagged and eased back up my shaft. Her gag reflex had always been sensitive, but I loved the feeling of the back of her throat tightening before she pulled away. Her hand on my balls was massaging gently but starting to roam, rubbing slowly down my seam and beyond. My eyes popped as I squirmed when a slicked-up finger circled my hole. I was too shocked to protest as her little finger slipped in.

I'm not a prude, but I've never done anything like that before. I'd heard locker room talk and now I fucking understood why. Her mouth sucked hard along my shaft as her finger moved causing me to buck my hips.

Oh fuck.

I was gasping and grinding my head into the mattress as she started to massage my p-spot.

"Are you okay with this?" Tama asked after she popped off my dick.

I bit my lip hard. "As long as you're doing this to me, fuck yeah."

She giggled and pulled her finger away, leaving me on the edge. I resisted the urge to ask her where she was going. I could hear her. She opened a drawer. The sound of the cap open and close made me bite my lip. And then her hands were back on my cock. I jerked forward when she slid a condom down my length.

I didn't know what to expect next, so I gasped when her finger was back, except it was a little bigger, creating a little bit of a burn that wasn't there before.

"Relax, you'll like it," she promised me.

Then I understood it wasn't her finger in me as soft vibrations made my eyes roll back. My mouth gaped open when she slid her hot pussy down my shaft. She was so fucking tight, the sensations of what was going on were almost overwhelming as she started to ride me.

She leaned into me, teasing my open mouth with her nipples. I sucked on them hard as my hips jerked into her. The light vibrations were blowing my fucking brain as she started to fuck me hard.

My orgasm started rolling up from my fucking toes and my ears tingled. The pleasure raced down my spine, up my legs, and converged making my whole body convulse as I pulled against the restraints.

"Oh fuck, oh fuck." I grunted as my cum filled the condom. My shoulders and thighs were shaking as my dick twitched, emptying my balls.

She tightened and came around me, prolonging my orgasm as she gasped above me. Latent tremors ran through my body as the vibrations stopped. I jerked my body forward as she pulled the toy out. I couldn't catch my breath as a warm washcloth cleaned my balls and thighs before my ankles were released. I felt too spent to move as my wrists were uncuffed. I dropped my hands to my stomach, still too lazy to even remove the blindfold.

Tama did the honors and kissed both my eyelids. I pulled her to lay on top of me as I kissed her again. She giggled against my mouth and worked her body off the mattress.

"I'm going to take a quick shower."

"Wait for me." I sat up too quickly and gave myself a head rush.

She grinned at me. "Has your rebound time improved so much that you're ready to go again?"

I chuckled and swatted at her bare ass. "Give me fifteen and I'll be ready."

It took me eight minutes before I was about to push inside her while the rain showerhead covered us both in warm water.

"Condom," she hissed against my lips.

"I'm clean and tested."

"Condom," she repeated.

I nodded, not arguing that we used to fuck condom-free. Okay for like a week in our lives, but I understood then why she insisted after our road trip. I was traveling everywhere, bunnies available in every city, we weren't exclusive, and I couldn't always test in time for her arrival. Now I was exclusively hers. I knew she had an IUD. I felt the strings while finding her g-spot, so wanting a condom wasn't about birth control.

Don't go there.

She leaned out of the shower and snagged a nearly empty box from the vanity. I swallowed the annoyance down. Tama was naked and wet in front of me, and I was about to fuck her against the tile wall.

By the time we turned the water off my knees were weak and my dick was happy. Her comb slid easily through her short hair, and she rubbed the access water away before slipping a band t-shirt on. Pulling back the covers, she snuggled against her pillows.

"Am I spending the night?"

"Your choice."

I grinned and grabbed my boxers from the floor, slipping them on before joining her in her bed. Her mattress was a million times better than mine. I reached for her like I used to and snuggled into her.

"I want to be clear about something," she said after a moment.

I kissed the back of her neck. "What's that?"

She let out a slow exhale. "We aren't in an exclusive relationship."

My body tightened.

Don't think about the nearly empty condom box and who she used the rest with.

"You still have a month of regular season and travel ahead of you. I'm not going to stand in the way if you find your future wife."

What the fuck? She's my future wife. I knew when I met her that she could be my wife. I ran from it and ignored it, but I knew.

I swallowed past the lump in my throat, refusing to say those words until I had proven myself to her. She'd never believe I could go a season without fucking around unless I went a season without fucking around.

"And so we are clear," I started. Her body became rigid. "I haven't slept with a single woman in over a year. I'm serious about wanting a real relationship. I'll spend however long you need until you see me as a person *you* can trust to be with."

Chapter 16

Tama

I peered over to Rhys while he slept. He still had that innocence about him while sleeping despite the stronger jaw and stubble that seemed to constantly adorn his face. The covers were pooled around his hips; his body turned to me. I was able to look at him uninterrupted, noticing all the things that had changed about him.

He was more muscular, thicker pecs and a more defined six pack, no doubt a side effect of having professional trainers at his disposal. His chest hair had also gotten thicker. It no longer was a sparse patch in the center of his chest and down his happy trail. Now it was evenly dispersed across those thick pecs, making him look impossibly masculine.

The biggest difference in his physique was the cluster of stars tattooed on the inside of his arm. He also had a tattoo over his chest on the left side that looked like a series of numbers and the words 'I knew'. I wanted to ask him what the heck his tattoo meant, but I wasn't sure if knowing would hurt me. God forbid it was a tattooed homage to Krista before she showed her true colors. The tattoo looked a few years old, so it was possible.

Trudy barked on the back patio. I grabbed my phone and unlocked the door. His heavy paws thumped on the hardwoods as he walked through the house shortly after the door beeped letting me know he was inside. My door rattled for a moment before it swung open. Trudy proudly sauntered in, stretching his legs in front of him in a yawn before walking over to my side of the bed. His head rested next to my arm. I turned my body to pet his velvety ears. He gave me the eyes that said, 'I'm hungry if you ignore me, I'll hit the buttons.'

I rolled slowly out of bed to not disturb Rhys. I brushed my teeth and slipped a robe on. My eyes closed at the reality that Rhys, of all people, was in my bed. After several rounds of mind-blowing sex, he wanted to spend the night. He wanted to prolong his time with me.

He told me he wanted me to be his girlfriend.

My stomach clenched at the thought. I wasn't ready to trust him like that again. Yes, our date was amazing, but it wasn't a real expectation for him to shelter me in a private room, so I didn't get pushed aside by the bunnies every time we went out. That wasn't my issue anyway. It had always been about not noticing or caring enough to notice how the women he was flirting with treated me.

He was a relentless flirt. It was embedded in his DNA to be charming. I had known him way too long to know that the way he speaks to women couldn't change overnight. He probably didn't even realize he was doing it. His charming smile, his body language where he leans forward, his inability to say no.

I could tell he was uncomfortable with Hailey hanging on him and kissing him, but he didn't say anything to her to tell her to stop or to create space between them. If the roles had been reversed the woman could have filed sexual assault charges, but because it was a woman doing it to a man, it was fine. I needed him to show me that he wouldn't put up with others disrespecting me. And then show me repeatedly.

But in order to do that he deserved a chance to prove he could. We needed to figure that out soon. My heart was falling into old patterns. Already craving the next time he slept next to me. That was a very dangerous, slippery slope if I wasn't careful.

Bending over to place Trudy's full bowl on the floor, he chased my hands with his snout. Rhys was off before he flew to Cleveland. Without a doubt he was waiting for me to say yes to meeting him in Tampa.

In all the years that he had lived in Tampa I only visited him once, his first game in the MLB. The same night he met Krista. I was worried about going back to the scene of the crime.

She was so awful to me and the other women in the bathroom encouraged her nastiness. I didn't want to go and be disappointed again, but I knew it would be a good test for both of us.

Trudy nosed his way over to the patio door, where I let him out. I had a feeling he was heading back over to Tom. It was confirmed when I saw a tennis ball fly to my side of the yard followed behind by my lumbering dog.

Rhys's arms wrapped around my waist as he pulled me into his chest. He kissed my shoulder and neck before turning me around. His blue eyes were hooded as he cupped my face to kiss my lips. I bit back a moan as he lifted me up and placed me on the counter. His tongue wrapped around mine as he stepped between my thighs. His boxers weren't containing his erection. The tented material rested on my bare thighs.

I wrapped my legs around his hips as he ground against me. "Reminds me of when we first started fooling around," he murmured against my lips. He tugged the tie of my robe loose. I wagged my brows as my thumbs pulled the waistband of his boxers down enough to free his leaking head and a part of his shaft.

My fingers slid up and down his length before grasping him in a firm grip. He grunted in my mouth as I slowly started to jerk him off. His hands moved from my hips to my knees and glided back up my thighs, past the hem of my Dumb Youths t-shirt that was the perfect amount of soft worn cotton.

His thumbs stroked me, spread my lower lips open, and pinched my clit. I moaned. His lips twitched into a smile.

Pulling my hips closer to his, he guided his head to slide up and down my clit, coating himself in my arousal.

"I want to fuck you like this."

"Get a condom," I murmured against his mouth.

He pulled his hips back, eyes lasered onto where we were almost connected. I could hardly see the blue of his eyes his pupils were so blown. He leaned back into me, kissing me hard. I slapped my hand on the counter, searching for my purse without stopping the dizzying way his tongue made me shiver with need.

Snagging the strap, I tugged it towards me. My hands rifled into the zipper pocket. I grinned when I tore the foil packet open. He growled in my mouth when I grabbed his dick to slow the way he was rutting his cock against me.

I broke the connection to glide the condom on. His tongue swiped his bottom lip as he watched me sheath his throbbing dick.

He gripped my hips, hands wrapping around to my butt as he pulled me onto him while pushing into me. I bit my lip to keep my moans down. If I made too much noise Trudy would come and investigate. I knew from experience from the last time Griffin visited he thought my moans meant I was hurt.

Trudy busted into my bedroom and pounced on Griffin while he was midthrust. Fortunately, he laughed it off and calmed my dog down before Trudy did any damage.

"I fucking love you like this." Rhys pushed my shirt up over my breasts. He rolled my nipples between his fingers before bending his head and sucking one into his mouth.

It made me clench around him.

"Fuck, baby, you're going to make me cum if you keep doing that."

I clenched harder as he rutted. His lips were parted as he panted against my chest. His warm breath made my wet nipples pucker into painful peaks. My eyes rolled back as he relentlessly hit the spot inside me that made my toes curl. I put my hand over my mouth and bit into my palm to keep myself from screaming. I was completely lost in him as he reached his climax. He thickened and pulsed into me as my orgasm slammed around him, prolonging the experience for both of us.

Rhys rested his head in the center of my chest as we caught our breath. The patio door beeped open, and I pushed Rhys to get off me. I righted my shirt and retied my robe as he pulled his boxers up. I hopped off the counter and dove for the fridge as Tom walked into my kitchen.

"Oh, sorry guys. Trudy was thirsty." He looked over to Rhys who was leaning casually over the counter hiding the slowly deflating tent in his boxers, still bare chested. "Didn't hear you come home last night, I guess I know why."

Rhys hummed.

"Would you like some coffee?" I checked the tie of my robe nervously. It was a little mortifying to have Rhys's dad practically catch us having sex while his son hung out in only his underwear.

"Yeah, that'd be nice. We are out next door."

I made a mental note to remind Rita next time we go to the store together. I poured him a mug and added a dash of milk and teaspoon of sugar before passing it off to him. He slurped loudly and looked between me and his son.

Awkwardness descended. I turned around and busied myself making Rhys his coffee, knowing they were having a silent conversation. I added half and half with a pinch of cinnamon for Rhys. The stare off was still going on behind my back.

"Trudy seems to love the gate. Thanks for playing fetch with him."

Tom nodded with a smile. "I love that dog. He helped me for an hour last night in the garage."

I grinned against my mug before taking a sip of plain black coffee. "He loves working, so if you need to borrow him, don't be shy." I turned back to the fridge. "I'm going to make some breakfast, any takers?"

I turned around to see a wide-eyed Rhys tipping his chin towards the patio.

Tom grunted. "I need to get back next door, but if you make those muffins…"

"I'll send some over with Rhys."

Rhys yawned and scratched his chest. He grinned at me when the patio door beeped again. "I don't know whether I love that you are so close with my dad that he feels comfortable letting himself inside or horrified he almost saw us fucking."

I groaned and cupped my cheeks. "Do I have sex hair?"

He chuckled. "No, baby, you look fine."

I shivered at the pet name. "What are we doing today?" Rhys asked.

"I have zero plans."

A predatory smile ticked Rhys's cheeks as he stalked towards me. "If that's the case then I can think of a thing or two to keep you occupied."

I laughed when he pounced on me, causing Trudy to give him a warning bark and walk towards me, nosing his snout between our stomachs.

"I'm not going to hurt your mom," Rhys promised. "I'm trying to convince her to fly to Tampa with me."

"About that." I bit my lip.

Rhys winced, closing one eye. "Can you at least let me give you another elevator pitch before you make your final decision?"

I wrinkled my nose. "You assume I'm telling you no."

He shrugged. "Don't want to get my hopes up."

I sighed. "I guess that's smart, but I was going to tell you that I am willing to go."

He pulled me into his arms again before I could finish my sentence. He kissed anywhere he could reach. When he set me down, I pushed him away so I could look into his eyes.

"This doesn't mean we are an exclusive couple. I am not your girlfriend. Tell the bunnies what you want if it makes you feel like they won't sexually assault you if you are attached."

He snorted. "They don't…" He looked off into space. "Oh fuck, I guess they do, huh?"

"Point remains. This," I waved my hand between us, "isn't official."

He hummed while narrowing his eyes to me. "How do I make it official?"

I tilted my head. "Give it time."

He groaned like a pestilent child. "Fine. I'm going to get rid of the condom and then help you make breakfast."

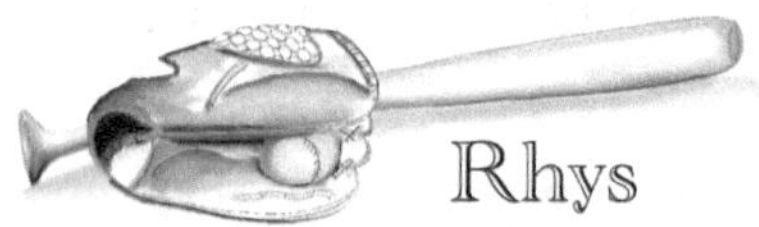

Rhys

I swiped through the pictures of Tama on my phone that I had taken over the past few weeks. She was so fucking beautiful no matter what she wore. I couldn't wait to see her in a few hours.

Nerves pricked my spine but excitement over sharing my Tampa home with her overshadowed all anxiety. I had wanted to show it to her since the moment I bought it, but I was already involved with Krista and didn't want to invite another woman to stay with me while I was dating her. Then living there alone for the past three years was a stark reminder during every sunset the one person that I wanted to appreciate the view with, never would.

"Who's that? She's hot as fuck." Kevin Hines, my teammate, craned his neck over to see my phone.

"Tama."

Kevin's eyes widened. He had known me since I was drafted. He was a second-round pick for Tampa the year before me. We were Biscuits together for a while. We moved up to AAA, and then he was traded to the Tacoma Rainiers when I was called up. He stalled a few extra years, making this his first official season.

"The fake wife that got away?"

I winced and swallowed. Yeah, he knew *all* about Tama. Out of habit, my thumb went to my right ring finger that held my rose gold band for so long. It still felt foreign to not wear it. "My best friend from college, yeah."

Kevin sighed. "You gonna seal the deal this time or get distracted by the first bunny that can form a sentence again?"

I cringed and tipped my head back. He may have been privy to my drunk ramblings before I met Krista about how Tama was going to be my wife someday, but first I needed to make it in our sport.

When I introduced him to my fiancée he immediately said, "Tama, right, I've heard so much about you." The rest of the conversation was awkward as fuck and caused a fight between me and Krista later.

I still couldn't tell you what the fuck I was thinking with proposing to Krista other than, 'I'm ready for a relationship, the girl I want isn't here, there's someone hot and capable, mine.' It was childish and stupid.

I was worried Tama would reject me again. Getting over her words after our road trip was tough, and they still haunted me. She still had a few years left of her PhD, and I'd never ask her to move for me especially since my job required me to travel six months of the year. Even though I had researched extensively PhD programs near me that accepted transfer students. I took it as another reason why my timing with her was never right. So, I proposed to the wrong woman.

"We are taking it slow, dating, but yeah if I have anything to say about it, I'm going to seal the deal."

There wasn't school or jobs holding us back. I had to prove myself trustworthy again, and I was willing to do the work. This trip was going to help.

"Slow is good, but didn't you string her along for years?"

I squinted. "No, we were not in a position to commit to each other."

He nodded and looked over my shoulder. "Well, if you are now, great. Just don't fuck around for another five years hoping to grow a pair of balls."

I rolled my eyes but didn't reply. The captain announced our initial descent.

We took the team bus to the hotel. The coaching staff was allowing me to stay in my house after I promised to meet in the hotel lobby every afternoon for the bus ride to the field.

I had a rental car waiting for me when we arrived. A few of my teammates wanted to come over to have a 'lowkey hang', but I knew what that meant. They wanted me to throw a rager with every bunny from my little black book to show up topless and ready for debauchery. Not only would that make Tama uncomfortable, but I wasn't interested in seeing plastic bunnies shoving their tits in everyone's faces while attempting to snag a professional athlete.

The rental car was borderline too small for my legs to fit. I made my way over to my house where Tama was due to arrive soon. I was happy as fuck to get there before her when I saw a few passed-out women floating in my pool and my old teammate sprawled ass naked on my lawn. I turned the sprinklers on watching Coleman jerk awake.

He stood up confused and then grinned when he saw me. Alister Coleman lived in the neighborhood, which is how he was able to get past the front gate security. He wouldn't party at his house. His younger sister had lived with him since she was a teen.

He walked towards me and went to give me a hug. I held up my hand to stop him. "I try not to hug naked dudes. What are you doing here, man? I told you I was selling the place and to stop throwing parties."

He chuckled and reached down to grab a pair of bathing suit bottoms. They appeared to be a woman's string bikini but at least his dick was covered. "I did. We've been keeping it in the pool area, don't worry your inside is pristine."

I growled. "No more fucking parties, and I need you and those two to leave right fucking now."

He chuckled and put up his hands in surrender. "No need to get testy. I'll clear out in like an hour."

I shook my head. "Don't have that much time. *Tama* is on her way."

Al's eyes widened as a huge shit-eating grin split across his face. "The Tama? Well fuck, why didn't you say so. I'll throw a party tonight to celebrate."

I gave him an unamused glare.

He chuckled. Nothing got to him, ever. "Fine, fine." He turned to the pool and let out an ear-splitting whistle. "Trixie, Cinnamon, time to go."

One blonde bleared her red rimmed eyes over to us. Al started clapping. When they didn't move, he grabbed the hose and sprayed them until they were scrambling to the edge of the pool, shrieking and squealing.

"You don't need to be such an asshole." One scowled and then noticed me. "Oh, hello there, I'm Cinni."

I held up my hand. "Get the fuck off my property before I call the police, *Cinni.*"

She turned on Al. "I thought you said this was your house."

He shrugged. "I lied, we gotta go though. This guy's woman is on her way here."

Cinni gave me what I figured were bedroom eyes. "Maybe your woman wants a threesome. Or maybe your woman should know the assholes you are friends with. Maybe I'll stay and let her know how many places I've left my cum around this patio."

My lip curled at Cinni. "Security will be here in five minutes." I strode into my house, locking the door for good measure.

Al tugged on Cinni's elbow to get her to leave. She crossed her arms and refused. Trixie appeared to be annoyed by the whole experience and left without any pomp and circumstance.

Al looked at me watching from the kitchen. He shrugged and walked out of the patio gate, leaving Cinni behind. She walked back over to the flamingo pool float and flopped back down. My phone was in my hand three seconds later, one minute after that security was carrying a screaming Cinni off my property.

As soon as the gates closed on my intruder, I went into action. It appeared Al was telling the truth as my house did look show perfect. It was my pool area that needed a hose down.

I snagged the two floats out of the water, popped them, and tossed them in the trash before taking the hose and blasting every surface that was even possible to fuck someone on. Then I grabbed a pack of shock that my pool guy left if I ever had a huge party and poured it into the water.

Sweat was gathering at the base of my spine as I finished up. I hadn't been away from Florida that long, but I somehow forgot about the unrelenting humidity and oppressive heat. A car door slammed on the driveway. Nerves coiled in my stomach as I poked my head around the gate to see Tama's wide eyes taking in the size of my house. I slipped back into my kitchen so I could let her in from the front door.

She bit back a grin as I held my arms out for her to run into. I picked her up and swung her around. It may have only been a few days, but I'd been waiting years to see her in my home. I kissed her hungrily as I pushed us into the house. Her chest heaved as she let out a sigh.

"It's so muggy outside. It's like basking in someone's hot breath. I don't understand how you lived here so long."

I chuckled. "I got paid a lot of money to put up with the weather. Where is your bag?"

She pointed behind herself back to the front steps of my house. I set her down and retrieved her luggage. She was looking around casually with her hands clasped behind her back.

I gave her the grand tour, leaving the pool for last in case she wanted to go swimming. I wanted the chemicals to have time to dissipate, and I didn't want to have to explain why I had shocked the pool in the first place. "You hungry?"

She stretched her arms overhead. "And tired, but food comes first and then maybe a nap."

I ordered Chinese food as we lounged on the couch. She snuggled against me and talked about her long flight and the turbulence over Kansas.

We ate our lunch while watching an old episode of a show we used to obsess over together. I kissed her head as she snuggled against my chest when she was done eating. "I'm going to take a quick nap, if that's okay."

She split off into one of the guest bedrooms. I paused, confused. She looked back to me when I hummed in question.

"What? Is there something wrong with your guest bedroom?"

I puffed my cheeks out. "Yeah, for one, I was going to nap with you. And I thought you were going to stay in my room after…"

Her cheeks went a beautiful shade of pink. "I didn't want to make assumptions," she whispered.

I walked up to her and cupped her cheeks. "Would it make you feel more comfortable to sleep in the guest bedroom?"

She chewed her lip. "I don't want to sleep where she did."

Oh, not what I was expecting.

"I got rid of all her things within an hour of the wedding, including the mattress. That's a nonissue, baby."

She still didn't look convinced.

"Let's do a comfort test, you sleep wherever you want, okay?"

She nodded tentatively. I followed her in the guest bedroom. She sat on the mattress and wiggled her ass before laying back. She swiped her arms up and down like she was making an angel and then her arms froze. Her face dropped into a horrified grimace as she pulled a condom wrapper from under the pillowcase.

I cringed. "That's not mine."

Her gaze flicked up to mine as she shot out of the bed.

"I told you my buddy has been throwing parties here, I guess the cleaners missed some trash."

She looked disgusted. "What if they've been using your bed too?"

I twisted my lips to the side. "That's a possibility. Let's change the bedding out. No big deal." I grabbed her hand and held tight, worried she was going to leave and led her into my bedroom. I deposited her to sit on my dresser as I stripped the sheets and replaced them with fresh ones. I settled into the bed first and motioned for her to join me. Her head rested on my chest. "Let's take a nap, baby."

"You weren't exaggerating. This sunset is exquisite."

Tama lounged next to me, staring at the horizon as the waves crashed below us. I looked at my beautiful friend as the golden light surrounded us. Overwhelming contentment filled my soul with Tama at my side. I clasped our hands together.

"What are we doing tonight?"

I gave her a confused look. "This, why?"

She hummed. "I figured you'd want to see your old friends or show your new team a good time."

I held back my shocked expression. "You expected me to go out tonight?"

She shrugged. "I'd be with you, obviously, but yeah. I figured your old team would have been clamoring all day to get you to come out."

They had, but I didn't want her to know that. I rubbed the back of my neck. "Is that what you want?"

I didn't want to subject her to any scene that was going to make her feel uncomfortable. The last time we had gone out to a club she had gotten so upset she left early. I'll be fucking damned to put her in the situation again.

"Sure, show me your town. What does Rhys Goodman do on his evenings off?"

It was a challenge and a curiosity all in one. I pulled out my phone and messaged a few old friends, knowing they'd be down to meet me. Al was the first to respond. Kevin was the second, he was confused and already chastising me for going out until I told him it was Tama's idea.

After a few minutes I looked up to her. "Okay, we can head out in two hours. I don't want to be out late. I do have a game tomorrow, but a few people are down to hang out."

"Perfect. I'll take a bath to relax beforehand." Her brow perked before she rose seductively from the lounge and bent down to kiss me sensually. "It would be a shame if you didn't join me."

Chapter 17

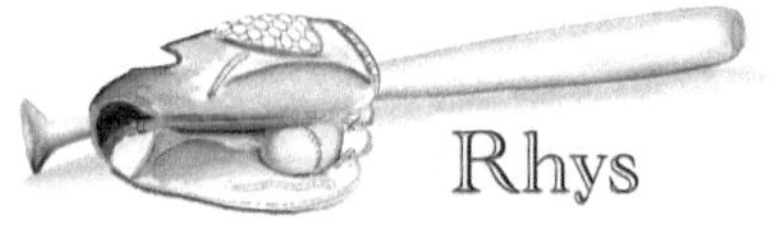

Rhys

My jaw flexed as Tama rubbed her ass all over my groin. We were in the middle of the dance floor of Al's favorite place to party. Kevin was sitting in the VIP section, a bunny on each knee. Al was making out with some girl. She was straddling him on the sofa, no doubt dry humping him.

We had been in the VIP section for an hour, bunnies and a combination of new teammates and old were hanging out.

The thing about baseball is most athletes know each other. Many were on each other's teams at one point in their life. Some competed all the way back to Little League, but you'd be surprised how many players personally knew their opponents.

I pulled Tama onto the dance floor after a woman kept sliding her hand up my leg while my buddies and I caught up on life. Tama didn't seem to notice that I kept swatting the random woman's hand away, but I didn't want to press my luck, so I tugged Tama away from the VIP section. Dancing with her was incredible.

My hands squeezed her hips as I yanked her harder into my growing erection. "You feel what you do to me?" I murmured into her ear.

She turned her face to mine and let me capture her lips before she smiled and went back to grinding on me. I kissed her neck. "We need to go soon, or I'll fuck you right in the middle of the dance floor."

She shivered against me before pulling her hips away. I gripped them and pulled her back. "Not yet, you're driving me wild, but I can't let you stop dancing on me yet. I've wanted you like this for so long, nothing is going to stop me from enjoying this a little longer."

Someone called my name before arms wrapped around my neck. I was pulled away from Tama quickly while a woman giggled in my ear.

"I can't believe you're here." Allison Coleman's arm squeezed hard and hugged me again. "Alister told me you were going to be in town, but I had no idea it meant tonight."

Allison was cool, smart, and pretty in the girl next door sort of way, but vulgar like a sailor.

"How the hell are you?"

She shrugged. "Same, Al is as protective as ever. Such a hypocrite. How do you like Seattle?"

"Amazing, I'm with my girl Tama. You'll love her." I turned around to introduce Tama to Allison, but my girl was nowhere to be found.

"Fuck!" I turned to Allison and winced. "Did you see the blonde woman I was dancing with?"

She shrugged. "I was too focused on you, why?"

"That was *the* Tama and the fact that she isn't right fucking next to me means she's pissed."

Allison cringed. "Oops. Do you want me to find her?"

My eyes squeezed shut until I saw static. "Check the bathroom for me, please."

My head swiveled on the dance floor as I looked for her. My heart was beating in my throat, worried as fuck that she saw Allison as someone trying to be disrespectful. I'd been so fucking careful all night and one fucking hug set her off. I should have fucking known. I should have immediately rebuffed anyone touching me. She didn't know who Allison was, and I knew how bad that hug looked. And there were two of them.

I flagged down a bouncer. "I'm looking for my friend. She's about five-foot, short blonde hair, little black dress."

"The one with you all night?"

Thank fuck I was famous enough to be noticeable. "Yes."

He spoke into his walkie. "She's waiting for a taxi."

"Fuck!" My fingers raked through my hair as I took off towards the exit. Pulling my phone out as I wove through the dance floor.

> *Me: It's not what it looks like.*
> *Come back inside*

Tama: I think you have the wrong
number.

> *Me: Please, Tama. That was*
> *my neighbor. She's the sister*
> *of Alister Coleman. I turned*
> *around to introduce you, but*
> *you were gone.*

Humid air smacked my face as I pushed past the exit door. Tama was next in line at the taxi stand, staring down at her phone. She shook her head and shoved her cell back into her dress. I reached out and grabbed her arm before she stepped forward to get into the next cab. She whipped around with a glare on her beautiful face.

"Ma'am are you okay?" some bro from the line asked. His eyes widened when he saw me.

"She's fine. My girlfriend forgot we valeted."

"Holy shit, can I get an autograph?"

I rolled my eyes. "Not right now, man." I tugged Tama away from the line and towards a quieter part of the sidewalk.

She pulled her arm away from me.

"You get my message?"

She shrugged. "Don't know, that text thread has been dead for three years. Hard to say."

My molars bit into my cheek as my throat knotted. I'd never seen her this mad before. The gravity of my situation made my heart drop. "Please baby, come back inside and meet Allison. She's not a bunny. She's not interested in me in the slightest."

"Don't call me that, and I'm ready to go. I'm surprised you noticed I wasn't near you. You seemed really into, what's her name, Allison?"

I blew out a breath slowly to calm my erratic heartbeat. "You have no reason to be jealous, Bully. I don't want her. I've never wanted her."

She rolled her eyes. "What did I tell you? I said it's not about jealousy or the approach; it's about how you handle people disrespecting me. She pulled you away from me with total disregard that I was there. I'm out. I'm done. You can call me a sensitive, jealous child, I don't care. Being in your orbit hurts, so I need to go."

Her eyes were a little glazed. I wasn't sure if it was because she was drunk or about to cry.

"Fuck". My jaw clenched and relaxed, making my temple bounce. She turned on her heel and stormed up the sidewalk. I followed her. "Please don't leave me again." I wasn't above begging her to stay. "Please."

Her shoulders dropped down as she shook her head.

"Let's go home. We can talk about it at home." I walked up to her, braided our fingers together, and tugged her to the valet stand. My phone was going off like crazy. I ignored it. This was way too important to deal with any distraction.

She was quiet the whole ride home while I rambled on about how sorry I was and who Allison is. She didn't respond. She had completely closed herself off.

"I get it, just stop," she finally said. "We aren't exclusive. I overreacted."

I swallowed the lump in my throat. "I'm fucking exclusive with you. It's not an overreaction if you feel hurt. Tell me how to fix it."

"I don't think you can." She turned to me as I closed the garage door. She gripped my hand in hers. Hope flared in my chest until I looked into her eyes. She was looking at the window, not me. "We are better off as friends, Rhys. I think you've always known that, too."

I shook my head. "No, I've always known you'd be my wife."

She squeezed her eyes shut. "Don't make this harder than it has to be."

"You can't break up with me."

She sighed patiently. "You're right I can't because we aren't together. While I believe that Allison is not someone competing

330

for your affection, I can't ignore how I felt back there. My reaction won't get better, and I don't want to make you choose."

"What's the fucking choice, because I'll pick you every single time."

Her chin quivered as she blinked rapidly at the tears that gathered. "You won't and that's okay." She opened the car door and walked swiftly into my home. My heart was in my throat, my body felt too heavy to move.

How did I ruin everything so quickly?

By the time I was able to make my way inside, Tama was wheeling her luggage into the living room.

"Please don't do this."

Her eyes were downcast.

"I'll do anything to prove to you I'm serious about us. I need to fix this, please let me fix it." Emotion clogged my throat as my voice cracked. "I can have Allison apologize. Fuck, I'll track down every fucking person that has ever been mean to you and make them say sorry. Please fucking stay." My chest heaved as my eyes welled up.

Fuck, I couldn't say the last time I cried.

I didn't shed a fucking tear for Krista, but this was breaking me.

I slipped to my knees and hugged her into me, burying my face into her chest. She was rigid in my arms for a moment before her fingers gently combed through my hair.

"I can't lose you again, please." My voice cracked again, my throat was too thick to clear.

"Don't make me regret this," she whispered.

My arms clung to her harder. I was not going to ever let her walk away from me again. Her heart pounded as I slowly moved up her body, kissing her stomach, shoulders, neck. I went to kiss her mouth, but she gave me her cheek.

Okay, that's okay.

She was still upset. I'd work my way up to kissing her again. She felt weightless as I carried her to my room. I turned the shower on and unzipped her dress.

"Rhys."

I shook my head. "Let me take care of you."

The desperation in my voice made her look into my eyes for the first time since we left the nightclub. I wanted to confess my feelings for her, that I loved her and was so madly in love with her, but it wasn't the right time for that. She'd see it as emotional manipulation and never believe that I was sincere.

"Please," I added softly.

She sucked in a deep breath. I leaned forward and kissed her cheek again, slipping the strap of her dress down. Kissing her shoulder, I watched goosebumps bloom as I worked her dress off her body.

She was letting out shaky breaths as I pulled her bra off next. Still in her sexy as fuck heels, I bit my lip as I kicked off my shoes and pants. My fingers were numb as I quickly worked the buttons, peeling my shirt off as quickly as I could. Tama was watching me, eyes zeroed in on my tattoos. I was waiting for her to ask, but she hadn't yet.

My fingers slipped into hers and I led her into my shower. I placed her directly into the water, knowing that if she got cold, she wouldn't tell me. I grabbed my soap and lathered it across her body. I wasn't going to do anything sexual. My dick didn't get that message, but I ignored him.

The shampoo lathered bubbles as I massaged her scalp. My own body got the quick treatment so I could get back to hers. I turned her around to face away from me. Seeing her bare body, wet and on display was wrecking my willpower. I kneaded my thumbs into her shoulders until she dropped her head forward.

332

My lips brushed the back of her neck as I turned the water off. I dried her body, squeezed the excess moisture from her hair and combed it out with the comb sitting on my vanity.

She watched me with a confused curiosity that I was too nervous to ask about. One of my t-shirts slipped over her head. She sniffed it and sighed.

I peeled back the covers and watched as she tentatively laid down. My chest painted against her spine. We'd talk more in the morning. It would be easier when emotions weren't as high, and she was sober. I wasn't going to lose hope because she didn't kiss me or initiate sex in the shower.

I held her tightly all night, refusing to let her go.

The ocean breeze felt nice compared to the unrelenting humidity that still hung in the air despite the sun just rising in the sky. The sunrise wasn't as impressive, though it was coming from the opposite direction of the water.

Rhys's house had a small path down to a beach. I had been sitting on the sand for an hour after I woke up and the sky was still dark. The sound of the waves was calming my brain. I was still upset about seeing Allison pull Rhys away from me. While in the sobriety of the day I can fully admit I overreacted, the fact that I had a viscerally painful reaction to it upset me more than the actual hug.

I had done exactly what I promised myself I wouldn't do. I'd let myself fall in love with him again. Pesky hope that I'd be enough had taken root. I knew it was pointless and would crush me when he realized I wasn't, but my stupid heart didn't listen to reason. Which meant my rational brain was going to have to work harder at removing romantic intent in all of Rhys's actions.

Yes, he said he wanted me to be his girlfriend, and yes, he'd been acting like that. But it was no different than calling me his wife so we could stay in a bed and breakfast in the middle of a small town. Everything felt exactly how it was in college. Him content with our friendship, me secretly longing for more. Despite acting like he was serious about the potential between the two of us, he'd never once hinted that he loved me.

What about what Kevin and Alister said?

I closed my eyes at the memory. Kevin was a little shorter than Rhys, nearly as handsome, but a little bulkier with muscle. He had that boy-next-door charm with brown curly hair and brown eyes nearly the same shade. His eyes lit up when he met me. He pulled me into a hug saying he was so happy to finally meet me.

"Rhys talked about you constantly when we were on the Biscuits together. I'm so happy for my friend to get his wife back."

The comment was jarring to my fuzzy, tipsy brain. He laughed at my confusion, cupping my ear like he had a secret to tell me. "He's so fucking in love with you, it's not even funny. Thank you for putting him out of his misery."

It was like I dreamed the words. He went to kiss my cheek, but Rhys was scowling at him and shook his head.

"No touch, Kev." Rhys had turned to me and asked me what he had said after Kevin sauntered off.

I shook my head. "I don't know. I don't think I heard him correctly."

Alister pulled me into a hug like we were old friends. He was taller than Rhys and had that rebellious vibe with his sleeve of tattoos that lined one arm. His smile was swoon worthy with dimples so deep my drunk brain told me to poke him right into one. Which I think I did.

"Fuck you're hot. Why the hell are you with Goodman again?"

I giggled and looked adoringly at Rhys who was talking to another former teammate. He winked at me before going back to his conversation.

"You're the one that got away, huh?" Alister said closely to my ear since it was so loud in the club.

I shrugged. "I didn't go anywhere."

He laughed and sighed. "Great, then maybe you'll let him catch you this time. He was one miserable motherfucker when you ghosted him."

His comment caused my stomach to twist. I closed one eye as my lip curled up. "He was getting married to someone else. And she hated me. I didn't ghost him. I was keeping the peace."

He threw his head back and laughed. "Your version is so much more innocent. I thought he was wrecked about Krista, but he didn't give a fuck when she started dating some basketball player two months after their wedding. I got him shit-canned one night while throwing a party at his house and he told me he was wrecked about you. I think we can agree on one thing. Our boy is a fucking idiot when it comes to you."

I laughed out loud, wanting to tell him he took the words from my mouth, but I kept it to laughter.

Both teammates knew all about me. That had to mean something, right?

He cried last night.

It was nothing compared to the way I had cried over him, but the tears that welled in his eyes were not fake. He was truly upset by the prospect of me leaving.

The way he took care of me.

Okay, yes, that was romantic and sweet too. He wasn't being nice to get laid. His erection dug into my butt for the better part of an hour after the shower, he never once pushed for more.

I stood up and walked against the shoreline, letting the cold water lick my toes. I was still only in his t-shirt but considering I'd noticed thong bikinis while enjoying the sunset, I was conservatively dressed.

What do I do about Rhys?

Slow it way down. We jumped way too quickly into our sexual relationship. We need to figure out how to be friends again. I need a little more space between us. His regular season still had a month to go. He'd still be traveling and it was looking more like his team was going to make the playoffs. Then he'd look for a house near the water, close enough to visit his parents, but too far away to pop in whenever he wanted. I needed to be strong and swallow my feelings for another month, maybe two. That'll be easy, I already had a decade of practice.

I turned back towards Rhys's house after another twenty minutes of walking. He was leaning against the railing, watching me. I ducked my head down and focused on the cold water again. By the time I had the courage to walk up the steps to his house he was no longer on the rail.

He smiled softly at me from the kitchen as I made my way past the pool and into the house.

"I ordered breakfast." He pointed to the paper bag on his counter. "Do you want to eat outside or in?"

"Outside, the heat isn't unbearable yet."

He chuckled and grabbed two mugs of coffee, tucking the bag of food under one arm, and led the way outside. "The heat does get pretty bad. It's hurricane season so the humidity is insufferable, but the weather is okay come November."

I snorted. "Yeah, sounds about right."

He passed me my sandwich and coffee before digging into his own food.

"About last night," he started.

I held up my hand. "I'm not ready to talk about that. I was drunk. I overreacted."

He licked his lips and blew out a breath. "I meant what I said. Allison is going to apologize to you today."

I closed my eyes at the sincerity and the embarrassment of a stranger apologizing to me for being sensitive. I shook my head. "That's not necessary."

"Yeah, it is. She didn't even see you, which is fucked up."

I twisted my lips to the side. "To be fair, I am small."

He snorted. "That's not an excuse. She feels awful about it."

I tried to focus on blowing the steam off my coffee.

We spent the rest of the morning making small talk. Which was fine by me. I wasn't ready to confront the bigger issue of why I overreacted. How it was a trauma response from years of perceived rejection from him and an echo of the night he met Krista.

I had already been on edge all night. I saw every single time someone touched him. He had swatted more than one hand away for my benefit. He had been so tense that I welcomed us moving to the dance floor in hopes that he'd relax. He had until I freaked out.

I went to his game as planned. I stayed away from the friends and family room after, opting to take a car back to his house. I had some writing to do, and he'd be a few more hours. I was getting into a writing groove when my phone went off.

Griffin: Honey, I'm coming home.

I grinned at the message. He was so weird.

Me: When should I expect you?

*Griffin: We are celebrating the end of
the tour now. Heading into the Red
Light District. My flight leaves tomorrow.
I can't figure out the time changes and
layovers. Hold on, let me ask Hawk.*

Hawk was his lead guitarist. His last name was Hawkins and since Griffin was named after a bird the label thought it would be cool to lean into that with all the members of the Dumb Youths. There was Griffin, the lead singer, Hawk on guitar, Phoenix on drums, and Talon on bass guitar. I had joined them on a tour the summer leading into my final year of my PhD program. They were good guys. All with severe Peter Pan Syndrome, but it worked for rock stars.

*Griffin: Gramma says tomorrow your
time around 4 I should be landing
in Seattle.*

That was thirty minutes after I landed from Tampa.

*Me: I'll already be at the airport.
I'll pick you up.*

338

Griffin: Who are you dropping off? Henry?

Henry had met Griffin a few times. He didn't particularly like Griffin. He was so protective of me. Especially after everything that happened with Rhys.

> *Me: No, landing from a trip to Tampa.*

Griffin: Why the fuck are you in the US's armpit? It's humid as fuck and there are alligators.

I giggled to myself.

> *Me: I'll tell you all about it when you land. See you tomorrow!*

The rumble of the garage vibrated through the wall. I sighed, knowing there was no way I could get back into my mental groove to write anything, and closed my laptop.

Rhys walked into the house, his head on a swivel, and walked right up to me. His smile stretched his lips as he leaned over to kiss me. I turned my face, still not ready to go there. His lips were my kryptonite. Always had been, always will be.

He kissed my cheek before dipping his mouth to my neck and kissing me there too. When he pulled away, he had a lustful look in his eyes as he stared at my lips. "Thank you for going to my game."

I smiled at him. "I had fun. It was hot, but the hotdogs were good, and my seat was in the shade."

His fingertip glided up the bridge of my nose. "Your freckles are coming out."

My cheeks flushed.

He hummed. "You're so fucking beautiful." He swung his body around and sat next to me, pulling my feet into his lap. "You get Allison's email?"

I shook my head. "I haven't checked my email today, so no."

His big hand circled my calf before he started to gently massage. "We aren't going out tonight, so don't even ask. I want a quiet evening with you. Did you eat?"

I shook my head again.

"I'll order us some food."

It was a nice, drama-free way to end my trip.

I was falling asleep while cradled against Rhys's chest when I remembered what he said about checking my email. Rhys was sound asleep behind me, breathing slow, deep breaths. I grabbed my phone and read through my email. I couldn't put my finger on how to feel at the end of her message.

Dear Tama,

I want to say I am so sorry for how I acted at the club. It was rude to assume that Rhys was dancing with someone insignificant. I didn't see you because I assumed it was some bunny like it has always been. When he told me it was you, I immediately understood my mistake. I feel terrible about it because I really understand how it feels.

My brother is a lady's man who is not afraid to sample everything offered to him. We are close, like way closer than most siblings because our parents aren't in the picture. He raised me from sixteen on. It was hard because I traveled with him from June to August when he was in AA and AAA. I was on my own a lot from March to June because I had school. Anyway, this is not a pity party, I'm trying to say we are close.

Ever since I have looked old enough to drink, I've been by his side after games. I cannot tell you how many cleat chasers have spilled drinks on me to get me to leave his side thinking I was some competition to get his attention. They are the worst combination of women; competitive, bitchy, lying, and pretty: pure sociopaths. Their one-track mind has made me feel unseen and insignificant on many occasions. To know that I evoked that with you makes me feel terrible, and I am so sorry.

I also wanted to say that I am a huge fan of your book. And if I ever get to meet you, I'd love you to sign my copy.

Once again, I am sorry. I hope you don't hold my actions against Rhys.

Allison Coleman

PS: Is Rhys your Jupiter?

Chapter 18

Tama

My eyes burned when I opened them from my nap. The flight had been long and my goodbye with Rhys was bittersweet. He tried to kiss me again and looked heartbroken when I rejected him. I wasn't ready for that.

I went into the bathroom and splashed water on my face. When my luggage made it around, Griffin had landed. I told him where I was parked, knowing that if I met him there would surely be photos of me posted on gossip sites. It happened a few times. The headlines were always '*Griffin DeMarco seen with Mystery Woman*' or some version of that. It was another reason why I didn't want my face plastered everywhere. People would make the connection to me, and I didn't want to deal with the added media attention for being someone's friend.

Griffin: I'll be at your car in five minutes.
I have two photogs following me.

342

I groaned and grabbed my hat and sunglasses and pulled them on. My car had eased out of the parking space when I saw him walking towards me. He wasn't joking about being followed. He dove into my backseat dramatically. I giggled to myself as I drove calmly through the parking deck to the exit.

He grinned at me and made his way up front. "You look good."

I perked my eyebrow. "I don't *feel* good."

He clicked his tongue. "Something to do with the reason why you were in Florida?"

I nodded.

"Tell me all about it."

"Rhys is back."

"Ah shit." He shook his head. "Rubbing his happy marriage in your face? Or let me guess she cheated on him, and he realized you're a fucking dime."

I blew out a breath. "Uh, the latter, sort of. She cheated on him at their wedding. He caught her before the ceremony. They never made it down the aisle. Anyway, he was traded to Seattle."

"Oh fuck. I take it he knows who you live next to."

"Yep. It's been a few weeks. He says he wants to be in a relationship with me, but…"

"He's played this tune before. Yeah, when we get home, I'm making you dinner and giving you a hug. Then we are getting drunk. I'll give you head all night long if you want."

I snorted. "I'll take everything but the head."

"Oh no, he took away your libido already? What a fuckface."

I whimpered. "Not exactly. It's still there, I'm banning myself from sex so I can think clearly."

He grunted. "Now I want to punch him for taking away my good time tonight."

I smacked his abs, hurting my hand in the process. He chuckled when I shook my fingers out and reached for them to give little kisses. "You're acting like you haven't had sex in weeks, not hours."

He held up one finger. "To be fair it's been almost a full twenty-four hours. I got pulled into a window."

I curled my lip at the idea of him sleeping with some prostitute for all the Red Light District to see.

He chuckled. "Calm down, I sat there and watched. It's a good story to tell, so I figured why not." He wagged his brows at me. "Now after the fact, a woman was waiting for me outside the window, and I went to her little apartment where she gave incredible head. Turns out she was born male, so it tracks that she understood the assignment. She was disappointed when I didn't reciprocate, but she'll get over it. It's not my thing."

I giggled.

"Anyway, after that blowjob, I was hungry, so I met Gramma for some pancakes. She says hi. Oh—" He paused and dug through the backpack he brought with him everywhere. It was beat up and worn, covered in patches from different cities. He pulled out a knitted gray dog. "She made that for Trudy."

I smiled at the gift. "Tell her I said thank you. Trudy will love it."

"Okay doc, start from the beginning. Why do you look like you're going through an existential crisis?"

I huffed. "Things were fine. I thought I could handle it. We slipped right to how things were, but this time he told me that he wants a relationship with me. And you know, fool me once shame on me, I've been resistant. He's had some interactions with fans that have left a foul taste in my mouth, and maybe I'm sensitive, but—"

"No, straight up, no. You aren't being sensitive. Not to toot my own horn, but I am internationally famous. I have shut it down any time someone has been rude to you."

I bit into my lip. He really had. He was like Henry in that regard. He'd make the person apologize to me right then and there. He'd check in on me to make sure I was mentally okay. It was exactly like Rhys did for his mother, but Griffin would do it for me.

"True, anyway, we slipped into old patterns pretty quickly."

"AKA fucking on every surface, got it."

I blushed. "And then there was this thing at a club. He didn't even want to go out. He knows, to an extent, how women around him have treated me for our whole friendship, so he didn't want to chance it. But I figured if he wants to be in a relationship with me then I need to see him in a situation with the most temptations and the highest probability for someone to be disrespectful to me to see what he would do."

"Fucker failed, obviously."

I groaned. "Not exactly. His neighbor came up and hugged him. We were dancing and she pulled him away. The smile on his face when he saw her killed me. I took off, not waiting to see what was going on."

"Yeah, good for you, Doc."

I whimpered. "It turned out to be innocent. She didn't see me. She wrote me an email apologizing. I overreacted, but I can't stop thinking about the next time when it's not his neighbor, and she doesn't apologize. I don't think I can handle that kind of rejection or uncertainty."

"Yeah, that sucks." He scratched his temple. "More fun for me though."

I smacked his stomach again.

He laughed. "Do you want advice, or do you want to vent?"

"I want to vent. I'm a psychologist, I know what I'm supposed to do. I want to feel my feelings."

He snorted. "Feel free to feel yourself all over me, Doc."

I groaned.

"What? You're my future wife if Reece's Pieces keeps fucking up. I gotta say, I'm liking my odds. Keep venting, Doc. Tell me all about how tiny his dick is, and how he can't satisfy you like I can."

I whimpered not wanting to admit they were comparable. "It's huge, and I'm not comparing the two of you. Comparison is the thief of joy."

He puffed out his cheeks. "That's fair. I don't need you telling me I'm the best you've ever had." He wagged his brows again. "Anyway, I'm craving brownies. I'll make you lemon chicken if you make me dessert."

"That's a deal."

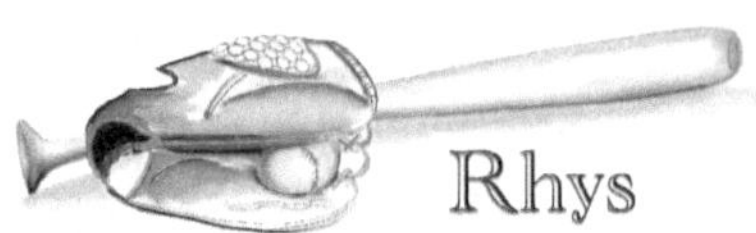

Rhys

Five days have come and gone since I said bye to Tama at the Tampa airport. She'd been distant, not giving me more than her cheek since the night club. I wasn't upset about it, I was worried. Ever since she landed, our conversations have been limited and awkward.

I tried Face Timing twice. She declined once saying she was with a friend and the other time she rushed me off the phone saying she was busy. I knew she was trying to write her outline of her new book, and she had shared with me that the teenagers at the high school had booked up all her timeslots. She had to complete her notes when she got home from school every day which took her a few hours.

I understood she was busy, but it didn't mean that I liked it. Our flight from Atlanta was delayed a few hours due to a tropical storm that had ripped through from the Carolinas. I was supposed to be home hours ago, now I was limping in at nearly dinner time, anxious and exhausted.

I shoved my luggage into the garage and went straight over to Tama's house, not stopping to see my parents. Trudy barked when I rang the doorbell. When the lock clicked, I went for the doorknob thinking Tama had remotely unlocked it, but then the door swung open.

My brows furrowed as a tall dude, built like a swimmer, long hair pulled up into a bun on the top of his head answered the door. He looked vaguely familiar. A charming grin spread across his face. He rubbed his bare stomach before sticking his hand out.

"We've never officially met, you're Rhys."

I wanted to swat his hand away, but I gripped it instead, applying a little more pressure than necessary. "And you are?"

"Griffin DeMarco. You don't remember me?"

That fucking name again. I squinted at him. Then it hit me. "The waiter from Maria Bella? You're a long way from Boulder."

He threw his head back and laughed. "I haven't been a fucking waiter in nine fucking years, but yeah, that's me."

I gritted my teeth when he opened the door to let me in.

"Come in, man. Tama's in the shower. She was feeling a little dirty after our day today."

My clenched jaw grinded my molars. Was this motherfucker the reason why my girl refused to be called mine? The reason for the condoms even though we were both clean and she was on birth control? The one my mom and dad fucking raved about?

"What did you do that made her so dirty?" My tone was thinly concealed rage. I wasn't mad at Tama. She'd been clear with me. We weren't exclusive and after the nightclub we weren't anything again.

"We took a hike with Trudy. Then you know how things are when you're already all hot and sweaty." He smirked at me.

I clenched my fist and pushed them into my thighs to not punch him in the smug fucking face.

Following him to the kitchen, he offered me a beer. I chugged it back. "What do you do now for a living, Griffin?"

He rubbed his eyes and yawned loudly. "Sorry, I'm still jetlagged to shit. I'm the lead singer of a little band. You might have heard of us, the Dumb Youths."

Motherfucker.

After I saw Tama wearing the shirt I had googled it to see why she loved it so much. The genre of music didn't seem like her type, but I downloaded some of their music and recognized a few songs.

"Only recently. What brings you to Tama's?"

He tipped his beer back and smirked again. "Visiting my fiancée. I haven't seen her in a few months. I tried to convince her to travel Europe with me again, but she said she was busy with her book. Have you read it? Shit's incredible."

My heart was in my throat. "Fiancée?"

"Yeah, as in a person that promises to marry you. We've been engaged for some time now."

My whole body clenched. Tama wasn't the type of person to cheat. I knew her way too well. But his answer was so confident, no way he was lying.

"You must be in an open relationship because I've been fucking her for weeks."

Griffin shrugged. "Sure, if that's what you want to call it." He cupped my shoulder. "Thanks for taking care of her. She gets needy."

I shrugged his hand off me.

Okay, so she didn't cheat, but she didn't fucking tell me either.

I don't know how I was still calmly standing in her kitchen while I wanted to break everything in sight. "When are you getting married?"

"We aren't," Tama called from the hallway. "Griffin, stop telling people we are engaged."

"But we are, Doc. You told me you'd marry me."

Tama stepped into the kitchen wearing my old t-shirt and cut off shorts. Her hair was wet and slowly dripping into the collar of the shirt. She walked up to me and kissed my cheek.

Warmth tingled where her lips landed. Her sweet scent surrounded me. I would have given anything in the world for her to kiss me properly in front of Griffin.

"I thought you'd have been here hours ago. You've met Griffin again, I see."

I couldn't swallow or talk so I nodded. She smiled softly at me and turned to Griffin, grabbing a towel and whipping him with it. "I told you I'd marry you if we are both single at forty so Gramma can see you get married. Stop telling people I'm your fiancée."

I let out a slow breath, easing my jaw muscles as he dodged her attack and chuckled. Trudy had walked in the kitchen and growled at him.

Good boy.

He held his hands up. "Don't bite me, Trudy Duty. Your mom is joking." He reached over to the counter and plucked up an apple and tossed it down to him.

Tama sighed and turned back to me. "I'm not engaged. He probably said that to rile you up."

Griffin threw his head back in laughter. "I love you so much. See, Doc, you know me so fucking well. It's why you have to stay single until forty."

She groaned. "I love you too, but I'm not talking about this." She turned to me. "Are you hungry? I'm making beef stroganoff at your dad's request."

My ears were buzzing at the love affirmation.

I wasn't fucking leaving now that I knew she had a male friend over trying to stake claim.

"Starved."

She grinned at me.

Griffin walked over to her and kissed her cheek. "I'm going to take a shower."

I watched him walk away, my neck craning to see which bathroom he was using. My shoulders unclenched when he walked into the guest bedroom. Tama watched me watch Griffin with a knowing look on her face.

"Don't be jealous."

I licked my lips. "That's fucking hard, Bully. How long has he been here anyway?"

She twisted her lips to the side and tapped her chin. "He landed a few minutes after I did from Tampa, what five days, I guess? He's flying to Vancouver tomorrow."

Thank fuck.

"How was your flight?" she asked brightly, like it was totally fucking fine that some dude was staying at her house for the better part of a week.

"Shitty."

She frowned. "Sorry about that." She pointed to my empty bottle. "Want another one?"

I shouldn't be drinking considering I had a game tomorrow. I wasn't going to have another off day for another thirteen days, but at least the next seven would be at home.

I needed to take the edge off after seeing her interact with Griffin. There was an ease between them that made me frustrated. I used to feel the same way when I saw her with Henry until I knew without a doubt they weren't sleeping together. But her and Griffin *had* slept together and that made me feel irrationally possessive of her. I wanted to pick her up and cage her against me until he left.

"Please." I tossed the empty bottle in her recycling.

Stewing in my own thoughts while she made dinner, I waited for Griffin to come out of the guest bedroom. I needed to suss out their friendship to see if I could tell if they hooked up. He was wearing sweatpants and one of my t-shirts that Tama had stolen from me in college. I flexed my jaw as my nostrils flared. He grinned when he saw me and looked down at the shirt, knowing good and well it was mine. It had my fucking name on the back for Christ's sake.

"Griff, can you make a salad? Rita dropped off all those tomatoes, lettuce, and carrots yesterday. We need to use them."

He saluted her. "You got it, Doc."

I stood up from the island. "I can help."

Tama giggled and shook her head. "Rhys you're the second worst cook of anyone I have ever met in my life, only behind Henry."

"Chopping vegetables isn't cooking."

Griffin smiled at me. "It's cool, man. If singing didn't work out for me, I was going to culinary school. I like honing my skills, and I haven't been able to cook regularly for almost two years because of this tour."

Great. My competition was charming, made Tama laugh, and could cook.

The patio door beeped as Trudy let himself in.

"Hello, hello," my mom called.

Griffin smiled brightly and went to give my mom a hug. She squeezed his ribs before pinching his cheek adoringly. "Such a sweet boy."

Oh, what the fuck?

"I thought you were flying out yesterday," my mom said. She looked around the kitchen. Her eyes landed on me and went wide. She turned back to Griffin with a look of guilt splashing across her face.

Griffin chuckled and swung his gaze to me. "Decided to stay one more day. You know how much I love Tama Bama."

Tama Bama? Great, an inside joke.

My mom shot a quick look over to me as my dad walked into the kitchen and yanked Griffin into a hug that pulled him off his feet. "Thanks for helping me find that part two days ago. I was able to finish the engine rebuild today."

I internally groaned. I told my dad weeks ago that I'd order the part, but I forgot. He turned around and saw me sitting at the island. "Hey son, when did you get in?"

"An hour ago. Came straight over to see my girl."

"I don't blame you man. I flew commercial while the rest of my band flew my private jet home so I could see her a day faster. She's one of a kind."

My dad grinned at Griffin and patted his shoulder before walking over to Trudy and petting his big head. Then after he greeted Tama he came over to put his arm around my shoulder.

"You've been playing well. I was a little worried when you struck out your last game in Tampa, but you hit that grand slam later to make up for it."

I nodded as Tama whirled around to look at me. "I missed your grand slam?"

I shrugged. "You were in the air." I turned back to my dad.

"You already added the star?" my dad asked.

I pulled up the sleeve of my t-shirt, revealing the cluster of stars tattooed in my inner arm. I pointed to a large one that was still a little red. "Got it in Atlanta."

Griffin pointed to me with a knife. "What do your stars represent?"

Tama looked over to me from the stove. I knew she was curious but had never asked. I had been waiting patiently, but she had more willpower in her pinkie than I had in my entire body.

"Small stars are home runs; big stars are grand slams since officially being in the MLB."

"That's dope as shit. Not only are you touring tattoo parlors around the US, you're documenting a cool feat," Griffin said.

I hated that he was so nice to me when I wanted to punch him hard in the face.

"On my first tour I did something similar." He pulled up the pant leg of his sweats, revealing his calf that was completely covered in tattoos. "Every state or country I toured I got the state or country flower. Covered my calf quickly, decided the next tour to slow it down."

"You got any other tattoos?" Griffin asked me.

I looked over to Tama. She was watching me through her lashes, her cheeks turned red when she saw me looking at her.

I rubbed my heart. "I do, but it's pretty personal."

Tama's brows furrowed before smiling brightly at the room. "Dinner is ready. Tom, since you chose, you go first. I set up the patio to eat at since it's supposed to be clear tonight."

Dinner should have been more awkward than it was. No one at the table but me seemed to have an issue with Griffin, so I stayed amicable. After dessert my parents made their way back across the lawns. Griffin slumped down on the sofa and turned the television on.

I wasn't ready to leave Tama, so I sat in her wide chair that easily fit two people and made sure to leave space for her to snuggle into me like she had a few weeks prior.

Tama rolled her lips in and looked back and forth between me and Griffin. Trudy's head bounced between the two of us before he walked over to me and climbed into the open spot. His heavy body crushed me into the side of the seat as Tama giggled. He rested his heavy head on my lap and let out a sigh like the weight of the world was resting on his shoulders.

"It's like that, Trudy Duty? I sneak you apples and wrestle with you."

Tama smiled and sat down on the opposite side of the sofa from Griffin, closer to me.

She reached over and scratched behind Trudy's ears. "He can probably smell Tom on Rhys. Lord knows Tom and Trudy are best friends."

Griffin sighed. "That's fair." With the remote in hand, he flipped through a few streaming services. "What are we watching?"

I didn't care what we watched. I was playing a game of chicken, not ready to leave until Griffin went to bed. I was there to make sure it wasn't in Tama's room, but my exhaustion got the better of me. I fell asleep huddled in the chair next to Trudy.

Tama's fingers running through my hair woke me up. "Go to bed, Rhys," she whispered.

I woke up again in Tama's empty bed, stripped down to my boxers. I yawned as I walked around her empty house. Relieved that at least Griffin was gone but still feeling out of sorts about everything.

Chapter 19

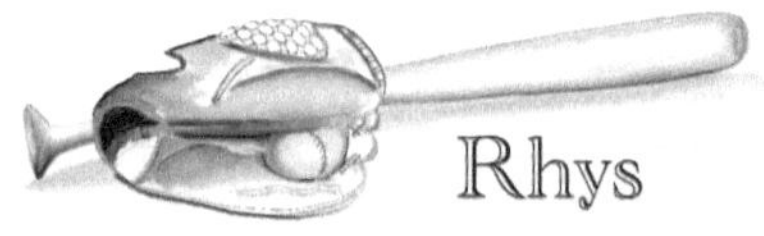

Rhys

"**Y**ou get things worked out with Tama?" Kevin asked. I removed my game socks and tossed them in the rolling laundry bin. "No."

"Bummer."

It had been eight days since I got home from Atlanta and officially met Griffin. I can admit I hadn't been spending as much time with her as I could have been, but I didn't know what to think or do.

Yes, I desperately wanted to be with her, but she seemed fucking content on having both me and Griffin. I wasn't going to share her, nor was I going to beg her to choose me.

We ate dinner together most nights, but my parents were also there. It wasn't exactly quality time. I spent the night a few times, but nothing sexual happened. She had successfully pushed me back into the boundaries of being her friend.

No kissing, no sex. The question had been burning my tongue for days: had she fucked Griffin while I was in Atlanta? She could have and I would have zero grounds to be upset, but the thought of it was making me nauseous. I simultaneously wanted to know and refused to ask.

"We are friendly, but that's it."

Kevin frowned. "Karma's a bitch sometimes, bro."

I scowled. "What the fuck is that supposed to mean?"

He rolled his eyes over to me as he peeled his sweaty jersey off and tossed it. "She wrote that book, right?"

I scowled. "And? What does that have to do with anything?"

He squinted at me before shaking his head. "Nothing…Just fucking with you. What's the plan for tonight? You lived in Denver for school, right?"

We were in the second game of a three-game series in Colorado. "I went to school in Boulder, but close. I'm meeting up with my college buddies. We are keeping it lowkey."

He hummed. "No bunny business?"

I rolled my eyes. The last thing I needed was a tabloid uploading unflattering pictures of some woman trying to touch me and Tama sees it. "Hell no."

Whinny and Nathan were waiting for me in the friends and family suite. I hugged them both, introduced them to a few players before we headed over to a pub near Whinny's house. He lived halfway between Denver and Boulder in a quiet town full of microbreweries and mountain air.

"You know, I figured you'd be happier with Tama in your life again," Nathan said after we hit another bout of silence.

I gulped down my beer. "I'm happy."

Whinny snorted and motioned for the bartender to get us refills.

"Sure sounds like it," Nathan said.

I tipped my head back. "It's complicated. I want to be with her, and she has some fucker named Griffin on her hook."

Whinny winced as Nathan's eyes narrowed. "DeMarco? Yeah, they're friends."

My eyes shot over to him. "How the fuck do you know that?"

He held out his hands. "I've visited her, remember, I was the reason she lives in that house. Anyway, Griffin was in town one of the nights I visited. He's cool as shit, but they aren't anything more than friends."

"They've definitely fucked."

Nathan shrugged. "And? It's not like you remained celibate the past three years. You left an emotional hole; she filled it with Griffin and her dog."

My jaw clenched at the remark.

Whinny snickered. "I've been meaning to ask what it feels like to be replaced by a dog, but I don't think you've realized it yet."

"I haven't been replaced by Trudy."

Whinny chuckled. "Let's list out some facts. Trudy is her protective, possessive best friend who leans on her for emotional support. She caters to his every whim; she cooks and cleans up after him. And that's just Tama. How about the fact that your mom babies him, and he helps your dad in the garage."

My face went slack. "Oh, what the fuck?"

Nathan laughed out loud. "Jesus, Whinny, when you lay it all out like that." He slapped my shoulder. "Tough break, man."

I was too gob smacked to argue. "Well, Trudy is an incredible dog, so I guess it's a compliment."

They laughed into their beers. "Change of topic, please."

Nathan grinned at me. "Back to Bully then. I say you stop being such a bitch about it and tell her how you feel."

I rolled my eyes. "I have told her how I feel. She said she needs time. And I'm going to give it to her, but it's fucking hard knowing that I have competition like Griffin."

"Griffin's not your competition and you haven't told her how you feel," someone said from behind us.

I turned around, my lip curling in confusion.

"What's up man? I haven't seen you in ages." Whinny stood up to shake Henry Foust's hand. "What are you doing here?"

Henry gave us all easy smiles. "Got in from Australia a few days ago. Ava wanted to take a break in Boulder before we start visiting friends. She has a few motivational speeches set up for the performance school at Pineview. And I'm here to talk to Rhys."

My mouth opened and closed.

"I hope you don't mind. Whinny posted a picture when you sat down. I recognized the place and figured there was no time like the present to talk to you without Tama or Ava knowing."

My brows rose, and I pushed out the available chair at our table. He took it and ordered himself a beer. He looked the same except instead of hoodies and jeans he was wearing an expensive sweater and khakis. He still had that smug look about him.

"Why so secretive?" Nathan asked.

Henry tilted his head. "I'm breaking the best friend code. Tama won't get out of her own way, and I'm not going to sit aside and let her bury her head in the sand with her emotions because she's too scared of this fool." He pointed to me.

My scowl deepened. "Why should I trust anything you have to say? You fucking hate me."

He lifted one shoulder as his head wagged from side to side. "I don't hate you. I didn't like that you strung my friend along for years, treating her like a fucking backup plan, but I never hated you."

"That's not what I did."

He held up both hands. "Semantics. I'm not going to argue about the past. I know her perspective on things, and I am entitled to my opinion. Regardless, I'm here to help."

Nathan elbowed me when I didn't say anything right away.

"Why?" I asked slowly. I couldn't hide the confusion in my voice.

"If it's between you and Griffin, I choose you for her."

I puffed my chest up.

He rolled his eyes. "Don't let it go to your head. You're only in the lead because you've told her you're finally willing to commit. Unlike Griffin who wants to string her along for another decade before he'll pull the trigger. She deserves better than some friends with benefits bullshit while she watches a man she loves fuck around."

I swallowed the lump in my throat. "She does love him then."

Henry shrugged. "Yeah, but she loves you, too."

I rolled my eyes. "Well, she's never told me that."

Henry gave me a flat stare. "You've never told her either, and between the two of you, you have always been the one to withhold how you felt. She's been following your lead."

"It doesn't change the fact that she loves another man."

Henry blew out a breath. "Would it change your mind if I told you she isn't in love with Griffin, but she is with you?"

I closed my eyes and shook my head. "How could you possibly know that?"

"For one, she's told me she's not in love with Griffin. But even if she hadn't, I'd still know. She doesn't care that he hooks up with other women. Shit, they joke about it. He shares embarrassing stories about his sex life with her all the time, and she thinks it's funny."

I shook my head. "She didn't care when I hooked up with other women before, and I haven't been with anyone but Tama in over a year."

Henry tilted his head at me, squinting. "You haven't read her fucking book, have you?"

I shrugged. "I've been meaning to. It's been a busy few weeks."

Henry gave me a stony look. "You can't tell me that you love her and not support her through her biggest professional accomplishment."

My lips formed a tight line. "I'm going to read it when the season is over. I support her, and I do love her. I don't understand how reading her book on grief is going to help me in this instance."

Nathan scoffed. "You can lead a horse to water, but you can't make it drink." He turned to me. "It's not about grief specifically. It's about heartbreak. And she wrote about her own heartbreak in the book."

"Yeah, she said that when Yolanda died, she was inspired and continued her senior thesis."

Henry let out a humorless chuckle. "All of that is the truth, but it was also misdirection. Read her fucking book, man." He downed the rest of his beer and slapped a hundred on the table. "I've gotta get back to Boulder before Ava questions my absence. If I don't see you in Paris, have a good life."

"What's happening in Paris?" Nathan asked.

I shrugged. "No clue." I squinted at my friend. "Have you read her book?"

Nathan and Whinny both nodded. "Yeah, she doesn't use the names of her participants, or specific details, but the language isn't so coded we couldn't figure out who was who."

I licked the front of my teeth. "What aren't you saying?"

Whinny winced. Nathan cleared his throat. "Read her book, and then I expect a phone call telling me that I was completely right about everything regarding her."

My temple bounced.

Whinny sighed. "Read it, man. If not tonight, soon. You aren't going to want to wait until the end of the season."

I rolled my eyes as I pulled my phone out and bought an eBook version. "Fine, I'll start it tonight."

Whinny smiled at me before ordering another round. "Our boy might figure his shit out."

Nathan nodded. "Unlike us."

"For now," Whinny said.

I finished drinking with my friends and took a cab to my hotel. I had a few hours before I needed to go to bed so I started Tama's book.

I had to pause and stare at the dedication:

To the good man that inspires me every day.

The book was somber, uplifting, relatable, and interesting. My heart sped up when I got to participant number 25.

Pluto's Heartbreak
I fell in love with my best friend

I grew up in a very sheltered environment. My mother was a widow, I was homeschooled, and my home was very secluded from normal society. Don't get me wrong, I had a very happy childhood, but I lacked normal childhood experiences.

I moved away from home to go to college. It was a scary and thrilling experience. For the first time in my life I was around people my own age, men my own age. I met Jupiter my first week of my freshman year of school. He was the second boy I had ever spoken to. I was immediately attracted to him, but he was larger than life, so I knew he'd never see me that way.

He ended up being my lab partner. It didn't take long for our friendship bond to become special and addicting. He would invite me to parties, hang out with me, talk to me all the time. Having positive male attention was a novelty and I reveled in it. While I was wildly attracted to him, he didn't feel that way about me.

We'd be at parties together and he would invite woman after woman into bedrooms, and when he was done, he'd come hang out with me. He'd shower me with attention, affection. He was the type of friend that I never thought I'd have. I never held it against him that he wasn't attracted to me like that. I was happy to be in his orbit.

It helped that he was not interested in having a romantic relationship with anyone. He had a steadfast rule, no girlfriend until he became a professional athlete. Knowing his dalliances were temporary and we were friends no matter what, helped.

The byproduct of his constant attention was the fact that no man would come near me. Jupiter was larger than life and intimidating. He was a top performing athlete, popular, and highly sought after. Women wanted him, men wanted to be his friend, so no one was crazy enough to come near me. By the second year of our friendship, we were spending the night at each other's place. He'd snuggle against me, and pillow talk with me every night. My other friends didn't understand our friendship, accusing him of using me as a backup plan. But I never saw it like that. I was his friend and happy to fill whatever role he needed to be successful.

My role in his life ended up being about emotional support. He needed affection and being adverse to relationships meant affection went to the wayside with his conquests. I provided the affection he needed, happily.

The first time he kissed me was one of the happiest nights of my life. I had never had any sexual experience, never been kissed, and in one night he kissed me and performed every sexual act short of penetration. He had given me my first kiss and orgasm at someone else's hand the same night. I woke up on cloud nine, happy our friendship had turned. The problem was he was too drunk to remember our night. It was devastating that something so important to me was forgettable for him.

I didn't hold it against him. I took a few days to let my ego heal and before I knew it, we were bed sharing again. I didn't tell him until much later about our night together, so, to him, life was back to normal. For me it was like seeing the beauty of the sun and then being shoved underground again.

As his senior year progressed our friendship also progressed. We turned into friends with benefits, but with no penetrative sex. I have no idea if he was monogamous with me, but I was with him. I never wanted to know. It would make me have to reflect on our friendship, and I wasn't ready to do that.

After all his hard work he was drafted. We spent a little over a week getting him to his destination city. One night on our road trip, the hotel we were staying at only allowed married couples. He bought us wedding rings, called me his *wife, and showered me in the type of affection I adored. He also took my virginity that night. It was a beautiful experience for me, and no matter how painful our story ended, I've never regretted giving Jupiter all my firsts.*

Before he started with his team, he made a joke about me staying with him. But I knew traveling would provide too many instances for him to explore other female options. He'd never asked me to commit to him and vice versa. He was still working to be at the peak of his chosen sport, and a girlfriend would get in the way.

If I would have stayed with him, I would have uprooted my education while begging for the scraps of his attention. He'd feel guilty and his game would suffer. I'd never want to be his obligation, and I would never throw my goals to the wind when my friend had proven he wasn't ready to commit.

Years went by. We would speak multiple times a week. We'd see each other every few months. Our 'benefits' remained for years. When he reached his professional goal, I was close to reaching mine. I knew he was going to be ready for a real relationship. Jupiter is nothing if not determined. If he said he was going to have a girlfriend after meeting his goals, then he was going to have a girlfriend.

We went through a stretch of time where we didn't see each other. I missed him but I knew he was busy with his new team. He had endorsement deals and was busy finding his footing in his new life. He asked me if he could see me and talk to me. A small hopeful part of my brain said, 'This is it. This is when Jupiter tells you that he feels the same way.'

And it turns out he was ready for a committed relationship. He introduced me to his girlfriend Mercury. I recognized her from months prior. She had made fun of me in the bathroom, telling me I was ugly and the pathetic girl that he kept around to stroke his ego. I feigned happiness for him while feeling my heart break with every beat.

I didn't get out of bed for a week after Jupiter told me about Mercury. A few months went by, and he called to tell me he was marrying Mercury. My week in bed months prior was nothing compared to the depression that gripped me when he told me he was dedicating his life to someone else. Mercury wrote me a letter telling me I wasn't invited to the wedding despite receiving an invitation in the mail.

Fortunately, my month in bed dealing with the crippling depression coincided with my summer break. Another friend came to my rescue when I hadn't answered any text or phone call in days.

On the day of Jupiter's wedding my friend didn't let me out of his sight. Keeping me occupied, and my mind off the love of my life choosing another woman.

It took me a long time to realize that my depression wasn't cut and dry and easy to fix with medication. I was in mourning. I was grieving the death of hope.

I tried to message him on his birthday to find my number was blocked. I had already mourned the death of our friendship, my future I hoped for, and my blind hope that he'd finally see me.

Another wave of mourning hit hard. I was practically catatonic while dealing with the loss of everything. He had been my beacon for so many years and losing him destroyed me. His ease to cut me from his life was a stark reminder to me.

To quote Maya Angelou, 'when someone tells you who they are, believe them'.

Jupiter never said he'd commit to me. He never implied I was anything more than his friend. He never told me he loved me. In the end I was the fool to fall in love with her best friend knowing he'd never reciprocate.

If I could talk to Jupiter, I'd tell him that I wish him all the happiness in his marriage and success in his career. He never did anything wrong.

I don't regret a moment of our time together, and I am grateful for the lessons learned. I know the capacity I can love someone. My hope is that I will find someone who can reciprocate all my feelings. Someone I would be enough for. Someone that would look me in the eye and tell me 'I knew the moment I met you that you were the one.'

My phone fell to my stomach as I absorbed what I had read.

I was her first.

A swell of pride pumped my chest. I thought back to all our sexual interactions and tried to remove the hazy veil of lust. She was so eager but tentative. I thought it was nerves because it could have changed our friendship. It was so much more than that.

I was glad we didn't have sex until that road trip. The constant blue balls were worth it knowing I was able to make that experience, and the days that followed, special. It was no less than she deserved. What she didn't deserve was how blasé I had been about her.

I crushed my best friend, and I had no idea. No wonder everyone had been trying to get me to read her book. All the side glances, and pinched expressions made sense. They wanted me to know how I had treated my friend. This was why she's been holding me at an arm's length. It was a hell of my own making.

She thought she wasn't enough for me. I had been choosing other women for years around her. No fucking wonder she didn't believe me when I told her I wanted her to be my girlfriend. It was so naïve of me to not think about how our past would influence her to be apprehensive.

I ran my fingers through my hair, itching to text message her. She had to know that I loved her. I didn't tell her, but I showed her all the time. I was a fucking idiot, but now I knew how she felt.

I could fix this. I had to fix this. She was going to be mine. All I had to do was confront every single one of her reasons why and prove to her that I was the right choice.

Chapter 20

Tama

Ava tackled me as soon as I opened the front door. Trudy was on both of us as we giggled. He licked both of our faces as Henry grumbled inside carrying their bags.

"When did you get in town?"

Ava was still hugging around my neck as we laid on the floor. "We came straight from the airport. We've been in The States for a week, but I had some speaking engagements in Boulder. I told Henry we had to stop by so I could see our bestie."

Henry gripped Ava's hips and hauled her up. My way back to my feet was far less graceful, but then I launched myself at Henry.

He chuckled as he patted my back. "Missed you, too."

Ava tugged on my elbow and hugged me again. "I'm so happy to see you, but I'm starving, and Henry has been complaining about how much he misses your chocolate chip cookies."

"Is that a hint?" I perked my brow.

Henry shook his head. "Not a hint, a plea, please Tama, make us cookies."

I giggled and led everyone into the kitchen to start a batch. "You're lucky I was taking a break from writing."

Henry wagged his brows. "Arguably the luckiest guy in the world." He squeezed Ava's thigh. "How's that going anyway?"

"Well, I have the outline down. It's difficult listening to the audio of people having sex. Sometimes the breathing is too heavy to understand the narration, but it is what it is. Fortunately, I had already dictated all the kink origin stories of the participants so about sixty percent of the book was written during the trial."

"This is your sex book, right?" Ava bit into a cucumber and gave Henry a knowing smirk.

My nose wrinkled but I didn't comment on their inside joke about cucumbers including me, too.

"Yes, it's about how different types of sex impacts the brain. I have it divided in three sections: being in love while having sex; sex with an acquaintance; and sex with some sort of kink. You remember I had everyone have sex twice."

Ava grinned and blushed. "Of course I do. It unlocked a new kink where we knew someone could hear us."

My face twisted in disgust. "I don't want to dwell on that, but I do think that people will be pleased with the results about how love and kink impact the brain during sex."

I creamed the butter and sugar together while going into detail about deadlines and the publisher's expectations.

When I had pulled the warm cookies from the oven Ava turned to me.

"Okay, spill. I've been patiently waiting for you to bring up Rhys, but you are a steel vault. Last we spoke you were having sex, and you were heading to Florida."

"Oh boy," I rubbed my forehead. "Well, we are no longer having sex."

I looked over to Henry. He already knew this story, so I wasn't sure why he hadn't told Ava. We had caught up my first night home from Tampa. Ava was working during our weekly catch-up call. I guess he did keep our private conversations between us.

Ava groaned. "What happened?"

I went into detail again. Ava whimpered at the right moments and grew indignant with me.

"I don't blame you for leaving, but…" She was chewing on her finger. "Now that you know that it was a misunderstanding, why are you still punishing yourself?"

I scowled at my friend. "I'm not punishing myself. I'm protecting myself. I'm drawing boundaries. You know the thing you both insisted I didn't do enough?"

Ava huffed. "No, you're punishing yourself by not allowing the possibility to be happy with Rhys. I get it, Tama, he's hurt you before. But as you have pointed out, he didn't know what he was doing. I don't understand why you are not jumping at the chance to be with him."

"It'll hurt too much when he finds the next Krista." My voice cracked as I admitted my biggest fear.

"Oh, Tama." Ava came over to my side of the island. She wrapped her arms around me tightly. "You can't think that way."

I bit into my lip as my eyes burned. "I can't help it." My quiet voice croaked against my knotted throat.

She held me out at an arm's length. She was the only person in my life that was as small as I was. It was odd to not have to look up to her.

"You are enough. If anything, you are too good for him. He knows it, but clearly you don't know it. Give yourself some grace and give him the benefit of the doubt."

I whimpered. "That's easy for you to say. Henry never hesitated to tell you he loves you. Within five months of knowing each other you had told each other how you felt. It's been a decade, and he's never told me he loves me, not even as a friend. I've heard him on several drunken ramblings telling Nathan or Whinny how much he loves them."

"That's all it's going to take?" Henry finally asked.

I shrugged and wiped the tear that had escaped. "I don't know, and I can't dwell on something like that anyway. If I keep him as my friend, I can't get hurt again."

"If you keep him as a friend, you won't be happy either," Ava said.

That was the inconvenient truth.

"Enough about that for now," Ava said. "Talk to me more about your book."

"You outdid yourself." Ava patted her tiny stomach. Henry's arm stretched around Ava's shoulder.

"We haven't had a home cooked meal in months."

Ava pouted. "I know, I've been too tired when I have gotten home from rehearsals or performances. Henry still can't cook worth a damn."

372

He nodded. "I took cooking classes and basically was asked not to come back. Did you know you can burn water?"

I giggled.

Ava snorted. "He didn't burn water, he forgot it was there and let all the water boil off while there was already pasta in the pot."

She shook her head. "His clothes smelled like it for days. His teacher asked him to try a beginning level course instead of intermediate."

Henry huffed. "The beginning level was boring. I wanted to learn the good stuff like making food, not boiling water."

"A lesson you probably should have paid attention to," Ava joked.

He leaned forward and kissed her. "I love this smart mouth, but it won't stop me from punishing you later."

She smirked at him and turned back to me. "Anyway, what are your plans for the next few days? I know we have dinner planned with Aunt Genevive and Weston tomorrow night, but other than that we are free."

"Rhys is landing any minute now. He'll be bummed he missed dinner, but he'll live. I'm sure he wants to hang out tonight, so if he does, please be nice." I looked over to Henry pointedly.

He raised his hands. "Best behavior. Besides, I'm always nice to him."

I rolled my eyes. "You've been calling him a douche canoe for the better part of three years."

He snickered. "Yeah, and he hurt you to the point of being comatose. But apparently it was a misunderstanding, and he's changed. My issue with him has always been and will always be not giving you what you deserve. And you're telling me he wants to commit. I'm giving him the benefit of the doubt."

I raised an eyebrow to him.

He grinned at me. "You deserve to be happy, Tam."

Ava gripped my hand from across the table. "You really do, and I think that he can make you happy if you let him. I know it's scary, but you have to try."

Trudy sat straight up and then walked over to the front door. He whined before going to his buttons. "Outside." Then he went back to the front door and sat.

"That's new." I sat my napkin down.

Trudy thumped his thick tail against the hardwood when I rubbed his head.

"We aren't going for a walk right now." He barked loudly and nosed the handle of the door. "Okay fine, let's see what's outside."

I opened the door to see Rhys walking up the sidewalk towards my house. Trudy went right for him and looped around him happily, tongue lolling.

I smiled. "He likes you. I guess he smelled you when you got home. He's been anxiously waiting at the front door."

Rhys chuckled and bent down to scratch his jaw. "You're a good boy, aren't you?"

He grinned at me. "At least your dog likes me." He stood up and walked over to me. His hug was warm. I closed my stinging eyes, and I drank in his woodsy scent. He sighed against my ear before kissing my cheek.

"It smells incredible in here. Please tell me there are leftovers."

"There are. Ava, Henry, and I just finished up."

He perked a brow at me as he craned his neck towards the dining room. "Do you want me to go?" he whispered.

I giggled and pushed him towards the table. "Go sit down, I'll make you a plate."

Henry and Ava greeted him. Rhys asked Ava how she was feeling about her newfound international fandom. They both commiserated about how hard their individual sports are to their bodies. I set Rhys's plate in front of him after I warmed his food up.

He smiled at me as he dug in.

"Feels like old times, huh?" Ava asked.

"The best time of my life was in college hanging out with Tama eating her food."

"She's one in a million," Henry said. "What's your game schedule looking like?"

"One more week of the regular season. We've already made the playoffs, so there's that. I have tomorrow off, and my next game isn't until Tuesday night, so I have about 48 hours to relax."

"Who are you playing?"

"Kansas and Dodgers this week."

Ava nudged me but continued talking to Rhys. "You have all day off tomorrow, huh?"

Rhys watched our interaction and smirked. "Yeah, I'm doing laundry and relaxing until this one gets off work. I was thinking about taking my girl and boy for a walk."

He nuzzled into Trudy's head. It made me hold back a smile at him calling Trudy his boy.

"I love this." Ava motioned between the two of us.

My cheeks heated up. I cleared my throat. "We're just friends, Ava. Chill out."

Ava wrinkled her nose. "Lame."

Rhys

I was nervous as fuck waiting for Tama to get home from work. I had rehearsed what I wanted to say to her, but I was worried everything was going to get all jammed up or not come out right. I had so much to say, apologize for, and plead my case about.

Taking a few days to reflect on my friendship with Tama through the lens of what I had put her through brought me clarity. The biggest thing I needed to do is convince her that she was exactly enough for me and that I've always known that.

I had set up something small for us to talk privately.

"You ready?" my mom whispered.

She had helped me plan my surprise for Tama. She was more than excited about the prospect of making Tama a member of the family. I was trying to reel her back, but she was thinking five steps ahead.

We had spoken a little about Tama's book. She had also gathered that I was Jupiter, and it was the biggest reason why dad wasn't completely sold on me being with her. It made a lot of sense now knowing Tama's perspective.

"As I'll ever be." I puffed out my cheeks. "I don't know what to do if she won't be with me after today."

My mom clicked her tongue. "Yes, you do. You stay patient."

"I know, I'll wait until she's ready. I hope that it'll be today."

Trudy's leash wound around my fist as I led us up the north trail towards our destination. My palms were sweating, and my heart was pounding. Tama was talking about her day and how crazy the teenagers at school were. I stopped when we were a few feet away from our destination.

I turned towards her and grabbed both her hands.

"I need to talk to you."

She blinked rapidly. "Okay."

Her easy demeanor stiffened as she pulled in a deep breath and bit into her cheek.

The spot I had created off trail was visible from where we stood. I had set up hundreds of flowers as a border and a blanket in the center. She gasped quietly and looked at me with wide eyes. When I pulled her to the center of the blanket everything I wanted to say went out of my brain.

She looked around. "What's going on?"

I licked my lips. "I'm in love with you, and I have been for a long time. I knew I loved you after meeting you in the biology lab. I knew I was in love with you when we were at Hot Springs. I should have told you then, but I was scared. It was stupid of me to think for one fucking second that we weren't in a relationship back then because we fucking were. When I tell people about you, I always refer to you as my college girlfriend."

She blinked rapidly at me. I plowed on.

"I should have asked you to be mine years ago, but I didn't want to ask you to move. I chalked it up to the timing being wrong, but the reality was, I was worried we couldn't find a compromise so we could be together. By the time I made it, you still had a few years of your PhD program, and I knew you couldn't move. I didn't want a half-life where we didn't see each other for six months at a time.

"I didn't want to ask you to change programs even though I looked at programs in Tampa. But every time I talked to you, you talked about how much you loved Seattle. When I realized I couldn't have you I sort of let Krista talk me into getting married. I never loved her. I knew when I proposed it was a mistake. When I saw her cheating, I was relieved. It wasn't until I realized you weren't there that I lost it. I thought I pushed my love for you away, but it was always there."

I started to unbutton my shirt.

"What are you doing?" she whispered. Her eyes were glassy as her chin trembled.

I swallowed thickly and pointed to the first group of tattooed numbers. "This is the date that I met you. It was love at first sight. That is why I couldn't stop being around you. You've had me from the first moment." I moved to the next line. "This was when you had your date with Griffin, and I acted like a jealous asshole. I realized I was completely in love with you." The next line down. "This was when we were at the Hot Springs. That night meant as much to me as it did to you, baby. It was when I knew I couldn't let you go."

Her brow pinched together as she rolled her lips in. A beautiful pink blush painted her cheeks.

I moved my finger down one more row. "This was my first game in the MLB. It was when I decided I was going to figure out how we could be together. I was going to tell you what I had learned from the PhD program near Tampa, but you left early, and I never got a chance to tell you."

She whimpered as a tear slid down her cheek. I leaned forward to kiss its trail.

"This last line was my wedding date. That was when I realized I lost my chance with the love of my life. Bully," I cupped her cheeks and looked deeply into her caramel eyes, "I knew the moment I met you, you were the one."

A few more tears escaped. "You read my book."

"I'm so fucking sorry for everything, but I promise you, I will spend the rest of my life making it up to you. You've always been enough for me. I choose you. It will always be you. It's always been you."

I held up my rose gold ring. "I wore this every day until I knew I lost you, but I kept it in case I ever had another chance with you. One of these days I'm switching it to my left hand because you and I are going to get married when you're ready for me."

She swallowed thickly.

"Tama Isla Bulris, will you please be with me. I'm yours, you're mine. No one else will ever hold my interest like you. You've held me captive for ten years. I love you with the depths of my soul. Please be mine."

She rose to her toes and kissed me. I picked her up and kissed her hard.

"I love you, too," she murmured against my lips. "Now take me home, the house is empty for another three hours, and it's been weeks since..."

I pulled my face away. "You and Griffin didn't..."

She giggled and shook her head. "It's only been you since you came back into my life."

"To be clear. I want it to be me and you, exclusive. We are together, boyfriend, girlfriend and everything that comes with that," I clarified.

"I prefer the term partner, but yes, I want that, too."

"I fucking love you," I leaned down and kissed her again.

She led the way to her home. Trudy trotted along happily, tongue lolling.

She pounced on me the moment the bedroom door latched shut. She was already tugging on the hem of my button up shirt that I never had a chance to button back up. It slid off my shoulders as I hungrily kissed her lips.

Our clothes were gone in a hurry as I walked her backwards towards her bed. She flipped the lock of her bedroom door and went to kiss me again. My eyes rolled to the back of my head when she started to slowly jerk me off. I pushed the last barrier of clothes off us and followed her to the mattress.

My lips trailed her neck, chest, stomach, before I licked her pussy. It was my favorite flavor in the world, and I moaned at her taste. Her hips bucked as I pushed two fingers into her and continued to flick her clit with my tongue while working her g-spot with my fingers.

Her moans were getting louder as Trudy started to howl in the hallway. I chuckled but dove back in when her fingers gripped my hair and yanked me back into her.

"Don't stop, please don't stop."

Her thighs started to bounce against my cheek, and I sucked her clit into my mouth. I moaned when her orgasm coated my chin and neck.

"You're so fucking sexy," I murmured against her thighs. My lips trailed up her body. She clutched my cheeks and kissed me hard again.

I gasped when she gripped my rigid cock and started to slowly stroke me. Her thumb smeared my precum around before she pulled her lips away and kissed the tip of my head.

"Fuck," I groaned as she swallowed my dick. Her hand moved in conjunction with her sinfully perfect mouth. My toes curled as she sucked me hard.

"Baby, get a condom. I want to fuck you."

She popped off me and pushed me to my back. Clasping our hands together, she pushed my arms over head. Her warm, wet pussy was all over me. She was still dripping from her orgasm, making us both slick with her cum.

"Get a condom, baby." I was close to begging.

She leaned forward and kissed me hard, letting go of my hands and gripping my shaft again. My eyes rolled back when she slid onto my hard cock, bare, hot, and wet.

"Oh, fuuuuck."

She was the only one in my life that I had fucked bare. She writhed on top of me, making my head grind back at how incredible she felt.

With my hands free I gripped her hips and helped her fuck me harder and faster.

She clenched around me, making my dick twitch. Her lips were feral against mine.

"I love you." Her gasps tickled against my chest as the fluttering of her pussy started. She squeezed me so tightly she pulled my own release out of me.

Her chest hit mine as her arms collapsed. Fingers combed through my hair as we caught our breath. She kissed my chest before tracing across my tattoo.

"You got this for me?"

My lips grazed the top of her head. "It's always been you."

I flipped us around, so she was on her back. I kissed her naked chest before resting my chin on her stomach and gazing up at her.

"I need a few minutes and then I'm going to make love to you all night long."

Epilogue

Tama

Six Months Later

I shook my arms out nervously. "I can't believe you talked me into this," I hissed to Henry. I had been convinced to throw the first pitch of the first home game for the Mariners. As a ridiculously unathletic person I should have said no, but Rhys was too excited about celebrating my second book with his team.

Henry chuckled and shrugged. "It's good publicity for the new book. Speaking of which, congrats." He leaned over and kissed my cheek. "You're back on the New York Times best seller list, not that I'm surprised, sex sells."

I whimpered. "See I don't need to do this for publicity."

He shrugged. "Whatever, it's already set up. There's no backing out now. Besides, you've been practicing with Tom and Rhys for a month now. You're ready."

Ava bounced into the room and passed me a bottle of water before grabbing my hands and inspecting them. "You are going to do fine. Are you feeling stage fright? I can go through some breathing exercises with you."

"Breathing sounds good."

A knock sounded at the door and the PR person for the Mariners walked in. "We are ready when you are."

I turned to Henry and Ava with a worried expression.

"You're going to kill it," Henry reassured me.

I couldn't feel my knees as I followed the overly bubbly PR woman through the bowels of the stadium.

"When you hear your name, you are going to wave as you walk up to the mound. Don't worry if you don't make it across the home plate. Most people don't."

I squeaked in response. She grinned at me and pushed my back as my name was called over the loudspeaker. The stadium lights were bright, almost too bright for me to see the crowd, but I could hear their applause.

Don't trip, don't trip, don't trip.

I made it to the center of the infield. Rhys had promised me that he'd be next to the mound to cheer me on, but I didn't see him. Kevin clapped and whistled loudly from his position. I gripped the ball hard into my sweaty palm. Tom had practiced with me almost every day since this silly thing was booked. Trudy loved that I was now a part of the game of fetch in the morning.

The catcher nodded at me, and I threw as hard as I could. He walked only a few feet in front of home plate and caught it. At least it was a respectable distance. The crowd cheered as I waved. The catcher walked back up to me to pass me the ball I had thrown. I recognized the swagger in his steps.

Rhys tipped his catcher's helmet off.

I giggled at him as he passed me the ball with a wink. Then he dropped to one knee.

My eyes widened at Rhys as the crowd went wild.

"I told you I wanted you to be mine forever, Bully, let's make it official and let the whole world know that I belong to you officially. Marry me, baby."

My wide eyes and quick nod should have been enough, but verbal communication was important. "Yes."

He slipped a rose gold band with a diamond solitaire on my finger. I recognized it as Rita's mother's ring. She had shown it to me before and lamented on how she wished her daughter would have it.

He scooped me up and kissed me hard. Arms wrapped around me that weren't Rhys's. I turned around to my mom and Beckett. They had Trudy on his leash. My mom was crying, and Beckett was shaking Rhys's hand. Trudy was wagging his tail pleased with the attention.

"No backing out now, Bully."

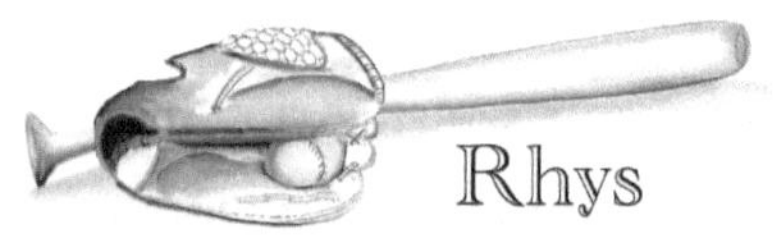

Rhys

Eight Months Later

"You look happy," Whinny said to me.

Nathan chuckled. "Nothing compared to the day we don't talk about."

I rolled my eyes, not wanting to think about my first wedding day.

"I'm glad you two recovered from last week. I've never seen you so drunk in my life."

My friends had treated me and several of the guys we went to school with on a crazy trip to Las Vegas. Ava, Lily, Will, Griffin, Henry, Matt, and Nicole had also planned a trip to Vegas, so we all hung out and got drunk. I knew my fiancée was a ringer at cards. I had no idea she was a fucking shark. She made ten grand and ended up getting our room comped.

Whinny grimaced. "We had to do your bachelor party right, bro. Though I don't think I can smell Fireball without feeling clammy again."

He and Griffin went to town on the liquor and then disappeared into some club after I called it a night. My friendship with Griffin was amicable, and I hated to admit I liked the fucker.

I chuckled as I straightened my tie.

Nathan grinned. "Last night got crazier than I thought it would."

Last night was my rehearsal dinner. Tama and I had decided to get married in Palm Springs so all her old neighbors from Friendly Village could attend. Gerty had set up a poker tournament and cleaned out all my groomsmen within two hours. Then she started betting on their clothes.

Ten minutes later my best friends and Griffin were down to their boxers and Tama was pulling the plug on Gerty's good time.

There was a small knock on the door to the groom's room. Henry poked his head in. Ever since our talk in Denver it had been easier to be around each other. I'd even consider him a friend because I understood he was firmly in my girl's corner, always.

"We are ready when you are."

I looked over to Whinny, Nathan, Kevin, and Alister. "Ready boys?"

"Shouldn't we be asking you this?" Al asked me with a curled lip.

I chuckled. "I've been ready for this for years."

I walked up the aisle where the justice of the peace was waiting. Everything about my wedding to Tama had been planned together. We agreed we wanted a party to celebrate with our closest friends. Our moms took over when we didn't have an opinion.

My mom and Melody had spent the better part of the week making floral arrangements with the residents of Friendly Village.

I wasn't nervous when the music switched and pair by pair our closest friends walked towards me. Alister walked down the aisle with Gerty and Thelma. They were the flower girls; a role they loved playing. He grumbled about walking the grannies, but after poker he had chilled and leaned into the flirtatious Gerty. He sat them down in the front row and joined me up front.

Nicole, who looked great considering she had a baby a month ago, and Kevin were next, followed by Lily and Nathan, last Whinny accompanied Ava. Ava who had married Henry a year ago in Paris after a four-year long engagement, and yes, I was invited to the nuptials.

I let out a slow breath when the music changed again to cue Tama's walk towards me. Beckett was crying as Tama patted his arm. She looked radiant as she beamed at me.

Our ceremony was short and sweet. Our vows were simple.

"I knew you were always meant to be mine."

"I know you will always be mine."

The End

While this concludes the Pineview University series, it is not the end for any of your favorite side characters.

Don't worry, I didn't forget about Holden Pierce. Stay tuned, he gets a whole series dedicated to him and his coworkers. Rules of the City Series is the next to launch!

Chapter 1

She cheated on me. *She cheated on me?* SHE CHEATED ON ME! Fuck, how could she? I've done everything for her. I've supported her both emotionally and financially for three years. Every single thing that didn't go her way I was there to hold her hand and shower her with praise and presents. When she wasn't voted her sorority president it was me that took her away for a weekend retreat so she could relax and reflect.

When she was failing her biology class, I was the one that helped her with tutors and quizzed her to keep her on track. When she got in a car accident, I was the one that paid the insurance premium so her dad didn't find out. When she wanted her tits done, I argued it wasn't necessary, but supported her because it made her happy.

I took off work to help her recover and swap out frozen peas even though what she had naturally was perfectly fine. Now, they were too big, looked fake, and were no longer sensitive like before. Essentially the procedure reversed an erogenous zone, which seemed even more wasteful to me.

I have been taking care of her for three years and she's been cheating the whole time.

I took a big gulp of the rum. Rum wasn't my drink of choice but it was there and I figured while in Barbados you drink fucking rum. I was walking along the beach at night. A different beach than the one that just blew my life up.

I was going to propose to her in two weeks! I was going to make a dedication of my life to hers. My whole romantic future fucking gone, up in smoke. A fact she wasn't privy to. *Nope because I found out while hidden in the forest like a creepy stalker overhearing a lover's quarrel.*

The showdown would happen, but not with witnesses. Lily had already seen too much, she didn't need to be involved in the end of my relationship.

I took another swig of rum. Head floaty, my anger mellowing out, I kept walking away from the resort where my cheating girlfriend was probably heading to my room to attempt to fuck me. I have no doubt Lily broke anything up before Lucy dug her claws into Will. *How could I have been so blind?*

Lucy told me she viewed Will as a brother. I believed her. Then again, she also told me that she would *never* cheat because how horrible Will's father was for cheating on his mom. Will's father had a second family, and when it all came out in the end, she told me Will didn't take it well. Will rebelled against his father and his new wife. That his new stepmom was framed as this villain, but she was just misunderstood. And the biggest culprit for villainizing Kim was Will. I believed all the bullshit. Even after I met Will and Kim. Even when I saw what a terrible person Kim was, I believed Lucy's version. At least until a seed of doubt was sewn that perhaps Lucy was lying and Will didn't lean on

Lucy for emotional support like she claimed. *What else did she lie about?*

I kicked the sand at my feet, shuffling through the shoreline. I looked up to the sky. It was a clear night, limited light pollution, and all the stars were twinkling. My foot slipped into a hole, propelling my body forward as I crashed into a sandcastle. Had I been watching where I was going I would have seen the manmade moat.

Fuck my life. I flipped my body around and looked at the sky. The sandcastle I had just destroyed was fairly sizable. A turret was propping one shoulder higher than the other. One leg was in the moat, the sand significantly damper than the rest of the structure. I knew my suit pants were going to be trashed. I didn't fucking care.

I just laid there in the wrecked castle and looked at the sky. *Maybe I'll just sleep here.* There was no way I was in the right state of mind to see Lucy right now. I was avoiding the inevitable conversation, but I needed to let my brain go to war for the night before I battled another person. Lucy was sneaky and a liar and I didn't have the energy to deal with her right now.

I had left my cellphone in my room after I dropped off my suit jacket and grabbed my wallet. I left the hotel quickly. I didn't give a fuck if I made Lucy worried. We would be over in the morning.

"Uh, are you okay over here?" a raspy feminine voice asked. A beautiful face filled my vision as she stood over me. I felt like perhaps I hit my head on a rock, and I was hallucinating because there is no fucking way Ariel from the Little Mermaid was asking me if I was okay.

I blinked up at her and slowly nodded. "Are you real or am I dead?"

Her throaty laugh made my chest feel tight. "I'm real. Do you need help up, or do you want to keep lying there?"

I held my hand up to signal that a little help would be appreciated.

She gripped my forearm with one hand and clasped our palms together with the other. My weight shifted a little too much as she toppled into my chest with an oof. She giggled in my ear. I closed my eyes at her perfume. She smelled like sandalwood with a hint of something sweet like jasmine and vanilla.

Our legs were tangled and torsos pressed together. She was tall, at least 5'9". Her long hair curtained around us as she pushed herself up. I didn't know whether to help her or not. Her sundress flipped up as she tried to right herself. She laughed when she stood back up and slapped her dress down that had exposed her little white panties.

"Let's try that again. I'll brace myself a little better."

She regripped my hand and instead of pulling her towards me like before I sat myself up and allowed her to pull me. When I was upright, she placed her hands on my shoulders and spun me around. In an almost violent attack, she swatted the sand off my back and butt.

"There." She wiped her own hands off.

I plucked up my bottle of rum and took a swig then offered her some. "Want to be my drinking buddy for the night?"

She shrugged, took a quick pull and passed it back. "I'll limit myself to that so I can drive home, but I have a good counteroffer."

I smirked at her. She was gorgeous and I was still not convinced this encounter was real. "What's that?"

She grinned. "I will happily be your snack buddy for the night. Have you ever tried BiBi's? It's a snack company here in

Barbados. I personally love their spicy plantain chips, but I could really go for a pineapple sugarcake. I have a little assortment if you want to noosh with me for a while." She wagged her eyebrows. I couldn't tell the exact color of her eyes, but I knew they were light.

I nodded. I wondered if she were a real-life siren, beautiful and tempting. "I could go for some food."

Her smile stretched across her lips, deep set twin dimples popped into her cheeks. "Perfect, I'll grab a blanket so we can make ourselves a nice little picnic." The sand twisted under her feet and the wind blew the skirt of her dress as she walked backwards up the beach towards the parking lot.

I felt awkward as fuck as guilt started to sweep in that I shouldn't be volunteering to talk to a random woman this late at night. I swallowed it down when she came back, arms ladened with food and a blanket. I reached out to help lighten the load.

"What a gentleman," she said with a fake little British accent. I chuckled. I wasn't feeling like a gentleman. I was feeling confused, but at least Ariel's presence was calming me down. None of it felt real, and if I were in a dream I needed to at least go with the flow. I gritted my teeth at the bitter reminder that I should not feel guilty about anything. My relationship with Lucy was over. I wasn't cheating, I was simply enjoying a gorgeous woman's company.

"I'm not feeling like a gentleman," I admitted. "I feel like we should at least swap names before I eat all your food."

She laughed and shook her head. "Do you think I'd let you eat it all? No sir, this is an equal partnership. And," she paused, twisting her lips to the side, "let's just keep it anonymous. No real names, just good vibes."

I ran my fingers through my hair and dusted off some sand from my hands. "Sounds good. I'll just call you Ariel," I suggested.

She laughed, "Because of the red hair?"

I shrugged. I didn't realize that was her hair color, but sure that works. "It sounds like you recently got your voice back. Do I need to be worried about Prince Eric looking for you? I got to be honest, I'm a little drama-ed out."

She smirked at me. "I kind of dig that you know so much about the Little Mermaid. And don't worry, no drama with me. Okay, so I'm Ariel, what should we call you?"

One shoulder lifted. "John Doe?"

Her lip pulled up unevenly. "Like an unidentified body in the morgue? No, that won't work for you. Let's call you Jack."

I grinned. "Like Jack Sparrow?"

She shook her head. "I wasn't going with the ocean theme, if I were I'd call you Bruce."

A confused expression furrowed my forehead. "Why Bruce?"

Her smile stretched again. "That's the name of Jaws," she said.

Come to think of it, I'd eat the hell out of her given the chance.

I gritted my teeth to keep my thoughts sealed and spread the blanket out onto the sand. She kicked her sandals off to hold down two of the corners and settled onto one side of the blanket, dropping her loot of snacks in the middle.

"Learn something new every day. Okay, so why Jack?"

"Because you look like Chris Pine from the Jack Ryan movie."

I couldn't be certain, but it looked like she was blushing. I smiled, "I'll take that as a compliment."

She leaned forward and opened a bag of chips. "Sweet potato?" she offered. I stuck my fingers into the small opening and pulled a few out. They crunched loudly, something I immediately tried to quiet down by covering my mouth. Lucy hated hearing someone chewing.

"Sorry, these are crunchy."

Ariel frowned at me and shrugged. "Yeah, they'd suck if they were soft. Crunch away, that's the best part." She took an exaggerated bite and crunched loudly. "So, tell me about your fake dreams Jack." Her words were muffled as she chewed her food.

I pointed to one of the bottles of water she had brought.

She nodded. "Help yourself, we are having a picnic at the beach. It's important to stay hydrated." Her wink made my stomach flip flop.

I chuckled. "I thought that had to do with sweating from the sun."

She shrugged. "The moon can make you sweat, probably." She made an unsure face and then smiled again.

"Maybe if I were a werewolf."

She giggled. "How do I know you aren't a werewolf?"

I pointed at the full moon. "I'm pretty sure you'd be dead by now."

She shook her head. "Nope, Twilight said that the werewolves didn't kill people, only vampires."

I chuckled. "Well, if we are going with Twilight werewolves then you would know that they aren't actual werewolves, but shape shifters that chose a wolf form because of its significance to their tribe."

Her eyes widened. "Are you are twi-hard?"

I shook my head. "Not in the tiniest bit. My girlfriend in high school on the other hand," I nodded, "she was a definite fan of the books."

Ariel hummed. "Well, I love books in general, so I have read them. It has been a while, but I think you are right." She dramatically wiped her brow. "Well, I guess you passed the werewolf test. So tell me about your dreams, Jack." She opened another two bags of chips and handed the entire bag to me and kept one for herself.

I thought about it for a moment. "Honestly, when I was a kid I wanted to be an astronaut. Like, how cool would it be to say you've walked on the moon?"

Her dimples were back. "It would be incredible considering no woman has been on the moon. It's been quite a sausage party since 1969."

I laughed. "The moon is the modern-day men's club. Maybe it actually stands for 'men's only orb of night.'"

She snorted. "So, it's a mooon, we've been saying it wrong all this time."

I chuckled. "Fine, men's orb of night, better?"

She nodded and crunched loudly, "Absolutely, if we are going to enforce the patriarchy in celestial satellites, I want it to be at least spelled correctly."

I pointed at her. "My apologies," I held up my bag. "These are freaking good, Ariel."

She snickered and nodded. "I love them. I was just coming from a friend's house after she made me some chicken soup and she gave me all of these as I was leaving." She waved her hand over the bags.

"It must be cool to live here."

She shrugged. "It's a paradise. The people are kind and hardworking. The tourists are okay. Even when they destroy sandcastles." She nudged my foot with hers.

I shook my head and gave her a half smile. "Not my finest moment. I'm going to blame the rum."

She nodded. "Some of the finest in the world. Okay, Jack, so you want to be an astronaut. What else?"

"Well obviously I live in Cape Canaveral, Florida because a good astronaut lives with his rocket."

I could barely hear her husky laugh over the sounds of the waves hitting the shore. "Wait, I thought astronauts would live in Houston because that is where they train for space." Her smile was contagious. Seeing her deep-set dimples made my own smile stretch.

"You caught me, I'm a space pirate. I live near the rocket so I can be a stowaway and take over the aircraft once we are in space."

"I knew it. That must be why you automatically thought of Jack Sparrow. You are a pirate at heart. So, Jack, once you have commandeered the ship, what are your plans going to be?"

I took a swig of rum and followed it up with a gulp of water. "Go to the moon, easy."

She nodded. "Well, Jack, then I insist you take me along for the ride. My name will live in infamy as the first woman to walk on the moon."

I stuck my hand out. "You've got yourself a deal. We can be the space version of Bonnie and Clyde." She giggled and clasped my palm with her own. It was warm and soft. It took willpower to not tug her closer to me. "What about you, Ariel, what do you do for a living?"

She wagged her head back and forth. "My mom and I run a donut ice cream shop. We started out with just donuts but noticed that we had an opportunity in the midafternoon for traffic, so we started making ice cream."

I leaned forward. "For real?"

She shrugged. "Why not? Not as lofty as an astronaut but people love donuts and ice cream. It's a stress-free job and you make someone's day a little better. I dare you to find one person that had either a donut or ice cream after a bad day and they didn't feel a little better."

I leaned back on my hands. "Well, now that I'm thinking about it, ice cream sounds good. And trust me, I've had a day."

She nodded. "I figured. Handsome men don't normally wander down the beach after midnight drinking rum and seem perfectly content in laying in the remains of a sandcastle they destroyed."

I shrugged and reached over to snag another bag of chips. My responding silence made her move the conversation along to lighter topics.

"What's the ice cream you'd drown your sorrows in?"

"I like mint chip."

She frowned and nodded. "I was going to diss your choice, but all that means is that you wouldn't eat my ice cream."

I grinned at her. "What's your ice cream choice?"

"Oh, that's easy. I love a good chocolate chip cookie dough."

I laughed. "Sorry to tell you, Ariel, but I would destroy your pint of ice cream. That's my second choice. I will be the one that seeks out all the cookie dough and leaves the vanilla ice cream full of tunnels where I stole the best part."

She clutched her chest and pretended to cry. "A man after my own heart. I am very guilty for doing that same thing." She stood up and wiped the sand from her calves and held her hand out to me. "Come on, Jack. Let's get some ice cream."

I let her pull me up. I was still taller than her, but I liked that she was closer to looking me in the eye than most women I knew. "Aren't all parlors closed?"

She shrugged. "Parlors, yes, but there is a twenty-four-hour convenience store that is about a ten-minute drive away. It's where I go when I'm hankering for some junk food late at night." She looked down at her watch. "Besides, the police will sweep the beaches in about thirty minutes to make sure no one is trying to sleep on the shore. From two to four the beaches are supposed to be empty. Unless you want to make your way back to your resort, then we need to go anyway."

I shook my head. "I have no interest in going to my room tonight."

She grinned and bent over to collect our snacks, trash, and the blanket. I grabbed the empty chip bags from her hands and walked over to the trash can near the parking lot path. She led the way, swaying her hips as her feet twisted in the sand.

Now that she was not watching me, I took a good look at her figure. I could already tell from the lower cut of her dress that her chest was ample. The dress she was wearing nipped in her waist and hit mid-thigh. She had an hourglass figure that many women paid for, but she didn't look the type to have cosmetic surgery to achieve her body. It looked natural. Her legs were long and lean as she shuffled through the sand.

She wasn't overly toned, but I could tell she stayed in shape. She probably didn't spend an hour and a half a day at the gym like Lucy did. She probably surfed and hiked to keep her physique, but she seemed too much of a free spirit to hold herself to any workout regimen.

Glancing over her shoulder, she caught me staring at her ass. Her grin split her cheeks as we stopped at the little spigot available to rinse sand from our feet. I rolled my suit pants up after she was done using the water.

There was only one car in the parking lot, an older Range Rover with three surfboards strapped to the roof. I settled into the front seat. Her car smelled like coconut and something familiar that I couldn't place. We made small talk as we drove to the little convenience store. It was just off the main strip where people were walking around the clubs and bars.

The bright fluorescent lights of the store made me blink after being in the darkness of nearly two am. Ariel was simply gorgeous in the light. Her hair was auburn with lighter fiery streaks and long, her eyes were a light blue. There was something familiar about her, but I didn't know why. I snagged a pair of flip flops and paid for our ice cream.

"Alright Jack, our adventure is all on you. Until you need to get back to your room, I am down to hang out."

I looked at her. Her white teeth were biting into her plump pink bottom lip. My throat felt thick and my tongue too big when I saw how beautiful she really was. "I could definitely use a night away from reality."

Her dimples popped as she opened the door to her Range Rover. "Okay then. There is this place that I know about twenty minutes away. The local high schoolers use it as a make out point, but after two the police stop checking it so they can monitor the beach."

"A make out point? I'm a gentleman," I pretended to be offended by clutching my imaginary pearls.

She giggled and shook her head. "You're a space pirate, but I'm not taking you there to seduce you. It has clear views of that sky you were so happy to look at."

I smirked at her. Making out with her sounded appealing, but stargazing was a good alternative. "Sounds good, let's go."

We talked the entire twenty-minute drive. She told me stories of local lore about roads we were on. She obviously loved living in Barbados. The SUV slowed down as we started driving up an incline and we stopped at the top of a cliff. She made a three-point turn so the back of her car was facing the cliff edge.

"You need a quick getaway?"

She chuckled and nodded. "Rule number one of space piracy, always plan for a quick getaway."

I smiled over at her, wanting to tell her my actual name and profession. There was a part of me that wanted to hear her say my name. I felt a connection to her that I couldn't describe. She made my stomach flip, and my head feel floaty. I hadn't felt that way about anyone since my first kiss with my first crush.

I wanted her to really know me. I doubted she'd be interested in my job; few people were. I can't even tell you how many times Lucy told me to stop talking about finance, stock options, and new companies.

The car was very quiet when she turned it off. "Alright, Jack, I am willing to share some of my ice cream, since you had a bad day."

I followed her to the back of the Rover as she opened the trunk and laid the beach blanket out. The back row was already folded down, making an open space for us to stretch out. She passed me my container of ice cream and clinked her spoon against mine before we dug in.

The coolness of the dessert felt good in the heat of the night. She moaned quietly with her lips wrapped around the spoon. I gritted my teeth and try to ignore what she was doing to my body. My brain was warring with my dick about what was right and wrong. My dick was one hundred percent on board with whatever happened tonight. My brain needed convincing.

"Close your eyes and open your mouth and I'll give you a big surprise." Her voice cracked and fried out at the end of her singsong request.

I squinted at her. "I don't know if we have that sort of relationship yet, Red."

She giggled and shrugged. "Suit yourself, but I found the Plymouth Rock of cookie dough."

I chuckled and opened my mouth and leaned over to her. She grinned and dug into her container and produced a pretty sizable chunk of dough. She watched me chew, biting her lip.

I nodded. "That's pretty good."

She grinned at me and leaned a little back. I hadn't realized that we were so close together. She licked her lips and turned her face down to concentrate on her ice cream. "Tell me a story."

I tilted my head. "What kind of story?"

She shrugged. "Dealer's choice. It can be something funny that happened, or it can be a controversial situation like 'am I the asshole'."

I took another bite of ice cream and thought. I grinned to myself after a moment. "I lived in North Florida until I was going into high school. There is this grocery store called Publix. Have you ever heard of it?"

She nodded slowly. "I've spent some time in Miami."

I nodded satisfied with the answer.

"Alright well my mom had some friends over for a barbeque or something. One friend had just moved to Florida from Oklahoma and was going on and on about how she bought this sal-mon at Publix and how wonderful the sal-mon was and how the Publix deli worker was so knowledgeable about sal-mon. And my mom says to her friend, 'the L is silent' and her friend said, 'oh it's pronounced Pubix."

She snickered under her breath and nodded. "I like an innocent story. Okay, my turn." She wiggled her fingers together. "When I was little, I was obsessed with sleeping in a top bunk. Like all I asked for on my birthday and Christmas was a bunk bed. Fast forward after a year of petitioning to get a bunk bed, my parents relent. I was five years old and literally thought I was the coolest girl in the world. A few months later I lost my first tooth, and my mom told me that in order for the Tooth Fairy to come I had to leave my tooth in the kitchen and cover it with a pillow.

"Now I was a curious kid, and I knew my friends were just able to put it under their own pillows in their bed. So, when I asked my mom, she said it's because the Tooth Fairy is afraid of heights. Being naïve I was like, yeah that makes sense. I legitimately believed that the Tooth Fairy, a fairy that flew around from house to house, was afraid of heights until I was like ten when the real Tooth Fairy was revealed to be my mom. Tell me why it took me until I was eighteen to realize my mom had me leave my teeth in the kitchen because there was no way she would have been able to get to my pillow without shaking the bed and waking me up."

I laughed to myself and shrugged. "That's really sweet though."

She nodded and bent her head back to look up to the sky. "Can you imagine though if the Tooth Fairy was real and was afraid of heights? The therapy bill must have been insane to get her to face her fears every day." She turned to me. "What are you afraid of?"

I ate a scoop of ice cream to stall. After a few moments of deliberation, I finally answered. "I was afraid of the dark until I was twelve. To this day my mom has a nightlight in the guest bathroom because I would refuse to go into the bathroom at night. The combination of the dark and a mirror still gives me the chills."

She gave me a wide-eyed nod. "Yes! Mirrors are creepy in the dark. Have you ever stared at your face so long that it starts looking weird?"

I shook my head. "I've never been the type of guy to admire myself for too long, but regardless I'd be too worried that the reflection would change without me moving."

She laughed and nodded again. "So true. Anyway, I'd say my biggest fear would be falling upstairs and cracking my teeth."

I winced. "Is there a story there?"

She shrugged. "Not that directly but I did have braces twice. I kept losing my retainer, and then I was born with three sets of molars like a shark, so I had to have oral surgery to remove them. The idea of anything happening to these chompers gives me the eebie jeebies." She showed me all of her teeth and then laughed when she couldn't hold her mouth open any more.

I chuckled. "You do have nice teeth."

She wagged her brows at me. "Thanks, so do you."

I smiled at her like an idiot. She leaned into me, and I made a decision that my brain was going to have to get on board with.

Setting my ice cream down, I cupped her cheek. Her lips were gentle and warm against mine. There wasn't urgency, but my whole face was tingling as my stomach started to feel light. Kissing her felt right. She tilted her head and slowly opened her mouth against mine. Her tongue was cold and tasted a little chocolatey. I immediately wanted more. My tongue slid against hers and her hands drifted into my hair.

Nails lightly scratched the nape of my neck, making goosebumps dance across my skin. She let out a little sigh when she pulled away. I watched her eyes flutter open as she leaned back. "You're a good kisser." Her voice was extra raspy.

I grinned and went to adjust the tent in my pants. I hadn't popped a boner from kissing a girl since I was fifteen. We both leaned against our respective sides of the car and finished our ice cream while talking about random things.

We made each other laugh, and after an hour of talking, my brain was sold that whatever happened with this woman was meant to be. I was going to enjoy wherever this night took me. I honestly couldn't remember the last time I had laughed this much. Our conversation lapsed into a silence, but at this point we were both on our back, head closest to the tailgate while we star gazed.

I saw her turn her head to me from the side of my eye. I mirrored her. "What?" I whispered, watching her strum her bottom lip with her teeth.

"I want to kiss you again, but I'm telling you right now I won't be able to stop. It's been a while, and you are quite possibly the hottest, sweetest, funniest guy I have ever spent time with."

I leaned into her and kissed her. It was not as gentle as before. It was feverish and desperate. I wanted to taste every inch of her, and in the back of her Rover, I did. And she tasted all of me. I almost blew my load when she started to suck me off. It was a sensation I hadn't felt in years. Lucy didn't like giving head, and I didn't complain about it.

When I got so close to cumming my jaw hurt from clenching I grabbed her arms and pulled up to kiss me. Her panties were long gone. I fumbled putting a condom on as she kissed me and as soon as I was sheathed she eased herself onto me. It was intense and no matter how hard I tried, I couldn't muster an ounce of guilt.

She snuggled into my chest when we were finished. She had unbuttoned my shirt and was running her fingers through my chest hair that I hadn't had time to trim since being in Barbados for two weeks. Her fingers circled down to the port wine stain I had on my hip. "Were you in a fight?"

I shook my head. "Birth mark."

She hummed and worked her body down to kiss it. She looked up to me from my hips. "The sun is going to be rising soon. We are on the wrong side of the island to watch it. So my question for you is, do you want another round now or at the beach?" She kissed my other hip. She made the decision for me when she licked me from root to tip.

An hour later I was so relaxed and satisfied as Ariel leaned into me and we watched the sun rise together. She had parked back at the original spot she found me. She turned to me and bit her lip again. I used my thumb to ease it away from her teeth. I leaned into her for a quick kiss. "What's on your mind?"

"Do you want me to drive you to your hotel?"

I shook my head. The reality was, it was possible that Lucy would be waiting for me somewhere near the resort and I didn't want her to see Ariel. It didn't matter if I was ending my relationship with Lucy officially as soon as I saw her, I didn't want Ariel to see Lucy and think I did something that I regretted.

"Okay," she sighed and stood up. "I need to get some sleep." She yawned and handed me a piece of paper. "I know we said we should keep this anonymous but in case you want to talk to a stranger, I'm available."

Shoving her number in my pocket, I watched her walk away. I started making my way down the shoreline and to my doom. I went over all the things I wanted to say to Lucy when I saw her.

She was sound asleep when I made it to the room. I started packing and wasn't until I was zipping my luggage did she wake. She grinned at me and then frowned when she saw my bags ready.

"What's going on?" Lucy asked, her green eyes looked beautiful in the morning light.

I shook my head. "I was on the private beach last night. I heard everything. Suffice it to say it's over. You've been cheating on me for the better part of our relationship, and I refuse to be with anyone out of pity." She tried to argue, but I walked away from our relationship knowing it was for the best.

Chapter 2

One Month Later

"I'm pregnant," Lucy said.

I blinked at her, confused. I had not seen her in a month, not since I left the resort. I was incredibly thankful that we never officially moved in with each other. It was a point of contention for me initially.

I had moved into an apartment that was halfway between Baylor, where she was going, and my office. It meant that my commute to work was forty-five minutes. I had moved there with the intent that we would actually live together. She said she didn't want to move that far away from campus, even though she only had classes one day a week and three other days a week she was working for a clinic that was twenty minutes from my apartment.

I was able to collect her box of stuff and leave it outside the door of my apartment so I didn't have to see her.

I had unblocked her number to send her the message to come get her things. Then I promptly blocked her again and went to hike the Cedar Ridge Loop. It was a trail I enjoyed on days when I had excess energy or I needed a quiet place to think and enjoy nature. Lucy was never a big fan of hikes because she didn't like to sweat outside.

The fact that she went on a hike while in Barbados shocked me. She didn't complain once. I thought it was because her best friend, who happened to be Will's half-sister and the bride of the vacation, spent the entire hike and vacation complaining and talking shit about Lily. Now I was thinking it had more to do with the fact that she wanted Will to think she was perfect. Not that he noticed because it would take a blind man to not see how perfect Lily was for him.

Lucy left a passive aggressive note on my door that I threw away without giving it much thought. It was the generic, *I'm sorry give me another chance,* bullshit. She was due for her botox injections that I paid for, so I figured that was her motive. She also started blowing up my social media. I had already erased every picture of her and me. Another red flag was she never posted a single picture of me and would untag herself in any picture I had her in. Within an hour my three-year relationship was gone from all social platforms. When she started blowing up my DMs, I deactivated my account.

And now after a month of not seeing her and refusing the lame attempts to talk to me, here she was. Lucy had stopped by my work and forced me to have lunch with her. She looked tired. The golden tan I had seen her with had faded. She was still beautiful, but I knew her beauty was tainted. Her hair looked like it was freshly dyed to cover her darker roots. I'm sure she was asking her dad to increase her allowance after telling him what a horrible boyfriend I was.

Her dad, Scott, had sent me a message a week after we had gotten home from Barbados. I really held myself back by not telling him everything. I kept it simple. She cheated on me, and I needed time.

"I don't understand."

She rubbed her overly plumped lips that I paid to have injected every few months and sighed. "I'm pregnant and it's yours. I haven't been with anyone besides you for a year."

I slowly nodded. "But you're on birth control and we always used a condom."

She shrugged. "Nothing is fool-proof, Holden." She took out a positive pregnancy test that was sealed in a sandwich bag.

My stomach felt like a lead weight was sitting in it. On one hand I had always wanted to be a father. She knew I had always wanted a family, but it was something she had said was going to have to wait. She wasn't sure if she ever wanted to have kids, which is why I used a condom on top of her birth control.

Of course in hindsight it was probably because she was fucking someone else.

I stared at the positive pregnancy test and took a deep breath. The reality was I didn't miss Lucy, but I did miss companionship. After my amazing night with Ariel, it put into perspective what my time with Lucy was. She didn't laugh at my jokes or ask me about myself. Every conversation geared back to her in some way. She didn't care about my job, she just wanted the security of my paycheck.

After I landed from Barbados, I was quick to unpack, throw my clothes in the laundry and drop my suits off at the cleaners. It wasn't until I was hanging my suit pants on their wooden hangers at home did I remember Ariel's number was still in the pocket. It had only been three days, but I wanted to text message her. The paper was completely smudged and unrecognizable from the cleaners. I felt like I was told my family pet had died and I had to deal with the loss silently.

"I can't trust you, Lucy."

She licked her lips and nodded. "I know I messed up. I was so stupid, and this test put a lot of things into perspective for me. For one, I looked up a great couple's therapist for us to go to. I know we can work something out for the baby."

I shook my head. "I don't want to be with you."

She frowned. "It was one mistake, and you believed Will without even asking me what really happened. I forgive you for taking his word over mine, but Holden, a baby deserves to have its father in their life. I am willing to go to therapy with you so we can make it past this."

I swallowed the knot in my throat and all the things I wanted to say. Like, I didn't believe only Will's side, I heard her confess everything. Or how I listened to her admit that she pitied me and that she had convinced Will that she was single for two of the three years we were together where she spent her summers continuing her affair. I didn't though because we were in the lobby of my office building, and nothing beats a gossip like a gossip from Texas.

But, she had a point. My child deserved to have me in their life so I agreed to therapy on the premise it would make co-parenting easier.

Three weeks later

These sessions are not about co-parenting.

It was about delving deeper into the root cause that Lucy felt the need to stray. Somehow, I was to blame for ninety percent of it. I was too available. I was too ready to do what she wanted. I didn't read her cues to fulfill her need to be chased. The other ten percent was how her parents never punished her, so it showed her that there were no consequences for bad behavior. Our therapist Nadia was insistent that what was best for the health of the unborn baby was to keep Lucy stress-free and my inability to accept responsibility in the downfall out of relationship was stressing Lucy out.

I didn't like that I was folding. I felt like I was understanding her on a different level. I felt like there was a possibility that we may have a future after all. She had already started her new job at the hospital and was liking everything so far. I wasn't ready for her to move in, but I was more open to having dinner with her once a week after our therapy sessions.

I wanted to be in my child's life. I wanted to be the father that they deserved and if it meant I was going to have to swallow a little pride to ensure that happens, I was willing to do just that.

Monroe

I let out a deep breath as I stared at the positive pregnancy test. The one night I let myself be free and have a one-night stand and here I was pregnant with no clue what the father's name actually was. He never called or text messaged me, which I took to mean the magic I felt was one sided.

I had no doubt that it was Jack's child. I hadn't been with anyone else in almost eight months. After I got back home, I had tried to go on a few dates, but nothing felt the same as what I felt with him. Our conversations flowed, he laughed at my corny jokes. He was funny too. It still felt like a fever dream, but I was staring at evidence that it definitely happened.

I had never wanted to kiss someone as badly as I did Jack within so quickly of meeting him. There was something about him that felt like we were deeply connected. I was normally the girl that only would have sex with her boyfriend after being together for a month.

I was a serial monogamous. I loved the feeling of falling in love. I loved the anticipation of being with that person. I loved getting to know my new boyfriend and the slow edging where we would do everything but penetration and that made it all worth the wait. But with Jack, there was no waiting period. And the sex, good lord the sex. The man was blessed from his incredibly handsome face all the way to his impressive dick.

I closed my eyes and tried to remember his face. He had blond hair, he was tall at least six foot two, which was great because I was five foot nine and I loved being in heels. I only caught a glimpse of his eyes when we were in the convenience store buying ice cream and then again when we were watching the sun rise. I felt certain he had green eyes. But the rest of his face felt fuzzy. I knew he was handsome. I knew I thought he looked like Chris Pine, but when I tried to imagine his face, it was blurry. I could still remember how he made me feel, but I wouldn't be able to pick him out of a lineup with *feelings*.

My stomach lurched again as I released the contents into the toilet. I had been feeling off for a few weeks. I noticed my period was late but chalked it up to traveling. I went from Barbados to New York to Cannes and then finally made it back to New York where I normally live.

My dad's resort in France was undergoing a minor expansion that we were trying to finish before the festival next year. It was not something that I would normally concern myself with. I had actually gone straight home from Barbados and after being home for two days dad asked me to fly to Europe. I ended up just taking notes about the negotiating he was doing with the various landowners.

I worked for my father in his finance department of the major resort company ML Properties. He owned 400 resorts throughout the world and my sister, and I were being primed to take over. Only she had decided to get her MBA after she was scheduled to graduate in a year. I wasn't upset about it. Between the two of us, she loved learning from books, and I loved learning through hands-on experience.

I was eventually going to take over for the CFO before Lily, my sister, and I took over as co-CEO. She was being primed as the COO. Both positions were being held by amazing people that weren't allotted to retire for years, giving us enough time and experience under our belts before we took over the helm when my dad was ready to retire.

A pregnancy was going to slow down my progress, but the CFO, Sue, was not set to retire for another fifteen years or there abouts. I would still have time to learn from the best, even if it meant I needed to take time off to raise this child… on my own.

Oh god! What was I going to tell dad? I knew my dad wouldn't be mad, he would probably wish I knew the father's name, but what was done was done. I couldn't exactly go back in time and demand the Chris Pine lookalike to tell me his actual life story.

I wiped my chin and swished water to get the bile from my mouth. My dad would support me. He would probably start looking for a nanny for me as soon as he found out. My child would be signed up for preschool before they were born because New York's preschools were elite and impossible to get into without waiting years.

My dad would do all the things I wouldn't even know to do. He raised Lily and me alone after my mom died of cancer. I was fourteen, Lily was twelve. I don't envy him the fact that he was the one that had the birds and the bees conversation with us. He also was the one to buy us all the feminine hygiene products and talked to Lily about what was going on with her body as she was going through puberty. I was lucky enough that my mom was still alive when I had started to change into a woman. I bestowed a traumatized Lily with the knowledge mom had shared with me.

What did I need to do first? I took a deep breath to ease the nausea and leaned against the vanity. I needed to talk to Lily. She had already started her final year of her bachelor's at Pineview, but at this point in the year she had just started her volleyball season. *Maybe I'll tell her over Thanksgiving.* That was the steadfast date when her season was normally over.

I swallowed back the bile. I would be showing at that point. I did the math. I'd be twenty-two weeks along. Oh lord, I'd know whether I was having a boy or a girl by then. Lily would be upset if I didn't tell her sooner. As it stood, I was already nine weeks along according to my period tracker. Okay, first things first, get a doctor's appointment. It was essentially Schrodinger's baby until I heard official word from a doctor.

I snatched my phone up and attempted to book an appointment. I was going to have to wait another week, no big deal. I could live in the limbo of both being pregnant and not pregnant for another week. I'd tell Lily and dad once I knew for sure. She was smart, she'd do the math and know it was my one-night stand.

She had been so understanding and encouraging when I expressed to her my desire to have casual sex for the first time in my life. Lily was my opposite. She hadn't had a serious boyfriend since high school when some tool named Geoff cheated on her.

I occasionally cyber stalked him. He peaked in high school. I never understood why people insisted on putting their socials on public. My account was completely private and even if you were my friend, all my posts were of my surroundings. Not a single picture had my face in it. I wanted the plausible deniability that any ex had found the correct Monroe Young.

How did this happen?

I whimpered when I sunk to my knees and pulled out the box of condoms, I had grabbed a strip from before I left for Barbados. My sister was staying in our family home there and was being bullied by her boyfriend's family for a variety of reasons. One of which was they thought she was poor and trash in comparison to her boyfriend, Will's ex, Lucy. It took some convincing for me to get her to let me come, but I went down for moral support.

Listening to her describe how she was being treated all because she refused to tell his family that she was real estate royalty pissed me off. I respected her right to privacy, so I didn't say anything and essentially hid myself away at my family compound. Well except at night when I pretended to be a local and apparently seduced hot tourists and got pregnant.

A tear slipped down my cheek when I saw my box of condoms were expired by six months. I had gone through a bit of a dating drought, but I didn't think it had been *that* long where checking the expiration was a necessary thing to do. A rookie mistake, apparently.

Didn't matter. I had the means, the mental fortitude, and the support to have this child whether I was going to raise this baby on my own or not. My dad would help me however he could. Lily would be my ride or die from Boulder. My support system was decent. I had good friends from work that were new parents. I had resources. I could do this. It was going to be fine. I was going to be fine.

Thank You

As soon as I wrote Tama's character in What are the Odds, I knew she needed her own story. It was so much fun having her learn and grow. From being naïve about everything to drawing boundaries and being her own advocate, it was therapeutic growth, that I hope you enjoyed.

Writing Rhys's character arc was a different sort of therapy. For all those out there that has known a fuckboy and saw his potential, Rhys was for you.

A million thanks to everyone that has read this book. I hope that you enjoyed it as much as I enjoyed writing it. Please leave a review and share. Reviews are the lifeblood of an author.

DB Jacobson

DB Jacobson is an American romance author. Her favorite writing companions are her dogs. She loves writing in the romance genre, but has branched into women's detective, romantic comedies, and sci-fi romance. She was born in the South and currently lives in Southern California. She often uses her experiences within those distinctly different cultures to guide her characters.

To get into touch with DB check out her website at www.dbjacobson.com

TikTok: DBJacobsonwrites
Meta: DBJacobsonwrites

Pineview University

What are the Odds

Matt is a senior with big league hopes. The only distraction he is willing to take on is finding her. A year ago, he ran into the perfect woman at a party. The problem? She was there was a total cheating jerk. He spends a year looking for her only to discover that she is in the math class he is a TA for.

Nicole is a sophomore that wants to focus on school because she spent her freshman year getting her heart broken by unfaithful jocks. Going into her second school year she is resolute in refusing to date another jock again. It's only a little complicated that the one jock she is willing to break her rule for is her TA.

Stressful, right? It doesn't help that some jerk keep stealing her
parking spot and making her life a living hell.

What are the odds is a steamy college romance. Tropes: enemies to lovers, second chance, baseball, forced proximity.

The Girlfriend Contract

Will just graduated school and has to attend his half-sister's wedding in Barbados. It doesn't help that Will does not get along with the bride or her mother. To make matters worse the maid of honor is 'the one that got away' and she is attending with her new boyfriend that Will suspects was the reason for their breakup.

Lily is Will's neighbor and friend. In a moment of weakness, she agreed to go to the wedding with Will. She knows all about Will's toxic ex, step-mother, and half-sister, so she's going and pretending to be Will's doting girlfriend.

The problem? Oh, just that she has a massive crush on Will and has for months. She just hopes she can get through the wedding with her heart intact.

The Girlfriend Contract is a young adult steamy romance. Tropes: fake relationship, vacation fling, forced proximity, one bed, friends to lovers.

Best Laid Plans

Henry is the reclusive dom who is recovering from a violent attack that ended his cousin's career before it even started. He's been busy trying to cope with the guilt of the attack and healing from a concussion. The last thing he wants to do is do anything that would jeopardize his friendships with the very people that saved his life.

Ava is Will's half-sister and just wants to escape the abusive shadow of her mother and sister. She lies to her parents about what school she is attending just so she can live her own life and be closer to Will.

Being only eighteen and doing everything on her own means she didn't know she needed to sign up for student housing. Luckily Will and Lily would never allow Ava to be homeless so they set her up with a place to stay.

The problem? Her roommate is Henry and he is without a doubt the most gorgeous man she has ever met. It make matters worse she's 'off limits' but that doesn't stop her from crushing on her brother's friend.

The Best Laid Plans is a steamy college romance. Tropes: brother's friend, roommates, forced proximity, dom/sub, first time.

The Missing Girls

A human trafficking ring is terrorizing the young women of LA. In the meantime, Caroline gets roped into helping a new friend find a missing person, who just might be the key to figuring out the trafficking ring.

Catching the Killer

A serial killer is on the loose in Southern California. Caroline works tirelessly to figure out who is guilty, so another woman does not fall victim to the SSS. While balancing her usual life with her nighttime investigations, her mysterious friend, Beck, keeps showing up when she least expects it. There is nothing like being attracted to a mystery man knowing there is no way for reciprocation.

Broad Day Gone

If a guy you were interested in a guy and they said you can't be with him until you knew who he was, you would invest the time to figure out who he is, right? Caroline finds herself compelled to take a deep dive into the mysterious Beck's background. She wants to figure out why he is so prone to believe he is not someone that can be loved

Running by Flight

Reeling from a break-up, Caroline is deep in a reckless well of depression. She is no longer careful with her investigations, putting herself in a perilous situation with a known rapist. After barely escaping, she is forced to face the one person that she is not ready to face. She is not ready for closure from her heartache, so she leaves before any confrontation could begin. There is nothing like a chase around the world and a good cold case of a missing woman to get Caroline back into the groove of life.

Dancing by Gaslight

Just when Caroline thinks she can put the whole human trafficking ring behind her, she gets roped right back into it. She gets tapped by an agency wanting to use her skills and her position as a board member from her bequeathed shares of KE. While investigating in Japan, she quickly learns what exactly Beck was doing during their six-month break-up and finds that something may still be going on with a gorgeous director of KE. Nothing like the crumbling of a personal life to complicate a professional one.

Chasing the Huntsmen

Grappling with the fall-out from the human trafficking ring, Caroline is trying desperately hard to rescue the women that were stolen and sold. After a particularly difficult extraction, she is forced to take a break from the gloom and doom of the victim's eyes. Just when she thinks she will be able to move past the depression that is looming over her head, a loved one is taken in an orchestrated scavenger hunt. Caroline is compelled to follow the clues, while being haunted by her past.

Dealing with the Devils

After running away from her life so she can find her center again, she returns home to realize that Beck is gone. She makes deals with two devils to find where Beck has hidden himself in the world. From the jungles to Colombia to the museums of Prague, she works tirelessly to get back to Beck. It gets complicated when she meets a man that is the spitting image of her late husband, John. Which would you choose: a man that ran away from you or a man that reminded you of the first love of your life?

To Have, Hold, Hide

Caroline and Beck are finally together again. Life is going great! Caroline and Beck are both expanding their businesses. Everyone is getting along in Caroline's large family, life couldn't be better. Beck even surprises her with her dream wedding and dream honeymoon. But just like any dream, when it's time to wake up, reality isn't always kind. She is confronted with an enemy she has wronged. She has to choose between staying with Beck and letting him know about what really happened in Prague. The decision is made when Roman is threatened, leaving Beck again without a trace.